THE GREENHAVEN ENCYCLOPEDIA OF

WITCHCRAFT

Other Titles in the Greenhaven Encyclopedia Of Series:

Ancient Rome

Greek and Roman Mythology

THE GREENHAVEN ENCYCLOPEDIA OF

WITCHCRAFT

Patricia D. Netzley

Daniel Leone, *President*
Bonnie Szumski, *Publisher*
Scott Barbour, *Managing Editor*

Greenhaven Press, Inc., San Diego, California

For Sarah, with thanks for all her help

Library of Congress Cataloging-in-Publication Data

Witchcraft / by Patricia D. Netzley
p. cm.—(Greenhaven encyclopedias)
Includes bibliographical references and index.
ISBN 0-7377-0437-3 (lib. bdg. : alk. paper)
1. Witchcraft—Encyclopedias. I. Netzley, Patricia D. II. Series.
BF1566 .W7377 2002
133.4'3'03—dc21

2001054533

10911 Technology Place, San Diego, CA 92127

Printed in the USA

CONTENTS

W

Y

PREFACE

Many scholars believe that while the history of witch persecution is deserving of study, the practice of witchcraft is not. Their view is that the aspect of witchcraft that involves attempts to manipulate supernatural forces (i.e., magic) is the product of superstition and therefore falls in the same category as unicorns and other mythological subjects. In other words, such scholars argue that the magical elements of witchcraft are a suitable focus for popular literature, but not academic works.

Moreover, some scholars believe that few people even practiced witchcraft prior to modern times. As evidence they cite the fact that most medieval and Renaissance victims of witch persecution were targeted for attack not because they professed to be witches but because they were different from their peers. Some were pagans who refused to abandon their deities for a Christian god. Others were uneducated women whose superior knowledge of illnesses and healing herbs angered the physicians of their time. Still others were physically disfigured or antisocial, or they had enemies who could profit from their execution as witches. In each case, these people were falsely accused and wrongfully convicted.

However, there is also evidence that some accused witches did indeed practice magic, believing their skills to be real. Most modern witches also believe that they have such skills, although they view witchcraft as being about far more than magic. Beginning in the 1960s, these witches began infusing religious elements into the practice of witchcraft, ultimately creating a witchcraft-centered religion called Wicca, and during the ensuing decades they successfully fought to achieve the same legal rights and protections in the United States as the members of other religions, and to gain tolerance from—if not acceptance by—mainstream Americans.

For modern American witches, then, witchcraft has been a social and religious movement, not just an aspect of world history. It is for this reason that some scholars believe that the practice of witchcraft does indeed deserve serious study. Furthermore, these scholars suggest that in order to fully understand modern witches one must examine not only their political activism and religious beliefs but also their magical practices, since magic is an important part of who witches are.

To this end, *The Greenhaven Encyclopedia Of Witchcraft* explores all aspects of witchcraft: magical tools, rituals, concepts, and traditions as well as witchcraft-related deities and historical events. It also offers information about important figures in the field of witchcraft, from witch-trial judges and other persecutors to people at the forefront of the modern witchcraft movement. Excluded from the work is information related to Eastern mysticism (i.e., the occult) except when necessary to clarify some aspect of witchcraft. The same is true for sorcery and sorcerers, which are only discussed in terms of their relationship to witchcraft and witches.

Essentially, this encyclopedia's goal is to help readers unfamiliar with Western witchcraft understand its history, traditions, and practices. In addition, an extensive bibliography provides both scholarly and popular resources for those interested in learning more about witchcraft. Lastly, a complete index will aid readers in locating their chosen subject.

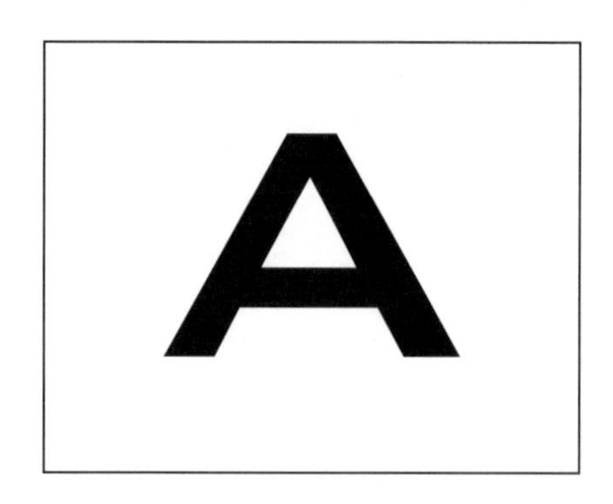

Aberdeen, witch trials of

The witch trials of Aberdeen, Scotland, were among the largest such events in the country's history, involving dozens of defendants. These trials were inspired by James VI, king of Scotland (as of 1603, known as James I, king of Scotland and England), who promoted the idea that witchcraft was aggressively practiced throughout Scotland, England, and Europe. Many Scots accepted this view and in 1596 began to seek out witches in their own communities. In Aberdeen most of those accused of witchcraft were elderly women. Some drew the attention of authorities as eccentrics and town outcasts, but the majority were brought to trial on the word of a condemned witch seeking leniency; she claimed to have attended a gathering of more than two thousand witches, several of them her neighbors.

Once accused, many were thrown into water with their hands tied. Those who floated were considered witches and urged to confess their crimes. Under coercion, several women admitted to activities that included making love charms and herbal cures, creating storms, spreading nightmares, bewitching livestock, dancing with demons, and attending meetings with the devil in groups of thirteen. One woman, Janet Wishart, was accused of killing one man and sickening another via magic spells.

In April 1597 Wishart was found guilty, as were twenty-two other women and one man. All of them were tied to stakes, strangled, and set on fire as a way to dispel their evil. A few of the accused escaped a similar fate by taking their own lives prior to trial or execution. Others were set free because the court lacked enough evidence of their guilt; however, suspicion that they were witches nevertheless remained so strong that they were branded on the face with a hot iron and told to leave Aberdeen forever. After the trials and executions, the families of the dead were forced to pay expenses. For example, the bill for the deaths of Janet Wishart and Isabel Crocker, dated February 1596, charged the women's families for the cost of peat, coal, and tar used to set the fire, stakes, ropes, an executioner, and the labor involved in carrying supplies to the hill where the women were burned. **See also** James I; Scotland, witch trials of.

abracadabra

Perhaps the most famous "magic word" in history, "abracadabra" is not used by modern witches or magicians; however, it was often employed in ancient times, when its primary purpose was to protect a person from illness. The word first appeared in print in a poem entitled "Precepta de Medicina" by Q. Serenus Scammonicus, a second-century physician who advised people to say or chant the word to cure fevers. Abracadabra was also commonly engraved on medallions worn around the neck to shield the wearer from harm. If no medallion was available, the word was written on parchment or some natural object, such as a stone or shell, to create a protective charm. Alternatively, it could be used to cure someone already sick. In such cases the written word was typically worn by the sufferer for several days, then cast into a stream so that the waters could carry the sickness away.

At first the word was simply written in a straightforward manner, but over time various rituals developed regarding how it should be written. For example, the eleven-letter word might be written on eleven lines, with each line containing one less letter so that the lines formed a triangle. The paper on which it was written might also be folded into a cross to add extra power to the word.

Although scholars are uncertain of the meaning of the word, they suspect that it originated in the beliefs of the Kabbalah, a system of Jewish mystical belief. Some therefore suggest that it might be derived from *Abraxas*, the Greek word for the Hebrew god, who could be called upon to protect people from physical injury. Others believe that the word is a Syrian Christian derivative of the Hebrew words *ab, ben, ruach,* and *acadosch*, which mean "father," "son," "holy," and "ghost." To Christians, the phrase "the Father, the Son, and the Holy Ghost" refers to God, Jesus Christ, who was capable of healing the sick. **See also** amulet; charm; Kabbalah.

Abramelin magic

Abramelin magic is a set of rituals and beliefs based on the writings of Abramelin the Mage, a Jewish magician from Würzburg, Germany, who lived between 1362 and 1460. Abramelin argued that the world was created by demons under the command of angels and claimed that these angels had told him how to control demons himself using names and number combinations with magical powers. He further claimed that his ideas were supported in part by ancient writings that formed the basis of Kabbalah, or Cabbala, a type of Jewish mysticism.

To share his knowledge Abramelin wrote three books, collectively known as *The Book of Sacred Magic of Abramelin the Mage*, in Hebrew in 1458. His original works have not survived, but evidence suggests that magicians began using Abramelin's complicated rituals during the Middle Ages to communicate with spirits and practice both white and black (good and evil) magic. A French version of Abramelin's writings appeared in the eighteenth century and an English version in the twentieth century. The latter influenced the beliefs of Aleister Crowley and Gerald Gardner, important witchcraft practitioners of the late twentieth century. **See also** Crowley, Aleister; Gardner, Gerald; Kabbalah.

adept

Among Wiccans, an adept is a witchcraft practitioner who through study and practice has achieved competency over various aspects of a particular Craft tradition. The degree of competency qualifying one as an adept varies, depending on the Craft tradition. In some traditions, an adept is an initiate who has completed at least a year and a day of training. In others, an adept is an initiate undergoing such training. In still other traditions, an adept is an occult master and/or someone who passes on the teachings of the Craft. **See also** traditions, Witchcraft.

Adler, Margot (1946–)

Margot Adler is the author of *Drawing Down the Moon: Witches, Druids, Goddess-Worshippers, and Other Pagans in America Today*, one of the most important books on the history of Neopaganism and Wiccan traditions in the United States. First published in 1979 and revised in 1986 and again in 1997, the book reports Adler's personal observations of religions and ritual gatherings throughout America. It also includes lists of rituals, festivals, publications, and organizations related to paganism and witchcraft. Adler herself is a practitioner of witchcraft, having become a Wiccan priestess in 1973. She has also been a journalist and radio producer since 1968. Currently she works for National Public Radio, both as a producer and as an on-air correspondent. In addition, Adler lectures on and leads workshops in paganism throughout the country. **See also** drawing down the moon; Wicca.

Ady, Thomas (dates unknown)

Seventeenth-century Englishman Thomas Ady authored one of the most influential books related to witchcraft trials. Entitled *A Candle in the Dark, or a Treatise concerning the nature of witches and witchcraft: being advice to the judges, sheriffs, justices of the peace and grandjurymen what to do before they pass sentence on such as are arraigned for their lives as witches*, this 1656 book argued that the Bible does not support the validity of witchcraft. Ady began by showing that the Bible defines a witch as someone who makes charms or tells the future in order to deceive others, rather than someone who bewitches people or consorts with demons. In fact, he pointed out that the Bible tells no stories of witches performing such evils. Ady then criticized all tests used by his contemporaries to determine whether or not someone was a witch. Ady's work convinced many judges and juries to reconsider their preconceptions about witches and witchcraft; Protestants found his arguments particularly persuasive because they generally believed that the Bible was the ultimate authority on such matters. **See also** Bible.

adytum

In some modern Craft traditions, the adytum is the most sacred spot within an area where a ritual is performed, usually at the center of a magic circle. Many witches consider the adytum to be the equivalent of an altar; thus they might place a candle on the spot or mark it with a pentacle. Some witches also place an actual altar there, an object that elevates ritual tools from the ground. This altar is usually oriented so that someone facing it is facing either north or east, both considered sacred directions. Ritual tools are selected and arranged on the altar in different ways depending on the Craft tradition being practiced. **See also** circle, magic; tools, ritual.

Agrippa von Nettesheim, Heinrich Cornelius (1486–1535)

German magician Heinrich Cornelius Agrippa von Nettesheim lectured and wrote extensively on the occult. He was educated as a physician at the University of Cologne in Germany, but had long been interested in the occult, and at age twenty-four he wrote *De occulta philosophia* (*On Occult Philosophy*), in which he argued that magic was produced by the human mind rather than via spirits or demons. Agrippa also insisted that various forms of predicting the future, such as astrology, were accurate and that certain gemstones had magic powers. For many years his writings remained unpublished, but he shared his beliefs by lecturing at universities and by establishing occult groups. According to some reports from the period, Agrippa also spent his time consorting with spirits, casting spells, and performing black magic. Nonetheless, in approximately 1530 he began speaking out against sorcery and the occult, arguing in a book entitled *Of the Vanitie and uncertaintie of artes and sciences* (translated into English in 1569) that magic did not work. People who disagreed with this position arranged the publication of Agrippa's ear-

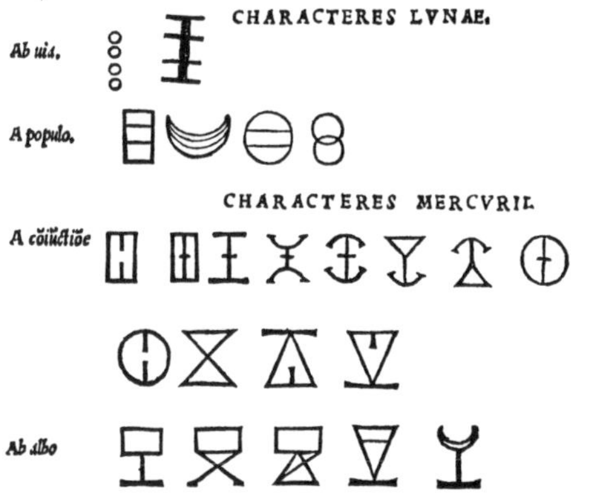
Caput LI.

CHaracteres etiã habent communitatem ſuã ex radiis cœleſti
cundum certum numerum in ſeinuicen peculiari quadam
etate coniectis,quę quidem cœleſtia,ſicut in diuerſis radioru
rum ictibus inter ſe aliter atq; aliter incidentibus,diuerſas conſpirant
tes:ſic etiã characteres, iuxta diuerſas eiuſmodi radiorum concurſus alite
aliter protracti,diuerſas ſubito nanciſcũtur operationes:ſępe etiã mu
ficaciores,q̃ phyſicalium commixtionum proprietates.Veri autem cha
res cœlorum,ipſa eſt ſcriptura angelorum,quæ apud Hebræos uocatu
ptura Malachim,per quam in cœlo ſunt deſcripta & ſignificata omna
libet ſcienti legere . Sed de his in poſterioribus . Iam uero etiam chara
ex Geomanticis figuris fabricant, uario modo ſingularũ puncta inter
ligantes,& iuxta earundem figurationum rationem ex quibus format
rint, planetis atq; ſignis illis attribuentes , horumq́; fabricam ſequens
la exponet.

CHARACTERES LVNAE.

Ab uia.

A populo.

CHARACTERES MERCVRII.

A cõiũctiõe

Ab albo

This excerpt from Heinrich Cornelius Agrippa von Nettesheim's De occulta philosophia *shows a table arranged according to the planets.*

lier work, *De occulta philosophia*, thereby discrediting his new views. Long after Agrippa's death in 1535, *De occulta philosophia* continued to be read, while *Of the Vanitie and uncertaintie of artes and sciences* was quickly forgotten. **See also** black magic; divination; sorcery.

air

Air is one of the four elements typically employed in the practice of magic. Modern witches typically associate each of these elements with a ritual tool; in the case of air, this tool is usually either the wand or a ritual knife known as an athame. Those who connect air with the wand point out that a wand is usually made from a tree branch that once swayed in the wind. Those who connect air with the athame note that the knife's blade slices through the air. In either case, air is generally thought to embody the male life force and is associated with thought, reason, creativity, illumination, and other aspects of mental energy. It is also connected with the color blue, the direction east, and the astrological signs Aquarius, Libra, and Gemini. The gemstones associated with air are the amethyst, sapphire, citrine, and azurite; the plants associated with air are the almond, broom, clover, eyebright, lavender, and pine. Incenses and fragrances associated with air magic include ambergris for love; lavender for purification, protection, and both mental and physical health; pine for money; sage for wisdom; star anise for psychic power; and sweetgrass either to protect against spirits or to summon them. Also associated with air are many spells and rituals related to calling or raising the wind. Originating in antiquity, their original purpose was to help sailors reach their destination. Such sailors would often visit witches to purchase a rope of knots; untying the knots was believed to release magic that powered the wind. **See also** athame; elements, four; knots.

airts, four

"The four airts," a phrase derived from ancient Gaelic, refers to the four directions—north, south, east, and west—integral to casting spells. The word *airt* actually means "east," the direction the ancients traditionally faced at the beginning of the casting of spells. The spellcaster then faced either *tuath* (north) or *deas* (south), depending on the spell, before turning *iar* (west). Moving from *airt* to *tuath* typically produced a curse, and from *airt* to *deas* a blessing. Many modern witchcraft practitioners also adhere to this belief. Like the ancient Gaels, they associate each of the four airts with one of the four elements—air, water, fire, and earth—and with one of four colors—red, white, gray, and black. Which airt represents which element and color depends on which tradition of witchcraft the spellcaster practices; however, most spellcasters place a candle at each of the four airts within a circle where magic is to be performed. **See also** circle, magic; elements, four.

Aix-en-Provence, witch trial of

One of the most notorious trials related to demonic possession took place in Aix-en-Provence, France, in 1611. The accused was thirty-four-year-old Father Louis Gaufridi, a priest who was said to have bewitched several nuns at the Ursuline convent in Aix-en-Provence and forced them to consort with the devil. The first supposed victim of Gaufridi was teenager Madeline de Demandolx. Gaufridi had long been a friend of Madeline's family, and it was rumored that he had been sexually involved with the girl prior to her entering the convent at age fourteen. When she was about sixteen, Madeline began having convulsions, fits, and hallucinations, and religious authorities concluded that she was possessed by a demon. They performed an exorcism to rid her of the demon; during this ritual Madeline claimed that Gaufridi was responsible for her condition. Afterward she continued to display signs of demonic possession, and other girls at the convent began to display them as well. More exorcisms were performed, also without success, and one of the other possessed nuns (Sister Louise Capeau) also accused Gaufridi.

In December 1610, Gaufridi was interrogated by church authorities, who decided that he was innocent. But as part of a subsequent civil investigation, Gaufridi was brutally tortured until he confessed to signing a pact with the devil and bewitching the girls. By this time, the nuns' behavior included not only convulsions and twitching but also hysterical rantings, and Madeline tried to kill herself several times.

On April 18, 1611, Gaufridi was found guilty of sorcery, despite the fact that he had by then recanted his confession, and was sentenced to be burned alive. He was further tortured in an attempt to extract the names of accomplices from him. The methods used for these torture sessions were particularly gruesome; during one session, for example, weights were attached to Gaufridi's feet and ropes to his arms, whereupon he was jerked violently and repeatedly up into the air. On April 30, 1611, Gaufridi was tied to a stake and set on fire, but church officials had convinced his executioners to strangle him first as an act of mercy. After his death, some of the nuns he had supposedly bewitched continued to exhibit strange behavior, and eventually authorities decided to imprison them. Meanwhile Madeline was declared cured, but in 1642 and again in 1652 she was accused of being a witch. Shortly thereafter she was imprisoned until just before her death in 1670. **See also** demonic possession; exorcism; France, witch-hunts of.

Akashic Records

Many modern witches believe in the existence of the Akashic Records, a permanent copy of all the energy that has been released on the earth throughout history. Within this energy supposedly lie ancient memories, stored in a region of the earth's magnetic field; a person who can psychically access the Akashic Records is said to be able to gain knowledge and improve intuition.

The name Akashic comes from a Wiccan word for spirit or spiritual ether, Akasha, which in some Craft traditions is considered a fifth element; the other four elements are Vayu (air), Tejas (fire), Apas (water), and Prithivi (earth). Each of these elements is associated with each of five tides believed to affect the energy flow within the region where the Akashic Records reside. Some witches therefore call this region a realm of cause and effect, and believe that its tides must be taken into account when accessing the Akashic Records or working magic. Spells that rely on the power of the air element, for example, gain strength by being cast when the Vayu tide is active. Each tide is active for twenty minutes within every two-hour period, beginning with Akasha after sunrise. **See also** elements, four; Wicca.

Albertus Magnus (c. 1205–1280)

Albertus Magnus was a respected theologian, scientist, scholar, and Dominican bishop who also practiced alchemy. Today some people believe that Magnus succeeded in his attempts to turn base metals such as lead into gold and silver, although he did not share his knowledge of this process with anyone and wrote only of the scientific properties of rocks and minerals. Some also think that Magnus practiced not only alchemy but also various forms of magic and sorcery; there is no proof of this, either. Magnus is, however, noted for influencing the thinking of Thomas Aquinas, whom he tutored and who in turn influenced thirteenth-century opinion on witchcraft and demonology. Magnus produced a large body of work related to science, philosophy, and theology, and lectured at various European universities. He was declared a saint by the Catholic Church in 1931. **See also** alchemy; Aquinas, Thomas.

alchemy

Alchemy is an ancient occult science by which base metals such as iron and lead are supposedly transformed into gold or silver using a combination of chemical and spiritual processes. In medieval times, most of the people who practiced this science, known as alchemists, believed in the necessity of employing magic along with these processes. In modern times, a few people still believe that alchemy is possible. They suggest that ancient occultists such as Albertus Magnus knew how to transform base metals via magic but did not share their knowledge. Most people, however, reject the notion that alchemy of any kind is possible.

During the Middle Ages, Renaissance, and Reformation, alchemists used various techniques in their attempts to transform metals, usually keeping their methods secret. Generally, however, they believed that metals are composed of essential elements, such as salt and sulfur, that can be separated and reconfigured using a substance called a philosopher's stone, which was supposedly composed of magical metals that alchemists refused to name.

Most medieval people believed that working to refine metals refined the human spirit as well. An alchemist was therefore said to be a more spiritual person, superior to nonalchemists, and so more closely connected to God. This idea may underlie the belief of many modern witches that gold and silver represent, respectively, female and male life forces or deities.

The forerunners of alchemists were ancient Egyptians who developed techniques to extract veins of gold and silver from surrounding rock. Word of the Egyptians' success in separating precious metals from ore spread to other parts of the world, inspiring the idea that metals could be transformed through some magical process. Ancient Greeks, Romans, and Celts all experimented with alchemy, as did ancient Chinese. In fact, a Chinese alchemist named Ko Hung published the first guidebook to alchemy in A.D. 320.

By medieval times, alchemy had become accepted as a science; most people believed that it was possible to create gold and silver from base metals. By the Renaissance, when perhaps the largest number of alchemists plied their trade, it was

An alchemist performs an experiment to make gold. Most people in medieval times believed that base metals could be transformed into gold or silver by employing magic.

also believed that certain by-products supposedly created during the alchemic process, including a black powder or liquid, could be used to create an elixir with the power to make people immortal. By the nineteenth century, however, scholars had largely decided that alchemy was impossible, since no alchemist had been able to prove scientifically that the process worked. **See also** elements, four.

alder

A member of the birch family, the alder tree (*Alnus glutinosa*) is sacred to witches. Its wood is sometimes carved into ritual whistles and flutes, and the sap of the European alder (also known as the black alder) has been employed as part of a process to produce red dye used to color ritual cords, ribbons, and bags. Some witches believe that fairies travel to their realm via a doorway hidden within the trunk of the alder tree. In addition, during pagan times various legends evolved regarding the alder's role as a tool of the gods. For example, the Celts said that the god Bran carried an alder branch into battle. **See also** trees.

aleuromancy

Aleuromancy is a form of divination in which fortunes are written on slips of paper and then stuck into dough. The dough in turn is pressed inside walnut shells. The shells are then mixed up, and people seeking to know the future select and open shells to learn their fate. Walnut shells are used because the ancient Greeks believed that walnut trees were associated with prophecy. **See also** divination.

Alexandrian Tradition

The Alexandrian Tradition is one of the largest modern Craft traditions, with hundreds of followers in both the United States and Great Britain. No two Alexandrian covens operate in exactly the same way. Generally, however, Alexandrian Wiccans practice ceremonial magic based on the Kabbalah, Angelic Magic, and Enochian Magic. All three of these magical systems call upon the power of angels. However, the Kabbalah is based on ancient Jewish beliefs, while Angelic Magic and Enochian Magic are based on early Christian ones, and because witches have long been at odds with Christians, far fewer witches historically have practiced Angelic and Enochian Magic. Most Alexandrian traditions have a hierarchical structure and meet at sacred times as determined by the Wheel of the Year as well as at the full and new phases of the moon. Some Alexandrian covens meet weekly as well.

Many Alexandrian covens allow interested guests to attend one of their meetings, as well as people who have not yet been initiated in the Craft but who plan to undergo initiation. (These newcomers to the Craft are called noninitiates or neophytes; once they have completed certain tasks and studied certain aspects of magic they are initiated into the first degree of the Alexandrian Tradition.)

Practitioners of Alexandrian Wicca use basically the same tools as members of the Gardnerian Tradition, although sometimes they use those items in different ways. Other similarities between the two traditions can be traced to the origin of the Alexandrian Tradition. It was originally established in the early 1960s by British witch Alex Sanders and his wife, Maxine, as an alternative to the Gardnerian Tradition. In fact, the Book of Shadows for the Alexandrian Tradition was largely copied from the Book of Shadows for the Gardnerian Tradition. Initially, however, Sanders claimed that the material had instead come from his grandmother, who he said was a hereditary witch. Sanders insisted that he too was a hereditary witch, but when his claim was later disproved by the people who had introduced him to the Craft he fell out of favor with many Wiccans, including many followers of the Alexandrian Tradition. Nonetheless, the tradition remains widespread today. **See also** Book of Shadows; Gardnerian Tradition; Sanders, Alex; traditions, Witchcraft; Wheel of the Year.

Algard

An American Witchcraft tradition established by Mary Nesnick in 1972, Algard is a blend of two older forms of Wicca, the Alexandrian and the Gardnerian Traditions. More than fifty Algard covens are currently active in the United States. **See also** Alexandrian Tradition; Gardnerian Tradition.

All Hallow's Eve

Celebrated on October 31, All Hallow's Eve is considered by witches to be one of the two greatest Sabbats, a time when deities are honored and rituals are performed. Most call this festival Samhain, thereby distinguishing it from the popular holiday that nonwitches call Halloween. **See also** Sabbat; Samhain.

Allier, Elizabeth (c. 1602–1639)

French nun Elizabeth Allier became well known in seventeenth-century Europe as the victim of demonic possession. Her body was reportedly taken over by two demons when she was only seven years old; in her twenties a Dominican friar named François Farconnet tried six times to exorcise the demons before declaring success in 1639. However, three days after this successful exorcism, Allier died. Shortly thereafter, Farconnet wrote about the experience, reporting that Allier's symptoms included convulsions and speaking in deep demonic voices. His writings spread Allier's fame beyond France, and some historians believe them to have inspired several other cases of demonic possession. Allier's possession was also unusual in that she accused no human individual of causing her distress. Typically, supposedly possessed nuns claimed that a priest, other male, or in rare cases their Mother Superior had sent their demons to torment them. Allier, however, said that her demons, which she named Orgeuil and Bonifarce, entered of their own accord, riding down her throat on a piece of bread. **See also** demonic possession.

alphabets, magical

During the Middle Ages, several magical alphabets were developed as a way to encode secret spells and as a means of increasing a spell's effectiveness. People believed that these alphabets, by virtue of the fact that they were created by magicians and employed solely for spells, were more powerful than ordinary alphabets. However, the idea that alphabets can have magical powers predates medieval times. The ancient Hebrews believed their alphabet had such significance, a concept reflected in their mystical system known as the Kabbalah. Many other ancient cultures held similar beliefs in the power of their alphabet. The ancient Celts made use of two alphabets believed to be magical, the Ogham alphabet and the Runic alphabet. Today modern witches use Runic characters, or runes, as talismans and to foretell the future. **See also** Kabbalah; runes; talisman.

Alphonsus de Spina (?–1491)

Living in fifteenth-century Spain, Franciscan friar Alphonsus de Spina wrote about demonology and witchcraft in a book entitled *Fortalicium Fidei (Fortress of the Faith),* which was published sometime between 1458 and 1468. Many historians consider this book to be the first work to offer descriptions of witches' activities, which included devil worship and the casting of evil spells. The book also identifies ten types of demons; one of the most significant is a demon that deludes women into believing they have magical powers, such as the ability to fly. Alphonsus's work had great influence on judges in witchcraft trials, both in his own time and decades afterward. **See also** demons; devil; Spain, witch trials of.

altar

For witches, an altar is usually a table or raised platform that serves as a focus for rituals. Witches typically place items of sacred significance on the altar. An altar might be used as a permanent shrine dedicated to a particular deity or aspect of a deity, or it might be a portable structure placed within a magic circle as part of the performance of rituals or magic. In the latter case, ritual tools are typically placed on the altar, although their exact placement varies according to Witchcraft tradition. In general, however, objects related to the Goddess are placed on the left side of the altar, which is dedicated to the feminine life force. Those related to the God are placed on the right side, which is dedicated to the male life force. **See also** circle, magic; tools, ritual; traditions, Witchcraft.

America, witch-hunts of

Most American witch-hunts took place during the seventeenth century, although a few isolated incidents occurred in the early eighteenth century as well. The phenomenon can be attributed in large part to the efforts of influential leaders such as Cotton Mather, the seventeenth-century Puritan clergyman who wrote extensively about the dangers that witchcraft posed to colonial society.

The best-known witch trials in America took place in Salem, Massachusetts, from 1692 to 1693, but the first witch execution took place in Connecticut. Alice Young was hanged as a witch there in May 1647,

An illustration depicts a seventeenth-century witch trial. Thirty-six Americans were executed on charges of witchcraft in response to the Puritan belief that magic is evil.

just five years after the first Connecticut laws against practicing witchcraft were passed. Over the next few years, a half-dozen more Connecticut witch executions took place, but they were isolated cases in various towns.

In 1662, the town of Hartford was the site of the first Connecticut witch trial involving numerous defendants. This case of mass hysteria was triggered by the accusations of a girl named Ann Cole, who claimed to be demonically possessed. While having a fit, Ann Cole named two women as witches, one of whom confessed to consorting with the devil and belonging to a coven. The confessed witch, Rebecca Greensmith, was executed, as was her husband despite his protestations of innocence. Hartford authorities then arrested at least nine people as possible members of Greensmith's coven. Most were soon hanged, although records are unclear regarding exactly how many. A few more witch trials, some resulting in hanging, took place in Connecticut from 1662 to 1697. The 1697 trial, however, resulted in an acquittal for its two defendants, probably because by this time the public had realized that many innocent people had been sent to their deaths in the Salem witch trials.

In fact, injustices connected to the Salem witch trials so profoundly disturbed most Americans that in their aftermath all witch persecution in the United States effectively ended. By 1694 most of the people responsible for the Salem trials had expressed regret over their actions, and no more witch executions took place. Moreover, although witch trials continued to take place into the early 1700s, along with some minor incidents of witchcraft-related hysteria, convictions were few and punishments mild. In all, during the seventeenth and eighteenth centuries, approximately fifty people were tried in America on charges of witchcraft; thirty-six were executed. **See also** Germany, witch-hunts of; Mather, Cotton; persecution, witch; Salem, witch trials of.

amulet

An amulet is an object believed by the possessor to protect against ill health or other catastrophes. It is typically worn or carried by the person desiring protection, but it also might be left in a place with significance to that person. For example, some people put their amulets on a home altar or bury them in their backyard.

Amulets can be either natural or manmade. Natural amulets consist of animal teeth and claws, stones, gems, crystals, or shells. Man-made amulets consist of small carved or sculpted animal figures, lockets concealing paper on which an incantation or other inscription has been written, or medallions marked in some way with symbols, pictures, or letters from alphabets such as the Runic alphabet, which are considered magical.

Witches disagree on how amulets gain their power. Many, however, believe that natural amulets derive their power from the circumstances or settings in which they were found, and that man-made amulets are either inherently powerful or derive their power by being created as part of a ritual or at a certain time of day, month, or year that has particular significance in Wiccan belief, such as midnight, or during a full moon, or Samhain.

Modern witches do not believe that an amulet attracts good luck; instead, its purpose is to ward off evil. For witches, a talisman is worn or carried to bring good luck or other positive things to its possessor. Talismans often bear symbols such as Runic characters. Some of the symbols used on amulets, such as the pentagram, can also be used on talismans, though, and witches consider an object displaying one of these symbols to be both an amulet and a talisman.

Both amulets and talismans have been used for millennia. The ancient Egyptians had seventy-five different traditional amulets to ward off evil, the most common of which was the scarab beetle. In medieval times, the Catholic Church tried to eliminate the use of amulets, except for those depicting images of Jesus Christ, the Virgin Mary, one of the Catholic saints, or the Christian cross. Gradually the idea that wearing these symbols conferred protection from evil was lost, and today most people view such items as religious jewelry rather than amulets.

Witches consider any jewelry bearing a symbol of their faith and/or magic to have some kind of power. In addition to the pentagram, the most common such symbols are the ankh, the eye of Horus, the cross, the feather, the Hecate Wheel, the key, and the Chinese yin-yang symbol. The power of each symbol is believed to be related to its area of influence. The ankh and the eye of Horus, two ancient Egyptian symbols, have protective power related to a long life and good health, respectively. The cross (with lines of equal length, as opposed to the unequal lines of the Christian cross) confers balance between sacred and secular, male and female, spiritual and physical, and the like. The feather is generally associated with truth and knowledge, although it can also represent the wind, the element of air, or the spirit. The Hecate Wheel is the symbol of the goddess Hecate, long associated with witchcraft; wearing such an amulet is said to protect a witch or to represent the eternity of witchcraft. The key stands for knowledge and new opportunities, while the Chinese yin-yang symbol represents the joining of male and female forces and therefore the whole of the cosmos; both the key and the yin-yang are generally believed to bring luck and prosperity. **See also** pentacle and pentagram; runes; talisman.

animals

Witches have historically incorporated animals into their rituals and magic. For example, body parts of various animals, including frogs and lizards, have been used as ingredients in potions and ointments. In addition, throughout the twelfth through the seventeenth centuries, depending on location, most people believed that every witch had an animal helper called a familiar who did the witch's bidding, and that these animals were actually demons or imps in disguise. The most common familiars were cats, mice, and hares. Black dogs were sometimes named witches' familiars, although they were thought of as tools of the devil and perhaps even the devil himself in disguise.

In attempting to demonize witchcraft, early Christians often said that witches could turn themselves into bats, animals often associated with Satan, or that they used bat parts in their potions. Also during the emergence of Christianity, witches were said to be able to turn themselves into owls, because owls had long been associated with paganism and sorcery.

The first associations between animals and witchcraft began with pagan rituals during which participants wore the skins, features, or horns of certain animals, or masks representing those animals, and acted like the creatures they represented. Some scholars have suggested that this is the origin of the belief that witches can transform themselves into various animals. However, ancient Greek epics describe the sorceress Circe, who was able to transform men into pigs, so the idea of transforming a person into an animal did not originate with medieval Christians.

In modern times, witches sometimes call on the spirits of animals in performing rituals, usually choosing an animal for which they feel personal affinity. Each animal is believed to have various traits connected to human qualities. For example, the bear represents stability, strength, and wisdom, the cat independence and secretiveness, the dog friendship and loyalty, the eagle the human spirit, the horse speed and power, the owl magic and psychic powers, and the wolf power, protection, and psychic energy. **See also** lycanthropy.

apple

Apple enchantment is a common theme in folklore, with references to magic apples or apple orchards in the mythology of the cultures of ancient Greece, Scandinavia, and England. During the seventeenth century, there were instances of people accusing a suspected witch of giving them an enchanted apple which upon being eaten bewitched them. Based on some of these accusations, innocent people were executed for practicing witchcraft.

Modern scholars believe that the connection between apple trees and magic predates recorded history, when many cultures considered such trees sacred. In addition, many Europeans have long believed apples to have divination powers. For example, in Austria people traditionally cut open an apple to predict their future. If one of the seeds has been cut, disaster will soon come; if two or more seeds are cut, death will soon come; if no seeds are cut and there is an even number of them, then marriage will soon come. Apples are used to foretell marriage in other European countries as well. Some methods involve counting the seeds, some counting the number of twists to remove the stem, and some slicing the apples and performing various rituals with the slices. **See also** hag.

Aquinas, Thomas (1225–1274)

Thomas Aquinas was an influential Christian theologian and scholar. Through some of his writings, Aquinas contributed to the witchcraft hysteria of the Middle Ages by insisting that witches consorted with demons. This concept quickly became a standard feature of witchcraft trials. Similarly, Aquinas's argument that the Bible includes passages suggesting that devil worshipers can fly—an idea that Thomas Ady, among other biblical scholars, later disputed—led witch-hunters to accuse some of their victims of flying to their meetings. Thomas Aquinas also believed in alchemy, having studied under the alchemist and scholar Albertus Magnus from 1245 to 1252. In 1256 Aquinas began teaching theology at the University of Paris, France, and in 1272 he left there to establish a Dominican house of studies at the University of Naples, Italy. He died in 1274 and was canonized in 1323. **See also** Ady, Thomas; Albertus Magnus.

Aradia

Largely because of the writings of American folklorist Charles Godfrey Leland (1824–1903), many witches believe that

Aradia was the goddess who brought witchcraft to mortals. In his 1899 book *Aradia, or the Gospel of the Witches*, Leland recounts an ancient Italian legend in which Aradia, whose parents were Diana (or Tana), goddess of the moon and queen of the witches, and Lucifer, god of the sun, is sent to earth to teach people witchcraft. In her book *Drawing Down the Moon*, Margot Adler expands on this story, calling Aradia the "messiah of the Witches" and saying that witchcraft was given to humans as a means to end oppression. Aradia is therefore a powerful figure for many witches, and she is often featured in rituals, particularly among Italian Witchcraft traditions.

To call on Aradia, witches sometimes go into the fields at midnight with a small red bag filled with salt, containers of water and wine, and a talisman. The water and wine are used in a ritual blessing, after which the person seeking Aradia recites a verse honoring the goddess while holding the bag and talisman. Some witches invoke Aradia as part of an esbat, a coven meeting taking place at the time of the full moon. Such witches believe that Aradia is a goddess of the moon, as is Diana.

Many witches believe that Aradia has the power to provide a witch with information about the future and about hidden or lost objects. She is thought to have other powers as well, such as the ability to heal a variety of illnesses, contagious diseases, and skin conditions, and to enhance love spells.

But despite witches' belief in Aradia, many scholars contend that Leland invented this deity himself. Others think that Aradia was fabricated, but not by Leland; they suggest that he derived at least part of his Aradia folktale from ancient sources. Still others believe that a fourteenth-century witch named Aradia actually existed, and it was she who inspired Leland's work. **See also** Adler, Margot; Diana; esbat; goddesses and gods; Leland, Charles Godfrey; Stregheria.

arcana

The word *arcana* refers to the Tarot cards, which are tools of divination and representations of magic. The word comes from the Latin *arcanus*, meaning "hidden or secret knowledge"; many people believe that the Tarot cards were created by sorcerers to pass on ancient wisdom related to magic. There are two types of Tarot cards within one deck, the major arcana and the minor arcana. There are twenty-two cards in the major arcana, and fourteen cards in each of four suits in the minor arcana. **See also** Tarot cards.

Arician Tradition

The Arician Tradition is an Italian Witchcraft tradition established in 1998 by Raven Grimassi, who based it on the Aridian Tradition that he established in 1981. Grimassi based both of these versions of Wicca on the folk traditions of Italy, which he believed were remnants of the religious practices of ancient pagans. In founding the Arician Tradition, he drew from the beliefs of people in the Arician groves of the Alban Hills near Albano Laziale, Italy. Their tales told of worshiping the god Tagni and goddess Uni; these deities are consequently featured in Arician rituals. **See also** Aridian Tradition; Grimassi, Raven; Stregheria.

Aridian Tradition

The Aridian Tradition is a Witchcraft tradition that attempts to re-create the beliefs and practices of ancient Italian pagans while still honoring many aspects of modern Wicca. To this end, its members celebrate not only ancient Italian agricultural festivals but also the festivals within the Wiccan Wheel of the Year. Aridian rituals involve the goddess Tana and god Tanus, both worshiped by ancient Italians.

The Aridian Tradition was established in 1981 by Raven Grimassi using historical writings and folk traditions from Italy. After Grimassi wrote about the tradition in his

1995 book, *Ways of the Strega*, its popularity increased and new members began to change many aspects of the tradition. This so dissatisfied Grimassi that in 1997 he abandoned the Aridian Tradition. The next year, Grimassi created a new Italian tradition similar to the original form of the Aridian Tradition, which he called the Arician Tradition. **See also** Grimassi, Raven; Stregheria.

Armstrong, Anne

In 1673, English maidservant Anne Armstrong was the catalyst for a witchcraft trial in Morpeth, Northumberland, England, that influenced public views on witchcraft, yet appears to have resulted in no convictions. Ironically, some historians believe that the people Armstrong accused really were practicing some form of witchcraft or folk magic, although Armstrong's stories about their activities were no doubt greatly exaggerated.

Armstrong claimed that her association with witches began when one of them, Anne Forster, came upon her walking late at night and forced her, via magic, to serve as a horse and carry her to a witches' Sabbat. After that, Armstrong supposedly carried Forster and several other witches to their Sabbats on a regular basis. At the Sabbats, Armstrong was also forced to sing and dance. She reported that these Sabbats were always large gatherings, with five covens of thirteen members each. Armstrong named many alleged members, who were promptly arrested by authorities.

At their trial, Armstrong offered lengthy descriptions of the coven meetings and the maleficia (harmful witchcraft) that participants had performed against innocent people. At least one other woman came forward to say that the witches had harmed someone she knew, a child who died for no apparent reason. Details of stories told at the trial later appeared as facts in texts about witch practices, and some of Armstrong's remarks about the covens' activities have led historians to suspect that she either unwillingly or willingly witnessed—or perhaps even performed—witchcraft herself. The accused witches, however, were found innocent and eventually released. **See also** coven; England, witch-hunts of; maleficia.

Arras, witch-hunts of

The Arras witch-hunts are an example of the initiation of witch-hunts as a form of religious persecution. They began in Arras, France, in 1459 as a direct result of attempts by the Catholic Church to stamp out an early Protestant sect established by Peter Waldo of the Vaudois region of France; followers of this sect were called either the Waldensians or the Vaudois.

Under torture for his religious beliefs, a Waldensian named Robinet de Vaulx confessed to consorting with the devil in the company of two witches from Arras. These people were arrested and tortured, and they in turn named five other witches in Arras. As time passed, the tortures grew more brutal (they included stretching the accused on the rack and setting their feet on fire) and the list of Arras witches lengthened. Each person who confessed—and most did, given the brutalities they suffered until they complied—was burned alive at the stake, unless he or she was rich enough to buy a pardon by giving over all land and property to church and town leaders. By the end of 1460, so many people in Arras had been executed that town businesses and trade began to suffer. Moreover, several influential French bishops denounced the events in Arras, and in 1461 the Parlement of Paris ordered an end to the persecutions. In July 1491 the Parlement officially declared the witch-hunts a mistake, condemned the methods of the inquisitor there (Pierre le Broussart), and asked the French people to pray for all those who had been killed unjustly. **See also** France, witch-hunts of.

Artemis

Artemis is the ancient Greek equivalent of Diana, an ancient Roman goddess honored in many Witchcraft traditions. She is associated with the moon, the tides, fertility, and magic, as well as with wild animals, the hunt, and vegetation. The ancient Greeks worshiped Artemis primarily as a goddess of a tree cult, of which there were many variations. Some emphasized the goddess's connection to vegetation growth, portraying her as the supervisor of tree nymphs who managed waters and springs. Others emphasized her connection to forest creatures, depicting her as the mistress of animals and honoring her wildness with lascivious dances. Modern scholars, however, tend to emphasize Artemis's role as a huntress, whereas witches generally view her primarily as a moon goddess and stress her connection to magic. This connection dates back at least to medieval times, and perhaps to antiquity. An inscription from an ancient temple of Artemis—"ASKI. KATASKI. HAIX. TETRAX. DAMNAMENEUS. AISON."—was used by medieval sorcerers as a spell against evil, and some historians believe it was similarly employed by ancient sorcerers. Modern scholars disagree on the meaning of these words, but many witches support a translation that reads "Darkness, Light, Himself, the Sun, Truth," although they differ in their interpretation of to what or whom these words refer. **See also** goddesses and gods.

ash

The ash tree (*Fraxinus excelsior*) is especially sacred to witches (along with the oak and thorn tree). Ash branches are often used as wands for magical rituals and for the sticks of traditional witches' broomsticks. A phrase witches commonly use in charging objects with magic is "by oak, and ash, and thorn."

Some modern witches further believe that the ash tree has powers related to divination, largely because according to Norse mythology the chief god, Odin, received the wisdom he needed to read runes, which are commonly used to predict the future, from an ash tree. The tree is featured in Greek, Roman, and Celtic mythology as well. According to Celtic lore, along with the oak and the hawthorn trees the ash is part of what is known as the Fairy Triad; fairies are said to dwell where the three trees grow together. **See also** trees.

aspect

Among witches, the word *aspect* is usually used to refer to one of the many manifestations of the deity. For example, the goddess Bridgit, also known as Brighid, is just one aspect of the Maiden, who in turn is one of three aspects of the Triple Goddess (the other two being Mother and Crone), who in turn is an aspect of the All. **See also** Bridgit; goddesses and gods.

astral plane

According to modern practitioners of witchcraft, the astral plane is a realm of existence composed of energy where spirits dwell. Parallel to the physical world yet invisible to the human eye, this realm can be reached through astral projection, a process whereby a person goes into a trance and sends his or her consciousness from the body. This traveling consciousness is called the astral body, because it is an exact though spiritual duplicate of the physical body. Experts in paranormal phenomena disagree on whether the astral plane and astral body truly exist, even though some people insist that they have experienced astral projection.

Modern witches have suggested that the ability to travel along an astral plane of existence is the basis of the many stories from witchcraft trials of witches flying through the air. In a few of these trials, the witches confessed to leaving their physical bodies behind and flying in spirit only, and apparently some of these confessions were given freely rather than under torture. Some modern witches argue that therefore these stories should be taken as fact, and a few further insist that they too fly in this manner. In addition, some modern witches report that they can use the same meditative techniques that they employ for astral projection to create an astral temple where their astral bodies can conduct rituals and cast spells. **See also** Akashic Records; flight.

astrology

Astrology is a form of divination that has been practiced by many witches for hundreds of years. The main concept behind astrological forecasting is that the placement of the stars and planets at a particular moment influences what takes place on earth, in regard not only to events but also to the formation of people's personalities. According to this theory, the location of the sun, moon, and stars at the time of a person's birth can be used to predict what that person's future will be and to provide a description of his or her character traits.

All birth dates fall under one of twelve zodiac signs, the zodiac being an imaginary belt in the stars that is divided into twelve parts. Each of these parts, or signs, is named after a constellation: Aries (March 21–April 19), Taurus (April 20–May 20), Gemini (May 21–June 20), Cancer (June 21–July 22), Leo (July 23–August 22), Virgo (August 23–September 22), Libra (September 23–October 22), Scorpio (October 23–November 21), Sagittarius (November 22–December 21), Capricorn (December 22–January 19), Aquarius (January 20–February 18), and Pisces (February 19–March 20).

Modern newspapers commonly print generalized daily astrological forecasts called horoscopes that are based on these twelve signs. Modern witches, however, construct much more specific astrological forecasts based on complex charts of the heavens, and they sometimes use their astrological work to determine when to perform certain rituals or cast certain spells.

Astrological divination has been practiced since ancient times. Historians disagree on where and when astrology was first used, but the prevailing view is that it was developed by ancient Egyptians. In any case, the Greeks knew of astrology at least as early as the first century B.C., when they referred to the belt across the heavens as the *zodiakos kyklos*, or circle of animals, and identified many of the signs with animals; for example, Aries was the Ram, Taurus the Bull, and Cancer the Crab. **See also** divination.

athame

Also known as an arthame, the athame (pronounced ath-AY-me) is a ceremonial black-handled knife approximately six inches in length. Its blade is double-edged and usually made of steel or stone; its handle is often decorated with symbols representing some word of significance to its owner—the owner's name, for example, or the names of deities, spirits, or objects believed to be powerful or magical, such as the pentagram. Used during witchcraft rituals, the athame is not intended to inflict injury to either people or animals. Instead, its purpose is to direct a stream of energy from within the wielder of the knife into the ceremony being performed, focusing power wherever the user points the blade. Most commonly, the athame is used to draw a circle around an area where magic is to be performed, or conversely to "dissolve" the magic circle when the ritual is over, but as an important ritual tool it is also employed during initiation ceremonies and while casting certain spells. In some cases it is believed to "cut reality," thereby opening a door into an otherworldly realm. In addition, some witches believe that wands that have been carved using an athame have more power.

Prior to each use, the athame is ceremonially cleansed to dispel any negative energy held in the blade. Also prior to each use, some witches recite a rhyme, the Call of Nine, over the athame to call power into the blade. Each line of the rhyme begins with a number, in sequential order from one to nine, followed by a request to the Goddess to take steps to descend into the athame and lend it her power. A different ritual is performed for newly made blades. Prior to first use, they are stuck into the earth, waved in the air, passed through fire, and dipped in water, to expose them to the four elements: earth, air, fire, and water. All ritual tools of witchcraft are believed to be associated with one of these elements, but witches disagree on whether the athame is a tool of fire (because its blade has been forged in fire) or air (because its blade slices the air during use). Air is the most common designation, but fire prevails in the Georgian Tradition and some other traditions. Most witches, however, agree that the athame symbolizes the male life force.

The use of the athame is apparently ancient. Witches are depicted holding athames in artwork of the mid–sixteenth century, and there is evidence of their association with magic and rituals as early as 200 B.C. A Greek vase from this period shows two women performing a ceremony with a wand and a sword that somewhat resembles traditional athames, although its blade is longer. **See also** circle, magic; elements, four; Georgian Tradition; pentacle and pentagram; sword; tools, ritual; wand.

autumnal equinox

Occurring sometime between September 20 and 23, the autumnal equinox is one of two moments in the year when the sun is precisely above the equator and the day and night are exactly the same length. (The other moment is known as the spring equinox.) During the day on which this exact balance happens, witches celebrate a major festival known as Mabon, which some refer to as the autumn equinox. **See also** Mabon; spring equinox.

Auxonne, demonic possessions of

A series of supposed demonic possessions occurred in a convent in Auxonne, France, from 1658 to 1663 that were unusual in their suspected cause; the person blamed was a nun, in contrast to most convent cases, in which a priest or other man was accused of controlling the tormenting demons. In the Auxonne incidents, the culprit was reputed to be forty-seven-year-old Sister St. Colombe (also known as Barbara Buvée), the Mother Superior of the Ursuline convent, and all of the eight supposed victims were nuns under her supervision. Their symptoms primarily involved sexually provocative behavior, which they said was the result of consorting with demons. At first investigators assumed that the possessions were caused by a priest who regularly visited the convent, but when the priest claimed that he too had been bewitched the investigators looked elsewhere. Eventually they settled on Sister St. Colombe, who had previously argued with church authorities. She was imprisoned in November 1660 and put on trial for witchcraft in January 1661. During her trial, the victims accused Sister St. Colombe of all manner of sexually inappropriate behavior. Fortunately for the Mother Superior, the authorties did not believe the young women's stories, noting that unlike most demonically possessed women they did not exhibit convulsions or speak in demonic voices, and after further investigation they ruled that Sister St. Colombe was innocent. In August 1662 the case was officially declared closed, and by the following year the nuns' odd behavior had ended. **See also** demonic possession; France, witch-hunts of.

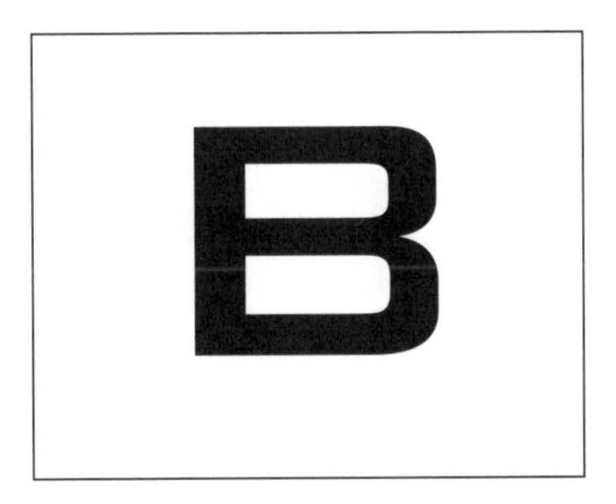

Bacchus

A Roman god, Bacchus has long been a symbol of intoxication and wild abandon. He has been adopted as an object of veneration by those modern witches who believe that the level of abandon with which he approaches his revels is something to emulate. In ancient Rome, Bacchus was also associated with the randy goat, and his Greek equivalent, Dionysos, was associated with the lusty bull. Both the Greeks and the Romans connected the god to grapes and wine, and the traditional image of Bacchus shows him with a crown constructed of leafy grape vines. Elsewhere in ancient Europe, this image inspired a pagan spirit known as the Green Man, a symbol of the wilderness. Witches, however, do not consider the Green Man and Bacchus to be the same entity, although they do sometimes honor them interchangeably. **See also** Green Man.

Bamberg, witch-hunts of

The witch-hunts of the principality of Bamberg, Germany, in the 1620s were among the most extensive of the many witch-hunts that took place in the country during the sixteenth and seventeenth centuries. They were also among the most brutal, thanks to Bamberg's ruler, Prince-Bishop Gottfried Johann Georg II Fuchs von Dornheim. Von Dornheim did not initiate the Bamberg witch-hunts; by the time he took control of the principality in 1623, 350 convicted witches had already been put to death since 1609 under the rule of Bishop Johann Gottfried von Aschhausen. However, von Dornheim did much to streamline the process by which accused witches were interrogated, tried, and executed. He established a witch-hunting organization comprising expert torturers, executioners, and attorneys whose goal was to gain convictions. He also built a new prison solely to house accused witches, and he directed that all accused witches be tortured both before and after confessing their crimes.

Von Dornheim's mandated tortures were so horrific that few of those accused could resist confession. For example, his professional torturers dunked suspected witches in boiling water mixed with caustic lime, forced them to kneel on spikes, crushed their bones using various devices, and/or burned their armpits. Convicted witches might have their right hands cut off or their flesh pinched or pierced in various painful ways.

Most defendants were wealthy. Bamberg witch-hunters targeted the rich because anyone found guilty of witchcraft was required to surrender all property and personal possessions to the head of the witch-hunting organization, Bishop Friedrich Förner, who in turn rewarded the witch-hunters according to the wealth they collected.

The trials were extremely short, and defendants were not allowed a lawyer. A verdict of guilty was virtually assured. It was particularly easy for witch-hunters to influence trial verdicts because witnesses against the accused were typically paid informants and investigators in the employ of the witch-hunting organization. Moreover, all accusations were kept secret at least until the suspected witch was arrested, and trials were closed to the public. Thus by the time most people heard of an arrest—if they heard of it at all—the accused had already been tortured and confessed and, in many cases, tried and executed. Testimony in defense of the accused was virtually impossible.

During the Bamberg trials, suspected witches were forced to endure terrible instruments of torture.

In any case, few would have wanted to defend an accused witch, because people who criticized the witch-hunting organization were usually accused of being witches themselves. For example, in 1628 the vice-chancellor of Bamberg, Dr. George Haan, was accused, tortured, and executed along with his wife and daughter because he opposed the organization. After his death, his torturers claimed that during his confession he had named as witches five other influential men who also opposed the organization, and they too were promptly tried and executed.

Meanwhile, affluent citizens were fleeing Bamberg in large numbers. From exile they petitioned the emperor of Germany, Ferdinand I, to end the Bamberg witch-hunts. In 1630 and 1631, he issued mandates that required all accusations to be made public and banned the practice of seizing a convicted witch's property. He also publicly spoke out against the proceedings in Bamberg.

Eventually the emperor's restrictions helped quell the witch-hunting. By then, however, thousands had died. Between 1623 and 1632 approximately six hundred people had been tortured and executed as witches in Bamberg. In the nearby principality of Würzburg, ruled by von Dornheim's cousin, Prince-Bishop Phillipp Adolf von Ehrenberg, nine hundred people—approximately three hundred of whom were children—were tortured and executed in accordance with von Dornheim's established practices. In the aftermath of these tragedies, Ferdinand I's son and successor, Ferdinand II, established new rules for the arrest and trials of witches; in particular, no accused person could be denied the services of an attorney, and no court proceedings could be secret. **See also** Germany, witch-hunts of.

banishing rituals

As part of ceremonial magic, witches and magicians use banishing rituals to dispel negative energy prior to performing other rituals, rites, or spells. The most common banishing rituals involve the pentagram, the five-pointed star that witches believe confers great protection to those practicing witchcraft. One example of a banishing ritual takes place before casting a magic circle, when the witch uses an athame or sword to repeatedly trace the sign of the pentagram in the air while facing first east, then south, then west, then north, then east again. Sometimes the blade is jabbed into the center of the visualized pentagram at the end of each tracing. After the completion of each of the first four pentagrams, the witch says the name of a deity, and after the fifth she or he recites a verse about the protection of the deities. Such verses vary, as do the names of the deities, according to Witchcraft tradition. Moreover, in some traditions the pentagram is traced on the witch's body or on the ground rather than in the air. **See also** athame; circle, magic; magic; pentacle and pentagram.

Baphomet

Baphomet is a demon whose image has been associated with witchcraft since medieval times. His appearance is that of a human with a goat's head and horns; his feet are cloven hooves, and in some cases he is drawn with wings (usually those of bats, but sometimes the wings have feathers). Although some Satanists have adopted Baphomet's head as their symbol, most modern practitioners of witchcraft reject him as a symbol of their beliefs. Nonetheless, witch persecutors of the fourteenth through seventeenth centuries often accused witches of worshiping Baphomet. The most famous reference to Baphomet in a witchcraft trial involved the Order of the Knights Templar. Members of this famed order of French knights were accused of devil worship and related crimes in the early 1300s, and under torture twelve knights confessed to worshiping Baphomet idols at their meetings. Their descriptions of these idols varied; for example, Baphomet might be represented as a painting, a carving with one face or three, or a human skull.

Historians disagree on how Baphomet came to be connected to the occult. Generally, however, they believe that he originated as an ancient Egyptian god of male fertility and sexuality, which had the appearance of a male goat. The name Baphomet possibly comes from the Greek words *baphne* and *metis*, together meaning "absorption of" or "absorption into knowledge." On this basis, some scholars believe that Baphomet represents not only fertility but wisdom. Others disagree, arguing that Baphomet was created by Christians seeking to mock Mahomet, or Muhammad, the founder of Islam. **See also** demons; Knights Templar; Satanism.

Barclay, Margaret (?–1618)

Seventeenth-century Scotswoman Margaret Barclay is an example of the mixture of misfortune, coincidence, and superstition that often led to a witchcraft accusation. Barclay disliked her brother-in-law, sea captain John Deans, and right before his ship sailed for France from Irvine, Ayrshire, Scotland, in 1617, she said she hoped it would sink. When the ship did indeed sink shortly thereafter, killing Deans and his crew, Barclay was arrested as a witch.

Also arrested was a man named John Stewart, who, when word spread that the ship was missing, said he was sure it had sunk. Under torture Stewart told investigators that he knew about the ship's fate because he had seen Barclay and two other women casting a spell against the vessel. He named one of the women, Isobel Insh, and she too was arrested. Her eight-year-old daughter was arrested as well; under torture the child said that the women had made figurines representing the ship and some of its occupants while in the presence of a demon dog.

Insh's daughter was eventually freed, but Insh died from a fall trying to escape imprisonment. Meanwhile Barclay was tortured, and the woman she named as her second accomplice, Isobel Crawford, was then tortured and executed in 1618 despite her protestations of innocence. Barclay was strangled and burned at the stake, even though she recanted the confession she made under torture. As for Stewart, he hanged himself in jail under sentence of execution.

Bargarren Imposter (1685–?)

The case of the Bargarren Imposter, an eleven-year-old girl who faked demonic possession, is a classic example of the power children sometimes gained by being witch accusers. Christine Shaw, who lived near the village of Paisley in Renfrewshire, Scotland, became the imposter in 1696, when she began accusing people of being witches. Her first targets were two people she particularly disliked: Katherine Campbell and Agnes Naismith. After that, she targeted others who displeased her or who were not well liked in her community.

Shaw's accusations were convincing because she made them while twitching and convulsing as though possessed by demons. Moreover, during her convulsions she vomited small objects such as pins, tiny bones, and eggshells, which she claimed she had been made to swallow by the spirits of these witches. (At the time, vomiting foreign objects was considered a sign of bewitchment or demonic possession.) Since two physicians could find no medical reason for her condition, in January 1697 the Privy Council of Scotland decided to investigate the matter as a possible case of witchcraft.

Meanwhile, Shaw continued to have fits and to accuse people of using witchcraft to send their spirits to torment her. In all, she named nine individuals, and some of these people—hoping for leniency from the court for their cooperation—provided additional names, so that the number of accused witches rose to twenty-one by some accounts and twenty-six by others. As the investigation into the Paisley witches proceeded, officials drew confessions from three of the accused, Elizabeth Anderson and James and Thomas Lindsay, who were children. Their confessions not only supported Shaw's accusations but added new stories of the witches' activities. For example, the children claimed that their grandmother, Jean Fulton, had taken them to witches' Sabbats, and Elizabeth said that her father, Alexander Anderson, had consulted with the devil on how best to murder Shaw by witchcraft.

These reports and others were introduced as evidence at a jury trial against the accused in April 1697. After hearing them, the jury deliberated for approximately seven hours before returning with a verdict of guilty against seven of the accused, including Katherine Campbell, Agnes Naismith, and James Lindsay, who was then fourteen. Their sentence was death by hanging followed by the burning of their bodies (a common practice to dispel a witch's evil).

After the executions, Christine Shaw's fits stopped; in 1718 she married a minister and in 1725 she brought thread-making machinery to Paisley that boosted both the economy of the region and her own popularity. Nonetheless, within a few years the Scottish people decided that Shaw had been faking her fits. In 1785 a prominent Scotsman, Hugo Arnot, dubbed her "the Bargarren Imposter." In 1839 two authors—Mr. Mitchell and Mr. Dirkie—inspected Shaw's childhood home for their book *Philosophy of Witchcraft*. The girl's bed was not only still there but still in its original location, and near its head, hidden by the frame, was a hole in the wall where the authors believe young Christine had hidden the small objects she supposedly vomited. **See also** Sabbat; Scotland, witch trials of.

Barrett, Francis (dates unknown)

Francis Barrett is a mysterious figure from the nineteenth century who some scholars believe established a school of the occult in Cambridge, England. In 1801 Barrett published a book entitled *The Magus*, which instructed readers in the performance of magic and summarized existing knowledge of the occult, including alchemy, numerology, talismans, healing herbs, and occult rituals. The book also called for people interested in learning magic to contact the author. In this way Barrett acquired at least a few students, teaching them in his home, and some evidence suggests that he might have found enough students to open a school. However, historians cannot confirm this, nor any other details of Barrett's personal life. **See also** alchemy; herbs and other plants; magic; numerology; talisman.

Barton, Elizabeth (c. 1506–1534)

Elizabeth Barton was a sixteenth-century English fortune-teller who was at first celebrated for her abilities but later condemned for them. She initially became famous after she suffered a series of seizures, then visited a chapel in Aldington, Kent, England, and claimed that the Virgin Mary had healed her there. As word of her miraculous healing spread, Barton became known as the Maid of Kent, and the chapel became a shrine visited by others wanting to be healed. Barton attracted many visitors herself, not only because of her cure but also because she claimed that the experience left her with the ability to see the future. Important people traveled long distances to visit the Maid of Kent and have their fortunes told, and Barton continued to profit from her gift until someone suggested that she predict what would happen to the king of England, Henry VIII, who had just divorced and executed his second wife, Anne Boleyn. When Barton predicted that the king would be punished for his treatment of Boleyn, she was arrested for treason and subsequently accused of being a witch. While in prison she confessed to faking her fits and her chapel healing at the urging of the Kent chapel's priest, who wanted the monetary donations that shrines typically attracted. Barton also said that her powers of divination were false, but the renunciation did not save her from execution. She was hanged in 1534. **See also** divination; England, witch-hunts of.

Basque region, witch-hunts of the

Known for its fiercely independent people, the Basque region of the Pyrenees Mountains of Spain and France was the site of extensive witch-hunting during the sixteenth and seventeenth centuries. Because the region was remote and rugged, Catholicism was slow to spread there, and its arrival in the Roman era did not completely supplant folk beliefs. Consequently, the open practice of magic was common among the Basques well into the sixteenth century. By this time the Inquisition, a Roman Catholic tribunal dedicated to eradicating witchcraft and other forms of heresy, had begun to target the Basques on the Spanish side of the Pyrenees. In the early seventeenth century authorities did the same on the French side of the mountains.

One French witch-hunter, attorney Pierre de Lancre, was particularly aggressive, reporting that he had executed six hundred Basque witches during just four months in 1609. As the executions mounted, rumors spread to the north of France regarding the possibly satanic activities of thousands of Basque witches. De Lancre fueled this hysteria by suggesting that the Basque witches were in league with other witches throughout Europe, were planning to eradicate Catholicism. Support for his witch-hunting efforts began to diminish after he executed several priests, who he said were supporting witches or were witches themselves. By this time, the Spanish had largely ended their own campaign against Basque witches, and the French people began to wonder whether de Lancre should do the same. Then a fleet of Basque fishermen who had been on a long sea voyage returned to find that many of their loved ones had been executed as witches. Their outrage convinced French authorities to recall de Lancre and put an end to the Basque witch-hunts. However, for the rest of his life de Lancre continued to insist that not enough had been done to eliminate the threat of witchcraft in the Pyrenees. He wrote several books in an attempt to reignite antiwitchcraft passions, but the French public failed to respond to his arguments. **See also** de Lancre, Pierre; France, witch-hunts of; Inquisition; Spain, witch trials of.

Bast

Also known as Bastet, Bast is an ancient Egyptian goddess of fertility still worshiped by many witches. She is particularly associated with spells and rituals related to sexuality. Since ancient times Bast has been depicted either as a cat or as a woman with the head of a cat. She is also commonly accompanied by a cat, which Egyptologists call her sacred animal but which modern witches often identify as her familiar. **See also** familiar; goddesses and gods.

bats

Bats were first associated with witchcraft during the Middle Ages, when many people decided that witches consorted with the devil. At that time Satan was typically depicted with the wings of a bat, probably because the bat is a creature of darkness, which in turn symbolized evil. Another connection between bats and magic is most likely derived from the fact that ancient Europeans thought the animal was related to dragons, magical, elusive creatures that lived in caves as bats did.

Because of bats' supposed magical qualities, medieval people thought that bat blood, bones, and wings were powerful additions to potions. Bats were also used to protect a person from witchcraft; for example, a bat bone was a popular amulet to ensure freedom from evil spells, and nailing a dead bat near the entrance to a house might keep evil from its occupants. Also in medieval times, the sight of a flying bat was interpreted as a witch in disguise, since some witches were believed able to turn themselves into bats to fly to Sabbat meetings. Alternatively, it was believed that witches flew on brooms smeared with bat blood.

Modern witches do not typically incorporate bats into their rituals, potions, or beliefs. Satanists, however, do use bats, both as ritual elements and as a symbol of their beliefs. In addition, voodoo practitioners sometimes use bat's blood as an ingredient in cures and potions. **See also** devil; potion.

bay

The ancient Romans considered the bay tree to be sacred, but since medieval times people have concentrated on the magical and medicinal properties of its leaves. They carried such leaves as protection against various diseases, particularly plague, and kept them near and within their houses to dispel evil spirits. Witches have also used bay leaves in various forms of divination. For example, some burn the leaves in a fire, then look at the flames' patterns and listen to their crackling to guide their responses to questions about the future. A certain number of crackles might mean the answer to a question is yes, another number might mean no. Primarily, however, witches employ bay leaves as ingredients in magical and medicinal potions and salves. **See also** herbs and other plants; potion.

Beelzebub

Beelzebub is a demon sometimes invoked in the performance of black magic. There is disagreement, however, over his origins and purpose. Some people believe that he and Satan are one and the same, because ancient writings refer to him as the Prince of Demons. Other people, however, believe that Beelzebub is either Satan's assistant or his immediate superior. *Beelzebub* is a Hebrew word that can be translated as "lord of the flies," although other meanings are possible. Perhaps this is why some people believe that Beelzebub has dominion over evils related to corruption or decay. However, while some Satanists worship Beelzebub, modern witches usually have nothing to do with him. **See also** demons; devil.

bees

In some cases, during the fourteenth through the sixteenth centuries, when witch-hunters could not extract a confession from an accused witch under torture, they blamed bees. Demonologists of these periods said that witches who ate a queen bee prior to their arrest would be able to withstand great pain for days. The origin of this belief is unclear, and there is no evidence that accused or convicted witches ever confessed to such a practice. Many scholars therefore suggest that the witch-hunters themselves made up the belief to justify killing witches who refused to confess.

As to why the bee was chosen for this supposed role, some scholars suggest that the reason lies in the obvious connection between human pain and the bee's stinger. In medieval times, such connections between animal traits and human responses to those traits sometimes inspired these kinds of stories. However, the connection between the bee and certain aspects of spirituality is well known. To ancient Celts the bee represented the underworld, and in ancient Greece it symbolized the soul. The ancient Greeks also associated the bee with the moon, which has itself been associated with witchcraft for centuries, and the queen bee was viewed as a symbol of the goddess known as the Great Mother. **See also** Celts; goddesses and gods; torture.

Befana

In some parts of Italy, the witch Befana is believed to fill children's stockings with presents on the eve of January 6, much the way many small children believe that Santa Claus delivers gifts on Christmas Eve. Apparently this tradition is derived from ancient times, when on the same date people would leave offerings of woven goods, such as stockings, for the goddess of fate. In fact, although today Befana is depicted as an old woman who flies on a broom or goat, she was originally a pagan goddess connected to the passage of time, one's ancestors or heritage, and the woodlands. Her transition from goddess to old witch is unclear; however, the goddess was sometimes depicted as a hunchback, an image later commonly associated with witches.

Italians honor Befana in different ways depending on the region where they live. One of the most common practices is to fill a replica of the witch with dried fruits, nuts, and candies, then break the figure open during a celebration, disperse the treats to the celebrants, and burn the figure in a bonfire. Some people believe that the burning of Befana symbolizes the return of a spirit to its ancestors. Others see it as symbolic of the passage of time, in particular the dying of winter in preparation for spring. Still others find it significant that the image of Befana is burned much the way women accused of being witches were burned during witch-hunting times, suggesting that Befana traditions were influenced by medieval Christians. However, fire was associated with pagan rituals long before witches were burned at the stake. **See also** hag.

Bekker, Balthasar (1634–1698)

Dutch scholar and Reformed Dutch Church clergyman Balthasar Bekker was a major force in preventing witch-hunts in seventeenth-century Holland. In 1691 he published *de Betoverde Weereld* (*The World Bewitched*), in which he argued, among other things, that it was impossible for witchcraft to work because spirits could not control the actions of human beings, that witches did not consort with the devil, and that anyone who believed in the power of witches was deluded. Bekker further suggested that leaders of Christian churches encouraged the public's belief in witchcraft so that they could justify the common practice of seizing the estates of wealthy people convicted of being witches. The leaders of Bekker's church did not support his views, and in 1692 they expelled him from his ministry, although they continued to pay the stipend he had been promised.

By 1693, when *de Betoverde Weereld* was reprinted in German, many Dutch people had accepted Bekker's beliefs despite the reaction of church leaders. Soon the majority of the public doubted the existence of any true witches in Holland; modern scholars believe this skepticism prevented the Dutch people from getting caught up in the witch hysteria that was then spreading throughout Europe.

After Bekker died in 1698, Dutch scholars and church leaders continued to argue the merit of his opinions. He left behind not only *de Betoverde Weereld* but another book entitled *Inquiry into Comets*, published in 1683, in which he argued that comets were a natural celestial phenomenon rather than a sign that something bad was about to happen, as was commonly believed.

bell, book, and candle

The phrase *bell, book, and candle* has long been associated with witchcraft. The connection began in medieval times, when the excommunication ritual of the Roman Catholic Church, often performed to cast a suspected witch from the religion, incorporated the use of these items. To excommunicate, or expel, someone from the church, a priest would ring a bell, read from and then close the Bible, and snuff out a candle to symbolize the end of the person's relationship with the church and therefore with God and his light. For many years, the phrase "bell, book, and candle" was used to refer to this separation of witches from God. However, in modern times many people mistakenly believe that the phrase refers to tools of witchcraft rather than the church, because some modern witches use bells, candles, and a book of rituals (usually known as the Book of Shadows) while practicing their craft. **See also** bells; Book of Shadows; candles.

bells

Bells are a common feature in modern witchcraft rituals, but ironically in the fourteenth, fifteenth, and sixteenth centuries they were thought to drive away witches. People at the time associated bells with church and therefore with God, and they believed that the sound of a ringing church bell would cause a flying witch to plunge to the ground. In fact, some villagers kept their church bells ringing all night long on dates when they thought it likely that witches would be flying to their Sabbats, such as All Hallow's Eve. Several suspected witches admitted—usually under torture—that this practice had indeed caused them to fall during flight.

Another common belief was that the sound of a pealing church bell could dispel spirits, which is one reason why church bells have traditionally been rung at funerals. The tolling bells supposedly send the spirit of the newly deceased on to heaven, while driving away any evil spirits who might seek to harm it on its journey. Other kinds of bells have been used to dispel spirits as well. For example, whereas today shopkeepers hang bells over the doors of their shops so they will know when a customer enters, the practice originated with a desire to keep evil spirits from entering the shop. For the same reason, people once commonly wore tiny bells as amulets on cords around their necks. Some bells, however, were believed to have the power to attract rather than repel spirits. Usually these bells were inscribed with magical symbols and/or were manufactured or initiated during some kind of magical ritual thought to give them power.

Fire festivals are held each year on May 1 to celebrate fertility, purification, and rebirth. Pictured are Druids reenacting the burning of a wicker man.

In modern times, witches use bells to mark certain points in witchcraft rituals. For example, in their book *A Witches' Bible: The Complete Witches' Handbook* (1981, 1984, 1996), Janet and Stewart Farrar describe a witch initiation ritual in which a handbell is rung three times in succession just before the initiate is lightly struck three times with a scourge (a type of whip). Bells are sometimes also rung to mark beginning and ending points in a ritual, and the number of times a bell is rung can have meaning within a ceremony. Generally, modern witches believe the bell to be the symbol of the Goddess they call upon in their rituals, and they consider it a tool that focuses their concentration via sound, thereby increasing their power. **See also** Farrar, Janet and Stewart; flight; rites and rituals.

Beltane

Also called Bealtaine or May Day, Beltane ("bright fire") is an ancient Celtic fire festival celebrated by most witches every May 1 as part of the Wheel of the Year. In ancient times, the festivities actually began the night before, on April 30, and its alternative names included the May Eve Festival or Walpurgisnacht ("Night of the Witches"). Beltane is one of four Celtic fire festivals; the other three are Imbolc, Lughnasadh, and Samhain. Beltane and Samhain are considered the two greatest pagan Sabbats, and they are opposite each other on the Wheel of the Year.

Bel was the Celtic god of light, the harbinger of the summer sun and the increased fertility it brought to the land, and many people believe that he was the deity in whose honor the festival was originally created. Indeed, Beltane traditionally involves large bonfires, although in modern times some witches make do with small fires or even candlelight for their celebration. A common practice during the festival is to jump over the fire as an act of purification. In ancient times, cows were driven over the ashes of a Beltane bonfire or between two bonfires to ensure their fertility and high milk production for the coming year. Similarly, women who wanted to become pregnant would leap over the fire to increase their fertility, and both women and men would make the leap prior to departure on a journey to ensure that they would arrive safely at their destination.

Beltane's association with fertility has also led some Witchcraft traditions to use the festival as a time of sexual abandon. The maypole, which schoolchildren in many parts of the world have traditionally danced around to celebrate May Day, is actually an ancient symbol of the sexual union of the God and Goddess, duplicated by some witches in a ritual known as the Great Rite. Many Witchcraft traditions recognize Beltane as the time of the year when the Goddess becomes sexually aware, making her transition from a Maiden to a Mother. Some modern witches celebrate Beltane by making a maypole and dancing around it and/or by decorating their homes with ribbons, flowers, and other signs of the spring season. In addition, since the festival is also associated with purification and rebirth, it is customary for witches to think of something they would like to eliminate from their lives, write it on a piece of paper, and burn the paper in a fire as part of a spell of purification. **See also** bonfire; Great Rite; Wheel of the Year.

Benandanti

The Benandanti was a secret Italian society that attracted the attention of the Inquisition between 1575 and 1647. Under questioning, its members initially insisted that they were not witches at all, but instead worked for Jesus Christ in fighting Malandanti, or the perpetrators of evil. The name Benandanti means "perpetrators of good," and some members of this sect claimed that they would go into trances to fight the Malandanti in the spirit realm. They further claimed that these battles were over the fate of the harvest and took place in the spring and fall—in other words, just prior to the growing season and the harvest season. In later confessions, members of the Benandanti admitted to being witches and engaging in pagan fertility rites, also tied to agricultural seasons. Some modern scholars have noted that many of the rites, rituals, and magical practices mentioned in Benandanti confessions have much in common with those of Wicca, and they believe this supports the notion that the Benandanti really were witches. Others argue that the Benandanti's initial denials reflected the truth, and that they only confessed to being witches under torture. **See also** Inquisition; Wicca.

Bergson, Mona (1865–1928)

Mona Bergson was a French occultist and goddess worshiper who, with her husband, Samuel Mathers, gave public exhibitions of occult rites honoring the ancient Egyptian goddess Isis. She and Mathers were also prominent members of an occult group called the Hermetic Order of the Golden Dawn, which was established in England in 1887. However, they were asked to leave the group when other members decided that the couple was using magic for evil rather than good purposes. In 1918 Mathers died, apparently of influenza, and Bergson decided to start her own Order of the Golden Dawn, which many believe concentrated on black magic. **See also** Golden Dawn, Hermetic Order of the.

Bible

For centuries, Christians justified their persecution of witches using references to the Bible. Today many people continue to oppose witchcraft as contrary to biblical

Many witch persecutors have justified their beliefs by quoting the King James Version of the Bible. The king's hatred of witches influenced the language his scribes used when translating the Bible.

teachings. However, scholars believe that prohibitions against witchcraft were not originally part of Scripture. The text that witch persecutors have used to justify their actions and beliefs was usually from or derived from the King James Version of the Bible, which is biased against witches. King James, who commissioned this translation of the Bible, so hated witches that he authored *Daemonologie*, a popular 1597 guidebook to witch-hunting. In translating the Bible into English, his scribes chose words intended to vilify witches, knowing they would please the king.

One example of this appears in chapter 22, verse 18, of the Old Testament Book of Exodus. As translated in the King James Version of the Bible, it states: "Thou shalt not suffer a witch to live." This was one of the most common justifications for executing witches, particularly after witch-hunter Matthew Hopkins quoted the verse in his 1647 book about the Salem witch trials, *The Discovery of Witches*. However, in the original Hebrew version of Exodus the word that King James's men had translated as "witch" was actually *chaspah* or *Kashaph;* in Latin translations this same word was *veneficus* or *maleficia*. The most accurate translation of these words into English would be *poisoner* or *malevolent sorcerer*, not witch.

Another significant passage relates to a nameless woman who has been dubbed the Witch of Endor. In chapter 28, verses 7 through 25 of Samuel I, King Saul of Israel hears that she is "a woman that hath a familiar spirit." Saul goes to her in disguise and asks her to "divine . . . by the familiar spirit" and bring forth the spirit of Samuel so that Saul might ask his advice. According to the Bible, the woman does indeed bring forth Samuel's spirit, but people of the sixteenth century debated whether this act was real or a trick. Many scholars, most notably Reginald Scot in his 1584 book *Discoverie of Witchcraft*, argued that the Witch of Endor was a fraud and her conjuring a fake, because he did not believe in witchcraft. However, King James I and others used the biblical reference to the Witch of Endor as proof that witches were real.

However, once again the King James translation of the Bible differs from earlier texts. By using the words "woman who hath a familiar spirit," King James's scribes were saying that the woman was a witch. However, in Hebrew she was *ba'alath ob*, mistress of a talisman, and in Latin she was *mulierem habentem pythonem*, a woman who used a spirit as an oracle. In other words, she practiced divination, but such people in ancient times were considered different from witches.

People of King James's time distinguished between diviners and witches as well. Divination was commonly practiced and not viewed as in any way offensive to Christianity. In fact, during the sixteenth century people used the Bible itself to practice divination. They would ask a question about the future, open the Bible at random, then read a passage and attempt to find in its words the answer to their question.

The Bible was also used as a tool against witches. One common test for witches was to weigh the suspected witch against the enormous Bible kept in most European churches. Someone weighing more than the Bible was considered guilty of practicing witchcraft. Certain passages of the Bible were also used as part of witchcraft tests. Suspected witches were asked to recite one of these passages—the Lord's Prayer was perhaps the most popular—under the belief that no real witch would be able to do so because the devil would never allow it. Such recitations were performed by memory; initially, suspects were considered guilty only if they were unable to remember the passage at all. Then witch-hunters made the test more difficult for the suspects by demanding that they get every word exactly right. Those who stumbled even slightly were considered guilty and usually executed.

The use of the Lord's Prayer in a variety of witchcraft tests was advocated by Heinrich Kramer and James Sprenger in their extremely popular 1486 guide to witch-hunting, *Malleus Maleficarum*. The first references to the prayer as a combatant of evil appeared in writings of the fourth century, and it was mentioned routinely after that. **See also** James I; *Malleus Maleficarum.*

bier right

The bier right was an unusual test demanded of accused witches being tried for murder. Beginning in the late sixteenth century, people believed that the body of someone killed by witchcraft would start bleeding upon being touched by the witch who committed the crime. Records of witch trials indicate that on several occasions when this test was administered, the body did indeed bleed. For example, during a series of trials of witches from the Pendle Forest area of Lancashire, England, accused witch Jennet Preston was ordered to touch the corpse of Thomas Lister, whom she was thought to have killed via witchcraft. When the body began to bleed, Preston's fate was sealed; she was executed as a witch in July 1612. **See also** Pendle Forest, witch trial of.

Bilson, Boy of

A boy named William Perry, commonly known as the Boy of Bilson because he came from Bilson, England, became famous in seventeenth-century England for perpetrating a hoax that involved demonic possession. Perry conspired with a Roman Catholic priest to fake possession so that the priest could exorcise Perry's demons, thereby raising the priest's stature in the church. To this end, the priest taught Perry how to behave to make himself appear possessed, encouraging the boy to fake convulsions, speak strangely, and pretend to vomit small objects. The first time Perry attempted the hoax, public officials became suspicious before an exorcism was performed, and the boy ended up confessing that his fits were not real. However, he never mentioned his co-conspirator, the priest. Perry then tried again, insisting that his new bout of fits was genuine. One prominent bishop, Thomas Morton, believed the Boy of Bilson enough to launch an investigation into his possession case. During this investigation, two events led officials to conclude that Perry was still a fraud. First, someone saw him putting ink into his urine to turn it black, because black urine was then considered one possible sign of demonic possession. Second, Perry claimed that his demons caused him to have a fit every time a particular biblical passage was read aloud to him. Investigators therefore tried reading the passage aloud in languages unknown to the boy, but they mixed in other, benign passages as well. When Perry thought they were reading the problematic passage, he began mimicking convulsions; other times he was unaffected. Unfortunately for his credibility, several times he made the wrong guess, and in the end investigators declared him a fake. Perry then confessed his association with the priest, and permanently abandoned his attempts to feign demonic possession. **See also** demonic possession.

binding spell

A binding spell, also known simply as a binding, is a spell used to restrict the actions of the person against whom the spell is cast. Many Wiccans believe that such spells are unethical because they curtail free will and therefore harm the human spirit. They base this belief on one of the main tenets of Wicca, the Wiccan Rede, which in effect advises the witch to do no harm. Some Wiccans further believe that employing a binding spell is dangerous, since Wiccans generally subscribe to the philosophy that whatever they do magically will come back to them threefold. In other words, anyone casting a binding spell would be likely to suffer a three-times-greater restriction of their own freedom in the future. However, some Wiccans condone a binding spell used to keep someone from committing an evil deed or evil magic, which falls into a different category than a binding spell used to curtail other types of free will, such as occurs when a love binding spell is used to bind one person's love to another.

Most bindings involve the wrapping and/or tying of ropes, cords, or ribbons around an image of the person being bound. The love binding spell is an excellent example. There are several ways to cast a love binding spell, but generally a doll is made from elm branches, red felt, and a photograph of the face of whomever will be bound. The completed doll is held above the flame of a red candle while the witch wraps red twine around the doll and chants a love-binding verse. The witch then keeps the doll in her possession, thereby keeping her beloved under her spell.

Candles are also a common part of the ritual that accompanies the binding spell. Red is the most common color for the cord, but the color of the candle varies depending on the intent of the spell. **See also** candles; knots; spells.

Binsfeld, Peter (c. 1540–1603)

German bishop Peter Binsfeld is the author of the 1589 book *Tractatus de Confessionibus Maleficorum et Sagarum* (*Treatise on Confessions by Evildoers and Witches*), which encouraged witch-hunts and was quoted by many European courts and religious authorities, both Catholic and Protestant, to justify their prosecution of suspected witches. Binsfeld's work named and described the activities of certain demons, but its main focus was the confessions of suspected witches. He argued that even confessions acquired through brutal torture were valid, and that any recantations of such confessions should not be trusted. He also suggested that while other criminals should generally be assumed innocent until being found guilty, suspected witches should always be assumed guilty until proven innocent, and the burden of proof was very high. Although Binsfeld died in 1603, his opinions continued to influence European judges until the eighteenth century. **See also** demons; Germany, witch-hunts of; persecution, witch; torture.

birch

Witches consider the birch to be a sacred tree. In that capacity they burn its wood at

Beltane festivals and make their brooms by tying birch twigs to a branch from an ash tree. Sweeping an area with such a broom is believed to purify it. Two types of birches are traditionally used for such tasks, the yellow birch (also known as the silver birch, or *Betula alleghaniensis*) of Britain and the European white birch (*Betula pendula*) of Europe and Asia Minor. **See also** ash; broom; trees.

Black Fast

The Black Fast is a term used during the sixteenth century to refer to a fasting ritual supposedly practiced by witches. In actuality, fasting has never been a prominent feature of witchcraft, if it is used at all. However, because fasting has always been practiced by Catholics, people of the sixteenth century assumed that witches fasted too. But whereas Catholics fasted as a way to honor Christ's suffering and thereby become closer to God, it was believed that witches fasted to improve their concentration, increase their power during rituals, and perhaps become closer to Satan.

The first reference to the Black Fast in witchcraft trials was part of the 1538 confession of accused witch Mabel Brigge. She reported that this particular fast required the elimination of all meat and dairy products from the diet, and she said that she had undertaken the Black Fast in order to improve her concentration so she could divine the whereabouts of a stolen object. However, her neighbor insisted that the Black Fast had instead given Brigge the power to kill a man and that she was plotting to kill another: Henry VIII, the king of England. Following her confession, the suspected witch was quickly executed. **See also** England, witch-hunts of.

black magic

Black magic is magic performed to call forth evil forces with the intent of causing harm or destruction. Most Wiccans and Neopagans do not practice this type of magic, believing not only that it is wrong to do so but also that its performance will bring equal amounts of harm to both the person employing the black magic and the person who is its object. However, black magic has been extensively practiced by Satanists, both in medieval and modern times. **See also** devil.

Black Mass

The Black Mass is a ceremony mocking the Catholic Mass, the central ritual of the Catholic faith, and as such is used to invoke Satan rather than God. Descriptions of the Black Mass vary, but generally involve sexually explicit words and behavior, incantations from the Catholic Mass said backwards, and tools from the Catholic Mass used in perverted ways. Many people believe that modern witches practice the Black Mass. However, the mass has never been a part of the Wiccan religion, nor does it appear to have been performed by any witch prior to the 1643–1715 reign of French king Louis XIV, and even then its use was minimal.

In fact, the idea of the Black Mass appears to have come not from practice but from fiction. Donatien-Alphonse-François, Comte de Sade (more commonly known as the Marquis de Sade) was one of several eighteenth-century authors who featured the concept of the Black Mass in their novels. In his 1791 book *Justine: ou, Les Malheurs de la vertu*, he describes a perverted mass performed by evil monks. Modern authors and filmmakers have also depicted the Black Mass as integral to Satanism, and there are Satanists today who do perform a version of the ritual.

Blanckenstein, Chatrina (1610–1679)

The case of accused witch Chatrina Blanckenstein is often cited as one of the most tragic injustices of the witch-hunts of the sixteenth and seventeenth centuries. Blanckenstein was a sixty-six-year-old German widow when she was arrested in 1676 on charges of murdering a baby through witchcraft. The death occurred four days after the child ate some of Blanckenstein's homemade jam and fell ill. During Blanckenstein's trial, which took place somewhere in the region of Saxony, Germany, other townspeople came forward to blame her for their misfortune. For example, one man said that Blanckenstein had used witchcraft to overturn his cart, even though the accident had clearly been caused by the man himself. Meanwhile, the court decided to authorize torture to extract a confession from the widow. Blanckenstein endured horrible suffering from such devices as thumbscrews and ropes twisted around her neck, but she refused to confess. Investigators then searched her body for a devil's mark, a skin blemish taken as a sign of proof that someone was a witch. When they found none they decided to dismiss the case, providing Blanckenstein would pay the costs of her imprisonment, trial, and torture.

Blanckenstein settled her debt and tried to resume her life, but her neighbors shunned her and she moved away. Later, however, she apparently returned to her hometown, where her daughter continued to live after Blanckenstein's death in approximately 1679. This daughter, whose name in court records is given only as "L—," was arrested on a charge of murder by witchcraft in May 1689. The reason for the charge was clearly L—'s family history; when a baby died unexpectedly and it was discovered that the infant's father had long owed L— money, townspeople assumed that Blanckenstein's daughter had in anger used the same witchcraft as Blanckenstein to kill the baby. But whereas Blanckenstein had withstood torture during her trial, L— confessed as soon as she saw the instruments of torture. Two days later she tried to hang herself in jail but her jailers found and revived her. Shortly thereafter she was burned alive. **See also** burning of witches; Germany, witch-hunts of.

blasting

Medieval Europeans believed that witches could magically destroy crops through a process known as blasting. To perform a blasting, the witch would supposedly first ritually kill and burn an animal (usually a cat or toad, but sometimes other animals were believed to be used as well), then employ magic to make blasting powder from its ashes. The witch would then sprinkle this deadly powder in the fields (perhaps while flying above the crops on a broomstick) in order to kill every plant.

Blessed be

Blessed be is one of the most commonly used phrases among modern witches. It is spoken as a greeting, in parting, in certain invocations, and as part of other rituals. A similar phrase, "Bright blessings," is used to say good-bye; the word *bright* refers to the glow of the moon. **See also** invocation.

blood

Because of its vital importance in supporting life, blood has been used in the practice of magic since ancient times, as well as in the performance of religious rituals. Animal and human sacrifices in which blood was intentionally spilled on an altar or other sacred spot were a part of many primitive cultures. Among ancient Vikings, for example, part of the sacrificial ritual involved smearing blood not only on the altar but on temple walls and the skin of participants in the ceremony. Blood sacrifices were also an important part of the religious practices of ancient Hebrews. Indeed, the Old Testament mentions many instances in which a blood sacrifice was used to ratify a covenant between man and God, and the Bible contains several stories in which God changes water into blood. Perhaps for this reason, an ancient magical system most likely originated by the Hebrews, the Kabbalah, used water to symbolize blood in various magical rituals, although actual blood was sometimes used instead.

Witches have similarly employed blood in magic rituals, believing that it adds power to their spells. In particular, they say that the letting of blood releases energy, and that when this is done within a magic circle the energy is held there for use during the ensuing rituals. Today most witches who practice bloodletting cut themselves to spill blood within the circle. However, some witches—such as Aleister Crowley in the 1920s and 30s—have sacrificed animals within magic circles during rituals. This practice is rare among witches today, but animal bloodletting is still common among practitioners of vodun, Santeria, and Satanism. Some Christians accuse modern Satanists of letting blood through human sacrifices, usually claiming that they use infants for this purpose. Christians made the same accusations against witches in the fourteenth through seventeenth centuries, and subjected accused witches to brutal torture to obtain confessions of human sacrifices and cannibalism.

During this same period, the connection between blood and magical energy led many witch-hunters to bleed suspected witches as a way of weakening their magic. This magic was believed to remain powerful and dangerous even after death, unless the witch's body was destroyed by burning. Therefore witches were typically burned to ashes, either while still alive or after having been killed.

Also during this period, witches were said to sign pacts with the devil using blood instead of ink, again because blood was believed to represent the essence of the witches' power. Some modern witches use blood as a substitute for ink in drawing magical symbols, but this practice is becoming less and less common. The same is true for the use of blood as an ingredient in potions and charms. **See also** circle, magic; devil; Kabbalah; potion; Santeria; vodun.

Blue Star Wicca

Blue Star Wicca is an American Witchcraft tradition that emphasizes the worship of goddesses and gods more than the practice of magic, although witchcraft is still performed. Which gods and goddesses are worshiped depends on the coven; however, many choose Celtic, Greek, or Roman deities. The tradition is highly organized, with coven officers and a defined set of beliefs, and membership includes families with children as well as adults. Witches newly initiated into the tradition are called Dedicants; with time and training they progress to becoming Neophytes and then Elders.

The Blue Star Tradition arose from a coven known as the Coven of the Blue Star. Established in 1974, this coven was primarily comprised of people who had been involved in the Pagan Way movement of the 1970s, which sought to make it easier for people to become practitioners of witchcraft. Some members of the Pagan Way had backgrounds in the American Welsh, Gardnerian, and Alexandrian Traditions, and the resulting Blue Star Tradition has many things in common with these traditions. However, the group is unique in that in 1983 some of its members created an album of music appropriate for pagan rituals. Today the Blue Star Tradition continues to feature such music in its rituals, as do other traditions it has inspired. These include the Blue Star Traditionalists and the Blue Star Nationalists. **See also** traditions, Witchcraft.

Blymire, John (c. 1895–?)

John Blymire was a self-professed American witch who committed murder because of a hex. His 1929 trial in the Pennsylvania Dutch region of Pennsylvania made him internationally famous for a time, as journalists issued regular reports on the sensational case. The murder victim was a witch named Nelson Rehmeyer. When Blymire was five years old, his father—a witch himself, as was his father—took him to Rehmeyer to be cured of an unexplained illness, probably anemia or some type of vitamin deficiency. The boy was soon well, and he continued to see Rehmeyer whenever he was sick. From the age of ten to the age of twelve, Blymire worked for Rehmeyer doing farm chores but he also learned some witchcraft, and later Blymire began performing witchcraft on his own. However, he did not earn any money as a witch, curing illnesses only as a favor for friends rather than as a business.

In 1912, Blymire began having health problems that made him so weak and tired he could barely get to his job as a factory worker. Eventually he decided that another witch—probably one jealous of his own witchcraft skills—had hexed him. For the next eight years Blymire visited other witches, asking them either to remove the hex or to help him find out who had caused his trouble. One of these witches told him that the perpetrator was someone he knew personally. Blymire suspected his wife for a time, and his relationship with her suffered as a result. Then in 1928 a well-respected witch named Nellie Noll named Rehmeyer as the culprit. Noll later said that Rehmeyer had also hexed two acquaintances of Blymire's—P.D. Hess and a teenager named John Curry—both of whom had already told Blymire they thought they had been hexed.

Together these three men went to confront Rehmeyer, along with Hess's son Wilbert. Once at Rehmeyer's home, however, the four lost their nerve and pretended they were just there for a friendly visit. The next day they returned to demand Rehmeyer's book of spells. When he said he had no such book, they attacked him, tied him up, and began punching him, kicking him, and hitting him with a board. Rehmeyer was killed, and his killers seized the opportunity to steal all of his money.

Because Blymire and his companions had told other people that they were going to visit Rehmeyer, the police easily connected the murder to them. Blymire immediately confessed, and in January 1929 he and his associates stood trial for first-degree murder. Just before the proceedings began, the judge forbade any of the attorneys from mentioning witchcraft in the courtroom. At the time he said his ban was meant to keep the jury from being prejudiced against Blymire, but later the judge stated that he actually wanted to keep his town from becoming known for harboring witches. In either case, the motive for Rehmeyer's murder was presented as robbery rather than anything related to witchcraft. The jury accepted this and found all of the defendants guilty.

Some historians believe that the verdict would have been different if the judge had allowed witchcraft-related testimony. At the time of the trial most people who lived in the area already believed that they lived among witches and that these witches could cure illness or bring bad luck down on others. In fact, self-professed Pennsylvania Dutch witches openly advertised that they could provide cures and hexes. The jury would probably have considered it possible that the men acted in self-defense, killing Rehmeyer to rid themselves of an evil curse. A few historians further speculate that this was the real reason the judge would not allow witchcraft-related testimony at the trial: He wanted the men found guilty. Curry and Hess served five years in prison, paroled from a ten- to twenty-year sentence; Blymire served twenty-three years of a life sentence.

Bodin, Jean (1529–1596)

Sixteenth-century French attorney Jean Bodin wrote one of the most widely read books on witchcraft of his time, *De la Démonomanie des sorciers* (*Demonomania of Witches*), published in 1580. As a young man, Bodin was a Carmelite monk; he then left the order to study law, eventually becoming a law professor. In 1561 he abandoned university life for the royal court, serving King Charles IX. After fifteen years in the king's service he published a work entitled *Six livres de la république* (*Six Books of the Republic*), in which he questioned the right of the king to rule the people. Naturally this suggestion lost him the favor of the king, so he left his post to become first a small-town attorney and then a prosecutor and trial judge. He also wrote extensively on politics and philosophy, but it was his work on witchcraft that gained him fame.

Démonomanie was published in roughly a dozen editions, including German and Latin translations. Like several other works of the period, the book offers descriptions of witches' activities. However, Bodin went further than previous authors on the subject by advocating that witches be tortured as brutally as possible. He suggested extremely painful methods and complained that the experience of being burned alive was not long enough. He also said that children should be tortured just as cruelly as adults to get them to speak out against their parents. He reported that as a trial judge he had often ordered that adults and children be burned with hot irons until they confessed to every charge leveled against them. In fact, Bodin argued that it was the duty of all judges to treat witches severely and then execute them by an extremely painful method, adding that anyone who showed mercy to condemned witches should be executed as well. Bodin's work was quoted by many judges seeking to justify their cruelties during witch-hunts. Ironically, Bodin died a painful death himself after contracting bubonic plague in 1596. **See also** torture.

bogey-man

The word *bogey-man* commonly refers to an evil spirit or demon who roams at night looking to cause trouble for people out alone. This spirit is said to particularly dislike children; in some folktales the bogeyman enters houses to snatch away youngsters who misbehave. In some regions, the bogey-man has traditionally been considered an agent of the devil, in others an agent of witches, and in still others the devil himself in disguise.

Boguet, Henri (c. 1550–1619)

French attorney Henri Boguet is the author of a legal textbook that helped guide judges in condemning witches. Entitled *Discours des sorciers* (*Discourse on Sorcery*) and published in 1602, this book included an appendix called "The Manner of Procedure of a Judge in a Case of Witchcraft," which offered detailed information on legal statutes and accepted practices during witchcraft trials. Boguet's book also offered details of witchcraft cases that Boguet himself presided over as chief judge in Burgundy, France. While he was on the bench, he oversaw the torture of an eight-year-old girl supposedly possessed by demons; she accused several people of sending the demons, thereby touching off a witch-hunt that ultimately led to the prosecution of more than forty suspected witches. As a judge, Boguet ordered a total of six hundred deaths, including the execution of numerous children. In many cases he decreed that the condemned be burned alive, even though the common practice at the time was to strangle the accused first before burning the body. (It was believed that burning dispelled evil.) Boguet also authorized brutal torture of suspected witches to extract confessions. His textbook was widely read, and his methods were copied by many other judges. *Discours* went through over a dozen reprintings by 1614, and was relied on as an authoritative work for several years thereafter. **See also** burning of witches; torture.

Boleyn, Anne (c. 1507–1536)

The case of English queen Anne Boleyn is a prominent example of the political use of witchcraft accusations during the sixteenth century. Boleyn was the second wife of England's King Henry VIII, who left his first wife, Catherine of Aragon, to remarry. The primary reason for the king's action was simple: He wanted a son and heir, and Catherine had not produced one. At the time, however, many people accepted the Catholic Church's doctrine, which held that Catherine was still Henry's wife in the eyes of God; these critics suggested that Boleyn had bewitched the king in order to usurp Catherine. Also opposed to Boleyn were members of the royal court who resented her influence over the king's decisions. Together these opponents fueled rumors that Boleyn was a witch and also that she was being unfaithful to the king.

Eventually the king himself came to believe these rumors, even going so far as to tell members of his court that his wife's body bore a devil's mark, some blemish believed to indicate an association with witchcraft. Historians disagree on the exact nature of this abnormality; some say it was an extra finger, a nub, on her left hand, while others believe it was an extra nipple on one breast. In either case, when Boleyn gave birth to a stillborn son (after having earlier given birth to a healthy daughter, Elizabeth), Henry called it God's way of punishing him for consorting with a witch. He ordered his wife arrested for treason, a charge based on her supposed infidelity, and she was quickly convicted and beheaded. **See also** England, witch-hunts of.

Perhaps the most prominent figure executed on charges of witchcraft, Anne Boleyn was accused of infidelity and bewitching King Henry VIII.

bolline

A bolline is a traditional witch's knife but is never used ritualistically; the ritual knife is the athame. However, the bolline is employed during rituals—as well as at other times—for ordinary tasks like cutting rope or carving wood. The bolline's first use was as a small sickle for harvesting herbs. Today the blade is not always curved, but the knife remains functional and plain in design rather than ornate. **See also** athame; herbs and other plants; tools, ritual.

bonfire

Since ancient times, pagans have used bonfires to celebrate certain festivals and as part of rituals related to fertility and the harvest. For example, the Celts lit bonfires in the spring to celebrate the return of life to the fields; ashes from the fire were scattered to encourage the growth of crops. During at least one of their festivals, the Beltane (also known as Bealtaine) fire festival, people would jump over a dying bonfire to increase their own fertility, bring themselves luck in finding a mate, or increase their chances of having a successful pregnancy or a safe journey. Farmers also drove their cows through the dying bonfire to ensure the animals would have healthy calves and produce large quantities of rich milk.

Three other fire festivals also sometimes feature bonfires: Imbolc, Lughnasadh, and Samhain. In addition, the Midsummer Festival, held since antiquity at the time of the summer solstice, can feature twin bonfires; passing between them is believed to confer the same luck as passing over a dying single bonfire.

Witches' bonfires created for sacred purposes are sometimes called balefires. Witches dance around them, either clothed or naked (or, as modern witches say, skyclad), both in celebration and to invoke deities. In addition, they often toss objects into the fire as part of spell-casting or rituals. For example, many witches write requests for certain items on pieces of paper that they then throw into the fire, in the belief that the smoke will carry their wishes to deities that can provide them. They might also pour wine into the flames to honor a particular goddess or god.

In recent years, most modern witches have chosen to perform such rituals indoors using a candle instead of a balefire or bonfire. They typically cite two reasons for this decision. First, finding space for and building a large fire outdoors in the close quarters of most cities is difficult today, and may actually violate ordinances regulating outdoor burning. Second, some witches fear that their outdoor celebrations will antagonize their nonwitch neighbors. On Halloween, however, in many parts of the United States and Europe bonfires are considered integral to the secular holiday's fun, not as having religious or magical significance. Many witches therefore feel free to hold their Samhain festival—which occurs on the same date—around an outdoor bonfire. **See also** Wheel of the Year.

Book of Shadows

The Book of Shadows is the hand-copied notebook or journal in which modern witches record their spells, charms, incantations, rituals, magical recipes, coven guidelines, and other Craft-related information. Some witches say that the title is derived from the concept that the book captures only the shadows of the realm in which magic resides. Others say it comes from the fact that magic must be performed in the shadows, kept secret from nonbelievers who might persecute the practitioners. In any case, a Book of Shadows is always secret; it is never left lying where anyone who cares to might read it.

Because the Book of Shadows usually includes personal observations and commentary as well as content passed on from other witches, each volume is unique, and most modern witches have one. In addition, each coven has a Book of Shadows that belongs to the group and is kept by its high priestess or priest. Coven members are allowed to copy information from the coven's book into their own, not all at once but in stages as the member ascends the coven hierarchy. A witch might also be permitted to copy passages from another witch's Book of Shadows.

When a witch dies, other members of that person's coven make sure that her or his Book of Shadows is destroyed, unless the deceased has previously named someone to inherit the book. Similarly, a coven's Book of Shadows is not supposed to leave the care of the coven; if the coven disbands then the book is either destroyed or bestowed on a worthy member or friend of the coven.

The most famous Book of Shadows is the one that belonged to Gerald Gardner, who claimed that in 1939 an English coven comprising hereditary witches gave him an ancient Book of Shadows containing centuries-old rituals. Gardner's claim has been questioned, however, since there is no evidence that early witches wrote their rituals down; the Book of Shadows appears to be a relatively modern invention. Nonetheless,

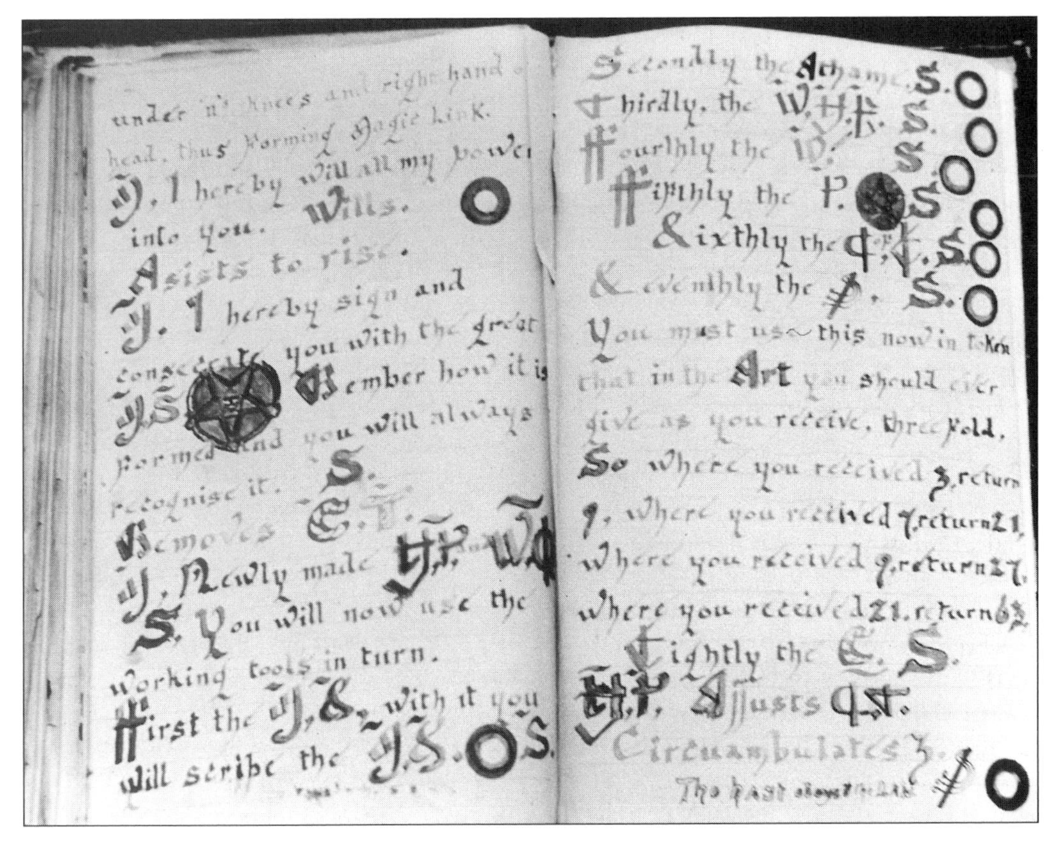

Modern witches record their spells, rituals, and personal observations in a Book of Shadows. Due to their secret nature, these books are never left on display and are typically destroyed after their owners die.

Gardner's Book of Shadows became the basis of a new Witchcraft tradition, the Gardnerian Tradition, after Gardner decided to share its contents plus his own additions first with other witches and then with the general public. **See also** Gardner, Gerald; Gardnerian Tradition.

Bridgit

The Irish Celtic goddess Bridgit, or Brighid—known as Brigantia in England, Bride-in in Scotland, and Brigandu in Celtic France—is worshiped by members of many Witchcraft traditions. To modern witches she represents the Maiden aspect of the goddess of the moon and is honored as part of the Imbolc fire festival in the Wiccan Wheel of the Year. Throughout history she has variously been known as the goddess of fertility, fire, smithcraft, inspiration, creativity, poetry, spirituality, wisdom, healing, and medicine. According to the Irish, Bridgit invented keening, the traditional grief-filled, sing-song crying of an Irishwoman in mourning. In most Irish legends, she is associated only with women; it is said that no man was allowed to enter her dwelling-place.

Among pagans, Bridgit was so popular that early Christian missionaries could not eradicate her worship. Shrewdly, they converted her to a saint, Saint Bridget, by spreading stories that she was a human daughter of a Druid who had been converted to Christianity by Saint Patrick. Saint Bridget continues to be honored by many Christians today. **See also** Celts; goddesses and gods.

British Traditional

British Traditional is a Witchcraft tradition that mixes elements of the Celtic Traditional and Gardnerian Traditions. In general, British Traditional covens draw on the writings of Janet and Stewart Farrar for their rituals, and members follow a structured path to work their way up through the hierarchy of the group. Deities featured in rituals and festivals might be those once worshiped by ancient people either throughout Britain or only in a particular region of Britain, depending on the coven. **See also** Celts; Farrar, Janet and Stewart; Gardnerian Tradition.

Brocken

The Brocken is a mountain where witches have long been rumored to meet, located in Germany's Harz Mountains. In ancient times the mountain was at first considered sacred and then magical, perhaps because mist often forms strange ghostly figures near the peak. By the mid–eighteenth century, most Europeans believed that the Brocken was the site of large witches' Sabbats that drew participants from all over Germany. The witches supposedly flew to the Brocken on broomsticks, which is why the symbol for the Brocken on some German maps is a silhouette of a witch on a broomstick. The biggest of these Sabbat meetings was believed to take place on the night of April 30, known in Germany as Walpurgis Night. Similar to Halloween, it is considered the time of demons, and townspeople in the Harz Mountains have historically avoided venturing out on this night. **See also** broom; Germany, witchhunts of; Sabbat.

broom

Also known as a besom (BEH-sum), the broom of a modern witch is used as a ritual tool. In some cases it is employed prior to certain ceremonies to sweep the area where spells will be cast or rituals performed, so as to dispel negative energy. In other cases it is laid across places believed to be thresholds to the Otherworld (where spirits dwell), such as the opening of a magic circle, in order to seal them. The broom is also often used as part of handfasting ceremonies, a rite that joins two witches in marriage; at the end of such ceremonies both participants jump over the broomstick to seal their union.

To nonwitches the broomstick has become a symbol of witchcraft, largely because of testimony given during European interrogations of suspected witches in the fifteenth through seventeenth centuries. Some accused witches confessed to sitting astride magical broomsticks to fly to their Sabbats; a few also insisted that they were given their broomsticks by Satan himself. According to their confessions, witches would coat the stick part of the broom with flying ointment prior to use.

Most Europeans of the period believed that witches regularly flew on broomsticks. In Germany, this belief was particularly strong. Germans first began using the image of a witch on a broomstick in 1280, when it appeared in the stonework of a cathedral, and by the eighteenth century this image was sometimes placed on maps to denote regions where witches were believed to reside. Nonetheless, most suspected witches insisted under interrogation that their broomsticks were not instruments of flight but might be straddled during ritual dances.

Ritual use of broomsticks goes back many centuries. Ancient fertility rites in what are now Great Britain and the European continent sometimes featured "rides" through fields on broomsticks or pitchforks, with the former usually representing the female life force and the latter the male. Broomsticks were also used in ancient rituals related to tree worship.

Witches' broomsticks from medieval times to the present have generally been made by using a cord of willow bark to tie birch twigs to a stick fashioned from an ash branch. In some parts of England, however, a birch-bark cord, oak twigs, and a hazel stick were more commonly used. Each wood used in making the broom had significance during ancient times, when certain trees were worshiped as sacred and powerful.

Prior to using a newly made broom, witches perform a ceremony to consecrate it and eliminate all negative energy from the wood. Modern consecration ceremonies differ according to Witchcraft tradition, but generally they involve subjecting the broom to each of the four elements. For example, the broom might be sprinkled with salt and water to represent the elements earth and water, respectively, then passed quickly through incense for air and a candle flame for fire.

Interestingly, during medieval times, ordinary household brooms—i.e., brooms not intended for use by witches—were made by attaching bunches of the broom plant, *Planta genista*, to any kind of stick, because *Planta genista* was thought to repel witches. In fact, such brooms were believed to be so repulsive to witches that no witch would cross a threshold where one had been laid. Even as late as the nineteenth century, some Europeans considered a broomstick a good luck charm for a house, undoubtedly a holdover from the earlier belief regarding the broom's effect on witches. **See also** flight; tools, ritual; trees.

Brossier, Marthe (c. 1573–?)

Marthe Brossier is known for faking demonic possession for profit, gaining fame in France but also fueling witchcraft-related hysteria. In 1598 she started going into rages, attacking friends and convulsing. Eventually she said she was possessed by the demon Beelzebub and needed an exorcism. Her parents took her from one French town to the next; at each stop Brossier had fits and spoke as Beelzebub while a priest tried to cast out her demons before a large crowd, which was then solicited for donations.

Her performances were very popular with the public, but officials of the Catholic Church easily determined that she was a fraud by administering standard tests of possession. For example, a possessed person was supposed to convulse when sprinkled with so-called holy water but remain unaffected when sprinkled with ordinary water. Brossier was tricked into doing the reverse. Similarly, a possessed person was supposed to convulse on hearing certain passages of the Bible, regardless of what language it was in. Beelzebub's examiners tricked her into reacting to nonbiblical passages recited in Latin.

In April 1599, King Henry IV of France imprisoned Brossier for fraud, and shortly thereafter she stopped exhibiting signs of possession. In May she was sent home and ordered to stay there. At the end of the year, however, a fan of her performances, who believed her to be truly possessed, kidnapped her and took her to be exorcised by the pope in Rome. En route to Rome, Brossier gave several demonic possession performances, as she also did before the pope. By some accounts, she continued to perform in Italy for the rest of her life, speaking as Beelzebub and having fits before large crowds. **See also** demonic possession; devil.

bruja

Bruja is the word used for a female witch, usually hereditary, among Mexican, Central American, and American Hispanic cultures. A *bruja* is valued for her ability to heal and protect others; she primarily works with herbs and amulets, although she might also deal with spells and curses. *Brujas* can often be found in the marketplace, selling charms that will cure sickness, bring romance, or solve any number of other problems for the buyer. The male witch, called a *brujo,* is believed to have far weaker powers than the *bruja* and generally does not peddle magical wares. However, he is still believed capable of performing magic to benefit others in his community.

Buckland, Raymond (1934–)

Raymond Buckland founded the Saxon-Wicca Witchcraft Tradition in 1973. He has also written extensively on the occult and is considered an expert on the modern practice of witchcraft. He began his writing career as an author of screenplays for television, first in England and then in the United States. Some credit him with introducing Gardnerian Witchcraft to America in the 1960s. Buckland's works include *Buckland's Complete Book of Witchcraft* (first published in 1986, with a twenty-eighth reprint in 1999), one of the most popular books on witchcraft published in modern times. **See also** Gardner, Gerald; Gardnerian Tradition; Saxon-Wicca Tradition.

Buirmann, Franz (dates unknown)

Seventeenth-century German judge Franz Buirmann condemned hundreds of suspected witches to death during the 1630s. He was particularly ruthless, even by the standards of the time, ordering tortures so brutal that many suspected witches died before reaching trial. Moreover, even those who refused to confess under torture were executed, because once Buirmann had determined guilt he did not let the lack of a confession stand in his way.

Many of Buirmann's victims were chosen simply because they were wealthy. He had been given authority by the prince-archbishop of Cologne, Germany, to travel the countryside to ferret out witches and confiscate their property. Not surprisingly, he targeted rich landowners.

So focused was Buirmann on money that during a series of trials in Rheinbach, Germany, in 1631, town leaders offered to pay him to abandon his witch-hunt there and move to someplace else. He accepted the bribe but returned in 1636 to conduct a new witch-hunt even more unjust and brutal than the last. By some estimates, the Rheinbach witch trials of 1631 and 1636 led to the execution of 150 people, out of only 300 families living in the region. All of the victims were burned alive, usually by confining them in a dry straw hut that was then set on fire.

Buirmann also had the power to override the objections of local civil authorities who opposed his actions. In fact, he had some of his opponents tried and executed as witches. One such person was Rheinbach's mayor, Dr. Schultheis Schweigel, who died before his execution could be carried out; the mayor expired after seven hours of constant torture. Such occurrences were not unusual. Buirmann was often merciless with people who angered him, regardless of their position in society. During his witch-hunt in Siegburg, Germany, in 1636, for example, he even convicted the executioner he hired of being a witch and had the man burned alive. **See also** burning of witches; Germany, witch-hunts of.

burning of witches

From the late fourteenth century to the early eighteenth century, people generally believed that the only way to dispel a witch's evil after death was through burning. Accordingly, in the late fourteenth and early fifteenth centuries it was common practice to burn witches' bodies after their execution. As the fifteenth century progressed, in continental Europe, Ireland, and Scotland hanging or strangling of the condemned witch prior to burning was eliminated except in rare cases in which mercy was shown (which usually depended on the convicted witch's confessing before the execution). In such instances, the older practice of strangling the witch first was followed. In most cases, however, the witch was burned alive, usually while tied to a stake in a public square. So many witches were killed this way that the period from the midfifteenth to early eighteenth centuries is now typically referred to in popular literature and in the work of some historians as "the burning times." However, the practice of burning witches alive was never adopted in England and the American colonies, where witches continued to be executed by hanging. Witches in England were burned alive, though, if they committed or attempted to commit treasonous murder, which was then defined as either a man or woman killing a monarch or a woman killing her husband. Some suspected witches were executed by burning under this charge as late as the eighteenth century.

Various estimates have been given for the number of witches that died during the burning times. The most reliable figure is for Germany alone: at least one hundred thousand. Given that many other countries burned witches, European deaths are likely to be several hundred thousand. **See also** Germany, witch-hunts of.

Burton Boy (c. 1582–?)

Born in Burton-on-Trent, England, and commonly known as the Burton Boy, Thomas Darling faked demonic possession because he wanted to be famous; unfortunately, his hoax resulted in the death of several innocent women. Darling's ruse began after he experienced a brief illness at the age of fourteen. Shortly thereafter he began having convulsions and reported seeing demons. One physician diagnosed his problem as worms, but others said he was bewitched, particularly since his convulsions

In continental Europe, Ireland, and Scotland, witches were generally burned alive to dispel their evil after death. This 1493 Nuremberg woodcut depicts Jews and Protestants accused of heresy and witchcraft.

grew worse over time. Asked to think about who might have bewitched him, Darling named an old woman with whom he had quarreled one day while in the woods. His family tracked down the woman, sixty-year-old Alice Gooderidge, and she was tortured to extract a confession.

Gooderidge refused to say she was a witch, but she was unable to recite the Lord's Prayer, at the time a failure considered to be proof of guilt. Her torturers continued to torment her until she gave them details of her witchcraft. Finally she broke down and said that the devil visited her in the form of a dog she had gotten from her mother, Elizabeth Wright. Wright was then accused of being a witch as well. Meanwhile a famous exorcist named John Darrell made a show of casting out Darling's demons, whereupon the boy's fits stopped. Three years later, Darling admitted that his exorcism was a fake, and some historians suspect that Darrell was involved in the fraud. Others, however, believe that Darrell truly thought that Darling had been possessed because of Gooderidge and her mother. Records fail to indicate what became of Elizabeth Wright, but Gooderidge died in prison while serving a twelve-month sentence for witchcraft.

Bury St. Edmonds, witch trials of

Several series of witch trials in Bury St. Edmonds (sometimes spelled Edmunds) in Suffolk, England, during the seventeenth century, resulted in the executions of dozens of condemned witches. One series of trials, in 1645, was presided over by Matthew Hopkins, one of the most famous witch-hunters of his time. But it is a single Bury St. Edmonds trial in 1662 that most scholars consider particularly significant, because writings about that trial later influenced judges in the famous Salem, Massachusetts, witch trials of 1692–1693.

The 1662 Bury St. Edmonds trial was extremely well documented; details of its proceedings were published in a pamphlet entitled *A Trial of Witches at Bury St. Edmunds*, and American witch-hunter Cotton Mather wrote about the case in his 1692 book *On Witchcraft: Being the Wonders of the Invisible World*. Many people in England and North America were thus familiar with the case.

The defendants were Rose Cullender and Amy Duny, elderly widows accused of using witchcraft to harm—and, in one instance, to kill—seven children. Duny was the first of the pair to be called a witch, after she baby-sat an infant boy and, without his mother's consent, nursed him. When the baby fell ill, his parents suspected witchcraft. They took the boy to Dr. Jacob, a man known for his witchcraft remedies, and were told to hang the baby's blanket inside their chimney and leave it there until the next day, then wrap it around the boy. Dr. Jacob predicted that when they did this, something would fall out of the blanket, and he instructed them to burn it in their fireplace. According to the parents later, a toad fell out; they grabbed it with tongs and stuck it into the fire. They claimed that it exploded like gunpowder. When Duny was seen the next day with a burn mark on her face, townspeople began calling her a witch and local girls began having convulsions, which they blamed on Duny. Some of the girls experienced lameness as well, and a few vomited pins and nails, considered a sure sign of bewitchment. One girl, ten-year-old Elizabeth Durent, died three days after being stricken with lameness and convulsions, during which she continued to insist that Duny's spirit was tormenting her.

Elizabeth's sister Ann also had convulsions, but she blamed Rose Cullender instead of Duny. Duny and Cullender were blamed jointly for the fits of nine-year-old Deborah Pacy, her sister eleven-year-old Elizabeth, and two other girls. As such accusations increased, Duny and Cullender were brought to trial, and adult townspeople came forward to blame the two women for other misfortunes that they believed had been caused by witchcraft, such as the unexpected overturning of carts in front of Cullender's home and the collapse of a chimney owned by someone Duny disliked. The jury took only thirty minutes to find the women guilty, even though Duny and Cullender insisted that they were innocent, and the two were soon executed by hanging.

By the time of the Salem witch trials in 1692, most people in England and America had heard of the case of Cullender and Duny. Historians suggest that this knowledge predisposed the public to believe the child accusers in the Salem trials. Historians further suggest that judges and juries who knew of the Cullender and Duny case were more likely to accept the idea that witches would target children as victims. **See also** England, witch-hunts of; Salem, witch trials of.

butter

From the fourteenth through seventeenth centuries, a woman was often suspected of being a witch if milk could not be churned into butter in her presence. When no witch was present and the milk would not churn, people suspected that somewhere a witch had cast a spell on it. To guard against this possibility, farmers employed a variety of charms and practices believed to protect the milk from witchcraft. For example, in some regions, churns were made only of rowan wood, thought to be impervious to magic. In other places, hairs from a black cat were dropped into the milk to ward off a witch's spell. (Interestingly, people in Sweden once believed that witches sent cats to steal food, particularly butter. According to this belief, the cats supposedly sampled so much of the butter on the way home that they threw up. Consequently the Swedish call the yellow bile that cats sometimes vomit "witch's butter.")

Butters, Mary (dates unknown)

In the early nineteenth century, Mary Butters was a witch who became the object of jokes after her magic almost killed her. In 1807 she was hired to cure a cow whose milk would not churn to butter. While the owner of the cow, Alexander Montgomery, and a friend stayed with the animal in the barn, Butters went into Montgomery's house with his wife, son, and another woman to mix a potion. When hours passed and Butters did not return to the barn, the two men went looking for her. They discovered that everyone in the house but Butters was dead; she herself was unconscious and near death. Investigators later decided that fumes from Butters's potion, which was cooking on the stove, had killed the victims, particularly since before making the potion—which included milk, needles, and nails—Butters had sealed the chimney and all of the windows. Butters, however, insisted that her magic was not to blame; instead she claimed that an intruder with a club had battered everyone to death. Few people believed her story. Nonetheless, despite its tragic outcome authorities found the incident so funny that when Butters was briefly charged for using witchcraft the court decided not to prosecute her.

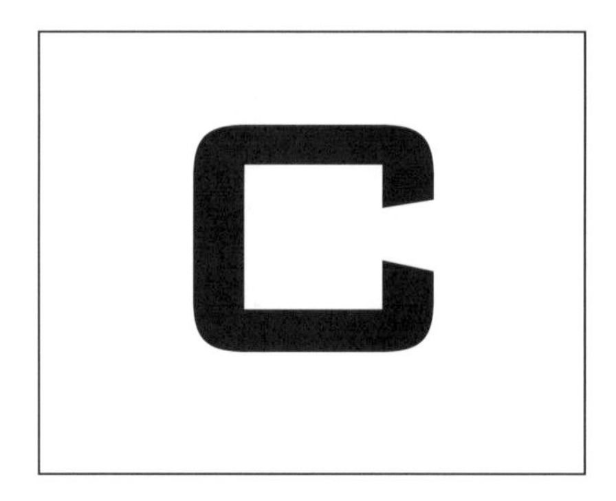

Cabot, Laurie (1933–)

Laurie Cabot is one of the best-known witches in America, in part because she has often appeared before the media in defense of witches' rights. She also serves on the board of the Chamber of Commerce in Salem, Massachusetts, a place that draws many tourists interested in witchcraft. Cabot has been the Official Witch of Salem since 1977, when the governor of Massachusetts awarded her that ceremonial title. In her role as Official Witch she hosts Salem's annual Halloween Witches' Ball, a costume party that she first held in 1973. In addition, Cabot's books on witchcraft are widely read by witches and by nonwitches interested in magic. These works include *Practical Magic: A Salem Witch's Handbook* (1986), *Love Magic* (with Tom Cowan, 1992), *The Witch in Every Woman: Reawakening the Magical Nature of the Feminine to Heal, Protect, Create, and Empower* (with Jean Mills, 1997), and *Power of the Witch* (1998).

Cabot became interested in witchcraft as a child, when she discovered that she had telepathic powers and began to read about paranormal phenomena and the occult. As a teenager she met a practicing witch who encouraged Cabot to take up the Craft. Cabot not only felt immediately comfortable in the role of witch but soon decided that she was descended from witches and had inherited some of their memories. Although there is no evidence that Cabot has witches in her family lineage, it is true that her ancestors came from a part of England—the Isle of Jersey—renowned for being home to witches.

To further connect to her heritage as a witch, Cabot moved to Salem in the 1960s and opened a witchcraft-related shop there. Now run by her daughter, the shop is a popular tourist attraction. Cabot herself is also popular with tourists, in part because her appearance fits the public image of a witch. Cabot wears long, black robes, has long, frizzy black hair, and uses a lot of black mascara, eyeshadow, and eyebrow pencil. Some modern witches have criticized her for perpetuating a stereotype, but Cabot believes that she is presenting the traditional—and therefore appropriate—appearance for a hereditary witch. Moreover, many of her activities are aimed at fighting prejudice and ending negative perceptions related to witches and witchcraft. In 1986 she created the Witches League of Public Awareness to educate the public about witches and to promote witches' rights. In 1988 she established a place of worship called the Temple of Isis, part of the National Alliance of Pantheists, where she continues to perform ceremonies. Cabot also established a new Witchcraft tradition, the Cabot Tradition, that emphasizes practical magic and Celtic beliefs. **See also** traditions, Witchcraft; Salem, witch trials of.

Cadìere, Marie-Catherine (1709–?)

Marie-Catherine Cadìere was the catalyst for one of the most sensational—and one of the last—witchcraft trials in France. In 1730, at the age of twenty-one, she accused a fifty-year-old Jesuit priest, Father Jean-Baptiste Girard of Toulon, France, of using black magic to bewitch and seduce her. Girard was the spiritual leader of an all-woman prayer and meditation group of which Cadìere was a member. The two spent time alone together, and Girard's letters to Cadìere suggest that they became romantically if not sexually involved.

At the same time, Cadìere desperately wanted to be declared a saint. She came from a religious household (two of her brothers were priests), had studied the lives of famous saints, and apparently decided to adopt some of their behaviors. For example, claiming she was receiving messages from God, she went into trances, had fits and visions, and exhibited stigmata, a phenomenon whereby a person spontaneously manifests the bleeding wounds of Christ. During this period Girard was allowed to be alone with her, in order to investigate her symptoms. What went on between them is unclear, but after a year Cadìere retreated to a convent, where she began exhibiting the violent convulsions and outbursts of someone being tortured by demons.

During an attempted exorcism, Cadìere accused Girard of bewitching her. Many historians believe that Cadìere's break with Girard was the result of his continuing refusal to certify her visions and other experiences as real. A few, however, suspect that the breakup had to do with their romantic relationship. In either case, one of Cadìere's brothers found other women who claimed to have been bewitched and seduced by Girard.

In January 1731 Girard was brought to trial. Cadìere provided lurid details of his seduction, along with key information about how he had bewitched her: by breathing into her mouth, which she said caused her to fall under a spell. Girard countered by saying that Cadìere was a liar who had tried to fool people into thinking she was a saint. Her stigmata, he explained, were merely ordinary unhealed sores. After ten months, the twenty-five trial judges decided that Girard had not bewitched Cadìere, but had engaged in improper conduct with her. He was reprimanded; she was sent home. **See also** demonic possession; exorcism; France, witch-hunts of.

Cagliostro, Count Alessandro (1743–1795)

Born Giuseppe Balsamo, Count Alessandro Cagliostro was an Italian occultist, astrologer, and alchemist who was convicted of sorcery although his real crime was being a con artist. Throughout most of his life, Cagliostro traveled throughout Europe defrauding people of their money. One of his most profitable scams was the selling of potions said to bring romance or long life. Authorities in France eventually expelled him from the country because of his schemes, whereupon he went to Italy. There he was caught up in a witch-hunt, the victim of his own too-convincing witchcraft ruses. After his conviction he was imprisoned until the end of his life. **See also** alchemy.

cakes and wine

In some Witchcraft traditions, witches share cakes and wine as part of a ritual in which the food and drink represent the body and blood, respectively, of a deity. According to Charles Leland in his 1899 book *Aradia: Gospel of the Witches*, European witches often blessed crescent moon-shaped cakes in the name of the goddess Diana as part of a ritual Sabbat meal. Leland reported that these cakes typically included wine and honey as ingredients. One of the most common occasions for modern witches to share cake and wine is at the completion of esbat rituals, although the ritual food is shared at other times as well. **See also** blood; esbat; Leland, Charles Godfrey; rites and rituals.

Cambrai nuns

The demonic possession of a number of nuns in a convent at Cambrai, France, has been cited by historians as proof that the Catholic Church sometimes inspired the very behavior it was trying to prevent. In December 1484, Pope Innocent VIII issued a papal bull, or decree, entitled *Summis desiderantes affectibus* ("Desiring with supreme ardor," a title taken from the first four words of the bull), which emphasized the reality of witchcraft, warned of its spread, and described some of its manifestations, including a mention of male and female devils summoned by witches to work evil. The publication of this document spread fear among many Catholics and triggered numerous witch-hunts. Within five years, the first cases of mass demonic possession appeared, usually among Catholics.

The incident involving the nuns of Cambrai is among the earliest—perhaps even the first—of these mass possessions. It began, as did subsequent cases, with one nun exhibiting fits that were immediately taken as a sign of demonic possession. Once this diagnosis was made, other nuns began having fits, and their behavior soon escalated to include barking and howling. As with most cases of mass hysteria, the nuns' odd behavior stopped abruptly, but not until after several of the nuns exhibiting the most dramatic symptoms had been accused of practicing witchcraft. **See also** demonic possession; France, witch-hunts of.

candles

Candles have a long history of association with magic and sacred rituals. Primitive people worshiped fire as a source of strength and power, and many ancient rituals took place around bonfires. Once candles were invented some of these rituals moved inside, with a candle's flame substituting for the bonfire as a focus of worship.

Candles are also commonly used ceremonially by many Wiccans and Neopagans as part of the practice of magic. In this situation, the candle usually represents the focus of the magic spell, whether this focus is a person, object, or goal. For example, if a witch wants a particular man to love her, she might cast a love binding spell that entails lighting candles representing herself, her beloved, and lust. The latter is a red candle, while the color of the candles for the two people would be chosen according to their astrological signs. Each sign has its own color; according to many Witchcraft traditions these are: Aquarius, purple; Pisces, aqua; Aries, pink; Taurus, orange; Gemini, violet; Cancer, green; Leo, red; Virgo, yellow; Libra, blue; Scorpio, gold; Sagittarius, red; and Capricorn, brown. Desires other than love are also linked to a specific color of candles. For example, in many Witchcraft traditions green candles are associated with fertility, money, and health, as well as with the attainment of personal goals. Blue candles are for increased creativity and peace of mind. Indigo is for wisdom and for strengthening psychic powers.

There are a total of twelve basic candle colors used in candle magic. One of them, gray, is rarely employed because it represents nothingness. Another, white, is an all-purpose candle that supports the work of others, while black candles banish negativity. Specialty candles are also sometimes employed for specific spells. For example, many Wiccans burn black candles shaped like cats to change their luck from bad to good. When the cat candle is red instead of black, burning it is supposed to bring luck in love. Green cat candles bring luck with money. Similarly, a seven-knobbed candle, burned so that one knob is melted each day, is supposed to make wishes come true after seven days.

The length of time that a candle burns is also important in candle magic. Generally, the longer a candle burns, the longer the spell will remain in effect. Wiccans also believe that candles used for magic should be anointed with oil prior to each lighting. Just as candle colors are chosen based on the intended purpose of the magic, so too is the oil selected. Various herbs and flowers typically added to the oils to scent them are believed to represent different desires and purposes. For example, cinnamon is used for prosperity, rose for love. To apply the oil, Wiccans usually start at the center of the candle and rub upward, then move from the center down. Throughout the process, the person about to use the candle thinks about the intent of the magic to come.

Candles are commonly used as the focus of magic spells and rituals. Pictured are witches of the Covenant of Earth Magic performing a ritual for Halloween.

Many Wiccans believe that this magic will be stronger if they make their own candles, particularly if magical herbs are embedded in each candle's core, or if they have marked their candles with magical symbols. However, even commercially produced candles with no herbs or markings are thought to be inherently powerful because they involve all four elements: Air allows the candle to burn; the candle's solid wax represents earth, its melted wax water, and its flame fire. Most Wiccans further believe that if a candle is blown out rather than carefully snuffed at the end of a ritual, the magic it produced will be blown away and the spell ruined.

These same beliefs apply to candles used in the practice of black magic, which is used by Satanists but not by Wiccans. In the fifteenth and sixteenth centuries, however, candle magic was often part of attempts to cause death or disease by magic. In some of these attempts, the wax of the candle was fashioned in the shape of the intended victim before burning. **See also** astrology; bonfire; cats; colors; elements, four; herbs and other plants; oils and ointments; rites and rituals; spells; tools, ritual.

Canon Episcopi

The Canon Episcopi was one of the first official documents of the Catholic Church to address the issue of witchcraft. Historians are unsure of its origin, but it was written prior to the tenth century and became part of church law in the twelfth century, remaining in effect until the mid–fifteenth century. Essentially, the canon stated that there was no such thing as witchcraft, because only God could have power over human beings; therefore anyone who claimed to be a witch or to have seen or experienced the effects of witchcraft had to be deluded. Moreover, the Canon Episcopi held that anyone who believed in witchcraft was a pagan and therefore a heretic who could be prosecuted as such. Those who claimed to be witches were accused of worshiping the pagan goddess Diana.

Naturally, the prospect of being accused of heresy discouraged a person from accusing another of being a witch. When such accusations did occur and a practitioner of witchcraft was brought to trial, the defendant was generally sentenced to pray and perform other duties to become reconciled with church teachings. In addition, many judges made a distinction between folk magic, which they classified as magic related to healing, romance, and household affairs, and witchcraft. Folk magic was usually excused, providing it harmed no one.

This tolerance for folk magic was a reflection of the times. Paganism was only reluctantly giving way to Christianity, so church leaders struggled to make their religion more appealing to the populace. Going against folk magic, which was extremely popular, would have alienated many of the people the new religion was trying to attract.

By the fifteenth century, pagan deities had been largely abandoned, and were no longer seen by church leaders as a threat to Catholicism. The fallen angel Satan, however, had become the personification of evil for Christians. Witches were no longer accused of worshiping Diana but of worshiping Satan. At the same time, people had come to believe that witchcraft was both real and dangerous. Unwilling to declare the Canon Episcopi, as an official church document, wrong, they said instead that Satan had taken advantage of the Canon Episcopi to encourage the sudden development of real witchcraft. A few suggested that over the years witches had become more powerful, which meant that although witchcraft had originally posed no threat, by the fifteenth century it was dangerous and therefore deserved to be dealt with severely. Eventually, Pope Innocent VIII in 1484 issued a new decree that reflected this view, declaring witchcraft real and encouraging witch-hunts. **See also** devil; Innocent VIII; persecution, witch.

Carolina Code

A set of laws governing territories under the control of the Holy Roman Empire, the Carolina Code was adopted in 1532 in part to direct witchcraft-related legal proceedings. Specifically, the five sections of the code define what is needed to prove that witchcraft or sorcery have been committed, how the questioning of accused witches should proceed, and what the penalty for a convicted witch should be. In regard to proof, the code says that reports of someone teaching witchcraft, associating with witches, and/or causing bewitchment (either directly or indirectly through an agent), as well as being named a witch by another witch, are all justifications for torture to obtain a confession. (Questioning under oath was deemed sufficient to extract further information, including the names of accomplices, from witches who had already confessed.)

Fortune-tellers were not to be tortured, nor sentenced to jail if convicted. Instead they were to be punished only if their actions had caused financial or personal harm, in which case jail might be appropriate. The same criterion was used to determine a convicted witch's sentence. A witch who had harmed others was to be burned to death, whereas one who had caused no harm would be sentenced to serve time in jail (the duration to be decided by the court) or to receive some other form of punishment. However, any witch displaying lewd behavior had to be killed, usually by burning, whether or not anyone else claimed to have been harmed by the behavior.

The Carolina Code remained in effect in many parts of Europe throughout the sixteenth century, although toward the latter part of the century many judges eager to execute witches ignored its restrictions regarding death sentences. **See also** persecution, witch.

Carpenter, Dennis (1954–)

American Neopagan Dr. Dennis Carpenter is co–executive director of the Circle Sanctuary, a Wiccan church and pagan resource center established by his wife, Selena Fox, prior to their marriage. Carpenter holds a doctorate in philosophy of psychology from the Saybrook Institute of San Francisco and worked as a school psychologist before joining the staff of the Circle Sanctuary in 1984. In addition to his administrative duties there, he is a groundskeeper for the sanctuary's two-hundred-acre nature preserve and edits its magazine, *CIRCLE*, as well as other sanctuary publications.

Carpenter first became involved with the Circle Sanctuary in 1982, when he went to the facility to hear a lecture by American witch Starhawk. At the time he had only recently become interested in paganism, having been raised a Protestant. Today he himself is a lecturer on modern paganism; his doctoral dissertation, written in 1994, is on the beliefs and experiences of modern pagans. **See also** Circle Sanctuary; Fox, Selena; Starhawk.

Carpzov, Benedict (1595–1666)

German judge and legal expert Benedict Carpzov is the author of *Practica Rerum Criminalum*, a 1635 book that presented case law and arguments to justify the aggressive persecution of witches. Carpzov believed that accused witches deserved fewer rights during a trial than other criminal defendants because of the danger they posed to society and to individual jurists. Therefore, Carpzov advocated a variety of brutal tortures to extract their confessions. At the same time, once they were convicted he believed they should be treated humanely until their execution. Carpzov's work continued to be used to justify witchcraft trial procedure for several decades after his death. **See also** Germany, witch-hunts of; persecution, witch.

Catholicism

Catholicism became the dominant religion and organizing institution in Europe during the Middle Ages. By this time, paganism had apparently disappeared, although some historians believe pagan worship merely went underground. Folk magic, however, continued to be practiced. At first the Catholic Church had tolerated folk magic because it was so popular.

However, as time passed and Catholicism became more firmly established throughout Europe, the church's tolerance for various aspects of paganism lessened. In particular, folk magic became something to condemn rather than simply ignore, especially since church leaders believed that people who put their faith in magic were less likely to put their faith in God. Therefore the church began to aggressively persecute anyone who practiced any form of folk magic or witchcraft, whether or not the practitioner followed church teachings in all other regards. Even the suggestion that someone carried a charm or amulet might be enough to place that person on trial as a witch.

The church continued to persecute witches until its political influence waned during the eighteenth and nineteenth centuries. However, even after it lost the power to arrest, convict, and execute witches, the Catholic Church continued to oppose all forms of witchcraft. Today the church generally holds that witchcraft is an expression of evil and that witches are aligned with Satan. **See also** paganism; persecution, witch; Satanism.

cats

Cats have long been associated with witchcraft, perhaps because since ancient times they have been objects of veneration and superstition. Ancient Egyptians, for example, considered the cat sacred and decreed that killing a cat was a capital offense; when a cat died, it was mummified for eventual entombment with its owner. The Egyptian goddess Bast, associated with marriage and fertility, was depicted as having the head of a cat, and the goddess Isis was often shown accompanied by a cat. Other cultures similarly associated cats with deities. For example, according to Norse legends, black cats pulled the chariot of the goddess Freya.

Some modern scholars suggest that the cat's connection with such pagan deities explains its identification as a symbol of evil, since early and medieval Christians tended to demonize many elements of other religions. In any case, medieval Europeans had many superstitions related to cats in general and black cats in particular, although evil was not always attributed to cats. For example, no sailor would throw a cat overboard because it was thought that doing so would bring a monstrous storm. Also, black cats were considered lucky to own, and if the owner of such a cat lost it, bad luck would follow.

Attitudes changed, however, and in the fourteenth century, authorities throughout Europe began to consider ownership of a black cat a criminal offense, in the belief that witches used black cats as familiars, animals that helped witches work magic. People also believed that witches could turn themselves into cats at will. The idea that cats might be witches in disguise persisted through the seventeenth century. Modern scholars believe that this belief had its origins in pagan rituals during which participants sometimes wore animal masks, thereby "transforming" themselves into cats and other creatures.

Witches, however, were not the only individuals who could disguise themselves as cats. Satan, it was believed, could also take the form of a cat: According to superstitions from Brittany, along the coast of France, if a person went to a place where five roads intersected and called for the devil, a black cat would suddenly appear. Other beliefs also associated the devil with cats. For example, some medieval Europeans said that the tails of black cats contained hairs from the devil. For reasons that are unclear, others thought that every black cat had a single white hair, well hidden, that would endow its finder with great power.

As the association between cats and black magic grew, the animal increasingly became the target of persecution. In some places cats were burned alive, in others they were shot with arrows. Often the carcasses were then marked with the sign of the Christian cross, usually by slashing.

Ironically, though witches were believed to favor cats, in the sixteenth and seventeenth centuries some witches confessed to killing cats, particularly by drowning, as part of their spell-castings. People of the period began to believe that the devil would steal the soul of anyone who killed a cat, just as he supposedly took the souls of people who practiced witchcraft. However, the reason that witches sometimes harmed cats in the performance of magic lay not in devil worship but in paganism. Many aspects of witchcraft originated in paganism, and cats were occasionally killed as part of pagan rituals. The Celts, for example, held a four-day divination ceremony during which cats were cooked alive.

Modern witches do not harm cats, but they do still keep them as familiars. However, they do not use familiars to perform tasks related to magic. Instead they consider them to be psychic partners that help connect them to nature and boost their ability to practice magic. Cats are particularly valued in this regard because many witches believe them to have stronger psychic and intuitive abilities than many other animals. **See also** animals; Bast; devil; familiar.

cauldron

A cauldron is a black, cast-iron pot, usually with three legs, used by witches to brew potions, cast spells, and hold offerings. It is associated with the four elements, all of which are involved in its use as a cooking pot. The element of water is necessary to create a brew; fire is necessary to heat it; air keeps the fire burning; and the earth provides raw ingredients, such as herbs and berries for potions.

Because of this connection to the four elements, many witches incorporate a cauldron into their magic, typically placing it on the altar within a magic circle or on the floor to the altar's left. There the cauldron typically holds earth, water, or fire as part of certain rituals. It might also be used for divination via a process called scrying, whereby the practitioner stares into a cauldron of water or other reflective object or liquid until a vision appears.

Alternatively, the cauldron might be employed as a place to burn written spells in the performance of magic. One example of the cauldron's use in a ritual occurs at the time of the winter solstice among witches of the Gardnerian Tradition. Adherents place a cauldron on their altar as a sacred object, fill it with dead leaves, wax, and alcohol, and set these ingredients on fire, then circle or dance around the cauldron while chanting. Sometimes people leap over the burning cauldron, much the way people leap over a dying bonfire.

In addition to its use in rituals, the cauldron is often seen as a symbol of transformation because it can change raw ingredients into food or potions through the cooking process. This concept appears in some legends related to magic cauldrons. For example, in the lore of the ancient Celts, the moon goddess Cerridwen brews a potion that confers wisdom; with only three drops the recipient is transformed by enlightenment and inspiration.

Because of her cauldron's power, Cerridwen keeps it hidden in the Underworld. Nine maidens constantly tend its fire, breathing on it when it begins to die out. There are also nine pearls decorating the cauldron's rim. The ingredients in its brew of enlightenment, which takes a year and a day to reach full potency, are a combination of flowers, berries, and sea foam, which can be deadly if administered in too large a dose.

The idea that magic cauldrons are likely to bring death is an ancient one. In fact, the first known reference to a witch's cauldron made this connection. It occurrs in ancient Greek legends related to the witch Medea, encountered by Jason and his Argonauts during their search for the Golden Fleece. Said to be a priestess of Hecate, the goddess of both the moon and witchcraft, Medea used her magic cauldron to brew a deadly potion with the intent of murdering a Greek prince. Similarly, the Aegean goddess Ceres was said to brew potions that left a poisonous residue in her cauldron.

Modern witches, however, view the transformative power of cauldrons in a more positive light. They consider their ability to change one thing into another as representative of nature's power to give life by transforming, for example, seeds into plants. In fact, many Neopagans consider nature to be a cauldron that creates and regenerates not only living creatures but also oceans, stars, planets, and the like. To most Wiccans the cauldron also symbolizes the feminine life force and the Goddess, because it is a vessel that creates and holds life. **See also** bonfire; Cerridwen; chanting; elements, four; Gardnerian Tradition; goddesses and gods; herbs and other plants; scrying.

Celtic Traditional

The Celtic or Celtic Traditional Witchcraft tradition is based on the religious beliefs of the ancient Celts and the practices of their Druid priests. Its deities come from Celtic lore and its rituals focus on nature worship, tree magic, and the four elements, earth, air, water, and fire. Runes are also featured prominently in Celtic Traditional magic and divination. **See also** Celts; traditions, Witchcraft.

Celts

The people known as Celts emerged sometime before 500 B.C., which is when Greek writers first mentioned their existence in the Alps, central France, and parts of Spain. From these places the Celts migrated throughout Europe and then into Asia Minor and the British Isles. A warlike tribe, they remained in control of their extensive territories until the Romans conquered them; this occurred in Britain, Scotland, and continental Europe during the first century A.D. and in Ireland in the fifth century A.D.

The ancient Celtic religion was initially polytheistic, meaning that it entailed the worship of multiple gods and goddesses. Many of these deities were local; those worshiped in Celtic Ireland, for example, were different from those in Celtic Spain. A few, however, were known throughout much of the Celtic world. These include Lugh, for whom the festival of Lughnasadh was named. Some local deities were associated with specific locations, such as a certain stream or hot spring. Others were worshiped as triads, which meant that each deity was considered to be one of three aspects of a greater deity. For example, the goddess Brighid (also known as Brigid or Bridgit) was considered the Maiden aspect of the Great Goddess, the other two aspects being Mother and Crone.

The Celts worshiped their deities on a daily basis, and many scholars of Celtic life believe that rituals honoring goddesses and gods took place at home as well as in public shrines. In Britain, Gaul, and much of Germany (but apparently not in Italy, Spain, or the Danube region), there was also a separate class of priests (which some historians believe included priestesses as well). Called Druids, they were typically of aristocratic birth and began training for the priesthood while young. This training could take as long as twenty years, during which the would-be priest, or initiate, had to memorize magic formulas, Celtic laws and historical information, and other important facts and concepts related to their priestly and social duties. These duties included establishing the times for public ceremonies, practicing divination, healing, and the magical arts, and acting as judges, arbitrators, and civil administrators. They also assembled in sacred places—usually in deep forests—to worship and make both animal and human sacrifices to various deities and spirits. Much of what the Druids did at their ceremonies remains a mystery, largely because they passed information down orally rather than via written texts. However, historians do know that Druids had a deeply held belief in reincarnation, certain that the souls of the deceased passed into the bodies of infants during birth.

Since the concept of dying and being reborn is central to Christianity, the Celts found it relatively easy to accept this new religion when it arrived in the British Isles, particularly since early Christians adapted many Celtic deities (such as Bridgit, who became Saint Bridgit) and festival times as their own. Because of the ready acceptance of Christianity, by the Middle Ages Druidism was only a memory in the British Isles. Then the surge of nostalgia for the old ways fueled a movement to revive Druidism (without its human sacrifices). By the eighteenth century, England had at least one major Druid organization, and by the twentieth century there were at least five. In the early 1960s several Neo-Druidism groups were established in the

Modern witches' Sabbats are often modeled after Druid ceremonies. Illustrated are Roman soldiers witnessing a Druid religious ceremony involving the cutting of mistletoe.

United States as well. Also in the 1960s, some Wiccan high priests began to view themselves as the modern successors to the Druids. Today many Witchcraft traditions have incorporated elements of Druidism into their own religious practices. For example, many traditions share the Celtic concept of the triple deity, wherein a lesser deity is viewed as one of three aspects of a greater deity. Similarly, modern witches' Sabbats are generally modeled after festivals once celebrated by the ancient Celts. **See also** Lughnasadh; Wheel of the Year.

censer

Also known as a thurible or incense burner, a censer holds a certain type of incense during Wiccan rituals. This incense itself is not flammable; it requires a base of coals to vaporize it. The censer is a receptacle for those coals. Censers come in many different styles and sizes, but regardless of type they are usually placed at the center of the altar within a magic circle. The censer represents fire and air, as does the incense it holds. **See also** air; incense; tools, ritual.

Cerridwen

Also known as Keridwen, Cerridwen is a Welsh Celtic goddess worshiped by many modern Wiccans as a Mother goddess and/or a moon goddess. When worshiped as a moon goddess, she is commonly personified as the Crone, the aged goddess representing the waning phase of the moon. In Celtic times, she was a goddess of the Underworld, as well as of enchantment and prophesy. According to Celtic lore, Cerridwen had a magical cauldron in which she brewed potions that could impart instant wisdom, awareness, and/or creative inspiration. Cerridwen was also said to be able to change shape at will, so that she might travel the earth as a bird, fish, or land animal. **See also** aspect; goddesses and gods; moon.

chalice

Usually made of silver, the chalice is a long-stemmed goblet employed during most witchcraft rituals. It might be filled with wine, with each participant in the ritual taking a sip before offering the rest of the contents to the Goddess, or it might be filled with the water that will be used during a ritual, usually for blessing and consecrating. The chalice is associated with both the Goddess and the element of water. It is also considered a symbol of the womb and therefore the receptacle of life or spiritual energy. In a ritual known as the Great Rite another ritual tool, a knife called the athame, is lowered into the chalice to symbolize the physical union of the God and Goddess. When placed on the altar, the chalice is typically positioned on the left side, which represents the Goddess. **See also** altar; athame; Great Rite; tools, ritual; traditions, Witchcraft; water.

Chambre Ardente

Sitting in secret from January 1679 to July 1682, the Chambre Ardente was a court established in Paris, France, to investigate the actions of people suspected of distributing toxic potions as part of an international poisoning ring targeting the rich and powerful. Eventually the court began to examine the possibility that these poisoners might be engaging in witchcraft. Within a short time, the affair developed into a major witchcraft scandal involving individuals at the highest levels of society.

The first indications that a poisoning ring was in operation surfaced in 1673, when two priests told authorities that they had heard confessions from several people who had killed or attempted to kill their spouses or lovers but had not been caught. The priests refused to reveal the names of these penitent poisoners, but said that the penitents had not concocted the poisons themselves, but had been provided them by someone else.

With no suspects named, at first authorities did nothing about the situation. Then in 1676 a French noblewoman, the Marquise de Brinvilliers Marie-Madeleine D'Aubray, attempted to poison her husband, who learned of the plan in advance and protected himself with an antidote. Shortly thereafter, French authorities found poisons among the marquise's possessions and discovered that she was also responsible for the deaths of her father and brother. D'Aubray was then arrested. Under torture she confessed not only to using poisons but also to practicing witchcraft. Later she said that many other French men and women of her social standing had experimented with witchcraft.

In 1676 D'Aubray was tried and convicted of being a witch, and promptly beheaded. After her execution, the police chief of Paris, Nicholas de la Reynie, found himself thinking about the other high-society witches that D'Aubray had mentioned and began to search for them, at first unsuccessfully. Then several other members of the French nobility were poisoned, and King Louis XIV ordered Reynie to conduct a full investigation. This eventually led the police chief to two fortune-tellers, Marie Bosse and La Dame Vigoreaux. They admitted to providing their socially prominent clients, who came to them regularly, with enough poison to rid themselves of unwanted romantic entanglements.

Reynie obtained the names of several such clients and arrested them. Soon he discovered that they had obtained poisons from other sources as well. Apparently there was a ring of poison providers, most of them fortune-tellers. When arrested, one of these people, Catherine Deshayes (also known as La Voisin), readily confessed to leading a coven and to celebrating Black Masses attended by socially prominent guests. When Deshayes began providing the names of those who attended her gatherings, the Chambre Ardente—or "Burning Room"—was established to secretly investigate whether these socially prominent people were indeed witches. Many were subsequently arrested or fled under fear of arrest, including dukes, duchesses, and other nobles who were friends of the king. In fact, one of the king's own mistresses, Madame de Montespan, was among the accused.

To ensure that no one was arrested without cause, Reynie brutally tortured Deshayes and some of her associates to see if they would change their stories about their witchcraft-related social events. Torture sessions were also used to extract the names of more witches, as well as further details about their activities. Meanwhile, police collected hard evidence related to these confessions, including poisons and books on black magic. Between the evidence and the confessions, the Chambre Ardente decided that 319 arrests were warranted; those arrested faced a variety of fates, from exile to prison to enslavement on a galley ship to execution. In all, thirty-six were killed. However, on the king's orders, anyone with noble blood was set free, as was his mistress. Louis also banned fortune-telling and limited the sale of poisons. In 1709 he commanded that all evidence of the existence of the Chambre Ardente be destroyed. Fortunately for historians his decree did not lead to the eradication of all evidence of the investigation. **See also** France, witch-hunts of.

Chanctonbury ring

Located in Sussex, England, the Chanctonbury Ring is representative of places that have retained an association with witchcraft throughout the ages. Today the site is a grass-covered rise ringed by trees. However, the word "Ring" in its name refers not to the trees, which did not exist when the spot was named, but to a ditch that encircled the rise in ancient times when a pagan temple stood there. As with some other aspects of paganism, this traditional place of worship became associated with Satan after the advent of Christianity. According to one legend, people who visit the Chanctonbury Ring at midnight might accidentally meet the devil there, and he will offer them food and drink. Anyone who accepts Satan's gift will become his servant. Legends also say that the Chanctonbury Ring is a site for witches' Sabbats. Indeed, according to Wiccan Doreen Valiente in her book *An ABC of Witchcraft*, some modern witches do meet on the rise. **See also** devil; Sabbat; Valiente, Doreen.

chanting

An ancient practice, chanting is the repetition of words or phrases in a monotone. Some modern witches chant to enter a state of altered consciousness. They also chant to honor or summon the Goddess/God and as part of the casting of spells. They generally believe that when a spell is chanted its power is increased. This belief goes back to the earliest witches, sorcerers, and magicians, who chanted their incantations. **See also** goddesses and gods; shamanism; spells.

Charge of the Goddess

The Charge of the Goddess is a speech delivered to the members of a coven during a Wiccan ritual called drawing down the moon. Not all Witchcraft traditions practice this ceremony and/or feature the Charge; it is primarily used by those in the Alexandrian and Gardnerian Traditions. Those whose traditions do feature the Charge generally believe that while giving the address the high priestess is actually a channel through which the Goddess herself is speaking. During the drawing down the moon ritual, the high priestess enters a trance, whereupon the high priest calls on the Goddess to enter the priestess and speak.

The words spoken by the priestess/Goddess were originally written by Gerald Gardner and Doreen Valiente in the 1950s. Many other versions have appeared since. Gardner based his work primarily on two sources, *Aradia: The Gospel of the Witches* by Charles Godfrey Leland, and the writings of influential modern witch Aleister Crowley. Leland's work concerns the legend of Aradia, daughter of goddess Diana, who is sent to earth to bring witchcraft to human beings. According to Leland, before leaving to return to the heavens, Aradia gave mortal witches some final instructions. It was these instructions that formed the basis of Gardner's Charge of the Goddess, but Gardner also incorporated phrases found in Crowley's writings. (Some of Gardner's followers defend this by suggesting that Crowley took his material from ancient writings in the public domain, a claim that has not been proven.)

Valiente revised Gardner's material to eliminate much of what was taken from Crowley. She also rewrote the Leland material in verse instead of prose. She later rewrote the Charge again to return it to prose, adding new material to make it more her own. Although some covens continue to use the verse version of Valiente's work, her prose version is the most popular Charge of the Goddess today. The full text of this version appears, among other places, in *The Witches' Bible* by Janet and Stewart Farrar. In general, it advises witches to gather secretly once a month—preferably when the moon is full—to worship the Goddess who has many names, to learn sorcery, and to dance, sing, and celebrate. **See also** Alexandrian Tradition; Crowley, Aleister; drawing down the moon; Gardner, Gerald; Valiente, Doreen.

charm

To modern witches, a charm is a series of words or phrases, or perhaps a verse, spoken over an object to "charge" it with magic for positive purposes. For example, a witch who wants to imbue a pendant with protective power might recite or chant a protection charm over it.

The earliest charms were chanted spells and incantations intended to convince evil spirits not to harm someone or to get them to stop harming someone. Indeed, the word *charm* comes from *charme*, French for "chant." In ancient times it was not uncommon for a sorcerer to stand over a sick person and chant the words of a charm to drive away the spirit(s) causing the illness. Soon charms served other purposes as well, including bringing love or prosperity, ending a bewitchment, or increasing fertility.

As oral tradition gave way to written histories, people began to write charms down, either on paper that they hid in protective amulets or directly on the amulets themselves. Gradually such an object also became known as a charm. This usage of the word remains common today, but not among witches. To them, a charm remains the spell and not the object itself. However, some witches use the phrase "love charm" to refer to a variety of herbs said to have aphrodisiac powers, and many witches use the phrase "charm bag" to refer to a small bag or pouch used to hold objects employed in the casting of spells. **See also** amulet; herbs and other plants.

Chelmsford, witch trials of

The town of Chelmsford in Essex, England, was the site of witch trials in 1566, 1579, 1589, and 1645. Considered in sequence, they reflect the increasing severity of verdicts in witch trials throughout Europe as the sixteenth century gave way to the seventeenth century.

In the 1566 trials, out of three defendants only one, Agnes Waterhouse, was condemned to death and hanged. Another, Eliz-

A 1589 English pamphlet published an illustration of Joan Prentice, Joan Cony, and Joan Upney being publicly hanged in Chelmsford on charges of witchcraft.

abeth Francis, was sentenced to just one year in prison (although she later received an additional year for bewitching someone else after her release from prison), and the third defendant, Waterhouse's daughter Joan Waterhouse, was found innocent. In the 1579 trials, out of four defendants three were hanged: Elizabeth Francis, who had received such a light sentence after the 1566 trial, Ellen Smith, and Alice Nokes. A fourth woman, Margery Stanton, was released for lack of evidence. In the 1589 trials, out of ten defendants, four were hanged, three were found innocent, and the sentences of the remainder are uncertain. In the 1645 trials, however, there were at least thirty-eight defendants and seventeen hangings, with an additional four deaths occurring in prison. Six defendants were found guilty but were spared execution; it is unclear how much prison time they served. It is also unclear what became of the other defendants, except for two who were declared innocent.

Besides the number of executions involved, the Chelmsford trials displayed an increasing complexity and aggressive prosecution. The 1566 trials took place over two days and were fairly straightforward. The defendants were accused of consorting with the devil and of committing maleficia, the harming of others via magic, through a talking cat named Sathan who was their familiar. Once confronted with the accusations, two of the women quickly confessed, while the third—Joan Waterhouse, the one who was ultimately found innocent—did not confess but instead begged for mercy, which was granted. In contrast, by the time of the 1645 trials the court was not only no longer inclined towards mercy but ordered the torture of the accused until they confessed to whatever charge was put before them.

In part, this change in approach was motivated by the desire to make money. Witch-hunter Matthew Hopkins initiated the 1645 trials because people concerned about the spread of witchcraft paid him for every witch he tracked down, but only if the accused was convicted. The motivations behind the 1645 trials thus appear to be very different from those in early Chelmsford trials, which primarily grew out of charges made by neighborhood children who disliked defendants. **See also** familiar; Hopkins, Matthew.

Church of All Worlds

The Church of All Worlds (CAW) is one of the oldest major Neopagan churches. Members of the church worship many goddesses and gods, but particularly Mother Nature and the deities of ancient Greece. They also celebrate the eight Celtic sacred days honored by most Wiccans: Samhain, winter solstice, Imbolc, spring equinox,

Beltane, summer solstice, Lughnasadh, and autumn equinox, collectively referred to as part of the Wheel of the Year.

The name Church of All Worlds was coined by Robert Heinlein in his science fiction novel *Stranger in a Strange Land*. Heinlein depicted "The Church of All Worlds" as a free-spirited, new form of church created by a man alienated from mainstream society. The founders of CAW, a group of friends that included well-known pagans Oberon and Morning Glory Zell-Ravenheart (then simply Zell, with Oberon previously known as Tim Zell and Otter Zell or G'Zell) were fans of Heinlein's work, and they incorporated some elements of his fictional church into the institution they created. For example, both churches comprised smaller units known as nests.

However, as CAW grew, it left some aspects of Heinlein's Church of All Worlds behind and added new elements not found in the fictional church. For example, in its earliest form CAW embodied the same freedom of spirit as Heinlein's church, but as time passed it developed more structure and its mission focused on environmentalism. To this end its leaders gradually increased the church's emphasis on the worship of Mother Earth.

Today CAW publishes a periodical, *Green Egg: A Journal of the Awakening Earth*, which is devoted to pagan issues. *Green Egg* originated in 1968, was abandoned in 1976, and resumed publication in 1988; from 1976 to 1988, CAW membership was falling, although the group established several related educational organizations. These include the Holy Order of Mother Earth (HOME), which focuses on living off of the land. During the same period, CAW merged with several other pagan organizations, such as the land-oriented Forever Forests. Today CAW is regaining membership as people become more interested in pagan forms of worship. **See also** paganism; Wheel of the Year; Zell-Ravenheart, Morning Glory; Zell-Ravenheart, Oberon.

Church of Wicca

The Church of Wicca is a religious institution with many doctrines similar or identical to those of other Wiccan churches. For example, the Church of Wicca calls for an adherence to the Wiccan Rede, which advises witches to do no harm, and celebrates the four main Wiccan sacred days—Samhain, Imbolc, Beltane, and Lughnasadh—as well as others in the Wiccan Wheel of the Year. Some practices of the church, however, are not widespread among Wiccans, in part because the church's founders, Gavin Frost and his wife, Yvonne, wanted the church to remain true to Gavin Frost's Welsh Celtic heritage. With this intent, in its early years the church was solidly Celtic in its rituals, and though it now incorporates some spiritual aspects of other cultures it is still primarily Welsh Celtic in nature.

Some of the church's stances were controversial. For example, at the outset the church banned homosexuals from membership, reasoning that the Celtic rituals the church followed were fertility-based and therefore emphasized male-female sexuality; however, they rescinded this position after it was severely criticized by many other Wiccans.

Another church position that is controversial with other Wiccans relates to Gavin Frost's vision of the deity. Most Wiccans worship a goddess and a god as the two elements of the ultimate deity, the All, believing that this deity has both a male and a female component. In contrast, the Church of Wicca does not accept the idea that the All has a gender. In fact, the church does not believe that the All can be described in any fashion understandable to humans. However, church members do create "stone gods" (which can be made of metal or other materials instead of stone) as figures or objects representing the deity, which they then "charge" with psychic energy. This energy can be released later during rituals to aid the working of magic.

The church shares information on its practices and beliefs via a correspondence school, the School of Wicca. Created by the Frosts prior to their establishment of their church, the school was the first to offer correspondence courses related to witchcraft. Today it provides information about other types of magic and rituals as well, including ancient Egyptian magic, divination, psychic ability, and other paranormal phenomena. The school also publishes books and produces videotapes and audiocassettes on Wicca-related subjects.

In addition, the Church of Wicca has been at the forefront of legal battles related to people's right to worship in whatever way they choose, particularly as this choice relates to the practice of Wicca. Of these battles, perhaps the most significant is a 1986 legal case in which a federal appeals court upheld a 1985 decision (*Dettmer v. Landon*) declaring Wicca a religion. In his decision, federal appeals court judge J. Butzher found that the Church of Wicca exhibited the same characteristics as mainstream religions, in that its members followed specific doctrines related to their spirituality. **See also** Frost, Gavin and Yvonne; Wheel of the Year; Wiccan Rede.

cingulum

A nine-foot-long cord typically wrapped around a witch's robe at waist level, a cingulum is used to store power that can later be released at key points during certain rituals. In those Witchcraft traditions in which it is worn, the cingulum is usually red in color and has nine knots, which are tied in sequence as part of a ritual that gathers energy. (Sorcerers and witches have long associated the number 9 with magic spells, believing it to be particularly powerful.) When these knots are untied in reverse sequence, each one is said to release an increasing amount of power. In this way the cingulum is similar to the knotted cords used as part of wind-releasing spells. **See also** knots.

Circe

According to Greek mythology, Circe was the daughter of Hecate, who was the goddess not only of the moon but also of witchcraft and enchantment. Today some modern Wiccans worship Circe in both or either of these capacities. Circe is widely known largely because the classical Greek poet Homer, in the epic poem, the *Odyssey,* told the story of how Circe turned Odysseus's crew into swine. This story has made Circe one of the best-known sorceresses in the Western world. **See also** goddesses and gods; Hecate; moon.

circle, magic

A magic circle is an area where witches perform rituals, work magic, and hold ceremonies to worship deities. The original purpose of the magic circle was to protect wizards, sorcerers, and magicians who were conjuring spirits. Medieval practitioners of Western ceremonial magic believed that if they created a magic circle and stood within it, no evil spirit would be able to penetrate the barrier to reach them. However, if during their conjuring of such spirits the magician placed even one small part of his body outside the circle, the spirit would capture him and carry him away.

Modern witches view the circle not as refuge from evil spirits, but as a sacred place that holds whatever energy is raised within it. Its perimeter is a boundary for a reservoir of power that witches can use in their rituals and magical work. Often spirits and deities are invited into the circle through invocation, so that their energy and support will enhance the rituals and magic being performed therein.

Modern witches typically create, or cast, a magic circle in much the same way that medieval sorcerers did. First they clear the area where the magic circle is going to be established, whether outdoors or inside. Then either the solitary practitioner or a coven's high priestess sweeps the area with a ritual broom to cleanse it of negative en-

Although magic circles were once used to guard witches from evil spirits, they are now believed to invite and hold energy raised through invocation. Pictured is a seventeenth-century woodcut of a witch invoking imps and familiars in her magic circle.

ergy. Sometimes salt is sprinkled on the area as well, for the same reason. The size of a magic circle ranges from nine to eighteen feet in diameter. In some Witchcraft traditions, two eight-foot circles are linked within a greater circle ten feet in diameter. In most traditions, witches cast circles at certain times in the lunar phase (usually as part of esbat meetings) or at Sabbats; in some traditions they might also consult astrological charts for the best times to cast a circle.

Prior to casting a circle, those who intend to use it prepare themselves mentally for the experience by meditating and/or chanting. When they are ready, one person—again, usually the high priestess—uses an athame, wand, or sword to outline the circle in a clockwise, or *deosil*, direction on the floor or ground. Sometimes the circle is outlined with cord or paced off with footsteps, either before using the ritual tool or instead of using it. As the circle is being traced, a "doorway" is left open so that participants in the upcoming ritual or magical work can walk inside the circle without crossing its boundary. The circle's altar and all ritual tools are brought into the circle via this doorway as well. Once everyone is inside, the circle is closed via the athame or other means; if someone wants to leave the circle during a ritual the doorway must be carefully opened in the same manner and then closed again.

Within the circle, the points of the four compass directions—north, east, south, and west—are known as the four quarters. Each of these quarters is typically marked with powerful magical symbols, words, or names, with objects of a certain color, and/or with an item symbolizing one of the four elements. For example, a bowl of salt might be placed in the quarter associated with earth, a bowl of water in the quarter associated with water, incense in the quarter associated with air, and a lighted candle in the quarter associated with fire. In the Georgian Tradition, the cardinal points of north, south, east, and west are marked by candles of green, red, yellow, and blue, respectively, before the circle is cast, and then the circle is drawn to connect these four points.

The significance and symbolism of each quarter varies according to tradition. For example, in some traditions, north is where the altar is situated within a magic circle, because most witches believe that this direction holds the most power. In other traditions east is the quarter for the altar, because this direction is associated with spiritual enlightenment. In still others, the altar is aligned with the northeast because this direction marks the border between light (east) and dark (north). In many traditions, north is also associated with the earth element, with death and rebirth, and with the colors black and gold. East is usually associated with the air element, with enlightenment, and with the color red or white. South is usually associated with the fire element, with energy and will, and with the color blue or white. West is usually associated with the water element, with creativity and fertility, and with the color red or gray.

Once the circle has been established, it is consecrated (ritually purified) using representations of the four elements. Those within the circle then call upon the Guardians of the Four Elements, also known as the Lords of the Watchtowers, to protect the circle. Certain deities and, if the circle is outdoors, nature spirits are invoked as well, to bring protection and power to the acts performed within the circle. Next the purpose of the circle is stated aloud, and actions fulfilling that purpose begin.

Once those within the circle have finished the ceremony, they typically share cakes and wine, offering some to the deities and spirits that were invoked. They then thank these beings for their presence. Finally, they dispel the energy created within the circle through a ritual that varies according to tradition. **See also** altar; cakes and wine; elements, four; Georgian Tradition; magic; rites and rituals; tools, ritual; tradition, Witchcraft.

Circle Sanctuary

Located on a two-hundred-acre farm in Wisconsin, the Circle Sanctuary is both a Wiccan church and an information center that provides material on all forms of paganism, past and present, to interested people throughout the world. To this end, the center holds retreats, workshops, and seminars as well as pagan rituals and is involved in both publishing and activism, promoting religious freedom and tolerance.

The sanctuary began with its church, established in 1974 by Selena Fox as a place to worship a religion she herself developed: Wiccan Shamanism, which combines elements of Wicca with those of Native American and African spiritualism. In 1977 Fox founded the Circle Network to disseminate information not only on Wiccan Shamanism but also on other forms of paganism, and to refer people to practitioners throughout the world. Circle Network is a membership organization that offers support to practicing pagans. It hosts an annual celebration of the summer solstice, the Pagan Spirit Gathering, at the Circle Sanctuary. Several other groups, or circles, are part of the Circle Sanctuary, each offering meetings and activities. Together these groups are known as the Circle Sanctuary Community. **See also** Fox, Selena.

Clutterbuck, Old Dorothy (1880–1951)

Old Dorothy Clutterbuck was the witch who supposedly initiated one of the most influential of modern witches, Gerald Gardner, into the Craft. Gardner reported that Clutterbuck was the leader of a New Forest coven that decided to share its secrets with him. However, there is no evidence that Gardner really did learn the Craft from Clutterbuck. In fact, for many years there was considerable doubt that Clutterbuck ever existed; instead people thought that Gardner had invented her to enhance the story of his early years as a

Wiccan. However, in 1982 another influential witch—Doreen Valiente, author of such important works as *An ABC of Witchcraft*—used official records to prove that Clutterbuck had indeed been a resident of the New Forest area of England in 1939, when Gardner claimed he had met her there. When she died in 1951, she left behind no personal belongings or writings related to witchcraft, giving rise to a new controversy over whether she was indeed a witch at all. **See also** Gardner, Gerald; Valiente, Doreen.

Cobham, Eleanor (?–1447)

In 1441, Englishwoman Eleanor Cobham, the duchess of Gloucester, was convicted of being a witch. Her husband, Humphrey, was the uncle of King Henry VI and had been regent since 1422, when Henry assumed the throne at the age of one. Some noblemen believed that Humphrey had too much influence over the king, and they decided that the best way to destroy the duke's standing at court was to charge his wife with being a witch.

Specifically, they accused Eleanor Cobham of using black magic to bring her husband political power—enough power, in fact, to eventually supplant the king. Their accusations were corroborated by scholar Roger Bolingbroke, who had been charged along with Cobham. Bolingbroke confessed under torture to being a master sorcerer and encouraging Cobham to take up black magic. He further confessed that he had taught Cobham some of his skills, including the use of image magic to hurt people. A wax figure had been found among Cobham's possessions after she was arrested, and her accusers noted that it looked a bit like the king. Cobham confessed to making the wax figure, but she insisted that it was not a likeness of the king but a fertility figure used to help her become pregnant. Despite her insistence, when the figure was produced during her trial, her judges decided that it had been used to work magic against King Henry. This evidence, along with the fact that all of the judges in her trial were allied with Humphrey's enemies, led to a quick conviction. Eleanor Cobham was sentenced to perform several acts of penance, including carrying a candle through London streets, then sent to prison, where she died under suspicious circumstances in 1447. **See also** image magic.

colors

To witches, each color has its own energy level and therefore produces a different effect in magic rituals. Consequently, witches choose the colors of candles, robes, ropes, and other aspects of a ritual very carefully in accordance with the desired results of a ritual. Beliefs about color correspondences vary according to Witchcraft tradition, but generally black is used for binding spells and banishing negativity; brown for grounding and strengthening magic; green for healing and fertility; blue for peace and tranquility; gold for money; pink for love or friendship; red for love or lust; silver for enriching spirituality; and yellow for increasing personal energy. White is an all-purpose color, enhancing others. Perhaps the most intricate beliefs about colors relate to the use of candles, where subtle differences in shades of colors are significant. **See also** candles; knots.

cone of power

Many witches use the phrase "cone of power" to refer to the energy they raise within a magic circle and then take into themselves. They visualize this energy in the shape of a cone, with its circular base on the earth and its point within the witch. In casting spells, witches release and direct the energy outward toward a specific desired outcome. When their work is complete, they typically perform certain rituals to dispel any leftover energy, a process that many call "grounding." Various methods of grounding, depending on Witchcraft tradition, involve saying particular words, making particular gestures, or employing salt, water, crystals, or other representations of the four elements (earth, air, fire, and water) ritualistically. **See also** circle, magic; elements, four.

consecration

Consecration is the ritual purification of an object or place to make it sacred and prepare it for magical work. Ritual tools, for example, are usually consecrated prior to use, by various methods. Some traditions expose the item or place to symbolic representations of the four elements. For example, an object might be sprinkled with water that has been mixed with salt (the water representing water and the salt representing earth), then passed through a flame (for fire) and the smoke of incense (for air). Other traditions simply sprinkle the object or place with salt. Alternatively, an object might be rubbed, or anointed, with oil; this is commonly the case with ritual candles. While performing any of these actions, the witch typically says certain words to call on a deity to ensure that the object or place holds only positive energy. **See also** candles; circle, magic; elements, four; oils and ointments; rites and rituals.

Cotswold Hills

The Cotswold Hills region of southwest England is a center of British witchcraft lore, largely because it contains an ancient circle of stones that was once a site of pagan worship. This same circle has also long been a gathering place for Cotswold witches, and for the most part the nonwitch residents of the area tolerate their activities.

However, in 1945 someone apparently felt threatened enough by one man's witchcraft to kill him for it. The murder victim was Charles Walton (1871–1945), who was found dead on Candlemas (a day sacred to Wiccans). His body exhibited signs of a ritualistic killing performed not just to end a witch's life but to destroy any evil that might linger after death. A knife had slashed a Christian cross on the body, which had also been stabbed with a pitchfork that held it to the earth. In addition, a great deal of blood surrounded the corpse. The murderer was never caught, although books and articles have put forth various theories about the identity and motive of the killer. British anthropologist Margaret Alice Murray was one of those who tried to solve the murder, exploring local rumors about witchcraft in the process. She also examined a similar murder, that of an elderly woman named Anne Turner, which occurred in the same area in 1875; in this case the killer had readily admitted that he was motivated by his belief that she was a witch who had worked magic against him.

The Cotswold Hills' long association with witchcraft is one reason why Cecil Williamson opened a witchcraft museum there in 1956. It contained books of witchcraft as well as displays that used wax figures to depict witches engaged in various activities. In the mid-1960s the museum was relocated to Cornwall, England, and moved again several times thereafter. It is now in Bocastle, Cornwall, England. **See also** Murray, Margaret Alice; Museum of Witchcraft.

Council of American Witches

The Council of American Witches formed and met from 1973 to 1974 for the express purpose of identifying a common set of Wiccan beliefs, under the presumption that presenting a unified front to the general public would serve two purposes. First, it would improve witches' image; second, it would prove to the public that Wicca is an organized religion.

The instigator of this effort was Carl Weshcke, a Wiccan priest and prominent publisher of Wiccan books. He assembled a council of dozens of Wiccans from diverse backgrounds and traditions, who in turn consulted with other Wiccans and developed a list of Wiccan principles. As reported by Margot Adler in her book *Drawing Down the Moon: Witches, Druids, Goddess Worshippers, and Other Pagans in America Today*, the group's stated principles of Wiccan beliefs are:

> 1. We practice Rites to attune ourselves with the natural rhythm of life forces marked by the Phases of the Moon and the Seasonal Quarters and Cross Quarters.
>
> 2. We recognize that our intelligence gives us a unique responsibility toward our environment. We seek to live in harmony with Nature, in ecological balance offering fulfillment to life and consciousness within an evolutionary concept.
>
> 3. We acknowledge a depth of power far greater than that apparent to the average person. Because it is far greater than ordinary, it is sometimes called "supernatural," but we see it as lying within that which is naturally potential to all.
>
> 4. We conceive of the Creative Power in the Universe as manifesting through polarity—as masculine and feminine—and that this same Creative Power lives in all people, and functions through the interaction of the masculine and feminine. We value neither above the other, knowing each to be supporting of the other. We value Sex as pleasure, as the symbol and embodiment of life, and as one of the sources of energies used in magical practice and religious worship.
>
> 5. We recognize both outer worlds and inner, or psychological worlds—sometimes known as the Spiritual World, the Collective Unconscious, the Inner Planes, etc. —and we see in the interaction of these two dimensions the basis for paranormal phenomena and the magical exercises. We neglect neither dimension for the other, seeing both as necessary for our fulfillment.
>
> 6. We do not recognize any authoritarian hierarchy, but do honor those who teach, respect those who share their greater knowledge and wisdom, and acknowledge those who have courageously given of themselves in leadership.
>
> 7. We see religion, magick, and wisdom-in-living as being united in the way one views the world and lives within it—a worldview and philosophy-of-life which we identify as Witchcraft, the Wiccan Way.
>
> 8. Calling oneself "Witch" does not make a witch—but neither does heredity itself, or the collecting of titles, degrees, and initiations. A Witch seeks to control the forces within him/herself that make life possible in order to live wisely and well, without harm to others, and in harmony with Nature.
>
> 9. We acknowledge that it is the affirmation and fulfillment of life, in a continuation of evolution and development of consciousness, that gives meaning to the Universe we know, and to our personal role within it.
>
> 10. Our only animosity toward Christianity, or toward any other religion or philosophy-of-life, is to the extent that its institutions have claimed to be "the only way" and have sought to deny freedom to others and to suppress other ways of religious practice and belief.
>
> 11. As American Witches, we are not threatened by debates on the history of the Craft, the origins of various aspects of different traditions. We are concerned with our present, and our future.
>
> 12. We do not accept the concept of "absolute evil," nor do we worship any entity

known as "Satan" or "The Devil" as defined by the Christian tradition. We do not seek power through the suffering of others, nor do we accept the concept that personal benefit can only be derived by denial to another.

13. We acknowledge that we seek within Nature for that which is contributory to our health and well-being.

Once its task was completed, the Council of American Witches disbanded. In the ensuing years, the group's work did indeed help to improve public opinion of Wiccans, and today the council's list of principles still represents the core beliefs of most Wiccans, regardless of tradition. **See also** Adler, Margot.

coven

A coven is a group of witches organized for the purpose of practicing their craft. Scholars disagree on the origin of the word, but most believe that it is derived from the Middle English word *covent*, or "gathering." The place where witches regularly meet is called a covenstead, and the members of a coven are called coveners.

The size of a coven varies according to the Witchcraft tradition to which it adheres. Most modern covens, however, either have thirteen members or set a maximum of thirteen for their membership, with a typical minimum of three. Some witches believe that a group of six men, six women, and a leader is best. In some Witchcraft traditions, an eight-member coven is considered best for experienced witches who are more involved in meditative work and higher states of consciousness. When this or any other size coven exceeds the limit, a new coven is usually created for the additional members. It is then considered a sister coven of the original.

The structure of a modern coven also varies according to Witchcraft tradition. Some traditions feature covens that are highly informal, with no one having an assigned position within the coven. Others have a rigid hierarchy, with members taking on certain specific roles; this is particularly true for covens based on the Gardnerian Tradition. Covens of the same tradition are usually structured in the same way, except within traditions that encourage variety.

The covens of some traditions are led by a high priestess and/or high priest; others rotate leadership or share it among many members. Some covens have a hierarchy through which a member must move before assuming a position of authority; others give new members as much authority as established members. The most structured traditions require each member to advance upward through three degrees, accomplishing certain tasks and learning certain knowledge and skills along the way, with the requirements of each degree taking a minimum of a year and a day to complete. Under such a system, only a third-degree witch can become a high priestess or high priest.

Initiation requirements and rituals that surround the joining of a coven also vary among traditions. Some covens admit any interested person into their group—although some covens are all-female—but most screen applicants and require them to train for a year and a day before being formally initiated into the coven. People who want to use magic for evil purposes are almost always rejected, as are people who want to use the coven as a social club rather than a place to practice serious magic and/or to express their religious beliefs.

On rare occasions, the members of a coven might decide to banish someone they have already accepted as a member. Usually this occurs when the member betrays the coven in some way, lies to its leaders, or breaks a fundamental law of Wiccan ethics. Once banished, a person who has been initiated as a witch remains a witch, because most Wiccans believe that the initiation into the Craft cannot be undone. Moreover, after a year and a day the banished person is allowed to petition for readmission to the coven.

Witches also leave covens voluntarily. Typically, witches who abandon their coven do so because they have decided that its practices and/or its tradition do not reflect their own beliefs or preferences regarding witchcraft. In such cases they might leave to start their own tradition. Many traditions have begun because of such dissatisfaction. At the same time, covens of various traditions sometimes come together for networking and other social purposes. Animosity among different covens of different traditions is rare.

Within a tradition, each coven functions autonomously, so the activities of coven meetings vary, but generally meetings feature rituals, celebrations, and the practice of magic (which members usually spell *magick*, to distinguish it from the type of magic tricks performed in stage shows). Magic is not performed at every meeting, but when it is performed it is usually intended to heal members or their relatives or pets, to improve members' lives in very specific ways, or to benefit society or the earth in some specific way. Celebrations usually take place on Sabbats, or holy days, that are part of the Wiccan calendar known as the Wheel of the Year. Other coven meetings are called esbats, sometimes referred to as working meetings to distinguish them from celebratory gatherings; the "work" involved is magical work as well as business related to the working of the coven. Esbats usually take place at the time of the full moon, although some covens hold working meetings every week or every two weeks. Sabbat and esbat gatherings can take place either outdoors or indoors, although certain traditions have strong beliefs regarding which type of location is best. Among some traditions, participants in rituals wear robes of a certain color, while others go skyclad or dress according to personal preference.

To guide participants in performing rituals, each coven and each member within a coven usually has a Book of Shadows. Each book includes the rules of the coven as well as procedures, texts, and chants for rituals and magic spells; an individual's Book of Shadows might also include personal observations and commentary regarding coven activities. When a witch dies, other members of that person's coven traditionally make sure that her or his Book of Shadows is destroyed, unless the deceased has previously named someone to inherit the book. Similarly, a coven's Book of Shadows is not supposed to leave the care of the coven; if the coven disbands then the book is either destroyed or gifted to a worthy member or friend of the coven.

The Book of Shadows is an important foundation for the coven's activities, but it is the high priestess who shapes the character of the group and guides its rituals, even when a coven includes both a high priestess and a high priest. The high priestess also usually has the duty of casting the magic circles in which the coven performs its magic spells. In some traditions, the high priestess has an assistant called a maiden, who usually takes over when the high priestess dies or becomes ill. Sometimes the maiden will leave to form her own coven. If this happens several times (more than three in some traditions, far more in others) and all of the new covens are allied with the old, the high priestess of the original coven takes on the title of witch queen.

In recent years, however, the trend has been not toward creating new covens but toward solitary practice. Many witches either leave their coven to practice witchcraft alone or choose not to join a coven in the first place. They study witchcraft on their own, using some of the numerous books available on the subject, and practice witchcraft in the privacy of their homes.

Some also turn to the Internet for the kind of group support that used to be available only through covens. Such online support is known as Cyber Wicca.

Literature on coven activities is fairly recent. The first witch to publish an entire Book of Shadows was American Wiccan Lady Sheba in 1971. Her *Book of Shadows* was condemned by witches who thought she shared too many secrets about witchcraft. However, Sheba was not the first witch to reveal the nature of coven meetings. During the 1950s and 1960s Gerald Gardner began the modern trend among witches of writing about the Craft in order to improve nonwitches' perceptions of them.

The first known references to covens in literature were extremely negative. They appeared in the twelfth century, when people were beginning to condemn witches for their activities. However, the concept that witches met in covens did not catch on until the fourteenth century, when discussions of these meetings began to be featured in witch interrogations and trials. By the middle of the fifteenth century, when aggressive witch persecution was widespread, references to covens were routine in the confessions extracted from witches.

Scholars disagree over whether the details given in these confessions are in any way based on the truth, and if so to what degree. One British anthropologist, Margaret Alice Murray, thought that witch confessions provided many accurate details about the activities of witches' covens because there were striking similarities among confessions from different parts of Europe and Britain. She further theorized that an organized witch cult existed during the witch-hunting times, with certain standard rules and rituals.

During the 1960s, 1970s, and 1980s, modern witches relied on Murray's work while establishing numerous Witchcraft traditions. Consequently, covens today function much like Murray said they did during pagan and medieval times. However, during the 1990s scholars largely dismissed Murray's theories for lack of reliable evidence to support them and have developed a variety of other theories regarding the origin of details about coven activities.

For example, according to over a dozen witch confessions (usually extracted via torture), a coven had to have exactly thirteen members—twelve plus a leader. Margaret Murray's argument was that these statements reflected the truth: Witch covens did indeed have thirteen members. This was therefore the model used by the first modern witches in establishing their own covens. Scholars, however, suggest that the concept of a thirteen-member coven came about as a result of Christian beliefs and/or ancient ideas regarding the number 13.

In many ancient cultures the number was considered unlucky, but it was also thought to have magical properties. For example, in Greco-Egyptian magical texts the number 13 was said to have the power to raise the dead. Such texts advised a magician to recite certain incantations while piercing a doll representing the deceased thirteen times or with thirteen needles in order to bring that person back to life. It is therefore possible that witch confessions featured the number 13 because of its association with magic. They might also have selected it because of its association with the moon and astrology; thirteen is the number of lunar months in the year as well as the sum of the twelve signs of the zodiac plus the sun.

Alternatively, the number 13 might have been drawn from the fact that during the Middle Ages, Christians associated thirteen-person gatherings with the Last Supper of Christ, which was attended by the Twelve Disciples plus Christ himself. Since this meal ultimately led to betrayal and death, a common superstition among medieval Christians held that if a person hosted a gathering with thirteen guests, it would likely result in betrayal and/or death—also a likely outcome, in the medieval mind, of a witches' gathering. Still another theory is that medieval Christians thought that witches met in groups of thirteen as a deliberate mockery of the Last Supper. Around the same period, witches were said to perform a ritual called the Black Mass, which mocked the Catholic Mass.

Today many witches dismiss scholars' suggestions that their preferred coven size is based on Christian concepts rather than pagan ones. Some continue to believe in Murray's work despite scholars' attempts to discredit it, unwilling to believe that the structure and activities of their covens might be based on flawed research into ancient forms of witchcraft. At the very least, they suggest that Murray's work deserves a second look. **See also** Book of Shadows; Cyber Wicca; esbat; Gardner, Gerald; Gardnerian Tradition; initiations; Murray, Margaret Alice; Sabbat; traditions, Witchcraft.

Covenant of the Goddess

Established in 1975 by Wiccans from several covens, Covenant of the Goddess (COG) is a nonprofit international organization for Wiccans of diverse traditions. Its purpose is to provide support to its members (both individuals and covens), to sponsor Wiccan activities, and to encourage an understanding of Wicca among the general public. COG holds celebrations and rituals on days sacred to Wiccans, such as the summer solstice, as well as national conferences in the United States and regional meetings throughout the United States and Europe. COG also provides monetary and legal assistance for Wiccan victims of religious discrimination and has become involved in other social issues, including environmentalism. The organization has its own website, www.cog.org, which provides valuable information about Wicca as well as links to other Wicca-related websites. **See also** Wicca.

Craft

The Craft is another name for Witchcraft, with a capital "W." It refers to witchcraft that is practiced as part of a magical religion with diverse traditions. The Craft can be practiced either by solitaries or by members of a coven, as long as it is approached in an organized and consistent manner. In other words, practitioners cannot change the meaning of a ritual from one day to the next, or approach the practice of magic in a haphazard fashion. **See also** witchcraft.

cross

The cross is an ancient mystical symbol, with over three hundred variations, some subtle, in design. The traditional Christian cross, formed by the perpendicular intersection of a short horizontal line with a longer vertical line, became a symbol of that religion in approximately the fifth century, but long before that time pagans used a cross with lines of equal length in the performance of magic and religious rites. This kind of cross was believed to represent balance between any two aspects of existence—sacred and secular, male and female, spiritual and physical. Pagan crosses are often marked on amulets intended to protect the wearer from harm. Cross motifs also appear on some ritual tools and might be employed in magical rituals. **See also** amulet.

Crowley, Aleister (1875–1947)

British magician and occultist Aleister Crowley wrote extensively on the occult, and many of his beliefs and theories relating to the practice of magic remain influential among modern witches. For example, Crowley came up with the idea of spelling *magic* as *magick* to distinguish the acts of a stage magician who performs tricks from the powers of a real magician. This distinction continues to be made by many practitioners of real magic today.

Even more influential were Crowley's theories on how magic worked. Expanding on existing ideas, he proposed that when a magician's personal will and imagination were heightened and focused through certain rituals, they could be used to access and direct nature's energy, thereby creating magic. His many writings on this subject led twentieth-century witches to increasingly emphasize the importance of the magician's will and personal spirituality as opposed to external forces in the performance of magic.

Aleister Crowley, a British magician and occultist whose theories are still influential to many modern witches, is pictured here wearing a Uracus serpent crown and displaying typical occult instruments.

Crowley's dozens of books on magic and the occult include a textbook entitled *Magick in Theory and Practice* (1929; sometimes reprinted as *Magick* or *Book Four*), *The Confessions* (1930), *The Equinox of the Gods* (1937), and *The Book of Thoth* (1944), a book about Tarot cards that was published with a deck of Tarot cards that Crowley created in conjunction with Lady Frieda Harris. Today this deck is one of the most widely used among occultists. A popular CD, *The Beast Speaks* (1993), features recordings of Crowley talking about the occult. Many collections of Crowley's poetry, essays, and other short works are also available, as are several biographies of the magician, including *The Great Beast* (1951; reprinted as *King of the Shadow Realm: Aleister Crowley, His Life and Magic* in 1989) by John Symonds, *Legacy of the Beast: The Life, Work, and Influence of Aleister Crowley* by Gerald Suster (1988 British edition; 1989 American edition), and *Do What Thou Wilt: A Life of Aleister Crowley* (2000).

Crowley first became interested in magic while a boy. The son of extremely devout Christians, he was so outspoken in his criticism of their faith that his mother nicknamed him "the Beast," a name some Christians use for the devil. Soon he was studying the occult and writing poetry based on this interest. In 1895 he enrolled at Trinity College of Cambridge University. There he was exposed to two books about magic, *The Book of Black Magic and Pacts* by Arthur Edward Waite and *The Cloud upon the Sanctuary* by Carl von

Eckartshausen, which directed his attention to the Hermetic Order of the Golden Dawn, a secretive occult society established in 1888. As he read about the occult, Crowley realized that he himself had some ability as a magician. In 1898 he dropped out of school, sought out members of the Golden Dawn, and was initiated into their order. He also bought a house on the shores of Loch Ness in Scotland in 1899, paid for with money he inherited after his father's death in 1887.

Under the guidance of the Golden Dawn, Crowley progressed well in his studies of the occult, but he also clashed with its leader, S.L. MacGregor Mathers. In 1900 he quit the order; by some accounts he then established his own order, by other accounts he struck out on his own to continue his occult studies. At the same time he embarked on a series of travels, going to Mexico in 1900, India in 1901, and Ceylon, Burma, and Paris in 1902 before returning to Scotland in 1903. There he married Rose Kelly, who participated with him in magic rituals, and in 1904 embarked on another series of travels with his bride, going to Paris, Naples, Cairo, and throughout India.

Crowley later reported that during a magic ritual Rose learned that Crowley would soon receive a message from the spirit world; this message was dictated to him by the voice of a spirit named Aiwass on April 8 through 10, 1904. The message comprised a three-chapter manuscript, its major premise revolving around one phrase, "Do what thou wilt," which according to Aiwass was "the whole of the Law" regarding how one should behave. This phrase, which has been interpreted to mean either "do whatever you want" or "do nothing more than what is necessary," was most likely the basis of Gerald Gardner's Wiccan Rede, "An' it harm none, do what thou wilt," which is a major principle of the Wiccan religion. Crowley called the phrase the Law of Thelema and published the manuscript under the title *Liber Legis* or *The Book of the Law*.

In addition to providing the Law of Thelema, *The Book of the Law* prophesied that a new era would soon ensue, a time when orthodox religions and traditional codes of morality would fall out of favor. This new era would belong to the young, and would therefore be called the Aeon of Horus, Horus being the child of the Egyptian deities Isis and Osiris. Crowley considered this prophesy vitally important, and throughout his life he continued to speak about it and to consider himself special for having received the message.

In 1909 he decided to share information about another subject as well: the secret rituals of the Hermetic Order of the Golden Dawn. He established a magazine, the *Equinox,* to publish articles about the order, along with his own poetry, and he continued to write about the secrets of the Golden Dawn until 1913 despite the numerous lawsuits Mathers filed to stop him. Crowley also traveled extensively through China, Morocco, and Spain, studying occult practices along the way. In 1912 he joined another occult order, the Ordo Templi Orientis, also known as the Temple of the Orient or the Order of the Eastern Temple, and became the head of its British branch. The following year he visited Moscow and the year after that the United States, where he continued to write poetry and books and in 1917 became a magazine editor.

In 1920 Crowley decided to establish his own center dedicated to the study and practice of magic. He selected a site in Cefalu, on the Italian island of Sicily, and called his center the Abbey of Thelema. Soon rumors abounded about the wild sexual activities, Satanic rituals, drug use, and other supposed abominations taking place there, and the international press ran stories attacking Crowley as evil. These attacks intensified after the publication of Crowley's 1922 book *Diary of a Drug Fiend*, which detailed his experiences as a drug addict. Finally, in 1923 Benito Mussolini, the Italian dictator, personally decreed that Crowley had to abandon his abbey and leave the country. By that time, according to statements he made later, he had used magic rituals to attain the Supreme Grade of Ipsissimus, the ultimate state of enlightenment under the beliefs of the Hermetic Order of the Golden Dawn. Since he claimed to have attained this state while working alone, however, there was no proof of his accomplishment.

In 1925, after spending time in Paris, Crowley was invited to return to the Ordo Templi Orientis as its international head. For the next four years, in addition to his duties for this order, he traveled through Germany, France, and North Africa before finally settling in France. However, Crowley was still a controversial figure, and the French government quickly expelled him from the country in 1929.

In the early 1930s Crowley gave up his position with the Ordo Templi Orientis and began a libel lawsuit against artist Nina Hamnett, who, in her memoirs (*Laughing Torso*, published in 1932), said that Crowley was a practitioner of black magic. Not only did Crowley lose the lawsuit in 1934, but when the details of his life became public during the trial he faced renewed condemnation in the media. Moreover, his legal expenses bankrupted him. Although he continued to lecture, to write, and to publish books, he never again regained his financial footing, nor did he shake his addiction to drugs. Crowley died in a boardinghouse in Hastings, England, in 1947. **See also** Gardner, Gerald; Golden Dawn, Hermetic Order of the; Leek, Sybil; Wiccan Rede.

Crowther, Patricia (1927–)

Wiccan high priestess Patricia Crowther is the author of several nonfiction books related to witchcraft, including *The Witches Speak* (1965) and *The Secrets of Ancient Witchcraft* (1974), both written with her husband, Arnold Crowther, *Lid of the Cauldron* (1981; latest edition 1998), and *One Witch's World* (1998). She also wrote a novel, *Witches Were for Hanging* (1992; reprinted 1999) and produced a British radio program, *A Spell of Witchcraft*, in 1971. The latter helped spread interest in witchcraft, as have Crowther's many lecture tours and media appearances.

Patricia Crowther's interest in witchcraft began in 1957 when under hypnosis she recovered memories of a past life as a seventeenth century witch. Crowther was convinced these memories were true because she also recalled several spells and later discovered them to be consistent with spells used in that time. Consequently, she decided that she was meant to be a witch in her present life as well. Meanwhile, in 1956 she met Arnold Crowther while performing theatrically as a singer and dancer; Arnold Crowther was a ventriloquist and stage magician. Crowther introduced her to his old friend Gerald Gardner, one of the most influential witches of modern times, and in 1960 she was initiated into Gardner's coven. The following year she became a high priestess and married Arnold Crowther.

In December 1961 the couple decided to establish their own coven, the first of many they ultimately formed throughout Great Britain. Together the Crowthers cast spells not only with fellow coven members but also for outsiders seeking help. Meanwhile Patricia Crowther was initiated into an ancient tradition of witchcraft from a hereditary witch who passed the information on in secret. She subsequently wrote her own rituals and Craft-related poetry. Today Crowther lectures and writes articles on both ancient and modern forms of the Craft. **See also** Gardner, Gerald.

Crystal Moon Wicca

Established in 1989 by Irish witches Talon and Firewalker shortly after they married, Crystal Moon Wicca is a Witchcraft tradition that employs a variety of deities, including Celtic, Egyptian, Greek, and Roman. Its members are free to choose their own practices, but generally Crystal Moon Wiccan rituals strongly emphasize nature, the moon, the four elements, and magic. Talon and Firewalker and other members of the Crystal Moon Tradition also teach Wicca by mail through their Order of the Crystal Moon International Pagan Fellowship. **See also** traditions, Witchcraft.

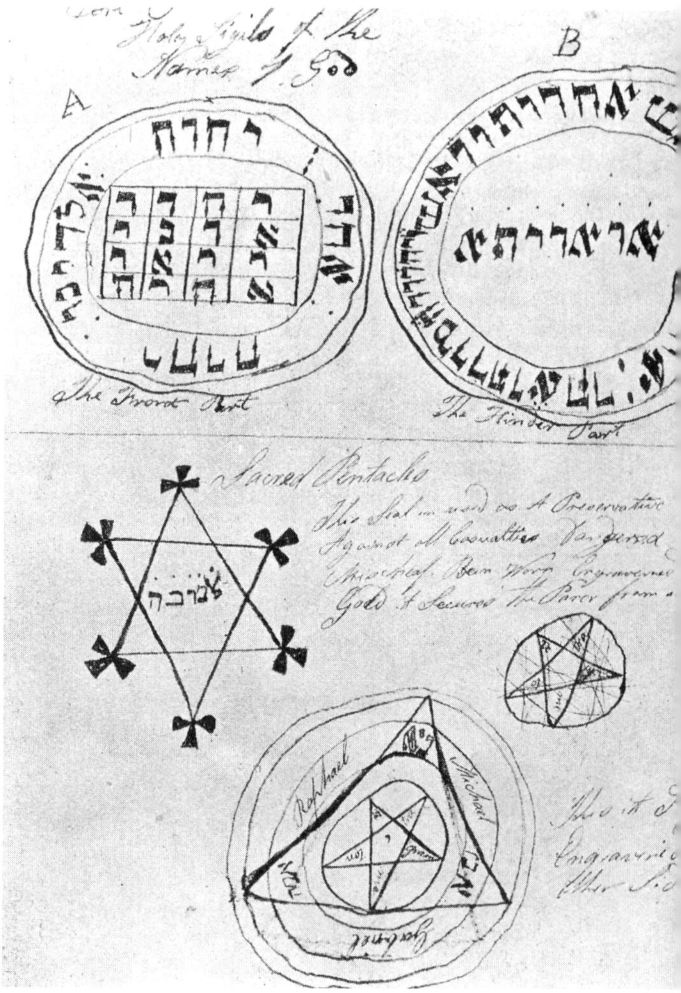

cunning man

Now rarely used, the phrase *cunning man* refers to a male white witch skilled in divining and healing. His female counterpart is the cunning woman or wise woman. The word *cunning* comes from *kenning*, Old English for "wise."

One of the most famous cunning men in history was England's James Murrell, who lived from 1780 to 1860. In fact, his name is almost synonymous with the term. He was the seventh son of a seventh son, a birth position believed to impart great powers of magic and healing to a child. Such children born into a family of hereditary witches are thought to be especially gifted. Murrell apparently came from such a family; however, he did not work seriously as a cunning man until his midtwenties. Until then he had a series of jobs, first as a surveyor's apprentice, then a chemist's assistant, then a shoemaker.

James Murrell kept a book of conjurations, sigils, and pentacles (pictured here). His name is now synonymous with the term cunning man.

Once Murrell did start working as a cunning man, he quickly became famous, attracting clients of all classes and economic standing throughout England. He charged fees for his services, which he divided into two categories: high magic and low magic. Low magic was traditional folk magic, involving amulets, talismans, charms, healings, and other objects and processes rooted in the natural world. High magic was rooted in the spiritual world, using spirits, angels, or similar beings to accomplish divination, mediumship, exorcism, and certain spells.

To aid him in his work, Murrell collected a large number of books and manuscripts on the occult, as well as ritual tools. Many of these items came into the possession of his son Buck some time after Murrell's death in 1860. Though Buck had no skill as a cunning man, he saved his father's possessions; unfortunately for historians, Murrell family heirs threw the items away in the mid-1950s.

Few people in modern times consider themselves to be cunning men or women. If they do dabble in the kind of folk magic that Murrell practiced, they generally call themselves something else, such as psychic healer. In fact, even when Murrell plied his trade in the nineteenth century "cunning man" was falling out of use, and prior to that time few people practiced the trade. Cunning men and women primarily appeared in England prior to the eighteenth century, mostly in small towns. Like Murrell, many owned occult books, if they could read, and/or came from families of hereditary witches where folk magic was traditionally passed down. Also like Murrell, they made money by serving the wealthy as well as the poor. It was not unusual for a well-to-do Englishman to travel some distance to visit a famous cunning man, seeking some charm, amulet, love potion, healing ointment, or a glimpse into the future.

Because of such patronage, for the most part cunning men were ignored during witch-hunts. Their female counterparts were usually less fortunate. Though they were just as helpful as cunning men, cunning women were often accused of consorting with the devil to commit evil. Some cunning men were accused of this as well, most typically if local church authorities considered them a threat to their congregation's adherence to Christianity. **See also** amulet; charm; oils and ointments; potion; persecution, witch.

Cunningham, Scott (1956–1993)

American Wiccan Scott Cunningham is the author of several books about witchcraft, including *Magical Herbalism* (1982), *Earth Power: Techniques of Natural Magic* (1983), *Cunningham's Encyclopedia of Magical Herbs* (1985), *Cunningham's Encyclopedia of Crystal, Gem, and Metal Magic* (1987), and *The Truth About Witchcraft* (1988). The latter, an expanded version of a booklet Cunningham published earlier, remains his most popular work and is often credited with spreading the practice of witchcraft among people previously unfamiliar with Wicca. Another of his books, *Wicca: A Guide for the Solitary Practitioner* (1988), is credited with helping to start the now increasingly common trend towards the solitary practice of magic, as opposed to magic performed as part of a coven.

Cunningham himself was a solitary practitioner, although during the early part of his association with witchcraft he was initiated into several different covens of different traditions. These include the Aridian Tradition, the Ancient Pictish Gaelic Tradition, and American Traditionalist Wicca. Cunningham first became a Wiccan in 1971, and after studying writing at San Diego State University during the early 1970s he began authoring witchcraft-related books. As his books became popular, he started lecturing on Wicca as well.

Cunningham particularly wanted to use his lectures to advance the status of Wicca as a religion distinct from the paganism practiced in ancient times and to promote its acceptance as a modern faith. After being diagnosed with cancer in 1983, Cunningham ended his public appearances. He died in 1993. **See also** solitaries; traditions, Witchcraft; Wicca.

curses

Curses are invocations of evil spirits or evil forces for the purpose of causing harm to whomever or whatever has been cursed. Modern witches do not typically use curses because they believe that the evil they send out to others will ultimately come back to them threefold. However, some witches accept the use of a specific curse, called a binding spell or binding, to stop an evil person from continuing to commit evil. A few Wiccans believe it is also acceptable to curse a murderer who has otherwise gone unpunished.

The idea that cursing is part of the realm of black magic, and therefore should not be performed by a witch, is a recent development. From the earliest times to the eighteenth century, cursing was a common practice among witches. In fact, many Europeans who were not witches also cursed spontaneously in anger. The typical words used for a curse varied widely; they included such phrases as "a pox on you" and "the devil take you." Such curses may not have been delivered with ill intent, but during witch-hunts, uttering such epithets openly and carelessly could be dangerous, because if someone died or took ill after being cursed—or if their animals died or took ill—the person who did the cursing was usually arrested and tried as a witch even in the absence of other evidence of witchcraft.

Cyber Wicca

A new trend among witches, Cyber Wicca is the sharing of Wiccan rituals and other coven activities over the Internet. Participants enter chat rooms where they exchange typed conversation, parts of rituals, and the like. Essentially, a solitary practitioner in this way becomes a participant in a virtual coven. People discover Cyber Wicca chat groups through a variety of sources, including message boards and links to websites of people involved in Wicca. Many links to such sites exist online, particularly at the websites of Wiccan organizations. Some of the most popular Wicca-related networking sites online are www.Wicca.com, www.witchesweb.com, www.witchvox.com, and www.witchcraft.net/ASP (the site of the Alliance of Solitary Practitioners). Sites that provide information as well as networking opportunities include www.BlessedBe.com, www.celtic-connection.com, www.cog.org (the site of the Covenant of the Goddess organization), www.CelticCrow.com (the site of the Witches' League for Public Awareness), and www.circlesanctuary.org/ (the site of the Circle Sanctuary organization). **See also** solitaries.

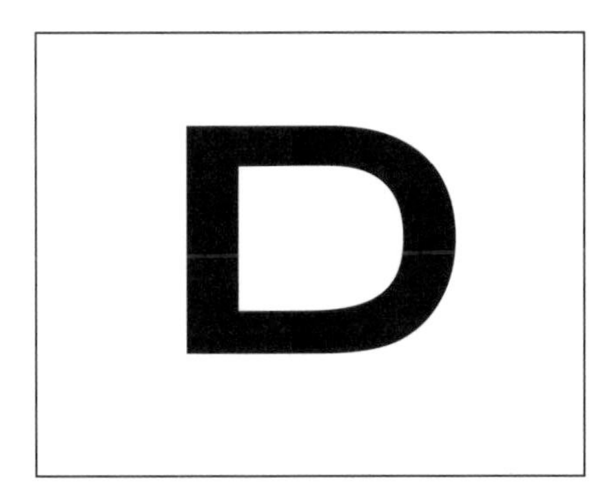

dancing

Dancing was part of the earliest pagan rituals, and it remains a part of witchcraft today. One guidebook for modern witches, *A Witches' Bible* by Janet and Stewart Farrar, mentions several ritual dances. These include the Corn Dance, during which a coven's high priestess dances while carrying a loaf of bread, and the Witches' Rune, a ring dance with participants arranged in a circle. In performing the Witches' Rune, the dancers stand side by side, with men and women in alternate positions to the extent possible. Dancers face the center of the circle and hold hands with one another so that each left hand is facing upward and each right hand downward. Sometimes the high priestess "breaks" the ring, so that she can weave the line in a complex pattern, then unravel it and reform the circle.

Many rituals call for dancing hand-in-hand in a circle, often around a bonfire or other flame. For example, in the Wheel Dance, participants dance around a bonfire to honor the winter solstice. In most circle dances, participants move in a clockwise direction. Known among witches as the way of the sun, or *deosil*, a Gaelic word that means "to the right," this direction is connected to good—or white—magic. Counterclockwise—known as widdershins, from the German word for "contrary way," or *tuathal*, from the Irish word for "to the left" or "wrong direction"—is considered the direction for black magic. However, some dances incorporate a few counterclockwise movements to symbolize going backward in time, but such movement is always balanced with a clockwise movement.

Another traditional style of dancing requires participants to move in pairs back-to-back with elbows linked. Some covens perform this dance at many types of celebrations, while others reserve it for the Imbolc, a fire festival and Celtic Great Sabbat held on February 2, thinking it to be the traditional Imbolc dance. Some scholars, however, believe that a different style of dance was performed at the Imbolc during ancient and medieval times: the Volta, in which individual dancers execute complicated steps and leap into the air or over fire. The ability to leap in this way was often cited by witch-hunters as proof that witches danced with the devil; only under the devil's influence, the witch-hunters argued, could witches dance with such abandon. Witches were also condemned for dances involving sexual activity, whether actual physical intimacy or merely suggestive gestures were involved. Some of these dances required female participants to "ride" a pitchfork or broomstick, and many scholars believe that this was the origin of the belief that witches fly on broomsticks. **See also** broom; chanting; circle, magic; Farrar, Janet and Stewart; Imbolc.

Darrell, John (c. 1562–1602)

John Darrell was a minister whose fraudulent exorcisms prompted the Church of England in 1603 to prohibit its clergymen from acting as exorcists. Darrell performed his first exorcism in 1586 on Catherine (also recorded as Katherine) Wright, who pretended to have fits to gain sympathy from her father-in-law. Darrell believed she was possessed by a demon. When he encouraged her to name the witch who must have sent it to torment her, she picked a neighbor, Margaret Roper. Darrell then performed a rite of exorcism to rid Wright of her demon. Shortly thereafter, apparently feeling guilt for her false accusation, Wright admitted that she had faked her fits.

For encouraging what turned out to be a falsehood, Darrell was threatened with jail by local authorities. Nonetheless, he continued his career as an exorcist and continued to associate with frauds as well. In 1596 he staged a series of dramatic exorcisms over the Burton Boy, who like Wright later confessed to faking his demonic fits. The following year Darrell and a priest named George More conducted public exorcisms of William Sommers, a man in his late teens or early twenties. Not uncoincidentally, Sommers had previously heard Darrell speak about the fourteen classic signs of demonic possession—including fits, obscene language and behavior, and foaming at the mouth—and then developed all fourteen of these signs. Darrell then made a show of casting out Sommers's demons, although he said they might come back unless Sommers could name their source. Sommers consequently accused thirteen women of sending the demons to torment him.

By this time, several people had begun to suspect that Sommers was a fraud, and they pressured him to confess that his accusations were false. When some of the women he had accused went on trial for witchcraft, Sommers finally told the truth: He had never been possessed. Furthermore, he said Darrell had coached him on how to fake possession. The archbishop of Canterbury and the bishop of London, among other Church of England leaders, launched an investigation of Darrell's activities. Darrell maintained that he had been unaware of Sommers's deceptions and had exorcised him in good faith. Nonetheless, in 1599 an ecclesiastical court removed him from the ministry and imprisoned him for several months as further punishment. He died in approximately 1602, continuing to protest his innocence to the end. **See also** Burton Boy; demonic possession; exorcism.

Dee, John (1527–1608)

John Dee was a well-respected English scholar, alchemist, astrologer, and occultist who became known as "Queen Elizabeth's Merlin" because he was the official magician of the Elizabethan Court. (In English legends, Merlin was the magician who advised King Arthur.) Dee also wrote extensively on the occult and collected books on the subject as well. Perhaps his best-known work is *Monas Hicroglyphia*, a 1563 book on numerology that he originally wrote in code. Although he was a prolific writer, producing nearly eighty books in all, only a few of his books were published in his lifetime, and most remain in manuscript form today. Nonetheless, many seventeenth-century people knew about him because of a popular 1659 book by Meric Causaubon entitled *A True and Faithful Relation of what passed for many years between Dr. John Dee and some spirits*, which told of Dee's experiences with the occult.

Dee first became interested in the occult while he was a student at St. Johns College in Cambridge, England, where he was studying science and mathematics. He left school to travel through Europe and learn more about the occult. Soon he became an expert in astrology, alchemy, and scrying. His interest in the latter two pursuits was inspired by his poverty at the time;

alchemy involves attempts to turn base metals into gold and silver, while scrying is a magical way to locate hidden or lost objects such as money.

Eventually word of Dee's skills in the occult reached England, and he returned there by royal request to serve King Edward VI, who assumed the throne at age ten after the death of his father, King Henry VIII. After Edward's death in 1553, Dee became astrologer for the next ruler, Queen Mary I, foretelling her future on a daily basis. He was a favorite at court for only a few months, however, because he befriended Mary's half-sister and rival, Princess Elizabeth, whom Mary hated. Once Mary became aware of this friendship, she had Dee arrested as a witch on manufactured charges that included killing children via magic and planning to murder the queen in the same way. Dee was imprisoned from 1553 to 1555. In 1558, Mary died and Elizabeth assumed the throne, whereupon Dee became the new queen's astrologer, numerologist, magician, and adviser. Some say he worked as her spy as well, telling the queen whenever he heard someone speak ill of her. He also worked as a geographer and map maker.

Alchemist, astrologer, occultist, and scholar John Dee attained fame when he became the official magician for Queen Elizabeth.

During this period Dee began collecting books on magic and the occult. His collection eventually numbered several thousand volumes, and included numerous tools that he used to communicate with entities many of his peers believed were spirits but which Dee insisted were angels. These tools include a piece of obsidian he called his "magic glass" or "magic mirror," and a pale pink crystal he said was given to him by an angel.

Dee had never actually seen the angels with whom he communicated, nor had he spoken to them directly. Instead his assistant, Edward Kelly (originally named Edward Talbot), let Dee know when they were present and received the messages from them. According to Kelly, the angels spoke in a strange language, Enochian, which he and Dee then recorded and translated.

At first Dee and Kelly communicated with angels for their own personal enlightenment, but at some point they began engaging in such communication for the benefit of others. From 1585 to 1589 they toured Europe as professional angel communicators, allowing other people to ask questions of the angels. Their tour ended when the two had a falling-out because Kelly was attracted to Dee's wife. Dee then returned to England and eventually found a new partner in spirit/angel communication, Bartholomew Hickman, but he and Hickman never achieved fame together. Dee survived on the favors of the royal court until Queen Elizabeth died in 1603, whereupon he lost his position and was thrown back into the poverty he had known as a youth. By this time, witch-hunts were increasingly common in England and Europe, and he began to fear that without royal protection he would be attacked for his earlier position as a magician. He petitioned King James I to publicly declare that he had never actually been a magician at all, but rather a scholar and scientist. He failed in his attempt but fortunately was not targeted by witch-hunters. Dee died of natural causes in 1608.

Today Dee's book collection can be found at the British Museum, along with some of the tools he used to communicate with angels. In addition, the Enochian language that Dee used in these communications is still used by some modern witches who believe it to be imbued with magic. One of the first modern witches to employ this language was Aleister Crowley, who in his book *Magick in Theory and Practice* advocated its adoption by all witches. **See also** alchemy; astrology; Crowley, Aleister; England, witch-hunts of; James I; scrying.

de Guaita, Stanislas (late nineteenth century)

Exactly when the nineteenth-century French marquis Stanislas de Guaita was born and died is uncertain, but he is best known for establishing a coven whose beliefs and practices were described in a popular 1889 work by Oswald Wirth, *The Book of Thoth*. De Guaita once got into a "psychic battle" with the leader of a rival coven, Joseph-Antoine Boullan, which involved each man sending demons to torment the other. When Boullan died, some of his fellow coven members challenged members of de Guaita's coven to a duel; this resulted in several injuries but no deaths. However, de Guaita's mental and physical health was poor because of heavy drug use. He died of a drug overdose at the age of twenty-seven.

de Lancre, Pierre (1553–1631)

French attorney and witch-hunter Pierre de Lancre was responsible for the death of over six hundred Basque men, women, and children on the French side of the Pyrenees Mountains in 1608 and 1609. King Henry IV of France ordered de Lancre to the region to hunt witches, alarmed by rumors of sorcery there. Within a short time de Lancre had decided that hundreds of Basque witches were conspiring to destroy every aspect of Christianity, and soon he was also suggesting that they were working in concert with witches throughout Europe.

De Lancre, long afraid that such a conspiracy would develop, had begun persecuting witches in the early 1600s and was adamant that all convicted witches be executed. During his interrogation of the Basque witches he obtained numerous confessions, in which the accused told of Sabbats in other parts of France and alleged that several Catholic priests were engaging in pagan and/or satanic activities. This type of information fueled de Lancre's already extreme passion for burning witches.

De Lancre wrote about his witch-hunting experiences in a huge volume entitled *Tableau de l'Inconstance des Mauvais Anges* (*Description of the Inconstancy of Evil Angels*, published in 1612). He wrote other books as well, including *L'Incredulité et Mescréance du Sortilège* (*Incredulity and Misbelief of Enchantment*, published in 1622) and *Du Sortilège* (*Witchcraft*, published in 1627). But although his works were popular for a time, eventually the French people began to consider his actions too harsh or even completely unwarranted, particularly after he executed several priests as witches. Government support for de Lancre's activities ended shortly thereafter, and de Lancre spent the rest of his life arguing for the resumption of witch-hunting to an increasingly uninterested public. **See also** Basque region, witch-hunts of the.

Del Rio, Martin (1551–1608)

Martin Del Rio is the author of *Disquisitionum Magicarum Libri Sex,* a book used by European judges to guide their handling of witchcraft trials. The book was first published in Belgium in 1599; a French translation was published in 1611. By 1747 there had been approximately twenty editions of the work. In it Del Rio, a Jesuit priest, argued that witches were a real threat to both individuals and society and should therefore be stamped out swiftly. According to Del Rio, any confessed witch should be considered guilty regardless of whether the confession was obtained under torture, and any judge who did not condemn a confessed witch to death should be suspected of being a witch himself. In fact, anyone who did not speak out against witchcraft in any form was suspect. However, Del Rio did believe that an accused witch should be allowed to have a lawyer during the trial.

In addition to such arguments, the *Disquisitionum* provided information on magic, alchemy, divination, amulets, exorcism, and ways to test witches to prove their guilt. Del Rio continued to write on these topics throughout his life. In all, he produced fifteen books, some of which were collections of his sermons. **See also** persecution, witch; torture.

demonic possession

According to some Christian sects, demonic possession is the possession, or taking over, of a person's body by one or more demons or the devil. Symptoms of demonic possession commonly include convulsions or fits, overt sexual behavior, verbal outbursts (often obscene), and physical changes in the body (such as a bloated belly or permanently grimacing expression). Some possessed people also supposedly demonstrate unusual abilities, such as unexplained knowledge of a foreign language, the ability to predict the future, or the ability to levitate. Today many people view demonic possession as the result of a mental illness that has nothing to do with demons or devils. Other people think that the symptoms of demonic possession are caused by ghosts or other types of spirits rather than demons or devils. Catholic dogma, however, generally continues to hold that demonic possession is caused by demons or the devil.

In the Middle Ages, the entity thought to have entered a possessed person was always the devil himself, but by the middle of the fifteenth century the prevalent idea was that the devil or one of the devil's agents had sent a demon to do the possessing. Magicians, wizards, and witches were all considered such agents, and were routinely accused of causing demonic possessions. However, it was commonly believed that the evil spirit could not simply be sent into the intended victim, but rather had to enter the body through the ingestion of food or the touching of some magical object. Amulets, potions, and ordinary foods, particularly apples or pieces of bread, were most typically cited as the tools used to cause a possession.

Some cases of possession—and the exorcisms performed to cure it—appear genuine. For example, in the early twentieth century Anna Ecklund demonstrated what appeared to be symptoms of demonic possession, including the ability to speak and understand languages to which she had never been exposed, and the exorcism performed appeared to cure her. Because her case was well documented, it is often cited by believers in demonic possession as proof that the phenomenon is real. However, many cases of apparent demonic possession have later been revealed as fraudulent. Instances in which some people faked demonic possession either for attention or for profit, demonstrating their symptoms in front of big audiences that sometimes paid for the experience, were particularly common in the sixteenth and seventeenth centuries. **See also** Bilson, Boy of; Darrell, John; demons; Ecklund, Anna; exorcism.

demons

According to Christian doctrine, demons are evil spirits led by the devil, also known as Satan. Outside of Christianity, demons have generally been defined simply as spirits, some good and some evil, the latter of which can be summoned and controlled by magicians intending to harm their enemies. Such magicians risk being harmed by the demons themselves, however, so they perform their work within a protective magic circle that keeps the demons at bay.

In the sixteenth and seventeenth centuries, demons were strongly associated with witches. It was said that some demons served as witches' familiars, while others were sent by witches to bewitch, torment, and take over the bodies of the witches' enemies as part of a phenomenon known as demonic possession. Still other demons were said to routinely enjoy sexual relations with witches. Stories abounded of wild revels involving witches and demons, particularly as part of Sabbats. Some of these stories came from witches' confessions; under pressure (usually involving torture) many witches admitted to consorting with demons as well as with the devil. However, witches do not traditionally involve demons in their rituals.

Sixteenth- and seventeenth-century Christian theologians gave names to many of these demons, usually choosing names already associated with pagan deities and spirits, such as Beelzebub and Astarte (a god and goddess of pagan Phoenicians also worshiped in ancient Israel) in order to vilify them. Entire books were devoted to describing these demons and defining their duties. For example, German physician Johann Weyer's *Pseudo-Monarchy of Demons*, published in 1568, described a hierarchy with 1,111 divisions of 6,666 demons each. **See also** demonic possession; devil; Weyer, Johann.

devil

Contrary to popular belief, the devil, or Satan, is not a part of pagan, Neopaganism, or Wiccan belief, nor is the devil a part of the practice of witchcraft. Rather, the devil is part of Christian belief and is considered the evil opponent of God. As such he is worshiped by Satanists, who practice black magic rooted in Christian traditions.

Nonetheless, people of the Middle Ages, Renaissance, and Reformation were certain that witches not only worshiped the devil but also signed pacts giving him their souls in exchange for magical powers and other benefits. Other groups of people who did not practice Christianity were said to have signed such pacts, and by the seventeenth century any evidence that a person either practiced folk magic or was not a devout Christian was considered proof that such a pact had been signed. However, witches were particularly singled out as Satan worshipers, and when pressured (usually under brutal torture) they often confessed to consorting with the devil as well as with various demons.

Common wisdom held that the devil often assumed the form of an animal in order to walk among humans. These stories usually referred to both the devil and demons, although the devil's most common animal form was supposedly a black dog while demons chose cats, mice, or other small household or field animals. In the Middle Ages, both the devil and his demons were said to take these forms to serve witches as familiars.

By the time of the Renaissance, people had begun to question why Satan would subjugate himself to a witch. By the Reformation, church authorities had decided that Satan controlled but was never controlled by witches; only lesser demons could be familiars, and they were given that assignment by the devil. Meanwhile the devil was said to preside over witches' Sabbats, sometimes sitting on a throne and often having sexual relations with the witches under his control. **See also** demons; familiar; Sabbat.

Diana

Worshiped in ancient Rome as the goddess of fertility, the moon, and the hunt, Diana today is considered by Wiccans an important aspect of the deity. They honor her as an aspect of the Triple Goddess of the moon, which also includes the goddesses Selene and Hecate. Diana is in charge of the new moon, Selene the full moon, and Hecate the dark moon. Diana is also the primary focus of an American and Western European Witchcraft tradition called the Dianic Tradition. Also called Dianic Wicca, this tradition has attracted many feminists because it diminishes the importance of or in some case eliminates the male aspect of the deity.

Indeed, the Diana of Roman myth is a strong female figure, a virgin warrior subservient to no man. The Greeks called her Artemis, and in their myths she was not only a huntress and a moon goddess but also the goddess who protected women during childbirth and avenged those who had been raped. Pagan women worshiped her well into the sixth century, when Christians began to demonize Diana/Artemis. In fact, many scholars believe it was the early Christians who first connected Diana with witches. By medieval times she was known as the patroness of witches and was said to take part in witches' revels, along with the devil.

In modern times, Diana has been a subject of controversy for researchers into the history of witchcraft, largely because of the work of British anthropologist Margaret Alice Murray. In her 1921 book *The Witch-Cult in Western Europe*, which was partially based on an 1890 book, *The Golden Bough* by James Frazier, Murray argued that a cult of witches dedicated to the worship of Diana not only secretly existed but thrived throughout the Middle Ages, Renaissance, and Reformation, creating a direct link between a Dianic cult known to have existed in the sixth century and modern witches who worship Diana. These modern Diana worshipers welcomed Murray's suggestion that their religious practices had been passed down from ancient pagans by way of medieval witches. In fact, Wiccan Gerald Gardner was so taken with the concept that he included it in his Gardnerian Tradition of Witchcraft.

Nonetheless, most of Murray's peers in the field of anthropology disagreed with her assertion, arguing among other points that it was impossible for such a large and well-organized cult as Murray described to have existed in secret, particularly during a time of aggressive witch-hunting. They further argued that Murray was wrong to rely on documents based on witch hysteria for proof that witches worshiped Diana in large, organized groups. In particular, Murray had cited the Canon Episcopi, a tenth-century document of the church, as support for her theory; the document railed against witches who consorted with "Diana, the goddess of Pagans." Those skeptical of Murray's theory insisted that Murray present more reliable evidence that a medieval Dianic cult existed.

In the years since Murray's book was published, many people have tried unsuccessfully to find this evidence. Most scholars and even some witches have concluded that Murray's theory was wrong. However, this does not diminish witches' and Neopagans' reverence for Diana, and it has not altered their worship practices. **See also** Dianic Wicca; Murray, Margaret Alice.

Dianic Wicca

Dianic Wicca is a major Witchcraft tradition practiced throughout the United States and to a somewhat lesser extent in Western Europe. Most of its practitioners are women, because most Dianic Wiccan covens exclude men.

The focus of Dianic covens is the Goddess, particularly the goddess Diana. Some of the covens feel a close personal relationship to witches of the fourteenth through seventeenth centuries, when witch burnings were common; this connection comes from their belief in British anthropologist Margaret Alice Murray's theory that a secret Dianic witch cult existed then, as well as from their anger over the historically documented persecution of women. Dianic covens generally encourage their members to be active and strong both personally and politically. Indeed, many members of the religion are also involved in feminist politics. At the same time, members are encouraged to nurture others on their quest for personal growth and identity. Dianic covens also generally celebrate the traditional Wiccan festivals of the Wheel of the Year, although covens vary widely regarding how they choose to celebrate and worship the Goddess.

During the 1970s, some covens routinely connected their rituals to events related to women's suffering in order to make a political statement. For example, they performed rituals in public after a sensational case of rape or murder involving a female victim. Today most Dianic covens do not participate in such events, and an increasing number of Dianic Wiccans are solitaries rather than members of a coven. However, many belong to a feminist religious organization based on the Dianic philosophy called the Re-Formed Congregation of the Goddess (RCG), which publishes a feminist newsletter/network called *Of a Like Mind*. The group has a website at www.goddesswoman.com.

The first Dianic Wicca coven was that of Zsuzsanna Budapest in the early 1970s. She called it the Susan B. Anthony Coven No. 1, after the noted American suffragist, and published several newsletters with articles about witchcraft and its relationship to feminism. These articles spread the ideas of Dianic Wicca to other parts of the United States, and soon other Dianic Wiccan feminist covens were born.

A variation of the Dianic Tradition, created by Morgan McFarland and Mark Roberts during the 1970s, worships many other goddesses besides Diana but keeps the feminist orientation of the Dianic Tradition. Called the McFarland Dianic Tradition, or MDT, it originated in Dallas, Texas, but is now practiced throughout the United States, with over forty high priestesses having been initiated into the tradition. **See also** Diana; Murray, Margaret Alice; traditions, Witchcraft.

divination

The word *divination* is typically used today to refer to the act of using magic to divine the future. However, the word *divine* not only means "to foretell" but also "to learn via intuition," so divination is also a magical means of finding hidden objects, like treasure, and of uncovering secrets. Witches and sorcerers perform divination along with other forms of magic, while diviners, also known as seers, specialize in divination alone.

Various methods are used for divination, but in most cases the diviner gains information by looking at either natural objects (e.g., the entrails of a sacrificed animal, the leaves left at the bottom of a cup of tea, the lines on the palm of the hand) or objects marked with man-made symbols (e.g., Tarot cards and runestones) to discern messages or images sent, presumably, by gods or spirits. Some modern witches believe that the images they see are really patterns forming in the currents of the astral plane, a realm of existence where spirits dwell,

A common method of divination is the reading of Tarot cards. Fortune-tellers claim the ability to receive images and messages from gods or spirits by interpreting these cards.

and that these patterns influence future events in the physical world. The same principle underlies a popular form of divination called astrology, in which the position of stars and planets at the time of a person's birth is believed to influence that person's personality and destiny.

Diviners believe that the future can be predicted, but most do not think that the future is fixed. Instead they believe that people can use information obtained by divination to either alter the future or assure the predicted events will occur. Christians, however, do not necessarily view the results of divination as helpful. Those who strictly adhere to Christian teachings believe that divined images and messages come from the devil and are therefore either lies or tools to entice the diviner to make a pact with Satan. This belief began in the sixteenth and seventeenth centuries, when witch-hunters routinely accused diviners of having made a pact with the devil in order to justify prosecuting them for witchcraft.

However, diviners have not always been viewed so negatively. In sixteenth-century England, for example, they were valued members of society. One of the most revered diviners of this period was John Dee, who held the unofficial title of royal magician because he regularly divined the future for Queen Elizabeth I. Dee used a magic glass or crystal for divination; when glass, crystals, crystal balls, mirrors, or other objects with reflective surfaces are used for divination, the process is called scrying. The most popular methods of divination in modern times are astrology, Tarot cards, runestones, and palm reading. **See also** astrology; Dee, John; runes; Tarot cards.

dogs

People today do not typically associate dogs with witchcraft, but during the witch-hunts of the fifteenth through seventeenth centuries Europeans generally believed that the devil sometimes took the form of a black dog. In fact, some accused and convicted witches confessed that the devil routinely appeared as a dog at their Sabbats. In medieval times, the devil was believed to have a black dog that accompanied him on hunts; any medieval Englishman out late at night who saw a black dog usually feared that the devil was after him.

The association between dogs and the supernatural goes back many centuries. In pagan times in England, the dog was believed to be the hunting companion of the Horned God, a fertility god, and therefore not particularly connected with evil. However, the Celts also thought that the dog enjoyed the companionship of fairies, who were sometimes mischievous. The idea that dogs associated with Satan was, along with Satan himself, a Christian invention.

Historically, some cultures associated the dog with death. The ancient Greeks, for example, thought that a three-headed dog guarded the entrance to the Underworld, and the ancient Egyptian god of the dead, Anubis, had the head of a jackal, a member of the dog family. **See also** Celts; devil; Horned God; moon.

drawing down the moon

The phrase *drawing down the moon* refers to an important act of ritual magic that employs a Wiccan invocation of the Goddess. During this invocation, a coven's high priest calls or "draws down" the goddess of the moon (usually the Greek goddess Selene) so she will enter the coven's high priestess. The goddess then talks through the priestess, traditionally giving a speech known as the Charge of the Goddess. Wiccans were not the first to draw down the goddess of the moon; writings of ancient Greeks and Romans specifically mention such a rite as well. However, the Charge of the Goddess is a modern creation written by Wiccans involved in the Gardnerian Tradition.

A similar though less common ritual is drawing down the sun, an invocation of the Horned God. In this case, it is the high priestess who calls the Horned God down into her coven's high priest. Once the Horned God has entered the high priest's body, he remains there until the magic circle is uncast. However, he does not deliver any particular speech or charge. **See also** Adler, Margot; Charge of the Goddess; Horned God; Neopagans.

Duncan, Helen (1898–?)

The witchcraft trial of Helen Duncan is often cited as the catalyst for the repeal of Great Britain's 1736 Witchcraft Act, which made it illegal to pretend to practice witchcraft. Duncan was not actually a witch but a medium who earned her living contacting spirits on request. In 1941, during World War II, she claimed to have spoken to the spirit of a sailor who had recently drowned at sea. Duncan's claim would have attracted little official notice except for the fact that the sailor's ship had indeed sunk. The event, however, had been classified as top secret so no one outside of the military knew about it. When Duncan's story hit the newspapers, the British government was forced to admit what it knew, and officials began to wonder what other secret information Duncan might reveal. Some historians believe this is why they put her on trial under the 1736 Witchcraft Act just as plans for the Allied invasion of Normandy were being finalized. According to this view, officials most likely wanted to use the trial to discredit Duncan so no one would believe her tales.

The government's main argument in the 1944 trial was that Duncan was a lifelong fraud who had never really been able to communicate with spirits of the dead. Dozens of witnesses testified to the contrary, however, swearing that Duncan had indeed contacted their deceased friends and relatives. Nonetheless, Duncan was quickly convicted. She spent nine months in jail, during which time public outcry against her imprisonment grew. This outcry continued even after her release, and finally in 1951 Parliament repealed the Witchcraft Act. Many modern witches hail this decision for giving them the freedom to practice witchcraft openly and to publish books on magic without fear of prosecution. In fact, very soon after the act was repealed Gerald Gardner began circulating his Book of Shadows, which inspired a resurgence of interest in witchcraft in England, Europe, and the United States. **See also** England, witch-hunts of.

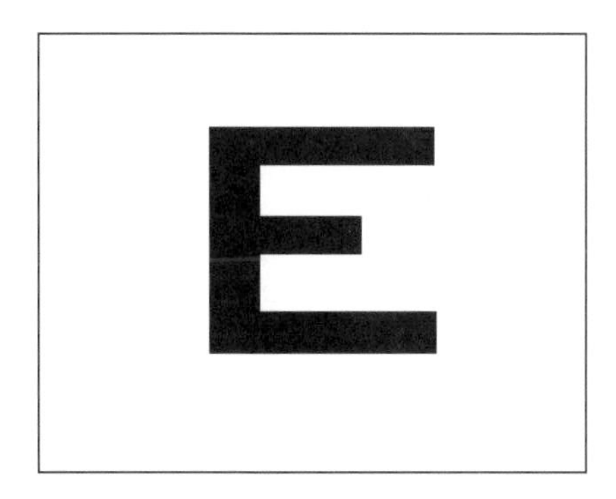

Early, Biddy (1798–1874)

Born Biddy O'Connor, Irishwoman Biddy Early became famous during her lifetime for using mysterious potions to cure people of a variety of ailments, and many people thought she was a witch. But while she was charged with witchcraft in 1865, her case was dismissed, probably because although church leaders denounced her as a witch the public revered her as a healer and considered her a good Christian for coming to their aid without asking for money in return. (She did, however, accept gifts of food, spirits, or household goods.)

Early first began using her potions in the 1840s, after her second husband died. She also began making predictions about the future, most of which came true. She claimed that both of her powers—the abilities to see the future and heal people—were due to a bottle that, when peered into through the neck, would magically show her future events or what potions to mix. Over the years, she told various stories of how she came to own this bottle, but usually she said it was a gift from fairies. She also refused to let anyone else look inside or even touch the bottle.

Throughout her life, Early continued to mix potions for people who needed healing. However, she turned away sufferers whose ailments were too severe for her to cure, not wanting to give anyone false hope. In April 1874 she herself became ill and knew no cure would help. She died shortly thereafter, whereupon a search immediately began for her magic bottle. When it was not found among Early's belongings, various rumors began to spread about where she might have hidden it, prompting some people to dive into rivers and dig up patches of earth. Nonetheless, the bottle was never discovered. **See also** potion.

earth

Earth is one of the four elements typically employed in the practice of magic. The element of earth is generally thought to embody the female life force and is associated with vitality, responsibility, perseverance, and authority. It is also connected with the colors yellow, brown, and russet; the direction north; and the astrological signs Capricorn, Virgo, and Taurus. The gemstones associated with earth are the moss agate, jasper, malachite, peridot, and tourmaline; the plants associated with earth are alfalfa, cotton, oats, and wheat.

Modern witches typically associate each of the four elements with certain ritual tools. Earth is linked with the altar, where all magic is grounded and the final product created, as well as the pentacle, the shield, the flail, and the horn. In addition, certain herbs, oils, and incense are generally used when practicing earth magic. These include honeysuckle, which is involved in spells to improve finances, and patchouli and vertivert, which are both used in spells to attract money or romance. **See also** elements, four; herbs and other plants.

Earthwise

Earthwise is a Witchcraft tradition based on the Alexandrian Tradition. However, unlike Alexandrians the members of an Earthwise coven believe that all members have equal rank and that each person must choose her or his own way to practice Wicca. At the same time, members must be formally initiated into the tradition, usually by a member of the opposite sex because the tradition believes in the balance of opposites. Since Earthwise covens have no hierarchy, once initiated each member is considered a priestess or priest as well as a practicing witch. Pre-initiates, though, must spend a year and a day learning the rituals, herbs, spells, deities, and other aspects of the Craft before going through the initiation ritual. They must also hand-copy the Earthwise Book of Shadows, which is largely Alexandrian in nature. **See also** Alexandrian Tradition; Sanders, Alex; traditions, Witchcraft.

Ecklund, Anna (c. 1883–?)

The case of Anna Ecklund is often cited by believers in demonic possession as proof that the phenomenon is real. A devout Catholic, Ecklund was fourteen years old when she suddenly could not bring herself to worship God or even walk inside a church. By the time she was twenty-six she was exhibiting signs of demonic possession, including having fits and becoming distraught in the presence of holy water. A monk named Theophilus Riesinger exorcised her in 1912, and for a time she seemed to have recovered. Then she got into an argument with her father during which he cursed her. (Eventually Riesinger decided that this was the cause of her original possession as well.) Shortly thereafter Ecklund's symptoms returned. In August 1928, Riesinger again tried to help Ecklund, isolating her in a convent, where, assisted by nuns, he attempted a second exorcism. Ecklund's demons apparently resisted his efforts. According to witnesses, she not only fought, screamed, and yelled but levitated from a bed to the wall above a doorway.

As days passed and the exorcism attempts continued, Ecklund's health began to fail. She refused all solid food, vomited bile, and experienced intermittent swelling in various parts of her body. These physical symptoms suggest that her condition was caused by some strange illness rather than demonic possession. However, other symptoms could not have been caused by illness: Ecklund developed the ability to speak and understand languages to which she had never been exposed, and she exhibited some telepathic ability as well. In addition, Ecklund's demons threatened a priest, Father F. Joseph Steiger, who was assisting Riesinger with the exorcism. Shortly thereafter he was injured in an accident. Nonetheless, Riesinger continued his work, talking to and praying over Ecklund's demons and exhorting them to leave her body. Finally in December 1928 they suddenly and unexpectedly complied. Ecklund cried out and, according to witnesses, the demons yelled as well. All signs of her possession were then gone, and she was able to pray again. **See also** demonic possession; exorcism.

Eclectic Tradition

The Eclectic Tradition was established toward the end of the twentieth century and takes bits and pieces from many other Witchcraft traditions. It is primarily practiced by solitaries, who use information found in books and on websites to develop their own unique version of Wicca. Practitioners of the Eclectic Tradition believe that there is no one right way to perform rituals or honor deities, and therefore each person must follow a unique path. **See also** Cyber Wicca; traditions, Witchcraft.

Eichstätt, witch trials of

In 1590 and again from 1603 to 1630, the town of Eichstätt, Germany, was the site of several witch trials, which, by some estimates, resulted in fifteen hundred to two thousand deaths of accused witches. The trial most often noted by scholars, however, is the one that occurred in 1637, because a detailed official record of its proceedings was published in 1811. By studying this material, scholars have gained insights into the great difficulty of proving one's innocence once having been accused of being a witch. Moreover, the case presents graphic descriptions of tortures that were common during European witch-hunts.

The defendant in the case was a poor, uneducated forty-year-old woman known only as N.N. (Today's scholars usually refer to her as the Eichstätt Witch.) Accused of attending Sabbats and practicing magic to a variety of ends, at first she protested her innocence, and it is clear that she did grasp the enormity of what was about to happen to her. She was then subjected to the most brutal of tortures, including the repeated crushing of her legs. After two weeks of agony, during which even her cries were written into the official record, she confessed to consorting with the devil and doing whatever else her torturers put before her. Her tortures then ended, whereupon she recanted her confession only to be tortured anew for what her judges called stubbornness. Finally, nearly insane with pain, she admitted all guilt and provided her tormentors with what they wanted most: the names of other witches who supposedly attended the Sabbats. Once the court was satisfied, the woman was found guilty and executed. **See also** Germany, witch-hunts of; Sabbat; torture.

eightfold path

Among witches, the eightfold path refers to eight types of training that must take place for someone to become skilled in magic. The first is learning to control the body, achieved through fasting and other forms of discipline in regard to personal habits. The second is learning to control the mind in regard to meditation and visualization. The third is gaining the ability to reach an altered state of consciousness. (Some witches believe that the altered state must be self-induced; others believe it is acceptable to use mind-altering drugs in moderation.) The fourth is acquiring personal willpower and strength of purpose. The fifth is acquiring knowledge of and a working familiarity with spells, magical symbols, rituals, and other practical aspects of magic. The sixth is developing psychic abilities, including those related to dream control, also known as directed dreaming, whereby a person trains the conscious mind to influence the dreaming mind. The seventh is learning to travel to other planes of existence through astral projection and other means. The eighth is becoming comfortable with sexuality in order to incorporate sexual elements into certain rituals. Not all Witchcraft traditions support this eighth point; some acknowledge that sexuality was once integral to magic because pagans considered fertility rituals to be of vital importance, but argue that in modern times it is no longer a necessary component of witchcraft. **See also** Great Rite; paganism; Wicca.

elder

The elder is one of several trees that witches consider sacred. However, the elder is unique in that it is more strongly associated with witchcraft than any other tree. This strong association is probably rooted in the fact that witches worship the Great Mother, also known as the Earth Mother, and in ancient times people believed that this spirit or deity lived within a European elder tree (*Sambucus ebulus*). Some people also believed that witches could turn themselves into elder trees at will. By medieval times, people became uneasy whenever they saw a single elder bush in an unusual place, thinking it was surely a witch in disguise. Others associated the elder tree more strongly with fairies, in the belief that these magical beings lived within the elder tree, or that the tree held the doorway to the fairies' magical realm. In any case, medieval people routinely asked permission of unseen spirits before cutting the branch of an elder tree.

By the fourteenth through seventeenth centuries, the view of elder trees had grown more complicated. Most Christians of this period would never think of bringing a piece of elder wood home, because they believed that it was connected not only with witchcraft but with evil. It was said that if a man wanted to invite the devil for a visit, all he had to do was burn an elder log in his fireplace. Still, some Christians also thought that elder wood could be used as an amulet to protect the soul from bewitchment. Others rubbed green elder wood on warts as part of a ritual to drive the warts away, or they wore elder leaves against their skin to prevent rheumatism. The idea that the elder could protect against or drive away evil probably came from the fact that many Christians believed that Christ had been crucified on a cross made of elder wood. **See also** trees.

elements, four

Four elements are typically employed in the practice of magic: earth, air, fire, and water. Witches working within a magic circle summon the forces of these elements, which together are believed to be the essence of all life, to consecrate their ritual tools and bring energy into the circle. Alchemists have also relied on the four elements in attempting to convert base metals into gold and silver.

Among witches, each element is associated with certain ritual tools, human qualities, colors, astrological signs, stones, plants, and other aspects of nature. In addition, each element is associated with a particular direction, which determines the placement of related objects within a magic circle. For example, witches typically associate air with either the wand or the athame; the male life force; mental energy; the color blue; the direction east; the astrological signs Aquarius, Libra, and Gemini; the metal silver; the gemstones amethyst, sapphire, citrine, and azurite; and the plants almond, broom, clover, eyebright, lavender, and pine. They typically associate earth with the altar and the pentacle; the female life force; vitality, responsibility, perseverance, and authority; the colors yellow, brown, and russet; the direction north; the astrological signs Capricorn, Virgo, and Taurus; the metal gold; the gemstones moss agate, jasper, malachite, peridot, and tourmaline; and the plants alfalfa, cotton, oats, and wheat. Witches associate fire with the sword, athame, or double-headed axe; ritual candles; the sun; energy, strength, power, and courage; the colors red and orange; the direction south; the astrological signs Aries, Leo, and Sagittarius; the metal gold; the gemstones ruby, garnet, diamond, and bloodstone; and the plants ginger, tobacco, and bloodroot. They associate water with the chalice and cauldron; the Goddess, birth, and fertility; the colors green and blue; the direction west; the astrological signs Cancer, Scorpio, and Pisces; the metal silver; the gemstones aquamarine, moonstone, and pearl; and the plants aloe, cucumber, gardenia, lily, and willow.

The elements are also associated with a hierarchy of spirits called elementals. Either good or bad, these spirits can be summoned to help witches perform either positive or negative magic related to the natural world. Wiccans call on only positive elementals, in accordance with their philosophy to do no harm. Some witches claim that they have actually seen these elementals, while others believe that elementals do not take on solid form and can only be seen, if at all, as images transmitted telepathically to the mind. Many witches also believe that the mind can create an artificial elemental, also known as a thought-form, that can assist in magical work in the same way a natural elemental can.

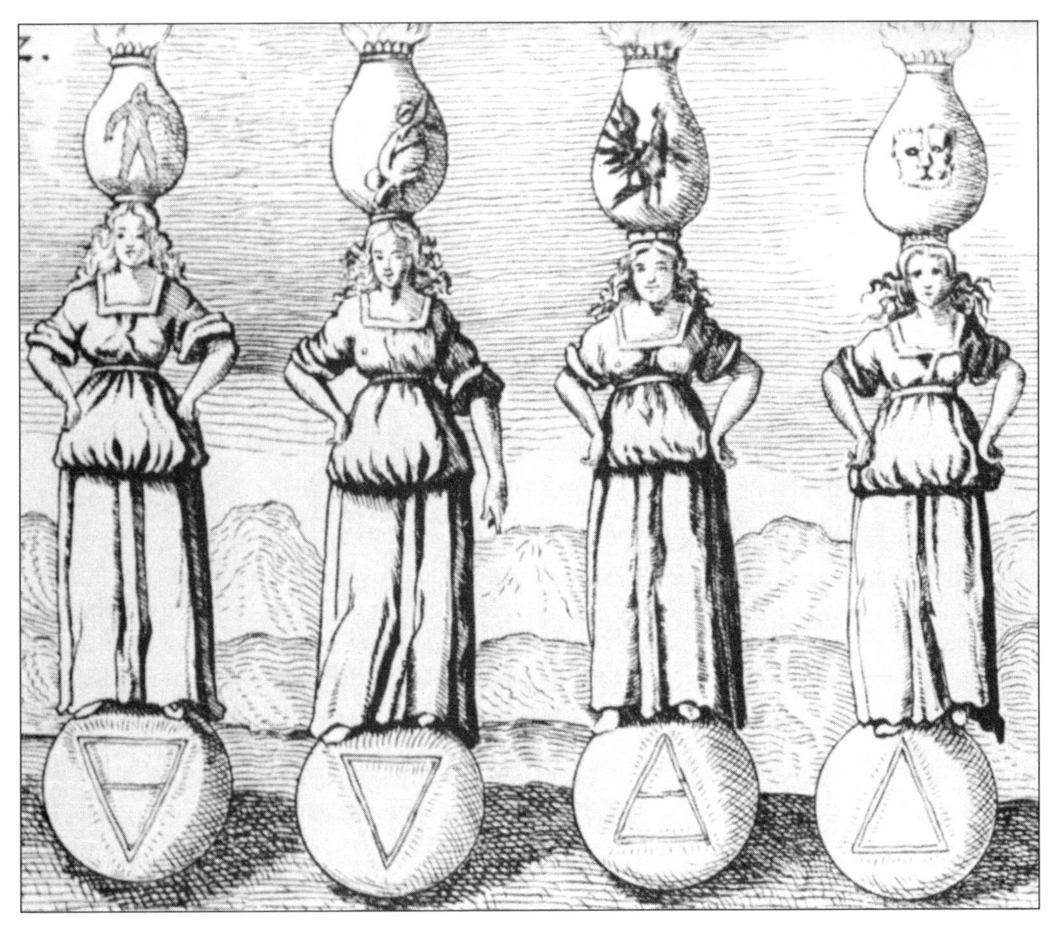

This seventeenth-century copper engraving depicts the four elements: earth, water, air, and fire. These elements are employed in many magic rituals and are believed to be the essence of all life.

Most witches and occultists consider the human spirit to be a fifth element, which they call the quintessence, life energy, the life force, or the occult force. The name quintessence comes from *quinta essentia*, Latin for "five element" or "fifth essence." On a pentagram, the five-sided star that has become the symbol of witchcraft, each point represents one of the elements; quintessence is represented by the lone point that in America is at the top of the star and in Great Britain and Europe is at the bottom of the star. This difference in orientation is perhaps due to the fact that American witches generally consider quintessence to be the ruler of all other elements, while other witches generally believe that earth, air, fire, and water—in balance with one another—dominate spirit. **See also** air; Akashic Records; earth; fire; water.

elm

Witches consider the elm tree (*Ulmus campestris*) to be sacred. It is associated with various aspects of magic, depending on the Witchcraft tradition. Some connect the elm with the Roman god Bacchus and/or the Green Man, while others believe the tree is the dwelling of elves or holds a secret doorway to an elfin kingdom. Still others view the elm tree as a symbol of death and rebirth. **See also** Green Man; trees.

England, witch-hunts of

England's approach to witch-hunting at the outset of medieval witch hysteria was far different from that of the countries of continental Europe. In thirteenth- and fourteenth-century France, for example, witches were routinely burned at the stake as heretics. Meanwhile, England was just beginning to put witches on trial, and witchcraft per se was not even a crime. The only witches prosecuted were therefore those who had used their craft to cause physical harm to another person and/or damage to that person's crops and/or farm animals, and they were treated just like any other defendant in the civil courts. In other words, the fact that the damage was supposedly caused by witchcraft made no difference in the way the case was handled. Moreover, any witch convicted of causing harm by malicious witchcraft, also known as maleficia, was punished in the same way as any nonwitch who caused similar harm by nonmagical means: with a fine, jail time, or some act of public humiliation, such as being put in a pillory for several hours.

By the fifteenth century, some members of the English government had begun lobbying heavily for a less lenient approach to witch trials. Largely as a result of their efforts, in 1542 a law was passed mandating stricter sentences, though still not death, for cases of maleficia. Just over ten years later, the Witchcraft Act of 1563 mandated execution for cases of maleficia whereby the accused had committed murder, and another act in 1581 mandated severe physical punishment for cases that did not result in murder. By this time, some scholars and government leaders had convinced the public that witchcraft was a serious threat, and witch hysteria rose accordingly. Correspondingly, the number of accusations of witchcraft increased dramatically. A number of sensational witch trials followed, including the Chelmsford witch trials and the trial of the Burton Boy. However, merely practicing witchcraft was still not a crime.

Then in 1604 King James I created an act that mandated death by hanging for all cases of maleficia, even first offenses that did not involve murder. The act also made it a crime to consort with the devil, make potions, or practice divination. In effect, witchcraft was banned. The act also effectively classified people in rural villages who practiced simple folk magic as witches and devil worshipers.

Once the Witchcraft Act of 1604 became law, the first professional witch-hunters appeared. They included Matthew Hopkins, who was responsible for the executions of over two hundred accused witches between 1645 and 1646. Ultimately, over one thousand people would be executed in England as a direct result of witch-hunting.

During the years that professional witch-hunters like Hopkins plied their trade, English law did not allow for the kind of brutal witch tortures then taking place elsewhere in Europe. Nonetheless, English witch-hunters still found ways to inhumanely pressure their victims into confessing and naming accomplices. One technique was to keep accused witches awake for days, during which they were refused food and water and made to walk continuously. Once they were exhausted and mentally confused, they might be interrogated in ways that would coerce or trick them into confessing. Another way to force a confession was to tie the accused witch up and throw him or her into deep water. Most people of the period could not swim, so the panic they felt at being tossed into a pond often led to a confession. Even if a confession was not forthcoming—and the accused did not drown—the victim might still be considered guilty, because it was said that witches always floated.

However, this practice of throwing suspected witches into water was so offensive to the English government that Parliament banned it in 1645. By this time, books like

Reginald Scot's *Discoverie of Witchcraft* (1584) were arguing that it was unlikely that any of the people condemned as witches had genuine supernatural powers. Gradually the English began to think of these people as innocent victims or deluded, misguided ignorants.

Eventually this view of witches affected public policy. Judges increasingly found witch trial defendants innocent or refused to take them to trial at all, and after 1684 no more witchcraft-related executions took place. The last such execution was that of Alice Molland, who was hanged at Exeter. A few years later, in 1712, Jane Wenham was condemned to death for practicing witchcraft, but her sentence was never carried out. The last person so condemned, she had been accused of being a witch by a minister's servant, Anne Thorne, who claimed that Wenham had been giving her fits and hallucinations. After her arrest, Wenham confessed to being a witch but not to harming Thorne, but the jury found her guilty anyway. However, the judge in the case, Sir John Powell, delayed her hanging until he could get the king to pardon her.

Wenham's pardon was very unpopular among the English public. In fact, long after judges and public officials had stopped persecuting witches—largely as a result of the replacement of the Witchcraft Act of 1604 with the Witchcraft Act of 1736, which sharply reduced the penalties for practicing witchcraft—the English public continued to attack anyone suspected of being a witch. Even as late as the early twentieth century there were stories of angry mobs trying to kill suspected witches. However, in 1944 it was public sentiment that compelled the British government to repeal the Witchcraft Act of 1736. The reason for the outcry was the government's use of the act to prosecute a clairvoyant named Helen Duncan who had been openly discussing government secrets. Parliament repealed the Act in 1944, but not until 1951 was all anti-witchcraft language stricken from British law. **See also** James I; Hopkins, Matthew; persecution, witch.

esbat

An esbat is a gathering of witches, usually held only on a night with a full moon; since there are thirteen full moons per year (one month has two full moons, the rest only one) this means that there are thirteen esbats per year. In ancient times, esbats were primarily for worshiping goddesses of the moon, usually as part of fertility rites. Ancient pagans generally believed that the light of a full moon imparted fertility, and that celebrating within this light increased the vitality of the body, particularly if the celebrant was naked. In some traditions, however, esbats are held on nights with either a full moon or a new moon, and/or whenever the need to meet arises. Witches who adhere to such traditions therefore use the word *esbat* to refer to any regularly scheduled coven meeting, regardless of whether it takes place monthly, bimonthly, or weekly.

Most covens consider esbats to be working meetings, in contrast to Sabbats, which are festivals and therefore celebratory affairs. Rituals are held at both types of gatherings, but esbats primarily feature practical magic. However, most witches believe that only three magical rites should be performed per esbat in order for each to have full power. During esbats, certain chants and rituals are used to "draw down" the Goddess so that she comes to earth to join in the festivities or rituals. Some Witchcraft traditions mark the end of each esbat by ritually sharing cakes and wine. **See also** cakes and wine; circle, magic; coven; moon; rites and rituals.

evil eye

The phrase *evil eye* refers to a particular look, stare, or glare with the power to hurt or even kill the person at whom it is directed. During times of witch persecution, accusations related to the suspected use of the evil eye often led to putting a suspected witch on trial. Originally people believed that the evil eye was only used in cases of covetousness—in other words, when the person giving the evil eye wanted something belonging to the victim. Eventually, however, people decided that the evil eye could also be given just for spite.

The concept of the evil eye has existed since ancient times, being mentioned in both ancient Greek writings and Hebrew Scripture. Witches, sorcerers, magicians, Gypsies, and many others trafficking in magic were the people most often accused of using the evil eye against their foes, but ordinary people with unusual eyes—ones striking in color or disfigurement—were sometimes accused of using it as well.

Throughout the centuries, a variety of amulets, charms, rituals, and hand gestures have been employed by people attempting to protect themselves from the evil eye. For example, in ancient times people sacrificed animals to counter an attack by an evil eye. In medieval times, amulets and charms were popular protections against an attack; after an attack it was believed that sticking pins in a wax figure of the perpetrator would break the spell. In later centuries, it became customary to chant spells against the evil eye or make countering hand gestures upon being attacked. This custom continues today among certain cultures, such as some in Italy and Romania. **See also** amulet; charm; spells.

evocation

An evocation is a ceremonial process by which spirits, demons, or similar entities or forces are called for the purpose of serving the caller, usually with the intent of causing harm. In this way an evocation differs from an invocation, where spirits or deities are called merely to be present at magic ceremonies and perhaps to confer protection on the participants during the proceedings.

Most modern witches, whose moral code calls for them to do no harm, do not evoke spirits for malicious purposes, but many ancient and medieval witches, sorcerers, magicians and others did so, as do modern Satanists. People who call on spirits for such purposes have traditionally made their evocations while within a magic circle that protects them from harm, since they are dealing with dangerous forces; the entity that has been summoned appears outside this circle and cannot enter it.

The evocation process also involves the use of ritual tools and the speaking of various words and phrases believed to have the power to evoke beings from the nonphysical realm. Modern witches generally believe that saying these words incorrectly or deviating from the correct form of the ceremony in any way can seriously harm the practitioner. **See also** circle, magic; invocation; tools, ritual.

Exeter, witch trial of

The 1682 witch trial of Exeter, England, is notable in two ways. First, it was one of the last witchcraft trials in the country, and second, the judge wanted to acquit the defendants but so feared the public's reaction that he condemned them to death instead.

There were three defendants in all: Susanna Edwards, Mary Trembles, and Temperance Lloyd. Poor, homeless, and old, they were arrested on suspicion of being in a coven led by Lloyd, who had been unsuccessfully tried twice previously for practicing witchcraft. The three readily confessed (some historians believe without torture, others with light torture) to being witches and consorting with the devil; Edwards even said that the devil himself had asked her to join Lloyd's coven. The judge was certain that these confessions stemmed from the defendants' physical and mental infirmities, but crowds outside the courtroom called for their death and he obliged. The women were hanged in August 1682. **See also** coven; devil; England, witch-hunts of.

exorcism

An exorcism is a ritual intended to drive demons, evil spirits, or the devil out of a human body. Throughout history, witches have sometimes been asked to perform such rituals, but during the fifteenth through seventeenth centuries, witches were often accused of causing demonic possessions, while Catholic priests came to be seen as the saviors who could end the victims' suffering by performing exorcisms. The Catholic Church developed a ritual that involved the use of holy water and readings from the Bible to cast out the demons, and the Church of England soon adopted this ritual as well. Unfortunately, some members of the clergy who wanted to make names for themselves staged fake exorcisms, sometimes involving the same "victim" again and again. One such minister was John Darrell, whose repeated fraudulent exorcisms prompted the Church of England in 1603 to prohibit its clergymen from acting as exorcists. Similarly, some "victims" of demonic possession faked their symptoms in order to get attention. One such fraudulent victim was a seventeenth-century English boy named William Perry, commonly known as the Boy of Bilson. In other cases, however, it appears that the exorcism was genuine. For example, in the early twentieth century Anna Ecklund experienced a demonic possession and exorcism seemingly without any evidence of fraud, and this well-documented case is often cited by believers in demonic possession as proof that the phenomenon is real. **See also** Bilson, Boy of; Darrell, John; demonic possession; Ecklund, Anna.

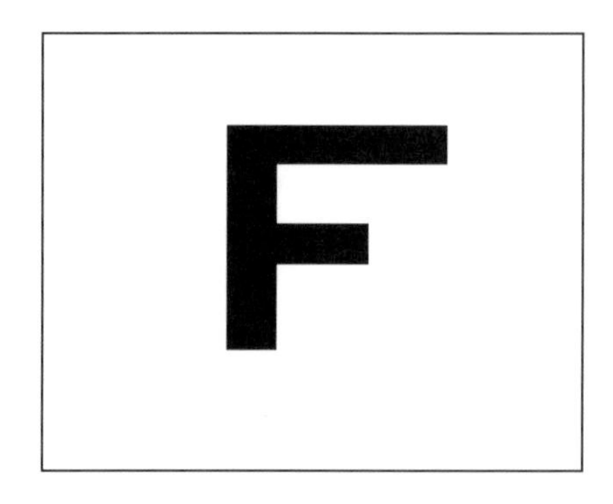

Faery Tradition

Founded by Victor Anderson in San Francisco, California, in the late 1960s, the Faery Tradition's followers call on a fairy entity or force called the Faery Power during rituals, believing that the participants in such rituals literally become enchanted and possessed by this Faery (alternately spelled Feri, Faerie, and Fairie) Power in a direct connection to the Divinity. To encourage possession, the tradition's ceremonies rely heavily on invocation and feature many chants and recitation of poetical and liturgical material. Much of this material was written by Victor Anderson and Gwydion Pendderwen, who cofounded the tradition.

In the working of magic (called circle-workings), the Faery Tradition employs a variety of ritual tools, techniques, and deities. These include pentacles (both upright and inverted), visualization of a blue fire, secret names, significant colors, and several deities. Of primary importance is the Star Goddess, from which emanates three pairs of other unique deities. There are also seven spirits called Guardians, associated with the four elements (earth, air, fire, and water) and the four directions (north, east, south, and west). Some of these deities can be found in other traditions, but most are unique to Faery. All of these spirits, as well as goddesses and gods, are considered real beings.

In addition, practitioners of the Faery Tradition have strong beliefs about how they should behave. Nature should be honored at all times. Moreover, most Faery covens ascribe to the warrior ethic, which means that members must be strong, stoic, directly honest, and unwilling to be subjugated by anyone. They also support risk-taking and behave with sexual abandon. Since fairies are sometimes said to be able to change their shape, or shape-shift, members of the Faery Tradition support the idea of changing identities and taking on new roles in life.

The Faery Tradition has also promoted change within its own belief system. Victor Anderson's original Faery Tradition coven was largely Celtic in nature, although it also included elements of folk magic of the American South because Anderson was married to a woman who had long practiced that form of magic. However, because each Faery Tradition initiate is encouraged to add something of her or his own interest into the practices of the coven, in the years since Anderson established the tradition it has developed many branches with influences as diverse as African and Haitian magic, Tibetan Buddhism, Native American shamanism, Kabbalistic magic, Santeria, and many other forms of magical and spiritual practice both ancient and modern. Some branches of the Faery Tradition are highly secretive, while others share many of their beliefs openly. **See also** fairies; Irish Faery-Faith Tradition; Pendderwen, Gwydion.

fairies

Fairies are tiny, magical beings from Western folklore that look like humans and live among them but are usually hidden or invisible. They use their magic capriciously, either to cause mischief or to leave gifts for deserving mortals, and they are said to be able to make time stand still. Some stories hold that they are also able to change their shape, or shape-shift, at will. In addition, they are portrayed as being vital to maintaining the life force of nature.

Ancient Celts of the British Isles thought that fairies lived within certain trees, or that certain trees held secret doorways to the fairy kingdom. Therefore a belief in fairies is integral to several Witchcraft traditions, particularly Celtic ones. For example, as the name implies, the Faery Tradition includes fairies in their rituals.

The first mention of fairies in literature occurred in England in approximately A.D. 800. Many scholars suspect that the concept was carried to England by the Romans, who conquered England around this time. According to this theory, the Romans had adopted the concept from the ancient Etruscans, whom they had conquered in the Mediterranean. Supporting this theory is the fact that Etruscan art from around 600 B.C. depicts small, winged, humanlike beings very similar to today's common image of a fairy. Also like fairies, these Etruscan beings were associated with the preservation of nature and were said to

Tiny, magical beings believed to cause mischief and enhance magic spells, fairies have been described as deities, angels, and spirits. This illustration depicts king and queen fairies from a fairy-tale book.

be able to make magic potions that could change the composition and shape of matter. However, they were typically depicted in the company of deities, and scholars disagree as to whether they were viewed as spirits of the dead, angels, or mortal yet magical beings.

Other scholars theorize that the Celts developed the idea of the fairy independently of the Etruscans, citing as evidence stories related to the Tuatha de Danaan. This apparently mythical race of short-statured people disappeared into the woods when the Celts conquered the British Isles. As with fairies, it was said that no matter how hard people looked for them, the Tuatha de Danaan could never be found unless they wanted to be found.

Throughout the Western world, fairies have been variously described as spirits of the dead, deities, angels, or nature spirits. Some people believe that these beings are just one class of magical, tiny, humanlike beings, while others think that every small, magical, humanlike being is a type of fairy. These other beings include brownies, elves, gnomes, goblins, leprechauns, and pixies.

Many witches believe in the existence of all of these beings, which have a variety of traits and magical powers but like fairies are deeply connected to nature. However, none of these beings has received as much attention among witches as fairies have, except perhaps for gnomes. Gnomes, which are typically depicted as small, old men, are considered an elemental, a spiritual representation of the earth element used in witchcraft rituals. Moreover, they are said to dwell deep in the earth, where they guard powerful gemstones. Therefore some witches consider them helpful in creating magic.

Also connected to magic are pixies, who are said to make magical pixie or fairy dust out of gold and silver. Some stories hold that this dust can make people fly, while others say it has the power to bring love, prosperity, or luck. Some witches make their own version of this dust out of a combination of dried herbs. They grind these herbs, which include jasmine and clover, into a powder, put the powder in a jar, set the jar where fairies will find it while reciting or chanting a spell over it, and then leave for several hours or days. Fairies, they believe, will then come and charge the powder with magic. The powder can subsequently be sprinkled over a person to make that individual fall in love with the witch, or it can be sprinkled around a house to bring it joy.

Witches also go to places where fairies are said to dwell in order to cast spells related to prosperity, luck, or the granting of wishes, believing that the fairies will enhance the magic of such spells. Sometimes witches have claimed that while at such a place the fairies have given them magical gifts. For example, nineteenth-century Irish witch Biddy Early said that the fairies had given her a bottle that had the power to heal people and to see the future. When peered into through the neck, the bottle would show her future events or what potions to mix to effect a cure.

During the Middle Ages, fairies were often said to spend their time not only creating magical gifts but making magical potions, casting spells, and flying about the countryside. Not coincidentally, these were all pastimes attributed to witches as well. This connection between witches and fairies continued into the witch-hunting times, when under torture some accused witches told of fairies participating in their Sabbats and acting as witches' familiars. Eventually leaders of Christian churches began associating fairies with the devil, just as they did witches. Nonetheless, among many people affection for fairies refused to die, and people continued to tell stories about their mischief. Some still do so today. **See also** Early, Biddy; Faery Tradition.

familiar

Prior to modern times, a familiar referred to a demon or imp that had taken the form of an animal to serve a witch, helping to carry out spells and other witchcraft-related tasks. Among modern witches, a familiar is an animal that has chosen to be the companion of a witch and has a psychic connection to that witch. Alternatively, modern witches use the term *familiar* to refer to an object, such as their brooms, with which the witch has formed a psychic bond. Many modern witches believe that having such a psychic connection with an animal or an object strengthens their magic and enhances their life in the Craft. They might therefore not only interact with their familiar regularly during daily life but also have their familiar present during rituals.

The concept of the familiar, which was undoubtedly based on earlier forms of animal worship, developed in medieval England and Scotland, then spread to a few parts of continental Europe and most of the colonies in America. By the seventeenth century, rules against keeping familiars had been included in witchcraft laws. In addition, many witch confessions and scholarly writings of the period offered elaborate descriptions of familiars and their activities. In most cases the familiars were given names, and usually they were animals commonly seen in households and fields: cats, mice, rats, owls, frogs, hares, and various insects. Sometimes dogs were named as familiars as well, but more often they were said to be servants of the devil rather than of witches, or even to be the devil himself in disguise.

It was also often said that the devil gave each witch a familiar upon her initiation into a coven, assigning the demon who would serve her. Some historians have suggested that this idea was a response to doubts about an earlier belief that the devil himself served witches. People wondered why such a powerfully evil being would be at the beck and call of women; to them it made more sense that a demon, as the devil's subordinate, would take on this role. Such demons were supposedly fed on their witch's blood, and any unusual mark found on the skin of a suspected witch was believed to be caused by the suckling of a familiar.

Today sorcerers in parts of Africa and in New Guinea continue to believe in spirit familiars, which typically take the form of snakes, frogs, hyenas, crocodiles, or jackals. Those who control these beings send them to fight or torment their enemies. **See also** cats; devil; dogs; marks, witches' or devil's.

Farrar, Janet (1950–) and Stewart (1916–2000)

British witches Janet and Stewart Farrar authored some of the most important books on Witchcraft in modern times. Of these, the most significant are *The Witches' Bible* (originally published as two books, *Eight Sabbats for Witches* and *The Witches' Way*), which incorporates information from Gerald Gardner's Book of Shadows, and *What Witches Do* (1971), which focuses on the Alexandrian Tradition.

The Farrars' contribution to the practice of Witchcraft was so significant that they were made honorary initiates in several Witchcraft traditions. However, they began their own practice of the Craft in the Alexandrian Tradition and subsequently created their own rituals, which are still used by many witches today. The couple met while they were members of the coven of Alex and Maxine Sanders. (Alex Sanders was the founder of the Alexandrian Tradition.) Stewart Farrar, who at the time was a novelist, joined their coven in 1970 after interviewing Alex Sanders for *What Witches Do*. Janet Farrar joined the Sanders's coven the same year, having become interested in Witchcraft after a friend took her to some of the Sanders's meetings. The couple married in 1972.

Eventually the Farrars decided to form their own coven in Ireland. Established in 1976, it inspired the creation of several other like-minded covens in the country. Once settled in Ireland, they began writing books together. They also went on speaking tours to actively promote the Neopagan movement. Stewart Farrar died in 2000, shortly after becoming part of the clergy of the Aquarian Tabernacle Church in Ireland, a place of pagan worship. Janet Farrar remains a member of the clergy there. **See also** Alexandrian Tradition; Gardner, Gerald; Sanders, Alex.

Faust

A character in numerous legends, plays, and books, Faust was always depicted as an elderly German magician who sold his soul to the devil in exchange for youth, passion, wisdom, and knowledge. Stories of his pact with the devil vary in their details and endings. The first book to feature Faust was *Dr. Faust, the Notorious Magician and Necromancer*, published in Germany in 1587. The English playwright Christopher Marlowe wrote *The Tragical History of Dr. Faustus,* which was first performed in 1589 and published sometime within the next three years. Perhaps the best-known Faust work is the play *Faust* by Johann Wolfgang von Goethe, initially published in two parts in 1808 and 1833.

Throughout the centuries since Faust first appeared in legend, much debate has taken place over whether the character was based on a real person, and if so, the identity of that individual. For several years many people believed that Faust was modeled after Johann Fust, a printer who lived from 1400 to 1466, but modern scholars have largely disproved this theory. Other, more likely candidates include Georgius Sabellicu Faustus Junior, a sixteenth-century German traveling soothsayer and alchemist, and possibly a magician as well, and Johann Faust, about whom little is known except that he was an early sixteenth-century German theologian. No proof of this exists, however, and "Dr. Faust" could have been a pseudonym for someone with a highly dissimilar name. **See also** devil; Germany, witch-hunts of.

fetish

A fetish is a type of charm or amulet believed to be magical by virtue of its shape or composition. The most common example of such an object is a wooden doll used in West African rituals. Fashioned in the image of a particular spirit, it is thought to possess the magic powers of that spirit. The same is true of dolls, called kachinas, in certain Native American cultures. Other examples of fetishes include certain types of bones, animal teeth, or unusual stones. No ceremony is required to imbue these objects with magic, because they are considered inherently magical by virtue of their appearance. **See also** amulet; charm; poppet.

Fian, John (?–1591)

In 1590 Scottish teacher John Fian was subjected to the most brutal tortures to force him to confess to trying to kill Scotland's King James VI via witchcraft. One of the first methods his torturers tried was tying a rope around his head and yanking on it several times. They then crushed his legs repeatedly. Shortly after this, Fian confessed to being the leader of a coven of witches who met in North Berwick, Scotland. However, the night after he confessed someone helped him escape from jail, and when he was recaptured he recanted his confession. (Rumors abounded about the identity of his helper in the escape, and about whether that person used magic against Fian to get him to recant and/or to shield him from pain during future torture sessions.) Once Fian recanted, his tortures began again, this time far worse. Perhaps the most excruciating involved the brutal removal of his fingernails, whereupon needles were jammed in their place. Still Fian refused to confess.

Periodically during his ordeal, he was brought before King James VI (then ruler of Scotland, later, as James I, ruler of both Scotland and England), who had been actively involved in Fian's case from the beginning. After Fian's arrest, many people came forward to accuse him of using magic against them and others as well, of worshiping the devil, and of grave robbing to obtain body parts for making potions. Presented with so many accusations, the court ultimately decided that Fian was guilty, even though he had recanted his confession. He was strangled in January 1591, whereupon his body was burned. **See also** James I; North Berwick witches; Scotland, witch trials of.

fire

Fire is one of the four elements typically employed in the practice of magic. Modern witches typically associate each of these elements with a ritual tool; in the case of fire this tool is the sword, athame, or double-headed axe, as well as ritual candles. The element of fire is generally thought to embody the sun, the source of all life's energy and power, and is consequently associated with energy, strength, power, and courage. It is also connected with the colors red and orange, the direction south, and the astrological signs Aries, Leo, and Sagittarius. The gemstones associated with fire include the ruby, garnet, diamond, and bloodstone; the plants associated with fire include ginger, tobacco, and bloodroot. In addition, certain types of incense and fragrances are generally used when practicing fire magic. They include allspice, which is involved in spells related to luck in gambling; basil, which promotes wealth; carnation, which promotes health; and rosemary, which promotes love and healing and confers protection. Candles used in fire magic are often anointed with frankincense oil prior to use, while orange oil is used to anoint the forehead of someone about to practice divination as part of fire magic. **See also** candles; divination; elements, four; herbs and other plants; oils and ointments.

Fitch, Ed (1937–)

American Wiccan Ed Fitch is one of the founders of the Pagan Way movement. In the 1960s he became a Gardnerian high priest, although his interests are currently with Norse traditions rooted in shamanism. Fitch has also written several books about Wicca, including *Magical Rites from the Crystal Well* (1984), *The Rites of Odin* (1990), and *A Grimoire of Shadows: Witchcraft, Paganism & Magic* (1996). **See also** Gardnerian Tradition; grimoire; Pagan Way; shamanism.

Flade, Dietrich (?–1589)

In 1588 German judge Dietrich Flade was arrested and charged as a witch himself because he had shown leniency to witches in his courtroom. The fact that Flade had been a highly respected jurist meant nothing to his main accuser, Johann Zandt, the governor of the city of Trèves (now Trier). Zandt wanted witches to be dealt with harshly, and when Flade refused to cooperate Zandt went before the archbishop of Trèves with a series of witnesses who testified against Flade. These witnesses claimed that they had seen Flade at witches' Sabbats and/or knew for certain that he was a witch. Ultimately Zandt convinced so many people to come forward that the archbishop had no choice but to arrest Flade. The judge was brutally tortured until he confessed to everything of which he had been accused and more. As a result, Flade was strangled and then burned in September 1589. **See also** Germany, witch-hunts of.

flight

Also called transvection, the power of flight was first associated with witchcraft in ancient Greece and Rome, when sorcerers and sorceresses were said to have the ability to turn themselves into birds. Beginning in the tenth century in Italy, the thirteenth century in England, the sixteenth century in Germany, and the seventeenth century in Scotland, scholars and witch-hunters wrote about witches who flew without changing shape, using magical instruments of flight such as broomsticks,

sticks, staffs, forked wands, long-stalked plants, or shovels. Some said that these objects (which were sometimes called "bune wands") were rubbed with a magical flying ointment prior to use. Others suggested that witches rode animals that supposedly had the power to fly; goats, black rams, and wolves were mentioned most frequently, perhaps because these animals were also supposedly associated with Satan. Medieval people also generally believed that a witch would fall off her flying broom if she heard a church bell ringing, so some European churches rang their bells throughout the night to protect communities from all forms of evil. Paulus Grillandus, a judge in medieval witch trials in Rome, wrote in 1525 about a witch who claimed to have been flying on a demon's stick when a church bell rang and she was thrown to the ground.

Witches were believed to have the ability to fly, using instruments such as broomsticks, shovels, or even animals.

Suspected witches of the period often confessed to experiencing episodes of flight, but some scholars of the period theorized that it was not the witches' bodies that took flight but their spirits. During the Renaissance this theory became prevalent enough to appear in reports of witchcraft trials. Reports by some scholars and physicians seemed to support this theory; they had observed women asleep or in trances who later claimed they had been flying to distant places while unconscious.

Modern witches refer to this flight of spirit as astral projection or an out-of-body experience, and experts in the paranormal believe this phenomenon is genuine. However, whether this was what led accused medieval witches to believe they had flown is unclear. Some people suggest that the medieval witches' spiritual flights were actually drug-induced hallucinations, particularly because a few of these witches confessed to anointing themselves with flying ointment prior to flight. It is possible that this ointment contained an herb or herbs with mind-altering properties. In fact, Francis Bacon wrote in 1608 that according to witches a common form of their flying ointment contained, among other things, hemlock and belladonna, both of which could have caused delirium. One German physician who tested some flying ointment on himself in 1603 reported experiencing a night flight atop a calf, and he believed it to be a real event rather than a hallucination. According to scholar Jean de Nynauld, writing about this incident in a 1615 book, *De la Lycanthropie*, the physician insisted that the calf eventually tossed him into the Rhine River.

Similar reports of flight caused through the use of flying ointment appeared in many other parts of Europe. One of the best-known accounts was that of Elizabeth Style, an Englishwoman who was tried for witchcraft in 1664. As part of her confession, she claimed that she and several companions would apply a greasy ointment to their foreheads and wrists and then recite "thout, tout, a tout, tout, throughout and about" to make themselves fly. Style went on to say that if they were going to a Sabbat, they would use different words: "Rentum tormentum." A Sabbat was the destination mentioned in most fifteenth- through eighteenth-century witch confessions involving flying. However, the majority of these confessions did not mention the use of flying ointment.

In fact, the majority of witches, past or present, laid no claim to the power of magical flight. Nonetheless, the image of a witch flying on a broomstick is common. This image most likely originated in thirteenth-century Germany, when it was carved in stonework; by the eighteenth century it was used on German maps to designate areas where witches were said to meet. However, witch confessions do not support the idea that broomsticks were instruments of flight; instead, accused witches said that broomsticks were straddled during ritual dances. Indeed, ancient European fertility rites sometimes featured "rides" through fields on broomsticks or pitchforks, with the former usually representing the female life force and the latter the male. **See also** bells; broom; oils and ointments; Sabbat; Somerset, witch trial of.

Fortune, Dion (?–1946)

Dion Fortune was the pseudonym of Violet Mary Firth, a British occultist who authored such nonfiction books as *Sane Occultism* (1929), *The Training and Work of an Initiate* (1930), *Psychic Self-Defense* (1930), and *The Mystical Qabbalah* (1936) and several novels with pagan themes, including *Goat-Foot God* (1936) and *The Sea-Priestess* (1938). Some modern witches use the rituals described in Fortune's novels in their own ceremonies. Fortune was also the founder of the Fraternity of Inner Light, which was inspired by and originally part of an occult society known as the Hermetic Order of the Golden Dawn.

In addition to her work in ceremonial magic, Fortune was interested in psychic powers. She believed that everyone possessed such powers but that few understood how to use them. Fortune first developed an interest in psychic phenomena in 1911, after she noticed that an argument with someone had left her mentally drained. She soon decided that her combatant had attacked her not only verbally but psychically. This belief led her to study research on the function of the human brain, and eventually she became a psychiatrist. Fortune turned to occultism when she realized that the field of psychiatry failed to address issues related to psychic powers. **See also** Golden Dawn, Hermetic Order of the; Kabbalah.

Fox, Selena (1949–)

American witch Selena Fox is a Wiccan high priestess and a leader in the modern Neopagan movement; as such she lectures and writes extensively on paganism, Wicca, and Wiccan Shamanism. The latter is a religion, created by Fox herself, combining elements of Wicca with those of Native American and African tribal spiritualism. Fox also established the Circle Sanctuary, a Wiccan church and religious organization in Wisconsin that provides information on all forms of ancient and modern paganism to interested people throughout the world.

Fox first became interested in witchcraft in 1970 after meeting a hereditary witch. By this time she had already experimented with Tarot cards and dream analysis and begun to develop psychic abilities, much to the dismay of her Southern Baptist parents.

In 1974 she established her own coven, which eventually grew into the Circle Sanctuary.

In the process of building the Circle Sanctuary, Fox became an activist in the areas of religious freedom, environmentalism, racism, gender bias, and other social issues. Also a spiritual healer, she received a masters degree in counseling in 1995 and is now a licensed clinical psychotherapist in Madison, Wisconsin. In addition, she is the author of such books as *When Goddess Is God*. **See also** Circle Sanctuary; Neopagans; Wiccan Shamanism.

France, witch-hunts of

Witch-hunting in France was aggressive during the Middle Ages and Renaissance, resulting in the deaths of thousands of suspected witches. The first French witch-hunts were conducted by fourteenth-century inquisitors of the Roman Catholic church, who technically charged people as heretics rather than as witches or sorcerers. During the 1320s, 1330s, and 1340s, ecclesiastical courts tried and condemned approximately six hundred people on such grounds. By the early fifteenth century, many more sorcerers and witches had been executed, usually in mass burnings; one of the most famous victims of church witch-hunting during this period was Joan of Arc, who was sentenced to burn at the stake in 1431.

The first secular witch trials took place around the end of the fourteenth century, beginning with the Paris Witch Trial in 1390. The main defendant in this case was Jehenne de Brigue, who confessed under torture to using sorcery to make a man sick, as well as to consorting with the devil; she was burned alive in August 1391. (Burning remained the most popular means of executing French witches throughout the country's witch-hunting period.)

As the secular courts became more involved in witch trials, the French government strengthened its antiwitchcraft laws to make convictions and executions more likely. For example, in 1579 the government mandated the death penalty for people convicted of practicing divination as well as other lesser forms of magic, real or fraudulent, thereby increasing the number of people snared in witch-hunts. At the same time, more accused witches meant more witch confessions, typically extracted under torture. This resulted in several mass witch trials followed by mass executions.

Mass witch trials, confessions, and executions fueled witch hysteria, as did the actions of professional witch-hunters like French attorney Pierre de Lancre. In 1608 King Henry IV sent de Lancre to the French slopes of the Pyrenees Mountains, home of the Basque people, to eliminate witchcraft in the region, and de Lancre eventually put over six hundred Basque men, women, and children to death. He also promoted the idea that hundreds of Basque witches were conspiring to destroy every aspect of Christianity, not only in the Basque region but throughout France and perhaps throughout Europe as well. Gradually de Lancre convinced the French people that large, organized bands of witches, both peasants and nobles, were consorting with the devil throughout the countryside.

This concept resulted in some sensational seventeenth-century witch trials involving noble defendants. In 1682 one such case, known as the Chambre Ardente affair, resulted in trials against numerous dukes, duchesses, and other noblemen and noblewomen who were friends of King Louis XIV, including one of the king's own mistresses. Eventually 319 people were arrested and 36 were executed. However, anyone with noble blood was set free on the king's orders, along with his mistress, and Louis announced that witchcraft was not real, signaling that the courts should stop pursuing such cases. This was largely what happened, although occasional witch trials continued.

Meanwhile the Roman Catholic Church had lost interest in hunting witches who had performed simple acts of maleficia, turning its attention instead to those seriously involved in devil worship and demonic possession. In the seventeenth century a rash of demonic possession cases surfaced in France, particularly in convents. The church always investigated these matters first, usually deciding to take them to trial. For example, in 1634 the church investigated and tried a case related to the demonic possession of nuns at the Ursuline convent in Loudun, France. The defendant, Urbain Grandier, was accused of consorting with the devil to cause the nuns' symptoms; an ecclesiastical court found him guilty and sentenced him to be burned alive.

In some instances, however, the church decided not to prosecute someone accused of causing demonic possession, whereupon the secular courts sometimes picked up the case. This was what happened in a 1611 trial in Aix-en-Provence, involving Father Louis Gaufridi, a priest accused of encouraging several nuns at the Ursuline convent in Aix to become consorts of the devil. The church decided that Gaufridi was innocent, but civil authorities prosecuted the case and convicted him anyway. Gaufridi was then executed.

By the end of the seventeenth century France had witnessed several cases of fraudulent demonic possession in which people pretended to be bewitched, either to gain attention or to support accusations of witchcraft against someone they disliked. Eventually, both ecclesiastical and secular authorities took a more skeptical approach to cases of alleged possession. Meanwhile the French people had grown weary of witch hysteria, and de Lancre's theory that Basque witches were organizing to destroy Christianity had largely been forgotten. **See also** Aix-en-Provence, witch trial of; Basque region, witch-hunts of the; de Lancre, Pierre.

Frazier, Sir James (1854–1941)

British anthropologist Sir James Frazier is the author of the 1890 book *The Golden Bough: A Study in Magic and Religion*, which influenced the development of modern Wicca as both a religion and a magical practice. The title of his book refers to a Greek and Roman myth in which a golden bough, or branch, broken from a sacred tree is used to gain entrance into another realm. Frazier's work discusses the connection between religion and magic, particularly the ways in which Greek and Roman mythology relate to later magical practices, and specifically addresses goddess worship and the cult of Diana. Gerald Gardner and many other Wiccans incorporated many of his ideas into their own works when they first began writing about witchcraft in the 1960s. **See also** Diana; Gardner, Gerald.

Freya

An ancient Nordic-Germanic goddess of fertility also known as Freyja, Freya is a popular focus of worship among modern witches, particularly those who are members of the Teutonic or Nordic Witchcraft Traditions. According to ancient legends, Freya rode in a chariot pulled by cats. Modern witches believe that a cat acts as Freya's familiar, as well.

Freya is also said to be a goddess of the Underworld and is strongly associated with divination. According to legend, she can also transform herself into various animals, an ability that has long been connected to witches and witchcraft. **See also** divination; familiar; goddesses and gods.

frogs and toads

Frogs and toads are animals that have been connected to witchcraft and magic for centuries. This connection began in ancient times, when the animals were used in rituals to honor certain goddesses. Scholars also believe that ancient people believed frogs and toads had the power to protect spirits of the dead from evil, because the animals' bones and mummified remains have been found in Celtic graves and ancient Egyptian tombs, respectively. Frogs were apparently associated with other types of protection, as well; the ancient Egyptian goddess Heket, who was called on to protect women in childbirth, was depicted with the head of a frog, and ancient Romans buried frogs in pots to protect their fields.

Beginning in medieval times, frogs and toads appeared in stories about witches' familiars in Britain and Europe. These stories described the animals—actually imps and demons in animal form—working as witches' servants in the performance of magic. Many medieval recipes for magical and medicinal potions and ointments included frogs and/or toads as ingredients, and the animals were used in rituals intended to cure drought. In addition, medieval and Renaissance people generally thought that witches could turn themselves into frogs and toads at will. The devil too was said to sometimes take the shape of a frog or toad, and Satanists have long incorporated these animals into their rituals. **See also** animals; devil; familiar; potion.

Frost, Gavin (1930–) and Yvonne (1931–)

American Wiccans Gavin and Yvonne Frost not only cofounded the Church of Wicca and the School of Wicca but also coauthored several books on witchcraft. These include *The Magic Power of Witchcraft* (1976; revised as *The Magic Power of the White Witch* in 1999), *Astral Travel* (1982), *The Prophet's Bible* (1991), *Who Speaks for the Witch?* (1991), and *Good Witch's Bible* (1991), earlier published as *The Witch's Bible*, a textbook the Frosts produced for students at their School of Wicca.

The Frosts teach and lecture frequently on topics related to Wicca. Political activists, they fight for Wiccan rights and work to educate the public on Wiccan beliefs. However, they are at odds with some Wiccans in their insistence that Wicca is not inherently a pagan religion because a Wiccan need not worship nature or a specific god or goddess as pagans do.

Gavin Frost, who holds a doctorate in math and physics, first became interested in witchcraft while studying at London University. In 1951 he was initiated into a small London occult group, and during the late 1960s he was initiated into a larger German occult group that focused on sorcery. He married Yvonne, whom he met while they were both working for an aerospace company in 1970.

By the time Yvonne met Gavin, she had already become dissatisfied with the Baptist faith in which she had been reared and was studying spiritualism. Shortly after their marriage the couple became involved with Wicca and established their School of Wicca. Their Church of Wicca soon followed; in 1972 it was granted tax-exempt status as a legitimate church. The Frosts continue to run the school and the church today. **See also** Church of Wicca.

Gaia

The earth goddess in Greek mythology, Gaia, also known as Mother Earth, is worshiped by many modern witches, Wiccans, and Neopagans because of her association with the environment and the balance of nature. Adherents invoke Gaia while performing magic or rituals related to nature, herbs and other plants, and environmentalism. The ancient Greeks believed Gaia was in charge of fertility; as such she had her own cult of followers. **See also** goddesses and gods; nature; Neopagans.

Gardner, Gerald (1884–1964)

British occultist Gerald Gardner is often cited as the founder of the modern witchcraft movement. In particular, Gardner established the Gardnerian Tradition, on which many other modern Witchcraft traditions have been based.

Gardner's connection to Witchcraft traditions began in the late 1940s, when he claimed that he had made contact with a coven of hereditary witches in the New Forest area of England who revealed the secrets of their religious and magical practices to him. Even before this encounter, Gardner had long been interested in magic, having studied the occult and written a novel involving goddess worship (*A Goddess Arrives*, 1939). Gardner elaborated on the story of his experiences, claiming that a witch named Old Dorothy Clutterbuck had initiated him into the New Forest coven.

For many years the existence of Clutterbuck was a subject of debate among both witches and historians who study witchcraft. Today, scholars know that a woman by that name did live in the New Forest area around the time that Gardner claimed to have met her. However, there is no evidence that she was a witch, and after her death she left behind no possessions or writings related to witchcraft. Witches argue that this does not mean Clutterbuck was not a witch, only that she was careful not to leave traces of her witchcraft practices for fear of being ostracized by friends and relatives. Opponents counter that the area of England where Clutterbuck lived was notorious for its acceptance of witches, suggesting that there would have been no reason for her to hide her witchcraft.

In any case, with Clutterbuck's background in doubt, scholars turned their attention to possible alternative sources of Gardner's ideas. Gardner wrote a Book of Shadows, which he claimed was based on a fragmented version of the New Forest coven's Book of Shadows. Today scholars know that much of the material actually came from the works of British occultist Aleister Crowley. Crowley involved Gardner in an occult order called the Ordo Templi Orientis, but it is unclear just how close Crowley and Gardner were. Some say that the two men collaborated in developing the Book of Shadows that became the foundation of much of modern Wicca. Others say that Gardner exploited Crowley's work, plagiarizing his material while Crowley was ill. (Crowley died in 1947, only a few months after meeting Gardner.) Still others believe that Gardner did not steal from Crowley at all, but that both men simply drew on the same, ancient sources for their writings. According to this theory, Gardner used this material only to fill in the gaps in the New Forest coven's Book of Shadows.

Gardner published parts of his Book of Shadows in a novel entitled *High Magic's Aid* (1949) under the pseudonym Scire. Marketed as a work of fiction, this book did not influence witch practices to the extent that a nonfiction book would have done, although some witches did use its rituals as a model. However, Gardner could not publish the book as nonfiction because under British law any promotion of or participation in witchcraft was forbidden. Upon the repeal of the Witchcraft Act in 1951, Gardner was free to practice witchcraft and share his beliefs openly, forming his own coven and establishing the Gardnerian Tradition of Witchcraft. Along with Doreen Valiente, then a member of his coven, Gardner wrote texts of rituals for his new tradition that are still used today in his and many other traditions. Gardner suggested that these rituals were best performed nude—or, as he said, skyclad—and many witches adopted this practice.

In 1954 Gardner published his first nonfiction book on witchcraft, *Witchcraft Today*. His most influential work, it advanced the idea that witchcraft stems from an organized pagan religion that survived the witch-hunts of the fourteenth through seventeenth centuries. This theory was first proposed by Charles Leland and expanded on by Margaret Alice Murray, but it was Gardner who promoted it in the modern media. Because of his many public appearances and articles related to his work, people previously unaware of witchcraft started forming their own covens, first throughout England and then in the rest of Europe and the United States. Instrumental in bringing Gardner's ideas to America was Raymond Buckland, whom Gardner introduced to the Craft.

Some of the covens that Gardner's work inspired followed his model as exactly as possible. Others took some parts of Gardner's new tradition but not others, creating variations of the Gardnerian Tradition. These variations spread along with the Gardnerian Tradition, influencing the development of modern witchcraft throughout the Western world.

But while many people lauded Gardner for inspiring the modern witchcraft movement, some members of his original coven objected to his popularization of the Craft. Dissension developed in the group, and many members abandoned it. Meanwhile, Gardner wrote a second nonfiction book on witchcraft, *The Meaning of Witchcraft*, in 1959. It was his last major work; he died five years after its publication. **See also** Clutterbuck, Old Dorothy; Craft; Gardnerian Tradition; traditions, Witchcraft.

Gardnerian Tradition

Established by Gerald Gardner in the 1950s, the Gardnerian Tradition is perhaps the oldest and certainly one of the largest modern Witchcraft traditions. According to Gardner, the tradition originated in pagan times as part of the Old Religion and was passed on to him by hereditary witches in a New Forest coven. However, scholars believe that he created at least some of the tradition's rituals and beliefs himself; his Book of Shadows, for example, contains excerpts from and adaptations of the works of Aleister Crowley and Charles Leland, among others. (Some Gardnerians, however, believe that Gardner did not take ideas directly from Crowley, but that both Crowley and Gardner acquired much of their material from the same hereditary witches.) Over time, English witch Doreen Valiente worked with Gardner to modify or rewrite parts of his Book of Shadows, and her contributions became an integral part of the Gardnerian Tradition. Moreover, much of the Gardnerian Book of Shadows, particularly its liturgy, has been used in establishing other Witchcraft traditions.

After Gardner shared many of its beliefs and practices in numerous books and articles on witchcraft, many people either created their own Gardnerian covens or adapted the Gardnerian model to form new traditions either closely or loosely based on the Gardnerian Tradition. However, only a member of the Gardnerian Tradition knows all of its rituals and practices, because the Gardnerian Tradition is an oath-bound tradition, which means that only someone who has been initiated into the Craft can learn all of its secrets. To gain access to this knowledge, a member of a coven must rise through the coven's hierarchy and complete three degrees of initiation. The member is then known as an elder and can "hive off" of the coven to create a new one; called a daughter coven, this new group is independent from the old but retains its characteristics.

Gardnerians emphasize the preservation of their heritage. As a result, although individual covens are autonomous, most adhere to the same structure and rules. Initiates are required to rigorously study various works (particularly the Gardnerian Book of Shadows), to memorize rituals and liturgical texts, to work diligently on their practice of magic, and to develop a deep relationship with the tradition's deities.

Gardner promoted the worship of the Horned God and the Great Goddess, the latter of which has been addressed by various names. He also used ritual tools that are now standard among many traditions: the wand, the athame, the sword, and the pentacle. Gardner's covens always met once a month, outdoors, to practice magic and perform rituals, with all participants nude (or skyclad, as he called it); his coven members incorporated sexual practices and light flagellation into their rituals. Today Gardnerian covens continue to worship and meet as Gardner's did, but sex is either far less prominent or nonexistent in coven practices. In addition, some Gardnerian witches wear loose clothing during ceremonies rather than go skyclad. **See also** Crowley, Aleister; Gardner, Gerald; traditions, Witchcraft; Valiente, Doreen.

garter

In certain Witchcraft traditions, both female and male witches wear garters to designate their rank within their coven. Most modern witches got the idea of doing this from British anthropologist Margaret Alice Murray, who argued that medieval witches had used garters as a secret form of identification that enabled them to recognize one another without alerting witch-hunters.

Many modern witches continue to believe that witches in medieval times adhered to this practice, although scholars do not. Historians do agree, however, that garters made of tied cord or cloth were used during ancient pagan rituals, and that this practice probably carried over into medieval times. Certain colors of garter seem to have been associated with certain magical powers. For example, red garters were said to protect the wearer from being bewitched. Some modern witches still use colored garters as part of their rituals as well as to designate rank within the coven. However, modern witches' garters are usually made of velvet, leather, or snakeskin, and some are decorated with buckles or other adornments. **See also** colors; Murray, Margaret Alice.

Georgian Tradition

Established in 1970 in Bakersfield, California, the Georgian Tradition is a Witchcraft tradition with highly structured covens in California, Florida, and Oklahoma. The Georgian Tradition can only be taught in a coven setting, with males instructing females and vice versa. Only someone who has been properly trained and initiated and has moved up the coven hierarchy to the priesthood can provide such training to others. In coven gatherings, Georgians worship both the Goddess and the Horned God and practice magic as well. This magic is worked only for the benefit of coven members or for people who have requested the coven's help. Moreover, magic can only be used for positive purposes. However, each Georgian is encouraged to write her or his own rituals and spells and to develop an individual approach to witchcraft.

The founders of the Georgian Tradition were Lady Persephone, Lady Tanith, and George E. "Pat" Patterson (1920–1984), also known as Lord Scorpio. Patterson called their first coven the Church of Wicca of Bakersfield. Out of this group came the Persephone Coven, the Aphrodite Coven, and several other covens, all of which retained their connection to the Church of Wicca of Bakersfield. In the late 1970s Patterson changed the name of this umbrella organization to the Georgian Church.

Patterson was first initiated into the Craft in 1940 as a member of a coven with Celtic roots. In setting up the Church of Wicca of Bakersfield, he drew on material from several traditions, including Gardnerian, Alexandrian, British Traditional, and various other Celtic-based traditions. He also became a minister in the Universal Life Church and obtained a doctor of divinity degree from the American Bible Institute, believing that these experiences would help him in leading the Church of Wicca of Bakersfield. To promote his church and provide information and support to its members, he edited and published the *Georgian Newsletter*.

After Patterson succumbed to cancer in 1984, his newsletter ceased publication and interest in the Georgian Tradition began to fade. However, in recent years there has been a resurgence of interest in the Georgians, fueled in part by former members who are using the Internet to locate other former members and bring in new members. **See also** Alexandrian Tradition; Celts; traditions, Witchcraft.

Germany, witch-hunts of

During the fifteenth and seventeenth centuries, Germany experienced the most extensive and aggressive witch-hunts in all of Europe. There, over one hundred thousand people were executed as witches, so significant a portion of the population that during the late sixteenth century, some villages ceased to exist as a result of witch-hunting, while others were left with few or no women (since far more women than men were accused of being witches). In one town alone, over one thousand witches were burned alive in an oven built especially for this purpose; some of the victims were girls as young as two years old.

Germany experienced such aggressive witch-hunting in part because all German states adhered to the Carolina Code, a 1532 papal doctrine mandating torture and execution for convicted witches. Though all countries subject to this doctrine suffered from witch-hunting excesses, Germany's tortures, including repeated crushing of the legs, were particularly vicious and resulted in a far larger percentage of confessions in which accused or convicted witches named supposed accomplices. This was the case, for example, in 1590 and from 1603 to 1630 in the town of Eichstätt, Germany, where witch trials involving brutal tortures resulted in approximately fifteen hundred to two thousand deaths. Eichstätt victims were tortured until they confessed and provided the names of other "witches"; if they later recanted their confessions they were tortured anew.

Even more brutal and extensive were the witch-hunts of the principality of Bamberg, Germany, from 1623 and 1632, when ap-

An October 1555 newsletter depicts the public burning of three witches in Durneburg. Germany experienced the most aggressive witch-hunts in Europe during the fifteenth and seventeenth centuries, executing over one hundred thousand witches.

proximately six hundred people were tortured and executed as witches. Bamberg's ruler, Prince-Bishop Gottfried Johann Georg II Fuchs von Dornheim, directed that all accused witches be tortured both before and after confessing their crimes; his mandated tortures were so horrific that few could resist confession. For example, suspected witches were dunked in boiling water mixed with caustic lime, forced to kneel on spikes, and subjected to burning and bone crushing using various metallic devices.

In Bamberg and elsewhere in Germany, the most popular targets of witch-hunters were wealthy citizens, because anyone convicted of practicing witchcraft was required to turn over all property and personal possessions to local authorities who in turn shared some of the booty with the witch-hunters. Witch-hunters, secular officials, and the church all stood to benefit economically from a witch trial conviction; not surprisingly, many German cities enacted laws and policies intended to make convictions easier to obtain. In particular, one person's accusation was considered enough evidence to warrant the arrest of a suspect, whereupon the accused witch was tortured so severely that a confession was virtually assured. Moreover, the children of convicted witches were customarily treated exactly like their parents, on the theory that they would eventually become witches themselves in keeping with family tradition, and they too provided information used to arrest and torture other suspected witches. In some German cities the number of child victims was quite high. For example, in the principality of Würzburg, approximately three hundred children were tortured and executed, along with about six hundred adults. (One of the child victims was the son of the town's ruler, the Prince-Bishop Phillip Adolf von Ehrenberg.) Here as elsewhere, the conventional means of execution was burning alive.

Often, any man who criticized such practices was accused of being a witch himself. For example, in 1628 the vice-chancellor of

Bamberg, Dr. George Haan, was accused, tortured, and executed along with his wife and daughter because he opposed Bamberg's witch-hunting organization. Meanwhile, German witch-hunting had numerous vocal supporters. For example, in 1635 German judge and legal expert Benedict Carpzov wrote *Practica Rerum Criminalum* to present case law and arguments justifying the aggressive persecution of witches. Carpzov advocated a variety of brutal tortures to extract witch confessions. He also argued that witches condemned to death should be treated humanely until their execution (usually by being burned alive), but his advice in this regard was rarely followed.

The last witch execution in Germany took place in 1775. However, public sentiment against witches remained strong for many years thereafter. **See also** Bamberg, witch-hunts of; Carolina Code; Eichstätt, witch trials of.

Gifford, George (?–1620)

Sixteenth-century English clergyman George Gifford is the author of two books on witchcraft: *A Discourse of the Subtle Practices of Devils by Witches and Sorcerers*, published in 1587, and *A Dialogue Concerning Witches and Witchcrafts*, published in 1593. These books were unusual in that they argued that witches did not have the power to hurt anyone; only the devil himself, Gifford believed, could work evil through supernatural means. Unlike most of his peers, Gifford thought that most self-professed witches were deluded, and that witch persecutors were acting primarily out of fear rather than reason. **See also** devil; persecution, witch.

Glanvill, Joseph (1636–1680)

English clergyman Joseph Glanvill is the author of *Saducismus Triumphatus,* in which he examined a 1664 investigation into witches' activities in Somerset, England. Published in 1681, Glanvill's work argued that the witches in Somerset had real powers, as did most witches, although they typically exaggerated their own abilities and importance. In particular, Glanvill suggested that although witches usually claimed that they could send the devil to torment people, in actuality it was the devil who always controlled the witches.

Glanvill's work convinced many of his contemporaries that the Somerset investigation and similar actions were justified. Nonetheless, the court handling the prosecution of the Somerset witches dismissed the case before a verdict was reached, on the grounds that there was no evidence that real witchcraft was involved. (Some scholars have suggested that the court's refusal to follow through on the confessions was not actually the result of disbelief but of a changing political climate, since during the mid–seventeenth century the public in England and continental Europe stopped supporting the prosecution of witches.)

For the rest of his life, Glanvill continued to argue that the case of the Somerset witches should have resulted in conviction and execution. He also continued to promote the idea that witchcraft was real and potentially dangerous. By the time *Saducismus Triumphatus* was published, he was already considered an expert on paranormal phenomena, having examined cases of poltergeist activity and mediumship, a process whereby people communicate with ghosts. Throughout his life he tried to approach such subjects as a scientist, using objective methodology. However, modern scholars who have examined his work now know that he allowed his beliefs to influence his conclusions. **See also** Somerset, witch trial of.

goddesses and gods

Wiccans and most other practitioners of witchcraft generally believe that the goddesses and gods worshiped by many cultures throughout history are aspects of the All, the spirit that created the earth. According to Wiccan beliefs, originally the

All was female, but then she created a male half and the two worked together, intertwined as one, to create the universe and everything on earth. The All remains both female and male, with the female half representing the nurturing, fertile aspects of existence and the male half the physically aggressive, lusty aspects of existence. Most Wiccans pay more attention to the female half of the All in their rituals because they are more interested in the gentler pursuits of the deity, and because they believe that most other religions, particularly Christian denominations, have neglected the female aspects of the All to concentrate on worshiping a male god.

Wiccans also generally believe that in worshiping any of the goddesses and gods of ancient cultures, a person is worshiping the All. Therefore rituals and magic can be performed in the name of any of these goddesses and gods, although many books on Wiccan magic recommend that a novice practitioner remain focused on goddesses and gods within one particular culture rather than intermingling deities from different cultures while performing rituals. Wiccans worship deities from many different pantheons—the deities worshiped in a particular culture—throughout the world. However, certain deities and pantheons are more common focuses of Wiccan worship than others. These are:

The Greek Pantheon. Along with the Roman pantheon, the Greek pantheon is most typically associated with witchcraft. The major goddesses of this pantheon include Aphrodite, the goddess of love, female sexuality, and beauty; Athena, the goddess of wisdom; Demeter, the goddess of the harvest and mother of Persephone, another goddess of the harvest as well as of fertility; and Hera, the goddess of older women and queen of all the goddesses and gods. Two goddesses are associated with the moon: Artemis, who is also the goddess of the hunt and of young women, and Hecate, who is also the goddess of magic. Another important goddess for Wiccans is Gaia, who is also referred to as Mother Earth. In ancient times, this goddess was relatively insignificant, but in recent years she has received a great deal of attention among people who worship various aspects of nature, and even environmentalists who do not practice any form of nature religion sometimes use the name Gaia to anthropomorphize the earth's ecosystem. Major Greek gods worshiped by Wiccans include Apollo, god of healing and the arts; Dionysus, god of wine and revels; Eros, god of sexual attraction; Hades, god of the dead and husband of Persephone; Pan, a god associated with fertility as well as pastoral life; Poseidon, god of the sea; and Zeus, god of the sky and king of all Greek goddesses and gods.

The Roman Pantheon. The Roman goddesses most commonly connected to witchcraft rituals include Ceres, the goddess of the harvest; Fortuna, the goddess of luck and destiny; and Venus, the goddess of love, female sexuality, and beauty. Three goddesses are associated with the moon: Luna, who can take on the form of a virgin, a mother, and an old woman; Diana, who is also the goddess of fertility and of young women; and Juno, the goddess of older women and queen of all goddesses and gods. The Roman gods most commonly connected to witchcraft rituals include Jupiter, god of the sky and king of all goddesses and gods; Mars, the god of war; Neptune, the god of the sea; and Pluto, the god of the dead.

The Celtic Pantheon. Goddesses and gods once worshiped by the ancient Celts are also commonly worshiped by Wiccans. Goddesses include Bridgit, the goddess of healing and creativity; Cerridwen, the goddess of the moon and the harvest, the Underworld, and enchantment; and Morrigan, the goddess of war and fertility (both of women and of plants). Celtic gods include Cernunnos, also known as the Horned God, who represents the male life force and its fertility; Herne, god of the dead; and Ogma, god of language. According to Celtic belief, Ogma invented a magical alphabet that was used by the Druids, who were the high priests of the Celts.

The Egyptian Pantheon. Modern Wiccans are increasingly turning to Egyptian goddesses and gods in their worship. Goddesses include Hathor, a goddess of female sexuality and beauty; Nut (also known as Nuit), a goddess of the sky; Isis, a goddess of the moon and magic; and Isis's sister Nephthys, a goddess of the earth and of nature. Isis and Nephthys are also both fertility goddesses. Egyptian gods include Amun (also known as Amon or Amen), the king of all gods whose name was sometimes added to the names of Egypt's rulers (pharaohs such as Tutank-amen); Anubis, a god of the dead; Geb, a god of the earth; Horus, a god of the sky and the son of Osiris, a god of fertility and the Underworld; and Ra, god of the sun.

The Hindu Pantheon. The Hindu goddesses most commonly associated with witchcraft rituals include Durga, also known as the Great Mother; Kali, goddess of both nurturing and destruction, as well as of the earth, and the wife of Shiva; Lakshmi, the goddess of beauty; and Sarasvati, the goddess of wisdom. The Hindu gods most commonly associated with witchcraft rituals include Agni, the god of fire; Brahma, the god of creation; Ganesha, the god who removes obstacles; Indra, the god of war; Krishna, the god of love; Shiva, the god of change and, like his wife Kali, of destruction; and Vishnu, protector and preserver of the world.

Other Goddesses and Gods. Some goddesses and gods from other religions are also revered by Wiccans, including Astarte, a goddess of both love and war who is worshiped in some Middle Eastern countries, and Freya (or Freyja) and Thor, a Norse goddess and god who represent female sexuality/fertility and male sexuality/fertility, respectively. Thor is also the god of thunderstorms. A few Wiccans also incorporate the Buddha, a figure who is the foundation of the Buddhist religion, into their worship rituals.

Wiccan guidebooks typically advise practitioners to develop a "personal relationship" with one particular goddess or god. To aid in this pursuit, Wiccans often buy images of their chosen goddess or god which they might place on an altar before performing a ritual. In addition, when choosing a magical name to use during rituals and spell castings, many Wiccans select the name of a goddess or god.

Also common among Wiccans is the concept of the Triple Goddess, the Goddess with three aspects. This female trinity is worshiped as three distinct goddesses, each typically representing a different female role: Maiden, Mother, and Crone. For example, in the Norse pantheon, the three aspects of the Triple Goddess are Freya, the goddess of love and beauty, who represents the Maiden; Frigga, the mother goddess, who represents the Mother; and Hel, the goddess of the Underworld, who represents the Crone. More commonly among Wiccans, the three aspects of the Triple Goddess are Diana for the Maiden, Selene for the Mother, and Hecate for the Crone. Bridgit is another common representative of the Maiden aspect among Wiccans. Each of the three aspects of the Triple Goddess also represents a different phase of the moon: waxing, full, and waning. Among some traditions, the Three-Goddess Ritual is held to acknowledge the three aspects of the Great Goddess. The consort of the Triple Goddess is the Horned God, but he is not considered a triple deity. **See also** aspect; Diana; Hecate.

Golden Dawn, Hermetic Order of the

From 1888 to 1915, the Hermetic Order of the Golden Dawn was a major occult society in England and parts of Europe; some of the splinter groups it inspired remain active today. The society began after London coroner Dr. William Wynn Wescott acquired a manuscript that partially described the activities of an ancient organization called Golden Dawn. The authorship of this manuscript was attributed to a minister, A.F.A. Woodford, but Wescott had no information as to when the author lived or when he wrote the manuscript. Nonetheless, he assumed it was very old and that the rituals it attributed to the Golden Dawn were ancient. Wescott worked with occultist Samuel Liddell MacGregor Mathers to expand on the rituals mentioned in Woodford's manuscript, expanding partial descriptions with details based on the two men's knowledge of the occult.

Without telling anyone else of their work, the two men then presented the material as the teachings of a secret occult order that they said had once been active in Germany. It appears that they also forged supplementary documents and writings to lend the Golden Dawn more solid substantiation. In addition, Wescott and Mathers used their teachings as the basis for their own Golden Dawn secret order, incorporating elements of other ancient writings into their approach to magic. These other works include the Hermetica, the Kabbalah, and Abramelin magic.

The Hermetic Order of the Golden Dawn officially began in 1888, when it initiated its first members, and quickly became notable for attracting members such as Irish poet William Butler Yeats. The organization was rigidly hierarchical, and members were required to work their way through levels of rank. These levels, called degrees, were divided into three orders, and to advance through the first a member had to learn information about various types of magic and other occult studies and be tested on them. Admission to the second order, however, was at the discretion of the leaders of the society—Wescott, Mathers, and some of their friends.

The barriers to advancement eventually led to destructive dissent within the order. Magician Aleister Crowley, who joined the Hermetic Order of the Golden Dawn in 1898, protested his exclusion from the second order, then tried to take over the group and was expelled. Shortly thereafter he began to reveal the order's most secret rituals, ultimately publishing some of them in a series of magazine articles. By this point, arguments within the society had resulted in the creation of several splinter groups. These divisions weakened the original order, as did the discovery by members that Wescott and Mathers had most likely fabricated much of the Golden Dawn's early history. By the 1940s the original Hermetic Order of the Golden Dawn and most of its offshoots were gone. Some of the order's rituals, however, survive within certain Witchcraft traditions, such as the New Reformed Orthodox Order of the Golden Dawn (NROOGD). **See also** Crowley, Aleister; Hermetica; Kabbalah; New Reformed Orthodox Order of the Golden Dawn.

golem

A variation on the familiar, a golem (sometimes spelled golum) is a creature created by a magician to do his bidding. The creature was first mentioned in the writings of the Kabbalah, an ancient Hebrew system of mysticism, but was subsequently discussed in other occult writings, and some people believe that these creatures still exist today. Descriptions of how to make a golem vary. Generally, however, the figure is made of clay or wood, then brought to life via a ritual that involves numerous incantations and a special mixture of herbs containing frankincense, myrrh, and gum arabic. At the completion of the ritual the golem is not yet alive, but over the next few days or weeks the magician's visualization of it as a live being gradually brings it to life. In other words, it is animated not only by magic but by the magician's will. Consequently the golem and the magician are psychically linked, which is how the golem always knows what the magician wants him to do. At the same time, the magician's will slowly becomes so much a part of the golem that if the golem is destroyed the magician will die. **See also** circle, magic; Kabbalah; magic.

Gowdie, Isobel (?–c. 1662)

In 1662 Scottishwoman Isobel Gowdie came forward with a confession that triggered a series of witchcraft trials in Auldearn, Morayshire, Scotland. Gowdie said that she had been part of a coven there, offering detailed descriptions of its activities and naming its thirteen members. Her descriptions included stories of dancing with the devil, using magic to create storms and kill enemies, traveling to the land of the fairies, changing into various animals, and flying to Sabbats on a beanstalk. Gowdie also said that every coven member had her own imp, a creature who would do her bidding.

In addition, Gowdie claimed that when she first met the devil in 1647, he nipped her shoulder to mark her as his, and upon examination authorities discovered that Gowdie did indeed have a devil's mark on her shoulder. She stood trial for witchcraft, as did the people she accused of being in her coven. Records do not indicate what became of these people, but most modern scholars assume that most if not all of them were executed; certainly Gowdie must have been, given her devil's mark and the customary treatment of witches in her time.

Scholars disagree on whether Gowdie's coven actually existed and on why she decided to confess, since no one coerced her to do so or even suspected her of performing witchcraft. Many believe that Gowdie was either deranged or desperate for attention. Those who propose the former typically point out that many of Gowdie's stories involved explicit, lurid details of her sexual activity with the devil, and argue that her obsession with sex was a mark of her derangement. Those who propose the latter note that Gowdie was young, pretty, and lively but married to a rather dull farmer, and so was likely bored and frustrated. Neither theory explains why she would invite death with a witchcraft confession; consequently, some scholars, most notably Montague Sommers, think that Gowdie really was a member of a coven, although she undoubtedly exaggerated their activities. According to this theory, feelings of guilt over her activities led her to confess. **See also** marks, witches' or devil's; Scotland, witch trials of; Sommers, Montague.

grave robbing

Grave robbing is the act of digging up a corpse to acquire something of value from it. According to magicians' writings and witch confessions from the fourteenth through eighteenth centuries, sorcerers sometimes used the body parts, hair, nails, and/or teeth of deceased humans to make magic potions and charms or to enhance magical spells. Although grave diggers and executioners could be paid to provide them, grave robbing was a means of obtaining these ingredients.

One of the most unusual magical uses for body parts was a charm called the hand of glory. Made by witches, sorcerers, and magicians from the hand of a hanged man, this charm was reputed to protect robbers while they were burglarizing a house. Many museums currently house examples of the hand of glory, some said to be taken from the pockets of captured robbers.

The most valuable corpses were those of people hanged on the gallows. Because such people were usually in the prime of life when they died, their bodies were believed to have more power than those who died of old age or other natural causes. Also believed powerful for the purposes of black magic were the remains of infants who had not yet been baptized into the Catholic faith, because they were infused with new life but were not part of the

Christian Church. Witches no longer profess to using any ingredients obtained from human corpses in their magical work. **See also** hand of glory.

Great Rite

The phrase *Great Rite* refers to the sexual union of the God and Goddess, a union also known as the divine marriage. In some Witchcraft traditions, this rite is always represented symbolically. For example, an athame (a ritual knife that symbolizes masculinity) might be lowered into a chalice (a cup that symbolizes femininity) as a way of showing the joining of male and female forces. In other traditions, human participants act as stand-ins for the deities. This typically occurs at major Sabbats, particularly Samhain, when the high priestess and high priest perform the Great Rite after drawing down the spirits of the Goddess and the Horned God, respectively. In some traditions, including the Gardnerian Tradition, the Great Rite is the central feature of a witch's third-degree initiation, in which coven members are welcomed into the highest level of training and responsibility within their tradition.

Actual reenactments of the Great Rite, as opposed to symbolic ones, are controversial among Wiccans, particularly when a physical union occurs as part of an initiation ceremony. Some Wiccans believe that this practice provides too great a risk that one of the participants—particularly the woman—will be sexually exploited. Moreover, many Wiccans fear the spread of sexually transmitted diseases. Others argue that the Great Rite is an important part of the Wiccan religion and that expressing male/female sexuality is a natural and personally beneficial way to raise energy for rituals and magical work. They also insist that within a coven it is easy to ensure that participation is voluntary and that participants' physical health is protected. **See also** athame; Gardnerian Tradition; initiations; Sabbat; Samhain.

Green Man

The Green Man is a pagan deity that represents the wilderness and the spirit of the trees and woodlands. The Green Man is also an ancient diety: Archaeologists have found evidence that a version of him appeared during the Neolithic period, which lasted from approximately 7000–3500 B.C. Agriculture had just begun at that time, and people began to pray to the gods of the lands they were clearing, including the Green Man. Scholars believe that this practice continued for centuries.

Ancient Greek art depicts the Green Man, who was called Dionysos, as a man crowned with ivy, laurel, vine leaves, or grape leaves, but it was the ancient Celts in Britain who created the image of the Green Man still known today: a man, sometimes with horns, peering through a thick bower of leaves that conceal all but his face. The earliest such image that survives appears on a fifth-century Celtic pillar. Interestingly, the image also appears in stone carvings on some early Christian churches, probably because they were converted from pagan temples.

In medieval times, the Green Man came to be viewed more as a woodland spirit than as a deity. He was also associated with wild, drunken revels, much like the Roman god of wine, Bacchus, who was yet another manifestation of the Green Man concept. Today witches and Neopagans consider the Green Man a symbol of nature. Nicknamed Green Jack, Green George, and Jack-in-the-Green, he appears on Neopagan jewelry and is sometimes featured in spring rituals, played by a man covered with leaves. **See also** Bacchus; Neopagans; Old Religion; paganism.

Green Wicca

Also known as Green Witchcraft, Green Wicca is a Witchcraft tradition that emphasizes herbalism, healing magic, and the worship of nature. Green Wiccans are attuned to the seasons, the phases of the moon, and other aspects of the earth's environment, and they are dedicated to worshipping earth gods and goddesses, primarily the goddess Gaia. Many members of the Kitchen Witch Tradition can also be said to be practicing Green Wicca, although Kitchen Witches primarily concentrate on practical magic and are primarily solitary practitioners, whereas Green Wiccans practice alone or in covens in roughly equal measure. In addition, most Green Wiccans are actively involved in environmental politics whereas Kitchen Witches are comparatively apolitical. **See also** Kitchen Witch Tradition; traditions, Witchcraft.

Grillandus, Paulus

Sixteenth-century Italian papal judge Paulus Grillandus is the author of the *Tractatus de Hereticis et Sortilegiis* (*Treatise on Heretics and Witches*), published sometime in the early part of the century. The work carried weight because Grillandus presided over numerous witch trials in Rome and was able to cite specific examples from those trials to lend authority to his arguments. Taking the position that witchcraft was real and witches were dangerous, Grillandus discussed such subjects as witches' ability to transform themselves into animals and to fly to Sabbats, the relationship between witches and Satan, and the signs of demonic possession. In Grillandus's opinion, witches' confessions should generally be accepted as truthful regardless of how they were obtained. His attitude was adopted by many of those who read his work, including many witch trial judges. **See also** flight; Italy, witch-hunts of; Sabbat.

Grimassi, Raven (1951–)

American witch Raven Grimassi is a leading author of witchcraft-related books as well as a leading figure in Italian Witchcraft traditions. His works include *The Book of Ways* (1981; two volumes), *Ways of the Strega* (1995), *The Wiccan Mysteries* (1997), *The Encyclopedia of Wicca and Witchcraft* (2000), and *Italian Witchcraft: The Old Religion of Southern Europe* (2000). Raised in the United States by an Italian immigrant mother, Grimassi was drawn to Italian Witchcraft, also called Stregheria, at an early age. As a teenager he began reading about the subject, and in 1969 he started studying Wicca after meeting a high priestess in the Gardnerian Tradition. This priestess, Lady Heather, soon initiated Grimassi into the Craft. In 1974 he studied Wicca under Lady Sara Cunningham, a psychic and shaman who founded a Kabbalah-based religious order called the First Temple of Tiphareth, which existed from 1957 to 1980.

In 1975 Grimassi joined Cunningham's order and began studying the Kabbalah. As part of his activities in the First Temple of Tiphareth, Grimassi met some practitioners of Brittic Wicca, a tradition combining elements of Basque Witchcraft and English Wicca. Soon Grimassi was initiated into Brittic Wicca. At the same time, he began studying ancient Egyptian magic as a member of a Rosicrucian Order. He then founded his own order, the Order of the Sacred Path, dedicated to the study of the occult. By 1979, however, he had decided to end his order and abandon his other studies so he could focus solely on Italian Wicca. In 1980 he started his own Italian Witchcraft tradition, the Aridian Tradition; one of his first initiates was Scott Cunningham, another notable author of witchcraft-related books.

Grimassi started writing about witchcraft in 1981 as a contributor to the *Shadow's Edge*, a magazine devoted to Italian Witchcraft. Within a few months he was writing for other magazines and producing books as well. Today he continues to write books and is the editor of and contributor to a witchcraft-related magazine called the *Raven's Call*. In addition, in 1998 Grimassi created the Arician Tradition, deriving it from the Aridian Tradition he had previously established. He currently runs a shop called Raven's Loft and has a retreat, Crow Haven Ranch, where practitioners of the Arician Tradition can meet. **See also** Cunningham, Scott; Gardnerian Tradition; Kabbalah; Rosicrucians; shamanism; Stregheria.

grimoire

A grimoire is a handbook of magic spells, formulas, rituals, and incantations. Some of the material in a grimoire might appear in a Book of Shadows, but unlike a Book of Shadows the grimoire is not used to establish a Witchcraft tradition, nor does it include the kind of personal and coven-related information typically recorded in a Book of Shadows. Nonetheless, some modern witches call their personal Book of Shadows a grimoire.

The first grimoires were circulated in the Middle Ages and Renaissance, and they became extremely popular with all kinds of readers in the seventeenth and eighteenth centuries. Reputed to contain knowledge from ancient times, they provided detailed information regarding how a magician should dress, live, perform rituals and sacrifices, and manufacture magical tools. Many also offered hierarchical lists of demons and spirits.

Among the best-known medieval grimoires are the *Key of Solomon*, which contains material regarding ceremonial magic and the control of spirits that was drawn from the Kabbalah and other forms of Hebrew mysticism; *The Book of Sacred Magic of Abramelin the Mage*, which describes the use of magical talismans and tells how to obtain knowledge from guardian angels; and the *Lemegeton*, a five-volume work telling how to summon various types of spirits. A popular seventeenth-century French grimoire was the *Grand Grimoire*, which contains information on black magic used to summon demons. *The Black Pullet* was an eighteenth-century grimoire dealing with magic talismans, while *The Book of Black Magic and of Pacts* was a late–nineteenth-century grimoire on black magic written by Arthur Edward Waite while he was a member of the Hermetic Order of the Golden Dawn.

Today several modern witches have published grimoires to help solitary practitioners of the Craft. These include *The Grimoire of Lady Sheba* by Lady Sheba (1974), *A Grimoire of Shadows* by Ed Fitch (1996), and *The Witch's Master Grimoire* by Lady Sabrina (2001). Whereas medieval grimoires primarily told how to conjure spirits and demons who would then serve the magician in both good and evil ways, modern grimoires typically focus on simple, practical spells designed to attract various forms of good fortune, such as a new romance or increased

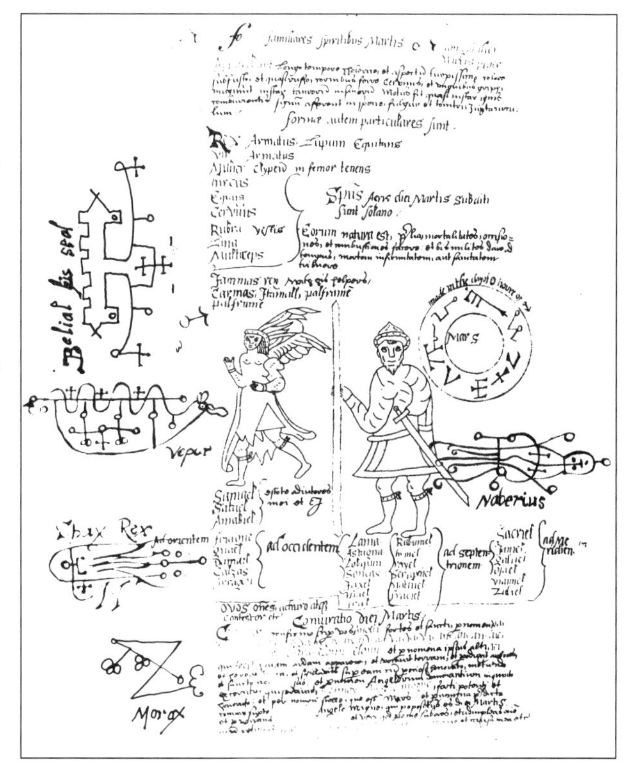

This page from an English grimoire contains sixteenth-century Latin text on demons with sigils of the spirits added.

wealth. **See also** Abramelin magic; Book of Shadows; Golden Dawn, Hermetic Order of the; *Key of Solomon*.

Guazzo, Francesco-Maria (c. 1600–1630)

Italian friar Francesco-Maria Guazzo is the author of the *Compendium Maleficarum* (*Handbook of Witches*), a 1626 book on demonology and witchcraft. As someone who had sometimes evaluated accused witches for the courts, Guazzo was considered an expert on witches and was therefore assigned the task of writing the *Compendium Maleficarum* by the bishop of Milan, who wanted to promote the idea that witches were a very real and very serious threat to society. The bishop was successful in this regard, and Guazzo's book remained influential even after he died in 1630. One of Guazzo's arguments, however, was unconvincing: the position that Martin Luther, the former monk who touched off the Reformation, was actually the son of Satan. **See also** devil; maleficia.

Gypsies

Gypsies are nomadic people who have long been reputed to use magic. Experts disagree on the origin of these people, but most believe that they initially migrated to Europe from India. It is clear that prior to the 1300s, Gypsies roamed throughout northwest India, and by the 1300s some of their number had migrated to Europe and the Middle East. By 1500 Gypsies could be found in England, and today they live in the United States and Canada as well. Their name most likely comes from the fact that when the first Gypsies appeared in Europe, many people there thought they were related to ancient Egyptians.

Traditionally, Gypsy bands spend the warm months of the year traveling from town to town, working at carnivals, fairs, or similar venues, where they typically sell handmade goods, tell fortunes, and provide various forms of entertainment. In the winter they live in large groups apart from other people. Gypsies typically do not marry outside of their culture, and so retain their own customs and language (Romany, which is derived from the ancient Indian language of Sanskrit).

Throughout history, Gypsies have been particularly famous for their divination skills and their potions. In fact, even today some people continue to consult Gypsy fortune-tellers and/or buy Gypsy potions. Gypsies traditionally use Tarot cards, crystal balls, tea leaves, or palm reading to predict the future, and the most popular of their many kinds of potions are love potions and love-charming oils. They also make pouches in which certain objects are placed and magically "charged" with spells to bring about a certain result. For example, a pouch designed to attract economic prosperity might include a gold coin, a magnet, and certain stones, herbs, nuts, and plant leaves. Gypsies also create charms and amulets, practice healing magic, cast spells, and make curses.

Some Gypsy rituals involve magic circles and broomsticks. Because witches employ these as well, along with practicing divination and potion making, it was relatively easy for sixteenth- and seventeenth-century witch-hunters to gain convictions against Gypsies. No one is certain how many Gypsies were executed during these centuries, but undoubtedly hundreds if not thousands perished for their beliefs. In addition, Gypsies were subjected to other forms of harassment because of their association with witches. In 1530 England's government began deporting Gypsies and enacted a law banning their entrance into the country. This law remained in effect until 1784. **See also** amulet; divination; England, witch-hunts of; Tarot cards.

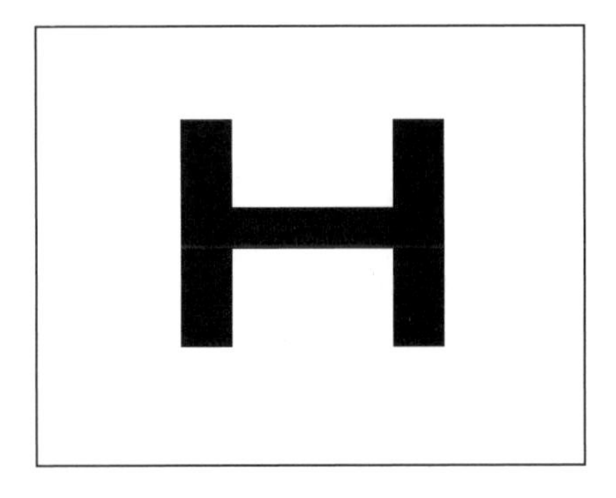

hag

From medieval times to the present, the word *hag* has often been used as a derogatory substitute for "witch." In this sense it means a sorceress who is old and ugly and has a stooped back. In ancient times, however, the word could also refer to a young, beautiful sorceress, priestess, or fairy. This connection to fairies remains evident in the way that "hagstone" is often used interchangeably with "fairystone" in Great Britain, in reference to a particular type of stone believed to have magic powers. **See also** fairies.

hand of glory

One of the most famous charms in black magic, the hand of glory is a pickled human hand that supposedly confers special powers and protection on its owner and is considered particularly beneficial to robbers. According to claims in medieval stories, a burglar carrying a hand of glory will not get caught, and door locks will magically open when he approaches them. In response, many medieval homeowners sought magical charms, potions, and ointments that, when put on windowsills and doorsteps, were said to prevent the hand of glory from working.

Throughout the fourteenth through eighteenth centuries, many books featured instructions on how to make a hand of glory. For example, the 1722 anonymous German work *Marvellous Secrets of the Natural and Cabalistic Magic of Little Albert* featured a popular recipe for the pickling of such a hand. Such recipes usually directed that the hand be pickled for two weeks, although other lengths of time might be recommended. The recipes also suggested that certain powders be added to the pickling solution and recommended specific days as best for drying the hand. Some of the recipes called for drying it in natural sunlight, others in a kiln or oven. In the case of the latter, some recipes suggested placing herbs in with the drying hand. Many also recommended that the hand be pressed prior to pickling, and that the extracted material be dried into a powder and inserted into the hand in its final stages of preparation.

All of the recipes agreed, however, that the only type of hand suitable for the hand of glory was one taken from an executed man, preferably while he was still hanging on the gallows. Magicians and witches typically bribed executioners to obtain such a hand, which they then wrapped in the same material used for shrouds so that it would remain powerful while they prepared it for pickling.

Once the hand of glory was finished, it was sometimes turned into a candle by placing wax and a wick between its fingers. Alternatively, the fingers themselves were lit. There were two main reasons for burning a hand of glory. First, such a hand was believed to increase the power of magical potions made by its light. Second, a burning hand of glory placed at a person's bedside was believed to keep that person asleep until the candle was snuffed out. This property was of particular value to robbers, who might arrange for an accomplice within the household to light a hand of glory beside the master of the house on a night when a burglary was planned. **See also** candles; grave robbing.

handfasting

A handfasting is a Wiccan wedding ceremony. As part of this ceremony, a man and a woman typically pledge to remain together as long as their love lasts. In some Witchcraft traditions, it is customary to handfast for a year and a day, whereupon the couple undergoes a handparting ceremony that dissolves their marriage.

The word *handfasting* is derived from an ancient pagan ceremony in which a couple's union was symbolized by tying their hands together with a cord or sash. Some modern handfastings also feature this practice, usually using a knotted cord. In addition, couples typically exchange gold or silver rings inscribed with the couple's names and/or some meaningful phrase or saying written in a magical alphabet. In some traditions it is common for participants to wear white robes, in some to go skyclad, and in others to wear whatever is comfortable. Different traditions recognize different times as the best for handfastings, but the majority hold them at times of a waxing moon.

The ceremony is usually performed by a coven's high priestess and/or high priest. If the priestess or priest has been authorized by local authorities to perform a wedding, then the ceremony is legally binding. Otherwise it can only be considered binding within the coven, not in society at large. **See also** coven; moon; skyclad.

hare

From medieval times through the seventeenth century, many Europeans believed that witches could turn themselves into hares at will. In particular, farmers often suspected that the hares in the fields that darted around their cows were actually witches trying to steal milk. Some farmers thought that it was useless to shoot at the hares, under the common notion that witches could only be harmed by pure silver bullets, which the average farmer found unaffordable. Others did shoot at the hares; in the event that a farmer grazed an animal and subsequently encountered a woman with any sort of injury he typically accused her of being the hare/witch he had just shot.

In confessing to practicing witchcraft, some Renaissance witches admitted to turning themselves into hares. In addition, witch confessions as well as stories about pagan rituals tell of a dance that featured women pretending to be hares as a man (usually a coven's high priest) pretending to be a hunting dog pursued them. **See also** animals.

hats

Contrary to popular belief, witches have historically not worn tall pointed black hats. Some modern scholars theorize that the misunderstanding came from the fact that the women who lived in Salem, Massachusetts, at the time of the famous Salem witch trials typically did wear such hats, as did women in other colonies settled by English Puritans. But other scholars note that the image of a witch in a pointed hat also appeared in Germany in the seventeenth century, when it was used to adorn maps of regions believed popular with witches, suggesting that the concept originated in Europe.

Whatever its origins, the stereotypical portrayal of a witch in a pointed hat is distasteful to modern witches. Some, however, embrace the popular image of the witch. For example, members of a short-lived American feminist group of the late 1960s (known by the acronym

WITCH), who professed to be witches dressed in flowing black robes and tall pointed hats when they staged feminist demonstrations. However, the group displayed such a complete lack of understanding of witchcraft that most Wiccans doubted its members' connection to the Craft and shunned them. Wiccans react similarly to witches who, for whatever reason, choose to wear such costumes. For example, American witch Laurie Cabot, who has been designated the Official Witch of Salem, has drawn criticism from other Wiccans for adopting a stereotypical version of witches' clothing. In actuality, there is no "dress code" for witches; their clothing has always varied widely, and in some traditions it is even customary to practice witchcraft skyclad—that is, wearing no clothes at all. **See also** Cabot, Laurie; skyclad; WITCH.

hawthorn

Also called the thorn tree, the hawthorn tree (*Crataegus monogyna*) is one of the most significant of all trees for witches. Its branches are used in May Day (May 1), or Beltane, celebrations, but are not to be cut on any other day but May Eve (April 30) or bad luck will follow. Some witches and Neopagans worship the tree as the personification of the Goddess, while others associate it with fairies. They consider the hawthorn to be one of the Fairy Triad, along with the ash and oak, and believe that fairies live wherever the three trees grow together. According to some Witchcraft traditions, the hawthorn tree hides a doorway into the fairy realm.

Reverence for the hawthorn goes far back in time. For example, pagans in ancient Britain also worshiped the hawthorn tree as representative of the Goddess. The uses other people found for the hawthorn's wood suggests they believed it had magical qualities. Ancient Germans routinely used the branches to build funeral pyres, while the ancient Greeks incorporated hawthorn leaves, branches, and flowers into wedding ceremonies. Ancient Romans traditionally built baby cradles from hawthorn wood, believing it would protect the newborn. **See also** ash; oak; trees.

hazel

Witches, particularly those witches involved in Celtic-based traditions, consider the hazel tree (*Coryllius avellana*) to be sacred. According to Celtic legends, the tree has various magical powers, including the ability to impart wisdom to people and animals. Consequently, from medieval times to the present, hazel wood has often been used to make witches' wands, divining rods, and other tools of magic. Hazel leaves are thought to have certain magical and medicinal properties as well. For example, they are used in potions and poultices to cure inflammatory disease such as rheumatism and lumbago. Ironically, some medieval people also used hazel to keep witches away, believing that if they hung a sprig of "witch hazel" over a doorway a witch would be unable to enter. **See also** herbs and other plants; trees; wand.

Hecate

Hecate is a goddess of Greek mythology still worshiped today by modern witches. Along with Diana and Selene, she is one aspect of the Triple Goddess of the moon, with Diana governing the new moon, Selene the full moon, and Hecate the dark moon. According to Greek mythology, Hecate also had some control over the three great mysteries—birth, life, and death—and the three realms—heaven, earth, and the Underworld. In addition, she held power over ghosts and phantoms, and was said to be responsible for determining whether or not mortals got their hearts' desire.

These qualities eventually led people to consider Hecate the patroness of magic and witchcraft. So thoroughly did this connection become embedded in the popular culture that plays and other works referred to Hecate in this vein. For example, in William Shakespeare's play *Macbeth* the three witches in the opening scene name Hecate as the goddess they worship.

Stories abound of witches meeting to honor Hecate, usually at a place where three roads meet. The reason they meet at crossroads can be traced back to ancient times, when statues of Hecate traditionally stood at such spots because of her association with the three phases of the moon, the three great mysteries, and the three realms. A goddess of threes, she was often depicted with three heads, each facing a different direction, and three arms. At the sites of her statues, ancient Greeks often left offerings of honey, eggs, and other foods, sometimes sacrificing animals as well. Rituals intended to honor and/or placate Hecate were typically performed when the moon was either full or dark. **See also** Diana; goddesses and gods; moon; Selene.

hedge witch

A hedge witch is a witch who practices alone rather than as part of a coven, and/or a solitary witch who has never been initiated into any Witchcraft tradition. A hedge witch does not typically have a mentor, but learns witchcraft through private study and experimentation. The connection between hedges and solitary witchcraft probably comes from the fact that in various mythological stories, certain goddesses are said to have private sanctuaries surrounded by hedges. **See also** coven; solitaries.

Henri III (1551–1589)

Henri III, king of France, is believed by many scholars to have practiced witchcraft while on the throne. He assumed the crown upon the death of his brother and ruled France from 1574 until his murder by a political fanatic in 1589. During his reign, Henri presented himself to his subjects as a good Catholic, but it was rumored that in private he performed pagan and/or satanic rituals. These rumors were fueled by the fact that King Henri surrounded himself with numerous handsome male retainers, and it was apparent that he was engaging in sexual activities with them. In that era, such activities were commonly associated with Satanism and witchcraft in the public mind. Nonetheless, there is no solid evidence to either prove or disprove that King Henri did indeed practice witchcraft. While some of the possessions the king left behind—including preserved human skin—suggest he very likely did engage in some kind of magic rituals, he was not an advocate of sorcery and did nothing to limit the persecution of witches during his reign. **See also** France, witch-hunts of; persecution, witch.

herbs and other plants

Herbs, tree leaves, and other plants and plant parts have been used in the healing and magical arts for centuries. Historically, a person well versed in the use of magical and healing herbs has been said to be skilled in wortcunning. Modern witches who specialize in wortcunning are Green Witches or Kitchen Witches; growing their own herbs and other plants is part of their craft.

Herbs intended for medicinal purposes are typically administered in salves, syrups, teas, poultices, and powders. Those to be used magically—whether for healing or other purposes—might be stuffed into special dolls called poppets or into charms that are carried or buried, or inside the wax of candles used in magical rituals. Certain combinations of herbs are also used to make suffumigations, which are magical incenses said to attract spirits, or witch's bottles, which confer certain types of protection on a household.

To create a witch's bottle, certain herbs are sealed inside a bottle, then buried under the doorstep. The number of herbs can vary from one to seven. The three most common herbs for witch's bottles are houseleek (*Sem-*

For centuries witches have used herbs to heal, protect, charm, and poison. This illustration depicts a witch shooting a twig through a man's foot, thereby inoculating him.

pervivum tectorum), which protects against lightning and other natural disasters, blackthorn (*Prunus spinosa*), which is generally protective, and St. John's wort (*Hypericum perforatum*), which protects against ghosts and demons. One popular seven-herb combination for witch's bottles involves herbs that were once sacred to the Druid priesthood of the ancient Celts. These herbs are believed to have especially strong magical powers when used together in spells and potions. They are mistletoe (*Viscum album*), vervain (*Verbena officinalis*), henbane (*Hyoscyamus niger*), primrose (*Primula vulgaris*), pulsatilla (*Anemone pulsatilla*), clover (*Trifolium pratense*), and aconite (*Aconitum napellus*).

When witches combine herbs for spells or charms, they generally believe it is better to use three, seven, or nine herbs, because these numbers have magical significance. Herbs that are employed singly, whether for medicinal or magical purposes, are called simples. Some herbs are only used singly, while others are used either singly or in combination. For example, two of the herbs used in combination in witch's bottles, vervain and henbane, are also often employed as simples.

Vervain is a flowering plant that has long been associated with witchcraft. In ancient times, it was thought to be a cure for depression as well as a charm against certain forms of illness. Other than putting it in witch's bottles, modern witches use it primarily in love potions. Henbane is another common ingredient in potions, even though it is poisonous. In judicious amounts it is said to aid clairvoyance, to act as an aphrodisiac, and to cure injuries caused by witchcraft. Henbane is just one of several varieties of bane; as deadly herbs, banes have historically been used in combination with other herbs to produce poisons.

In the seventeenth and eighteenth centuries, one of the most popular magical plants was yarrow, which was believed to add power to love spells. Another popular herb was St. John's wort. As well as being used in witch's bottles, it has long been used medicinally to treat cuts, burns, and depression, and magically as part of spells to banish evil spirits, as well as in love charms. The word *wort* comes from the Old English *wyrt*, which means "plant," and the appellation of St. John's relates to the fact that the herb is believed most powerful when harvested on St. John's Eve.

Other common herbs and plants that have been used in witchcraft, either alone or in combinations, are:

Angelica. During the fifteenth century, Europeans wore leaves from the angelica plant as a charm against plague or to guard against evil. However, the plant's connection to magic dates back to antiquity, when Norwegians employed it in a variety of potions.

Bay. In medieval times, bay leaves were believed to have magical and medicinal properties. People carried such leaves as protection against various diseases, particularly plague, and bay trees were planted beside houses to keep away evil spirits. Bay leaves were also used in divination. People burned them in a fire; by looking at the flames' patterns and listening to their crackling they believed that they could discern the answers to questions about the future. For example, a certain number of crackles meant yes, another meant no.

Elder. The European elder tree has been associated with witches and fairies since pagan times. Since medieval times, green elder wood has been rubbed on warts as part of a ritual to drive the warts away, and elder leaves have been worn against the skin to prevent rheumatism. Medieval Christians thought that elder wood could also be used as an amulet to protect the soul from bewitchment.

Hazel. According to Celtic legends, the hazel tree has various magical powers, including the ability to impart wisdom to people and animals. Hazel leaves are thought to have certain magical and medicinal properties, as well. For example, they are used in potions and poultices to cure rheumatism and lumbago. Ironically, some medieval people also used hazel to keep witches away, believing that if they hung a sprig of "witch hazel" over a doorway a witch could not enter.

Hemlock. Hemlock is a poisonous plant that was once used judiciously in brews and potions to cure lover's quarrels and animal infertility. During medieval times it was also said to be an ingredient in witches' flying ointment. Most modern witches, however, avoid this highly toxic plant.

Lily. The lily is a flowering plant used in spells to counter black magic. When mixed with bay leaves, it is employed in spells intended to cause someone mild harm. It has also been used medicinally to treat skin sores and blisters.

Mugwort. Also called the mother of herbs, mugwort (*Artemisia vulgaris*) is an herb associated with healing magic, divination, meditation, and psychic powers. It is often brewed as tea but might also be placed within protective charms. Some witches drink mugwort tea as part of certain rituals and ceremonies. Others rub mugwort juice on magic mirrors to enhance their ability to foretell the future. Similarly, an incense made with mugwort is said to improve scrying spells.

Nightshade. Nightshade is a poisonous plant whose berries are said to enable people to see into the future. However, an overdose of these berries will cause death. Small amounts of nightshade are used in many spells and potions, and in medieval times the plant was said to be a main ingredient in witches' flying ointment.

Periwinkle. Also known as sorcerer's violet, periwinkle is a popular ingredient in love potions.

Rue. Rue (*Ruta graveolens*) is a sacred herb of witchcraft that has been employed since ancient times as protection against evil magic. In Italian Witchcraft traditions, it is ingested or carried as a charm for protection against enchantment and to strengthen psychic vision.

These plants and others are typically planted during a new moon, which witches believe is the best time for all things related to new beginnings. The time to harvest a particular plant is determined by its intended purpose. A plant intended for constructive magic is best harvested during the waxing moon, while a plant intended for destructive magic is best harvested during the waning moon. Plants intended for white magic are the most powerful when harvested during a full moon, while plants harvested during a dark moon are best for black magic. Sometimes a witch harvests only the blossoms, sometimes only the leaves, sometimes only the roots. In any case, witches traditionally cut the plant using a knife called a bolline, and in many traditions it is believed that the plant must be harvested with only one stroke of the blade or its magical properties will be diminished. **See also** bay; bolline; charm; elder; Green Witch; hazel; Kitchen Witch Tradition; moon; potion; scrying.

Hereditary Tradition

Practitioners of the Hereditary Tradition of Witchcraft are all hereditary witches, ones whose genetic connection to other witches can be traced through many generations and who have been taught the Craft by a living relative. Their covens usually comprise only close relatives. Most believe that their knowledge and power as witches is inherited, although sometimes they adopt people into their coven if a family line is dying out. **See also** traditions, Witchcraft.

Hermetica

A collection of ancient books related to the occult, the Hermetica has influenced many Witchcraft traditions and helped inspire the creation of occult societies like the Hermetic Order of the Golden Dawn. The books were written in Greek and Latin sometime between the third century B.C. and the first century A.D., most likely as an ongoing work with several contributors. The collection was called the Hermetica, however, because the Greeks of the Hellenistic age originally attributed it to just one author, Hermes Trimegistus. His name means "The Thrice-Great Hermes," in reference to the fact that he supposedly had three roles: priest, king, and philosopher. Hermes Trimegistus was once believed to be a real person, but historians now think he was a mythical person based on two gods, Hermes and Thoth (a Greek messenger god and an Egyptian god of magic, respectively). First linked by the Greeks, Hermes and Thoth were both said to have authored sacred texts, which is probably why Hermes Trimegistus was credited with authoring the Hermetica.

The Hermetica is said to have originally consisted of forty-two books. Historians place the books into two categories: popular Hermeticism, which deals with the occult and astrology, and learned Hermeticism, which deals with philosophy, science, and other scholarly subjects. Most of these works have been lost, but historians have discovered material from ten books related to Egyptian religious practices, four to astrology, six to medicine, and various others to philosophical, scientific, and legal subjects. Evidence of the Hermetica exists primarily as fragments that appear within other works, such as *The Divine Pymander*, which includes most of the Hermetic concepts regarding magic and mysticism.

Another writing considered part of the Hermetica is the Emerald Tablet, which first appeared in ancient Arabia and was said to have been copied from a tablet in Hermes Trimegistus's tomb. Its text is convoluted and confusing, but it begins with a sentence that forms the basis of an important tenet of witchcraft known as "as above, so below." The sentence reads: "That which is above is like that which is below and that which is below is like that which is above, to achieve the wonders of one thing." Witches interpret this passage to mean that the spiritual realm is expressed in the physical realm and vice versa, with the Creator and the Creation so intimately connected that alterations in the physical realm can impact the spiritual realm and vice versa. It is for this reason that magic is believed able to influence objects and human events.

There are several other important principles of Hermetic occult science. Foremost is that everything currently in existence was mentally created by the divine spirit. Second, every natural and supernatural force has a particular energy vibration that can be employed to work magic. Polarity, the pairing of opposites, and the balance of male and female forces are also important. The

Hermetica also addresses various types of cause and effect. For example, it tells why certain herbs have certain magical effects and discusses how one magically charged object might affect another. **See also** Golden Dawn, Hermetic Order of the.

hex signs

Hex signs are magical signs and symbols usually used to protect buildings or household objects from destruction. Witches and other practitioners of folk magic use hex signs in the casting of spells. There are many different kinds of hex signs, but the most common are simple drawings derived from ancient cultures. These include various symbols for the sun and moon, stars with varying numbers of points, different shapes of leaves and flowers, hearts arranged in various patterns, rudimentary outlines of animals such as roosters and hares, and crosses, including the "rolling cross," or swastika.

Hex signs were first used in medieval Germany and Switzerland, where they were put on barns and houses, respectively. People who emigrated from these countries to America brought hex signs with them. They then expanded the use of these signs, painting them not only on barns and houses but also on all sorts of household items, furniture, and farming tools in order to protect them. In addition, they drew hex signs as part of spells to bring luck, health, wealth, and good weather.

high priestess and high priest

In most Witchcraft traditions, the high priestess and high priest are the female and male leaders, respectively, of a coven. In rituals, the high priestess represents the Goddess, while the high priest represents the Horned God.

High priestesses and priests have various duties, depending on their Witchcraft tradition. For example, in many traditions the high priestess is in charge of creating each magic circle. She sweeps the area intended for the circle with a ritual broom, then sprinkles it with salt to cleanse it of negative energy, before using an athame, wand, or sword to outline the circle in a clockwise, or *deosil*, direction on the floor or ground. In some traditions, however, members of a coven take turns casting the magic circle. Similarly, in some traditions the high priestess always leads the dancing, whereas in others this duty is shared by coven members.

In the Alexandrian and Gardnerian Traditions, the high priestess is always the only one responsible for delivering a speech called the Charge of the Goddess during a ritual called drawing down the moon. While giving this speech, the priestess is believed to be a channel through which the Goddess herself is speaking. Also in the Alexandrian and Gardnerian Traditions, the high priestess and high priest together re-create the sexual union of the Goddess and God, a union also known as the divine marriage, in another ritual called the Great Rite.

In these and many other traditions, a person can take on the designation of high priestess or priest only after working upward in responsibility and knowledge through three degrees of initiation. The most structured traditions require each member to take tests of skills along the way, with each degree taking a minimum of a year and a day to complete. In such traditions, only a third-degree witch can become a high priestess or high priest.

In some traditions, the high priestess has an assistant called a maiden and the high priest an assistant called a summoner. The maiden and the summoner might take over the duties of a high priestess or high priest, respectively, who becomes ill. In addition, in some traditions the maiden is allowed to form her own coven. If this happens several times (more than three in some traditions, while other traditions require far more) and all of the new covens are allied with the old, the high priestess of the original coven takes the title of Witch Queen.

In most Witchcraft traditions, it is considered acceptable to have no high priest, or even to have no men in a coven at all. However, it is unacceptable to have no high priestess or to have an all-male coven. In their book *The Witches' Bible*, Janet and Stewart Farrar explain the rationale behind this practice. They report that most witches believe that witchcraft does not come naturally to most men, whereas every woman is considered a natural witch. Moreover, such witches believe that most men can only connect to the Goddess through the efforts of a woman. Therefore, the Farrars report: "That is why Wicca is matriarchal, and the High Priestess is the leader of the coven—with the High Priest as her partner. They are essential to each other, and ultimately equal . . . but . . . Wiccan working is primarily concerned with the 'gifts of the Goddess,' so the Priestess takes precedence; for woman is the gateway to witchcraft, and man is her 'guardian and student.'"

In a few other Witchcraft traditions, however, covens have neither a high priest nor a high priestess, preferring to rotate leadership or share it among members. In such cases, they either give new members as much authority as established members or require members to display certain levels of knowledge and/or skill before assuming a position of authority. **See also** Alexandrian Tradition; coven; Gardnerian Tradition.

hocus pocus

Hocus pocus is a phrase once commonly used by stage magicians during the commission of their tricks, and has nothing to do with the practice of magic by witches. Historians disagree on the origin of the words, which apparently are nonsensical. However, the use of the phrase dates at least as far back as the seventeenth century when, according to Thomas Ady's 1656 book *A Candle in the Dark, or a Treatise Concerning the Nature of Witches and Witchcraft*, a magician used a spell that began with "hocus pocus" to literally blind people to his illusions. In recent years, the popular media have used the phrase to refer to witches' magic, fostering the misconception that witches actually say the words as they work. One example of this usage is the 1993 movie *Hocus Pocus*, which concerns three witches who bewitch most of a town as part of an attempt to steal its children. **See also** Ady, Thomas; magic.

Holt, Sir John (1642–1710)

English attorney and judge Sir John Holt is notable in that he was more inclined than his peers to find suspected witches innocent rather than guilty. He insisted that no one be convicted of witchcraft without strong, well-documented evidence, and many of his peers on the bench subsequently adopted this approach as well. Sometimes this position brought trouble. For example, in 1701 he found a woman innocent of witchcraft, after she had been accused of causing fits in a young blacksmith. Public sentiment was against this verdict, so some people immediately called for his removal from the bench while others threatened the innocent woman's life. Later, however, the blacksmith was proved to have been faking his fits. **See also** England, witch-hunts of.

Hopkins, Matthew (c. 1621–c. 1647)

Professional witch-hunter Matthew Hopkins is one of the most notorious figures in the history of witch persecution. Calling himself the Witchfinder General, he profited by fueling witchcraft-related hysteria in England from 1645 to 1646, and in that one year was responsible for the executions of over two hundred accused witches. Moreover, he brought hundreds of people to trial who would not even have been accused as witches without his involvement.

Hopkins worked hard to increase the number of witches he caught and thus secure his reputation as a witch-hunter. Money also likely played a role in Hopkins's motives. His fee was forty shillings for each witch investigated, and he received a bonus for each witch convicted; his profit per job was anywhere from four to twenty-six pounds sterling, depending on how many witches he could uncover and convict. (As a frame of reference, most people of the period made wages of sixpence a day, with twelve pence equaling a shilling and twenty shillings equaling a pound.) By encouraging fears of witchcraft, Hopkins obviously profited considerably; some of his cases involved dozens of investigations. For example, he initiated witch investigations in Suffolk, England, against approximately 200 people, resulting in roughly 125 arrests and 68 executions by hanging.

Notorious for his relentless pursuit of suspected witches, Matthew Hopkins profited by hunting and torturing accused witches throughout England.

To achieve such numbers, Hopkins typically singled out a few people as suspected witches and then tortured them until they confessed and provided the names of people they claimed to have seen at witches' Sabbats. His favorite torture was to keep his victims awake for days, during which he made them walk continuously and refused them food and water. Once they were exhausted and mentally confused, he would interrogate them in ways that would coerce or trick them into confessing. When coercion or trickery failed, he would try beatings and other, more brutal methods of torture, including tying victims up and throwing them into deep water. Only those who sank were considered innocent, because it was believed that witches could always float. In theory, the person who sank was then supposed to be pulled up by a rope tied around the waist, but in most cases designated rescuers were not fast enough and the innocent person drowned.

Hopkins did not learn his witch-hunting methods from any expert on the subject; in fact, he had little or no experience with witches prior to establishing his witch-hunting business. He was a struggling lawyer when, in 1645 at the age of twenty-four, he started advertising his services as a witch-hunter, working with assistant John Stearne. (Later he added a second assistant, Mary Phillips, who searched female witches' bodies for blemishes known as devil's or witches' marks that indicated a relationship with Satan.)

The first suspected witch that Hopkins investigated was Elizabeth Clarke, who was put on trial in Chelmsford, England. Like most of the people he accused, she was aging, infirm (she had only one leg), and disliked by her neighbors. Under torture she named five accomplices, and eventually they and about a dozen more people were executed as witches.

But although Hopkins got results, his methods troubled some people, and others were upset by his high fees. One of those opposed to his work, John Gaule, published a book attacking Hopkins's investigations and trial proceedings, *Select Cases of Conscience Touching Witches and Witchcraft* (1646). After the publication of this work Hopkins's business began to fall off, and his assistants quit. In 1647 he attempted to repair his reputation by self-publishing a pamphlet entitled *The Discovery of Witches*. In it he defended his actions and insisted that his motivation for becoming a witch-hunter was not money but a desire to rid his country of evil.

Shortly after this publication Hopkins disappeared. No one knows for certain what happened to him, although various theories have been proposed. According to one, Hopkins was himself accused of witchcraft and executed. More likely, however, he died of illness, given that contagious and often fatal diseases were common during his time. In any case, many historians believe that Hopkins the witch-hunter is the same Matthew Hopkins listed in public records as being buried in Manningtree, Essex, England, in August 1647. **See also** torture; water; witch-hunter.

Horned God

Also called the Horned One, the Horned God is featured in many Wiccan and Neopagan rituals as the consort of the Goddess. He was also the god of ancient pagans who practiced the Old Religion, on which much of modern Wicca is based. Some Witchcraft traditions feature him in a myth related to the earth's seasonal life cycle. In this myth, the Goddess gives birth to the Horned God, who grows up, unites with her, creates a new child, and dies, whereupon she awaits his birth so the cycle can begin anew.

The idea that the god has horns probably originated with the primitive practice of tribal priests of wearing an animal-horn headdress. This practice connected horns with magic and spirituality in the minds of the members of the tribe. Many ancient kings wore animal-horn headdresses as well, which led to their association with ruling power. Horns are also associated with male fertility, because in most horned species, the largest horns belong to the mature males.

In various Witchcraft traditions the Horned God has the horns of a goat, a bull, or a stag. The latter image was the one employed by ancient Celts, because it connected the Horned God to the forests in which they worshiped. Many modern Wiccans also prefer this image; in some of their rituals the high priest wears stag horns or carries or wears a horn or piece of horn. Both in modern and ancient times, the Horned God has traditionally symbolized not only the male life force and fertility, but also the sun. **See also** goddesses and gods; Old Religion; Wheel of the Year; Wicca.

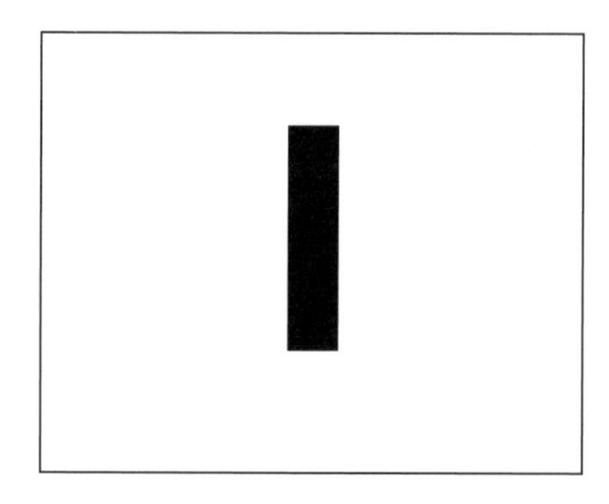

image magic

Image magic employs an image of a person against whom a spell is being cast. For example, in a spell designed to attract and keep, or bind, a specific person's love, the one casting the spell makes a doll (also called a poppet) representing the victim from elm branches, red felt, and a photograph of the victim's face. The completed doll is held above the flame of a red candle while the spell caster wraps red twine around the doll and chants a love-binding verse.

The basic principle behind image magic is that whatever is done to the image will affect the real person represented by that image. This is taken to its extreme with image magic performed to physically hurt the intended victim of a spell. In such cases, a wax, clay, wooden, or straw doll is made in the likeness of the intended victim, then enchanted and subjected to a variety of tortures that will cause the victim to suffer. For example, a wax doll might be melted over a candle to bring about the victim's death, or a straw doll might be pierced with numerous pins to subject the victim to a series of sharp pains. Modern witches do not typically perform this type of image magic, which is also known as sympathetic magic, because they adhere to a moral principle that requires them to do no harm. However, it is a common practice among vodun priests and others involved in black magic. **See also** binding spell; poppet; vodun.

Imbolc

Also called Imbolg, Candlemas, the Festival of Brighid, or the Feast of Lights, Imbolc is a Celtic fire festival celebrated by witches on either February 1 or February 2, depending on the Witchcraft tradition. The name Imbolc actually means "within the womb" or "in milk"; both meanings are references to the festival's connection to the birth of the first lambs of the spring season, which causes their mothers' milk to flow. The festival celebrates the expected arrival of spring and, in most traditions, the transformation of the Goddess from Crone back to Maiden. In many traditions the Maiden aspect of the Goddess honored at Imbolc is the goddess Brighid, whom many witches ritually invite into their homes at this time. In some traditions, Brighid is believed to be pregnant with the God's child during Imbolc.

Since Imbolc is viewed as a time of new beginnings, customs connected with this event relate to spring cleaning of the home as well as ritual cleansing of the body and of ritual tools. Imbolc is also a time for rites of initiation and consecration. The colors most commonly associated with this time are lavender, white, silver, and red. The herb lavender is used in many Imbolc rituals, as are candles, candle wreaths, and candle wheels in traditional Imbolc colors. Among some Witchcraft traditions and Neopagans, milk is poured onto the earth as part of an Imbolc ritual to encourage the start of spring. **See also** candles; consecration; goddesses and gods; herbs and other plants; Wheel of the Year.

incantation

An incantation is the recitation of words or phrases, usually rhymed, as part of a ritual to produce magic. Incantations are typically performed as part of magic spells, but not all spells feature incantations. The main purpose of an incantation is to help focus the intent of the person casting the spell. However, some witches believe that if incantations are performed at certain times of the day or of the lunar cycle, they will increase a spell's power. **See also** moon; spells.

incense

Witches use incense in ritual and magical work because they believe that it attracts spirits that will add power to their rituals and spells. Some also believe that the incense will carry the spell up into the spiritual realm. In addition, the smoke of incense is used to represent the element air in many rituals.

Incense can be made of many different herbs, spices, and woods, either singly or in combination. These substances contain oils that release fragrances and smoke when burned. In homemade incense mixes, witches add additional scented oils and colored dyes. All of the ingredients in such mixes are selected in accordance with the type of magic the witch is going to perform. For example, in many Witchcraft traditions sandalwood is associated with granting wishes and increasing spirituality. Allspice berries are used as ingredients in incense intended for spells related to money and good luck. Star anise improves psychic power, bay leaves are for protection and purification, and lavender flowers are for love. Lavender buds and lavender oil are also ingredients in an incense designed to attract romance; its other ingredients are sandalwood, basil, orris root, and rose oil. Some witches further believe that the time the incense is made affects the kind of power it holds. Love incense, for example, should be mixed during a new or full moon, protection incense during a waning moon.

Homemade incense is generally in powdered form and is not self-combustible. This means that it must be sprinkled over coals that are then lit to get it to burn. The holder used for the incense and coals is called a censer. Store-bought incense is formed in the shape of sticks, cones, or squares, and can be burned in a variety of holders. Most types of incense can be bought in craft and gift stores and candle shops, although only specialty shops catering to witches sell suffumigations, which are special blends of incense burned to attract spirits so that they will materialize. **See also** air; censer; rites and rituals.

initiations

Practitioners of witchcraft who belong to a coven typically have to undergo several initiations as steps to becoming a full member of the group and to learning various degrees of magical arts. Each initiation is a magical rite that invokes cosmic powers to aid the witch on her or his path within the coven.

Initiation rites vary according to Witchcraft tradition, but the concepts behind these rites are essentially the same. For example, each initiation represents the witch's personal and spiritual transformation. Therefore in many traditions the initiation incorporates a great deal of symbolism related to death and rebirth. However, this symbolism varies widely. In some traditions it might take the form of certain gestures or words, in others it might be manifested through some physical struggle. For example, in some traditions the initiate is bound with a cord and required to struggle to crawl along the ground, symbolizing the journey through the birth canal, whereupon the person leading the initiation ceremony severs the cord to symbolize the cutting of the umbilical cord at birth.

Witchcraft traditions also share the concept that initiation involves a substantial commitment of time, patience, and study. Most traditions will therefore not formally initiate someone into a coven until that person has spent a year and a day in preparation. During this time the apprentice studies the rules and rituals of the coven and is trained in the basic practice of magic. The path from one level to the next, and one initiation to the next, as the witch gains increasing knowledge of the Craft, involves similar commitment.

Most traditions share the belief that initiations should take place within a magic circle. In many traditions the initiate must enter this circle blindfolded with hands bound. One member of the coven leads the initiation; in most traditions, a female must be initiated by a male and vice versa. However, some traditions allow a mother to initiate a daughter or a father to initiate a son. In most cases, the coven requires initiates to be over the age of twenty-one, believing that this is the point at which people are fully able to take on the responsibility and secrecy that being a part of the coven requires.

Another belief shared by most traditions is that the initiator should be of a degree higher than the person being initiated. In other words, a second-degree witch can be responsible for a first-degree initiation but not a third-degree one; a third-degree witch can be responsible for any degree of initiation, while a first-degree witch can be responsible for none. In some traditions, however, every member of the coven is on equal footing with all other members and can perform all rituals as high priestesses or priests once they have themselves undergone first-degree initiation.

The largest number of initiation variations among traditions relates to such minor details as which ritual tools are used or the exact words that are spoken. However, the Gardnerian Tradition, on which many other traditions are based, serves as a model for many covens, Gardnerian or not. In the Gardnerian Tradition, the first-degree initiation begins with an act called the taking of the measure. A red thread or cord is used to measure the initiate from the crown of the head to the heel of the foot, and this thread is then tied around the left arm.

Red is the color typically used for first-degree initiates because it symbolizes the passion that person applies to learning the Craft. Cords used in rituals associated with second- and third-degree initiations are usually green and blue, respectively, because green symbolizes being a part of the earth and blue a part of the heavens. Many traditions use cord colors, particularly those tied around robes, to designate a person's level of experience or initiation. Alternatively, each level might be designated by a different number of knots in the cord, or a different number or color of beads strung on the cord.

The cord used in the first-degree initiation is usually given to the initiate after the ceremony to keep as a symbol of the experience. However, sometimes the thread or cord is retained by the coven to show that the person is bound to the coven. Some traditions use the cord to work magic against any member who betrays the coven.

Loyalty to the coven is an important part of most traditions. In fact, coven members usually take an oath of loyalty at their first- and second-degree initiations. According to Janet and Stewart Farrar in their book *The Witches' Bible*, the oath in the Gardnerian Tradition is as follows:

> I, [initiate's name], in the presence of the Mighty Ones, do of my own free will and accord most solemnly swear that I will ever keep secret and never reveal the secrets of

> the Art, except it be to a proper person, properly prepared within a Circle such as I am now in; and that I will never deny the secrets to such a person if he or she be properly vouched for by a brother or sister of the Art. All this I swear by my hopes of a future life, mindful that my measure has been taken; and may my weapons turn against me if I break this my solemn oath.

Initiations based on Gardnerian practices also emphasize the importance of ritual tools, both through their use and their presentation to initiates. Both the first- and second-degree initiations involve bell ringing, and the initiate might be anointed with oil. The first-degree initiation includes a ritual presentation of the new witch's working tools, such as the athame and sword; in the second-degree initiation the initiate must use each of the tools in the appropriate fashion as part of the ceremony, following the lead of the initiator. In many traditions, the second-degree initiation promotes the first-degree witch to the status of high priestess or high priest (whether in the original coven or, if the initiate so chooses, in the establishment of a new coven), so it is important for the witch to demonstrate a firm working knowledge of the ritual tools.

According to the Gardnerian model, another part of the second-degree ritual is the descent of the Goddess, which requires the initiate to recite a legend involving the descent of the Goddess into the Underworld to seek the answer to life's mysteries and to learn magic from Death. In addition, the ritual requires the initiator to will power into the initiate, thereby exposing the first-degree witch to a new level of energy that will enhance future magical work. Once again, this associates the initiation ceremony with transformation. To symbolize this transformation, most witches take a new name during the ceremony.

The third-degree initiation exposes the initiate to the highest levels of energy and knowledge within a coven. In many traditions this is the time for the Great Rite, when the Goddess or God is called down into the initiate for the purpose of physically uniting with the high priest or priestess, who is also filled with the spirit of the deity. In recent years, an increasing number of covens have been performing this rite symbolically rather than physically. In either case, the third-degree witch is believed to have the closest connection to the deity, and with this connection comes the ability to perform the most powerful magic. **See also** coven; Gardnerian Tradition; rites and rituals.

Innocent VIII (1432–1492)

Born Giovanni Batista Cibo and elected pope in 1484, Innocent VIII is particularly notable in the history of witchcraft persecution because of an edict—officially known as a bull—he issued to encourage aggressive witch-hunting. Called the Bull of 1484 or *Summis desiderantes affectibus* ("Desiring with supreme ardor," the first three words of the bull), it required officials in Germany under control of the Roman Catholic Church to "remove all impediments" hindering witchcraft inquisitions so that witch-hunters might "exercise against all persons, of whatsoever condition and rank, the said office of the inquisition, correcting, imprisoning, punishing and chastising, according to their deserts, those persons whom they find guilty."

Requested of the pope by two Dominican inquisitors, Heinrich Kramer and Jakob Sprenger, the bull not only specifically ordered local ecclesiastical authorities not to interfere in any way with inquisitors' proceedings, but also called on these authorities to offer any support deemed necessary by the inquisitors. Kramer and Sprenger had encountered many obstacles to their witch-hunts in Germany; the bull effectively ended their difficulties with German authorities. Moreover, after they published the bull as the introduction to their 1486 guide to witch-hunting, *Malleus Maleficarum*, knowledge of the pope's edict spread beyond Germany, influencing church officials elsewhere in Europe. The bull continued to be seen as encouraging witch-hunting long after Innocent's death in 1492. **See also** Inquisition; *Malleus Maleficarum*; persecution, witch.

Inquisition

A tribunal, or court, of the Roman Catholic Church, the Inquisition was established in the twelfth century to investigate and prosecute heretics, people who publicly rejected church doctrine. By the end of the fourteenth century the Inquisition had expanded its activities to include cases involving sorcery and devil worship, although it continued to prosecute defendants as heretics. By the end of the sixteenth century, the Inquisition was directly responsible for the executions of at least thirty thousand witches, and indirectly for far more as laypersons gradually took over the job of witch-hunting from the Catholic Church with church support.

France, Italy, Germany, Spain, and parts of Switzerland all experienced witch-hunts and witch hysteria under the influence of the Inquisition. For example, during the 1320s, 1330s, and 1340s, French ecclesiastical courts tried and condemned approximately six hundred suspected witches on the grounds of heresy. In Italy, so many witch executions took place under the Inquisition that the leaders of several city-states, including Venice, complained to church authorities. In one city, Valcanonica, the Inquisition investigated over five thousand suspected witches, and in Como over three hundred were killed.

Religious officials watch as two men are burned at the stake. People suspected of sorcery and devil worship became targets of the Inquisition by the end of the fourteenth century.

Inquisition witch-hunters were priests who worked directly for the pope. Two of the most notorious were Heinrich Kramer and Jakob Sprenger of Germany. Their complaints about local officials' lack of cooperation led Pope Innocent VIII to issue a bull in 1484 mandating more support for witch-hunting among regions under the control of the Roman Catholic Church. Kramer and Sprenger then wrote a popular guide to witch-hunting, *Malleus Maleficarum*, that included arguments in favor of witch trials and executions. These arguments were used by witch judges for years to justify their actions.

Many investigators for the Inquisition promoted brutal torture, usually in three sessions, as a way to obtain witch confessions. The most stubborn prisoners were subjected to squassation, whereby the victim was fitted with weights as heavy as six hundred pounds, hung by the arms, and repeatedly dropped to the floor and jerked upwards, so that the shoulder bones dislocated and many other bones were broken. When squassation was performed more than three times, the victim usually died.

In response to concerns that innocent people might be tortured by mistake, inquisitors like Kramer and Sprenger insisted that if someone was accused of witchcraft they were far more likely to be guilty than innocent. Almost everyone who was tortured did indeed confess, which, the witch-hunters believed, proved their point.

At Inquisition trials, accused witches were not provided with lawyers or allowed character witnesses, and little or no evidence was required other than one witness's word that the defendant had practiced witchcraft and/or consorted with the devil. In many cases, the accuser was a spiteful child or a condemned witch who had been brutally tortured to name supposed accomplices. In either case, a conviction was usually inevitable. In fact, a summons from the Inquisition was virtually a death sentence. The only way for a person to avoid the sure path from accusation to execution was to bribe the inquisitor to drop his or her case; however, since inquisitors already had the authority to confiscate the money, possessions, and property of a condemned witch, this tactic rarely worked.

Executions were typically carried out by secular, local authorities, and eventually the secular courts began holding their own witch trials, as well. They usually followed the model provided by the church, with the same brutality and unfairness. As the secular courts increased their involvement the inquisitors stepped back to become paid advisers to their secular counterparts. By the seventeenth century inquisitors were largely uninvolved in actual witch trials and turned instead to writing witch-hunting guidebooks. **See also** Innocent VIII; *Malleus Maleficarum;* persecution, witch.

invocation

An invocation is a ceremonial process by which a goddess, god, spirit, or other such entity is called to witness a religious ritual or rite of magic and to protect those participating in the ritual or rite. The invocation differs from an evocation in that the entity being called is not being asked or commanded to act as a servant, only to confer positive influences.

Wiccans commonly invoke the Goddess and the Horned God during their rituals. This occurs, for example, during the event known as drawing down the moon, in which the high priest calls down the goddess of the moon. Also common is the invocation of the spirits of the four elements: air, fire, water, and earth. In some rituals, invocations begin with the phrase "by leaf, and stem, and bud" to call on the forces of nature. The words refer to the gradual process by which plants are born: Leaves push through the soil, then the stem grows, and finally buds appear. **See also** drawing down the moon; evocation; rites and rituals.

Ireland, witch trials of

Ireland experienced very few witch trials during the times of witch hysteria in England and continental Europe. In fact, there were only eight witchcraft-related trials during this period, despite the fact that in 1586 the Irish Parlement criminalized the practice of witchcraft. Moreover, the first Irish witch trial, that of Alice Kyteler in 1324, was actually based not only on charges of witchcraft but also on charges of heresy (defined as going against the teachings of the Catholic Church).

Modern scholars speculate that the reason for the lower number of witch trials in Ireland has to do with its relative isolation from the source of witch hysteria: books written by European witch-hunters. Ireland did not import many books during this period, and even those that were available could not be read by most of the population because of the high illiteracy rate. Therefore, the Irish did not hear much about the supposed dangers of witchcraft. In addition, the Protestant Church in Ireland, fairly strong in the northern part of the country, was not interested in witch-hunting, although elsewhere Protestants did rival Catholics in their zeal to rid the countryside of witches. In any case, the last Irish witch trial took place in 1711, although the law against witchcraft was not repealed until 1821. **See also** Kyteler, Lady Alice; persecution, witch.

Irish Faery-Faith Tradition

The Irish Faery-Faith Tradition is based on ancient Celtic religion, Irish folklore (both written and oral), and modern folk beliefs and practices regarding fairies (which members of the tradition spell *faeries*). In addition, trees figure prominently in the tradition because fairies are believed to live in forests. The tradition organizes its courses of magical study into units called groves, each of which is associated with one type of tree and with a particular holiday, color, type of wisdom, and so on. Each initiate into the Irish Faery-Faith Tradition selects one tree and its grove as a focus of study, then learns lore and magical skills and takes tests centered around the knowledge inherent in that tree and grove. It is said that each member of the tradition has a natural affinity for one particular type of tree, although sometimes a person selects more than one grove as a course of study. Members of the tradition further believe that fairies guide them in their studies and magical work. **See also** Faery Tradition; fairies; traditions, Witchcraft.

iron

Since ancient times, people have believed that iron repels evil. Ancient Egyptians put iron objects in tombs to protect their loved ones from evil spirits during the journey to the afterlife. Much later, medieval people routinely put horseshoes over their doorways so that evil spirits and witches could not pass through. Even today, many people believe that horseshoes hung ends-up above doorways bring luck.

Iron has also been used in the practice of magic. Its value as a magical substance was most likely based on the fact that it could be both attracted to magnets and itself magnetized. Medieval witches therefore used objects made of iron to fortify their magic circles, believing that when magnetized the iron would draw power. Similarly, they used iron nails as ingredients in potions and as part of magic rituals. Iron was also used as a protective amulet, under the theory that it would draw and absorb any evil magic directed at the wearer before that magic could do its work.

Iron's connection to witchcraft was not lost on witch-hunters. Girls claiming to be possessed by demons were said to vomit iron nails, and when they did this it was considered proof that the demons had been sent by witches. **See also** amulet; circle, magic; demonic possession.

Isis

An ancient Egyptian goddess of fertility, the moon, and magic, Isis is one of the most popular goddesses among Wiccans who worship deities of the Egyptian pantheon. Such Wiccans often wear the symbol of Isis, a design similar to the ankh that is known as the Isis knot, on bloodstone amulets that confer long life. In ancient Egyptian mythology Isis is the sister of Osiris, god of the Underworld, and also his lover. **See also** goddesses and gods.

Italy, witch-hunts of

As the stronghold of the Roman Catholic Church, Italy experienced witch persecution under the Inquisition. This Roman Catholic tribunal, or court, was established in the twelfth century to prosecute heretics (people who openly opposed church teachings). By the fifteenth century the powerful Inquisition was addressing cases of witchcraft and sorcery as well. Sorcery had been a crime in Italy since ancient times; however, witchcraft continued to thrive in rural areas of Italy until the Inquisition began taking aggressive measures to combat it. In 1484, Pope Innocent VIII issued a bull that encouraged diligent witch-hunting, and shortly thereafter mass trials and executions of witches became commonplace in Italy. In 1520 the government of Venice complained about the number of deaths that were taking place across the country due to witch trials. (In one mass execution of witches in Como, for example, three hundred were killed, and in Valcanonica the Inquisition investigated over five thousand suspected witches.) The church's response, under Pope Leo X, was to voice support for its inquisitors. Not until the sixteenth century did the Inquisition's role in Italian witch trials end, although secular courts continued to prosecute witches there until the eighteenth century. **See also** Innocent VIII; Inquisition; persecution, witch; Stregheria.

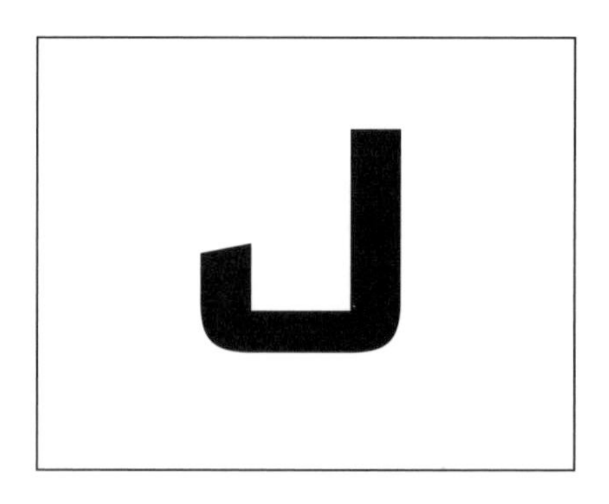

James I (1566–1625)

James I was king of Scotland from 1567 to 1625 (as James VI) and of England from 1603 to 1625. During his reign in both countries, he influenced public views on witchcraft and enacted laws and policies that at first encouraged and later discouraged witch-hunting, in accordance with his changing views on the matter.

In his early years on the throne, James was convinced that witchcraft posed a real threat both to society and to individual safety, partially because of an incident that occurred in 1589–1590. During that time, James and his new wife, Anne of Denmark, experienced several storms while aboard various ships at sea. Shortly thereafter, a coven of witches from North Berwick, Scotland, was put on trial. James, who had long been interested in witchcraft, decided to examine the accused witches himself. One of them confessed that the coven had used magic to cause the storms because the devil had commanded them to kill the king, his worst enemy on earth. Though James believed in witchcraft, he did not believe this confession, until the witch proved her powers by relating private information that only the king and queen would have known. James assumed that the witch had received this information through divination, a magical way of learning secrets that many people believed required the help of the devil. Once the king was convinced of their authenticity, the witches were condemned and executed.

Having been confronted with what he thought was clear proof that witches had real power, James became even more fascinated with witchcraft and demonology. In addition, he wanted to make sure that his subjects also knew that witchcraft was real. Several books had recently been published arguing that the opposite was true, including the 1584 book *The Discoverie of Witchcraft* by Reginald Scot. King James countered such works by writing his own book in 1597, *Daemonologie,* in which he described a variety of witches' powers, including—understandably—the ability to create storms. It also suggested ways to identify and test witches, along with guidelines for their trial and execution. The book was often quoted by witch-hunters to justify their actions.

Daemonologie went through several editions and was translated into many languages. A second English edition of the work was published in 1603, a Dutch edition in 1604, and two Latin editions in 1604 and 1607. Meanwhile King James tried to have all copies of Reginald Scot's book destroyed.

King James next turned his attention to opposing witches in the legal arena. Under his guidance, Parliament enacted a new statute, the Witchcraft Act of 1604, that established harsher punishments for condemned witches and broadened the definition of prosecutable witchcraft. Previously, the emphasis in witchcraft trials had been on maleficia, the causing of harm to people, animals, or property; judges based convictions on whether the accused witch had hurt anyone. Under King James's new law, however, judges were allowed to consider evidence related to devil worship, which made it possible to prosecute people even when there was no victim available to testify.

The 1604 Witchcraft Act also increased the punishment of a convicted witch. Under earlier laws, a first offense brought a sentence ranging from a year to life in jail. Under the new law, a first offense brought a death sentence. King James's Witchcraft Act, which remained in effect until 1736, therefore resulted in thousands of deaths. Interestingly, however, the majority of these deaths occurred after the king died. The reason for this lies in part with King James's growing doubts that witchcraft was a real threat. During his reign, the king encountered many supposed witches who were discovered to be frauds, as well as innocent people who had been unfairly accused of practicing witchcraft and/or consorting with the devil. Eventually the king began openly voicing his concerns about possible injustices in his courts, putting judges on notice to be more careful in their evaluation of evidence. They complied, and the number of convictions dropped. In fact, fewer than forty people were executed as witches while James was king, and only five people were executed as witches between 1616 and 1625, the year of his death. **See also** England, witch-hunts of; persecution, witch; Scotland, witch trials of.

Joan of Arc (c. 1412–1431)

Young Frenchwoman Joan of Arc heard voices and saw visions that eventually led her to go into battle against the English. Joan's voices and visions began when she was thirteen years old. At that time she told people that she had been contacted by three saints (Michael, Margaret, and Catherine) who told her to go to the dauphin, as the son and heir to the throne of French king Charles VI was known. She was to tell him that her destiny was to lead French troops against the English, who then controlled

Mocked for her claim to have had visions of saints, Joan of Arc was sentenced to death for heresy. She is pictured here at the siege of Orléans.

part of France and were disputing the dauphin's right to the throne. According to the saints, if Joan did this then the dauphin would ultimately be crowned king.

It took Joan three years to act on the saints' message. In 1428 she traveled to the town of Vaucouleurs, where the dauphin was staying, and tried to see him. She was turned away. The following year she tried again. This time she was able to convince the captain of the dauphin's guards to take her to him. Once in his presence, she convinced him that she was receiving messages from heaven by repeating his daily prayer, which no one but he and God could have known. This so astonished the dauphin that he gave Joan an army to lead into Orléans, where the English were defeated. Shortly thereafter the dauphin became King Charles VII of France.

Lauding Joan as a heroine, the new king sent her to lead troops into other cities still held by the English. During an attack on Compiègne in May 1430 she was captured and taken before a bishop intent on proving that she was a witch. Her arrest was politically motivated: If Charles VII had gained the crown of France by witchcraft, the English could argue that he was in league with the devil, thereby discrediting his claim that God had granted him the right to rule. However, Joan did not exhibit any of the characteristics of a devil worshiper. She was clearly pious, and she could pray and read from the Bible without torment from demons. Moreover, many people stepped forward to attest to her goodness and deny that she had ever dabbled in magic.

Unable to support a charge of witchcraft, an ecclesiastical court tried Joan on charges of heresy, since claiming that voices and visions came from anyone but Satan was contrary to church teachings. Moreover, it was also against church teachings for women to wear men's clothing, which Joan did before leading troops into battle.

With such clear evidence of heresy, in 1431 the court found Joan guilty and sentenced her to burn at the stake. Joan eventually announced that she had only been pretending to hear voices and have visions. She promised that she would obey church teachings from then on; when Joan signed a confession to this effect, her sentence was commuted to life in prison. This angered many Englishmen, who wanted her killed for leading the French against them. Historians suspect that Joan's prison guards deliberately refused to give her women's clothing to wear so that she would be caught in men's clothing again and again charged with disobeying church teachings; her original sentence of death was reinstated. Now certain she was going to die, Joan retracted her confession. On May 30, 1431, she went to her death once more insisting that her messages had come from saints. Less than twenty years later, Pope Calixtus III declared Joan's death sentence to be unjust and annulled it. By this time the English were gone from France, and the people were once again lauding Joan as a heroine. Almost five hundred years later, in 1920 Pope Benedict XV declared her a saint. **See also** England, witch-hunts of; France, witch-hunts of.

John XII (c. 1245–1334)

Baptized Jacques Duèse or D'euze, the Frenchman who became Pope John XII spent his life convinced that sorcerers and witches were trying to kill him through the use of magic and demons. On becoming pope, he attempted to stamp out witchcraft, going to greater lengths than any of his predecessors to accomplish this. In August 1320 he ordered a French Inquisition to aggressively seek out and punish anyone who practiced sorcery or witchcraft or who worshiped devils or otherwise consorted with or invoked them.

Pope John XII issued regular edicts, called bulls, to flesh out his definition of witchcraft and to put forth new ways to pursue the prosecution of witches and sorcerers as heretics. For example, a bull of 1318 ordered that if someone suspected of being a heretic or witch died before being brought to trial, the trial should still take place so that others would know of the person's guilt. A bull of 1326 emphasized that divination was a form of witchcraft and was to be considered a serious threat to Christian society. This bull and others of 1323, 1327, and 1331 also ordered new witch-hunts throughout southern France.

Ironically, Pope John himself was accused of heresy after he began preaching that saints in heaven would not be allowed to see God until the world ended and every human had been judged for worthiness (a concept known as the Last Judgment). This was contrary to the teachings of the Catholic Church, which held that saints in heaven were in the presence of God. Because of Pope John's divergence from church doctrine, actions were under way to remove him from his position when he died in 1334. **See also** divination; France, witch-hunts of; Inquisition.

Jones, Margaret (?–1648)

A physician in the Massachusetts Bay Colony, Margaret Jones holds the distinction of being the first person executed for witchcraft in the American colonies. There is no evidence that she ever practiced any form of witchcraft. However, if her patients refused her prescribed cures then she would warn them they would soon get worse, a diagnosis taken by some people as a threat: Accept my medicine or die. When some of her patients did die, Jones was accused of using witchcraft to kill them. During her trial, anyone who had experienced physical suffering while under her care testified against her. Her show of anger at their testimony was held up as proof that she was in league with the devil, a conclusion confirmed in the colonists' minds when a huge storm broke right after Jones was executed in 1648. **See also** America, witch-hunts of; devil.

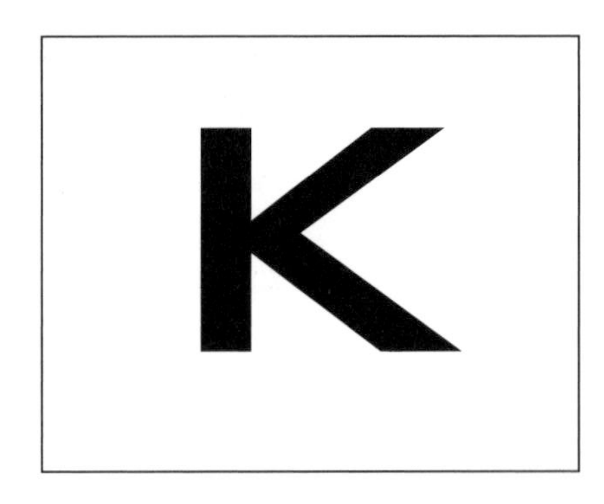

Kabbalah

Also known as Cabala, Kaballah, Kabalah, Quabala, or Qubalah, Kabbalah is an ancient and complex system of ceremonial magic and a form of Jewish mysticism whose concepts have been adopted by some occult orders and Witchcraft traditions. It is also a collection of anonymous writings recorded at various times from the eighth through thirteenth centuries. These works include *Sefer Yezirah* (Book of Creation) and *Zohar* (Book of Splendor).

The main concepts behind Kabbalistic teachings are that God not only created the universe but *is* the universe, filling every part of being; that from God emanate angels, humans, animals, and every other manifestation of creation; and that certain numbers, letters, and names can control these manifestations—even angels—when uttered as part of incantations within rituals.

To guide them in this magical work, Kabbalists use a visual representation of God's emanations. This visual representation is the drawing of a tree, the Tree of Life, with lines connecting various aspects of God. Under Kabbalah belief there are ten such aspects, each called a sphere, which on the drawing of the Tree of Life are interconnected by twenty-two lines called paths. These aspects include Hokmah (Wisdom), Hesed (Mercy/Love), Gevurah (Judgment/Power), and Hod (Majesty/Glory). Each sphere is associated with a different color, gem, flower, tree, herb, planet, angel, or other part of existence, and each sphere controls a different aspect of human nature, emotion, and activity. Moreover, each sphere is paired with another for balance. Under Kabbalah, all aspects of God are believed to have a male force and a female force; when Kabbalists unite these forces they create magic, just as a male and female unite to create life. Consequently when Kabbalists use the Tree of Life as a guide to performing ceremonial magic, they work not only with the sphere that controls their desired object or goal but also with its opposite. This not only creates magic to bring the Kabbalist the desired outcome but protects the Kabbalist from harm, because under Kabbalism it is believed that throwing the tree out of balance allows the Qliphoth—the destructive forces of the universe, as manifested by demons—to invade the Kabbalist's life.

Because of their knowledge of such things, during the Renaissance the Kabbalists were considered the most powerful magicians in the world, and their influence was widespread. At the same time, some Christians began using the Kabbalah under the belief that its power came from Christ. Kabbalists themselves believed that the source of their knowledge was God himself, who sent his angels to share the teachings of the Kabbalah with the first man, Adam. Kabbalists therefore saw the Kabbalah as a way to get closer to God. Meanwhile, alchemists were interested in the Kabbalah because of its supposed power to control the elements, believing that it could help them in their attempts to turn base metals into precious ones.

In the sixteenth century, however, the Kabbalah began to be associated with witchcraft and started to fall out of favor with Jews and Christians alike. Study of Kabbalistic teachings did not become popular again until the late nineteenth and early twentieth centuries, when occultists such as Aleister Crowley began to employ its principles in working magic. Today some witches and Neopagans also follow Kabbalistic principles.

In addition, most witches believe that the Tarot cards they use for divination were first created as symbolic representations of elements of the Kabbalah. According to this theory, ancient occultists from throughout the civilized world gathered in Morocco in approximately A.D. 1200 to develop a way to pass on their teachings; the earliest Tarot cards were their solution. As such, these cards contained the occultists' images and symbols, including those related to the Kabbalah. This would explain why the group of Tarot cards known as the major arcana are twenty-two in number. There are twenty-two letters in the Hebrew alphabet, and each of these letters corresponds to a path on the Tree of Life. **See also** arcana; *Key of Solomon*; magic; names, significance of; Tarot cards.

Key of Solomon

Titled *Clavicula Salomonis* in Latin, the *Key of Solomon* is perhaps the most famous magical spellbook, or grimoire, in history. Supposedly dating from the time of King Solomon, who ruled Israel from approximately 970 to 933 B.C., the work contains material regarding ceremonial magic and the control of spirits that was clearly drawn from the Kabbalah and other forms of Hebrew mysticism. However, since the *Key of Solomon* did not surface until the seventeenth century, when a copy of the book was taken from a woman accused of practicing witchcraft, modern scholars disagree on the true age of the book's contents. Nonetheless, two Witchcraft traditions—Gardnerian and Alexandrian—incorporated many of the symbols and rituals found in the *Key of Solomon* into their own grimoires, and witches from these traditions often use symbols from the Kabbalah and the *Key of Solomon* on talismans. **See also** Alexandrian Tradition; Gardnerian Tradition; Kabbalah; talisman.

Kitchen Witch Tradition

The Kitchen Witch Tradition of Witchcraft involves rituals and magic related to domestic concerns, e.g., the home and healing, which usually take place indoors. Herbs and other plants figure prominently in this tradition, as does a respect for nature. In recent years, Kitchen Witches have applied their practice of magic to concerns in the workplace as well. It is primarily a tradition of solitary practitioners, although friends might perform rituals together. The Kitchen Witch Tradition is particularly popular in urban settings, where it is more difficult for witches to practice rituals outdoors. **See also** Green Wicca; herbs and other plants; traditions, Witchcraft.

Knights Templar

A religious order of knighthood, the Knights Templar (also known as the Order of the Temple or the Poor Knights of Christ and of the Temple of Solomon) was the target of a fourteenth-century witch-hunt launched by its political enemies. The order was founded sometime between 1118 and 1188 by French knights in the Holy Land seeking to protect Christian pilgrims traveling to Jerusalem and to drive non-Christians from the region. At first the knights lived in poverty, helping others with no expectation of reward. As time

A member of the Knights Templar.

went on, however, the knights accepted the money and gifts offered to them by grateful travelers and others who applauded their order's work. Individual knights turned such rewards over to the order as a whole, which in turn invested the money and became wealthy and powerful.

By 1307 two people had begun to covet the order's wealth and felt threatened by its power: King Philip IV of France and Pope Clement V. Together the two saw to it that over two hundred Knights Templar were arrested on a variety of charges, including devil worship, even if they were living outside France. The knights were then tortured, whereupon many confessed to consorting with demons or doing other things offensive to God. These confessions were then used against the entire order. In fact, in trials throughout Europe from 1311 to 1312, simply belonging to the Knights Templar was evidence of practicing devil worship and witchcraft. Many were executed, including the head of the order, unless they were willing to admit wrongdoing and speak out against the order. Meanwhile all money and property belonging to the order were seized, either by the monarch or by other religious orders.

Most scholars believe that the assets of the Knights Templar were the motivation for the accusations against them. However, in recent years a few scholars have suggested that the Knights Templar actually did begin to incorporate non-Christian elements into their secret rites and rituals and perhaps might have been dabbling in witchcraft as well. The leader of the Knights Templar, Grand Master Jacques de Molay, went to his death insisting that all charges against the order were false. However, according to some stories, while Molay was being burned alive at the stake he said that God would provide proof of the knights' innocence by bringing about the death of both King Philip and Pope Clement within a year, and both deaths did indeed occur within the allotted time. **See also** France, witch-hunts of; persecution, witch.

knots

Since ancient times, witches have incorporated knots and knot tying into their magic. Knots are used primarily to bind spells, holding and releasing energy as needed. For example, even as late as the early nineteenth century, sailors would buy knots from witches who had imbued them with magic related to the winds. The actual object was typically three knots tied in a rope or handkerchief. Untying one of the knots would release a spell to create a brisk wind. Untying a second knot would create a much stronger wind. The third knot untied would produce a gale.

A similar knot spell popular in modern times involves the tying of nine knots in a red cord. Before tying the knots, the spell caster writes a statement of intent on a scroll. This statement is a declaration of what the person intends to achieve or obtain, with the help of the spell. As the knots are tied, the spell caster concentrates on the scroll and recites a nine-line spell, then says, "By the Goddess's hand, this thing is mine," to mark the completion of the spell casting. At this point, the spell has several variations. In one, the cord and scroll are kept on the witch's altar until the magic works and the spell caster's intent is realized, whereupon the scroll is burned. In another variation, the cord is buried instead of being placed on the altar. In still another, the knots are untied one by one at a rate of one per day, under the belief that when the last is untied, the spell's intent will be realized.

In addition to using knots to get something, in times past some witches tied knots to cause others harm. For example, in ancient Rome, knots placed under a couple's bed were believed to cause trouble in their marriage. Another belief historically related to knots is that intricate ones attract evil spirits, who can become trapped in them; untying the knot releases the spirit. Modern witches sometimes employ this concept by casting binding spells, which are used to restrict any evil magic created by the person against whom the spell is cast. In such spells, a cord is wrapped around a doll or image of the intended target of the spell, so that the target will not be able to send evil magic out into the world.

In practicing cord or knot magic of any type, color can be particularly significant. The cord is selected in a color that relates to the intended outcome of the spell. For example, a red cord would be used for spells related to love. Green is generally for healing and fertility. **See also** binding spell; colors.

Kyteler, Lady Alice (dates unknown)

The fourteenth-century case of accused witch Lady Alice Kyteler is significant for several reasons. First, hers was the first major witchcraft trial in Ireland. Second, her prosecution was based not only on charges of witchcraft but also on charges of heresy, defined as going against the teachings of the Catholic Church; at the time of Kyteler's prosecution, nearly all witch trials throughout Europe focused on witchcraft alone. Third, this case offers one of the many examples of witch accusations prompted by greed. Fourth and finally, it provides a rare instance where the accused witch was able to exact revenge on her accuser.

The accusations against Kyteler began with poisonous potions. An extremely wealthy and influential woman, she was married to her fourth husband, Sir John Le Poer, when he fell ill and decided she was poisoning him for his money. Her three previous husbands had also died of illness, and the men's children also suspected Kyteler of poisoning their fathers. These suspicions were confirmed when Le Poer searched their house and found a hidden sack of mysterious powders. He sent them to a bishop, Richard de Ledrede of Ossory, Ireland, who confirmed that they were tools of black magic. After further investigation, the bishop determined that Kyteler was part of a coven. He ordered all thirteen of the coven's members arrested, but Kyteler had powerful friends who helped her escape to Dublin, and on to England, where she lived out the rest of her life.

Meanwhile, the suspected coven members who failed to escape arrest were interrogated. They included Kyteler's son William Outlawe and Kyteler's maid Petronilla. Under interrogation and torture, some of the supposed coven members provided details of their activities. They said that they met to sacrifice animals to the devil, leaving the animals' dismembered bodies at crossroads, and to perform other rituals in opposition to the Catholic Church. In addition, both collectively and individually the witches had used magic and poisons to harm others and improve the fortunes of themselves and their families, cooking their potions in a skull instead of a pot.

Based on the details that the supposed coven members provided, some modern scholars believe that they really were witches. Others adamantly disagree. However, after Petronilla was convicted of witchcraft in 1324 she refused Christian last rites before being burned at the stake. The remaining alleged coven members met a variety of fates: burning at the stake; escaping the country; spending time in jail and/or being ordered to say specific prayers and serve the church through hard labor and community service. While these sentences were being carried out, Kyteler began exerting her political influence, which was considerable even from outside Ireland, to exact revenge on Bishop Richard de Ledrede. Under pressure, the bishop's superiors questioned his activities and accused him of heresy. He was then sent to the pope for further questioning. While he was gone the Crown seized all of his property. It took the bishop fifteen years to clear his name and regain his lands. **See also** Ireland, witch trials of.

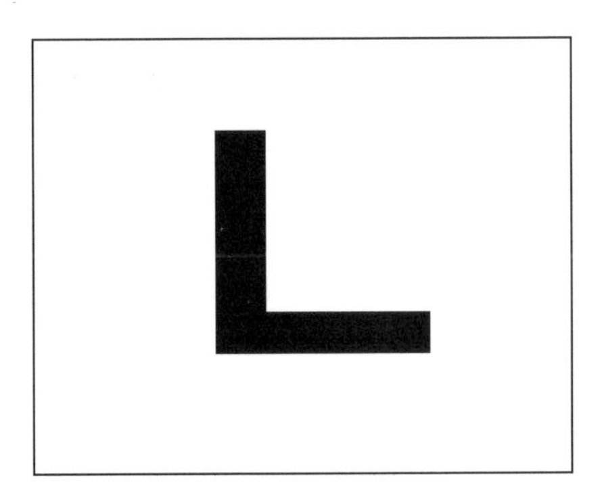

Ladywood Tradition

Established in 1982, the Ladywood Tradition arose out of the Pagan Way movement and incorporates many aspects of other traditions into its practice of the Craft. However, it emphasizes healing magic and environmentalism more than many traditions. The Ladywood Tradition is also unusual in that it encourages its practitioners to open their rituals to the public, and it promotes various projects designed to educate the public about Wicca. **See also** Pagan Way; traditions, Witchcraft.

Lamb, John (?–1628)

Seventeenth-century English doctor John Lamb became famous not only for his medical skills as personal physician to the first duke of Buckingham, George Villiers (1592–1628), but also for his abilities as a sorcerer. By the time he became the duke's physician in 1624, Lamb was already known in England as an occultist, having been convicted twice on charges related to sorcery. His first conviction was for using magic to kill a nobleman, the second for using magic to consort with demons. Both times he received what was a light sentence for the times: jail rather than execution. It is unclear who ensured that Lamb's life was spared, but it is likely that the duke was involved. The duke's wife was rumored to be a witch, and the duke was said to have dabbled in magic at least as early as 1625. In any case, in 1624 Lamb received a full pardon for his crimes and immediately went to London to work for the duke.

Rumors abounded about what exactly Lamb's work for the duke entailed. Many thought that in addition to medicine the physician was practicing magic on the duke's behalf; all manner of sorcery was suspected, and people began referring to Lamb as "the duke's devil." Finally in 1628 public sentiment against Lamb was running so high that when a crowd spotted him leaving a London theater they attacked him. Within minutes he had been beaten to death. Shortly thereafter his assistant, Anne Bodenham, published a book of incantations based on Lamb's magic. She also began billing herself as a fortune-teller and healer. Her activities were taken as posthumous proof of Lamb's guilt, particularly after Bodenham was put on trial for witchcraft in 1653. This trial included testimony that she had turned herself into a black cat, helped the devil acquire human souls, and sold poison to a woman wanting to commit murder; by accusing Bodenham of bewitching her, this woman was able to avoid a trial for her own crime. Meanwhile Bodenham was convicted and hanged. **See also** England, witch-hunts of.

Leek, Sybil (1923–1983)

English witch Sybil Leek fueled interest in witchcraft among the general public with the publication of her 1969 book *Diary of a Witch*, which she promoted heavily via mass media. Leek went on to write dozens of books related to witchcraft, including *The Complete Art of Witchcraft* (1971), as well as an internationally syndicated newspaper column. Leek claimed to be a hereditary witch whose lineage could be traced back to eleventh-century Ireland. She also said that occultist Aleister Crowley was a family friend during her childhood, and that he predicted she would become a prominent occultist herself.

Leek lived in the New Forest area of England, a region where witchcraft had long been accepted. New Forest was also home to many Gypsies, and while in her twenties Leek lived with some of them to learn about herbs and potions. After she left their group she became the high priestess of a New Forest coven. She also ran an antique shop in the village of Burley. There she gained fame by promoting witchcraft, and as her notoriety grew, tourists came from all over England to visit her shop. The crowds caused many problems in her small town, and her neighbors encouraged her to move elsewhere. Eventually she settled in the United States.

Once in America, in addition to pursuing her writing career, Leek became a professional astrologer. At the same time she continued to make media appearances promoting witchcraft. Leek was often accompanied by her pet bird, a jackdaw named Jackson who was said to be her familiar. He had great significance to Leek, because the ancestor with which she most identified—a seventeenth-century witch named Molly Leigh—had a jackdaw herself. **See also** Crowley, Aleister.

Leland, Charles Godfrey (1824–1903)

American folklorist and occultist Charles Godfrey Leland is the author of several books on Gypsies and witchcraft, including *Gypsy Sorcery and Fortune Telling, Illustrated by Numerous Incantations, Specimens of Medical Magic, Anecdotes, and Tales* (1891) and *Aradia: Gospel of the Witches* (1899). Both are notable for being among the first widely published books to provide specific information about Gypsy and witchcraft practices, respectively, including the words of incantations and spells.

Leland became interested in the occult as a boy, when he was exposed to family servants who believed in fairies, vodun, and similar manifestations of the magic realm. When he was eighteen he started studying occult texts, and in his forties he traveled throughout Europe studying Gypsy culture, becoming an expert in the subject. In the early 1880s he studied Native American spirituality, then returned to writing about Gypsies. While traveling through Italy in 1886, he met a hereditary Italian witch who provided him with information about Italian witchcraft, and he began writing extensively about this subject as well. His influential book *Aradia* is a work from this period.

In the preface to the book, Leland explained that *Aradia* was drawn from a manuscript containing the doctrines of an Italian society of witches that had survived since ancient times. This manuscript told of witches gathering naked under full moons to worship the Roman goddess Diana, perform magic, and ritually share cakes and wine. Leland presented this material in his book, providing details about the rituals, spells, and incantations practiced by Italian witches. Much of this information influenced modern witches like Gerald Gardner when they were developing their own Witchcraft traditions.

Throughout his life, Leland gave few personal details about his experiences with the Craft. In particular he refused to reveal the name of the witch who had given him the manuscript upon which *Aradia* was based, calling her only Maddalena. Various theories regarding her identity have surfaced over the years, but today most scholars suspect that she was a Florence, Italy, fortune-teller named Margherita Talanti. A few scholars also believe that while studying Italian witchcraft, also known as Stregheria, Leland was himself initiated into the Craft, although he never admitted to this. Leland was working on another book about Italian witchcraft when he died in Italy in 1903. **See also** Aradia; Gypsies; Stregheria.

Loudun nuns, demonic possession of

The demonic possession of nuns at the Ursuline convent in Loudun, France, in 1634 resulted in one of the most notorious witch trials in history. The defendant was Urbain Grandier, who had served as a priest in Loudun since 1617. From the outset of his appointment there he had been a problem for the Catholic Church because of his indiscriminate sexual activities. Many of the town's most prominent young women were reputed to be his mistresses, and in 1630 he was found guilty in the secular court of fathering a child out of wedlock—with the daughter of the prosecutor. Only the intervention of the Archbishop Sourdis of Bordeaux, one of Grandier's few supporters, allowed Grandier to escape jail.

Grandier was also an outspoken critic of Cardinal Armand-Jean du Plessis Richelieu. Chief minister to King Louis XIII, Richelieu was an extremely powerful duke with considerable influence in both the church and France's legal system. Many historians now believe that Grandier's outspokenness against Richelieu, as well as the priest's womanizing, eventually led to his undoing.

In 1633 Grandier's enemies apparently convinced the Mother Superior of the Loudun convent, Sister Jeanne des Anges, and several of her nuns to fake the classic symptoms of demonic possession and to blame their condition on Grandier. Once the nuns began convulsing, screaming obscenities, and speaking in strange tongues, two of Grandier's enemies in the Catholic Church, Father Mignon and Father Pierre Barre, staged an exorcism at which Sister Jeanne claimed that Grandier had sent the demons to torment her. She also accused Grandier of sending her all manner of depraved dreams.

When Grandier heard these accusations, he convinced Archbishop Sourdis to once again intervene on his behalf. The archbishop sent a physician to examine the girls, decree that there was nothing wrong with them, and end the exorcism. But Cardinal Richelieu was even more powerful than the archbishop, and he arranged for a new round of exorcisms to be conducted, this time in public. He also appointed a special investigator to look into the matter. Once this investigation began, many of Grandier's mistresses came forward with tales of his sexual escapades. The priest's debauchery was considered evidence that he had been consorting with the devil and had most likely sent depraved dreams to the nuns. The investigator ordered Grandier to send his demons from the nuns during yet another exorcism, but the procedure failed and Grandier was arrested as a witch.

Once Grandier was imprisoned, his conviction was virtually assured. He was searched for devil's marks and supposedly some were found; supporters present at the examination insisted that Grandier had no such marks. Officials of the court—all of them under the control of Cardinal Richelieu—ignored their complaint, along with the fact that some of the nuns who had blamed Grandier for their demonic possessions were now recanting their accusations. The court dismissed these statements as tricks of the devil, and Cardinal Richelieu offered to pay the nuns a pension in exchange for their testimony. In addition, some of Grandier's supporters were threatened with arrest on witchcraft charges themselves unless they kept quiet.

In August 1634 Grandier was found guilty and sentenced to be burned alive. He was then tortured so he would confess and name accomplices. Even under the most brutal agonies (including the crushing of several bones) he refused to comply. At his execution, he tried to make a last statement but several priests doused him with holy water and made noises so that his words would not be heard.

After Grandier's death, some of the nuns who had accused him continued to exhibit the most outrageous signs of demonic possession. Historians now believe that they did this because it brought them public attention, since their symptoms came to an abrupt end when Cardinal Richelieu punished their antics by cutting off their pensions. However, Sister Jeanne went on to become a prophet and a healer, and at times displayed stigmata, the physical manifestation of Christ's wounds on the cross, until her death in 1665. **See also** demonic possession; France, witch-hunts of.

Lughnasadh

Also called Lammas or Lammastide, Lughnasadh (pronounced *LOO-NA-SA*) is a harvest festival dating to the times of the ancient Celts. It is one of three such festivals in the Wheel of the Year, along with Mabon and Samhain. The word *Lughnasadh*, which means "Lugh the Long-Handed," refers to the Irish god Lugh, considered the Lord of Light. This festival celebrates bread, grain, corn, and all other by-products of the harvest season. Traditionally held on August 1, Lughnasadh features berry picking, baking, feasting, and ceremonial dancing. A common decoration at Lughnasadh festivals is the sunflower, probably because it comes into full bloom right before the festival. **See also** Wheel of the Year.

lycanthropy

While scientists believe that lycanthropy is a mental illness that causes a person to believe himself to be a wolf, most witches believe that it is a form of magic that allows a person to physically transform himself into a wolf. Just as many stories arose during the Middle Ages of witches transforming themselves into cats and other animals common to households and fields, so too did stories circulate about their use of lycanthropy. At the same time, medieval scholars and theologians debated passionately whether lycanthropy was possible; people were aware that at least some of the individuals claiming the ability to become wolves were deranged.

Except during periods of witch hysteria, such individuals were usually sent to insane asylums. But witch-hunters often promoted the idea that lycanthropy was a real magical skill whose practitioners deserved execution. Two such witch-hunters were sixteenth-century French attorney Jean Bodin and sixteenth- and seventeenth-century French witch judge Henri Boguet. Anyone suspected of using lycanthropy who was unlucky enough to encounter one of these two men was usually convicted of witchcraft and put to death, rather than being sent to an asylum. In support of their approach to lycanthropy, these witch-hunters cited stories of farmers wounding wolves only to find a woman in their village displaying a similar injury the following morning. Such a woman was typically arrested, tried, and convicted as a witch.

One variation of lycanthropy is involuntary transformation into a half-human, half-wolf creature called a werewolf. Werewolves were generally believed to be servants of the devil, and in most places persons suspected of being werewolves were prosecuted and punished like witches. In at least one case, however, the accused came up with an unusual defense that brought him a light sentence. In Livonia, near the Baltic Sea, in 1692, a suspected werewolf named Thiess insisted that he and all other werewolves deserved praise rather than prosecution because they did battle with witches and hated the devil. He described ferocious fights in which the agents of Satan were overcome by bands of werewolves from throughout Europe. Thiess's unique defense brought him only ten lashes and no imprisonment, but his positive view of werewolves failed to catch on. Even today, werewolves continue to be associated with evil. **See also** Grillandus, Paulus; hare.

Mabon

Also known as the autumn or autumnal equinox or Harvest Home, Mabon is the second harvest festival in the Wheel of the Year, after Lughnasadh and before Samhain. It marks the day when the hours of darkness and the hours of light are exactly the same, an event which occurs sometime between September 20 and September 23. The name Mabon probably refers to the Celtic god Maponos, who represented music and peaceful contentment. Scholars do not know for certain why many modern Wiccans began calling their autumnal equinox festival by the name Mabon, and members of some Witchcraft traditions passionately reject the association because they believe that the ancient pagan festival it honors was never called by the name Mabon.

But regardless of what this Sabbat is called, many Witchcraft traditions hold that it is associated with a gradual descent that the Goddess makes to the Underworld to try to recover her newly deceased consort (the God or the Harvest Lord, depending on the story). Such stories symbolize the fact that the bounties of the Goddess on earth are slowly disappearing and the dead of winter is approaching.

Mabon festivals recognize this change through various rites and rituals. There are feasts and offerings to gods and goddesses, usually to give thanks for the harvest, and group canning and preserving of food. Some traditions associate Mabon with grapes and wine, and their Mabon celebrations typically involve much drinking in honor of gods associated with wine, such as Bacchus or Dionysus. Other traditions honor the goddess Ceres, who represents agriculture. The most common colors associated with Mabon are those of fall leaves: yellow, red, and orange. **See also** goddesses and gods; Lughnasadh; Samhain; Wheel of the Year.

Magee Island, witch trial of

The 1711 Magee Island witch trial is notable for being the last such trial in Ireland. It also illustrates the fact that even when presented with rather striking evidence of witchcraft, people of the eighteenth century were inclined to deal with convicted witches far more leniently than would have been true in earlier times.

The case began on Magee Island, near the town of Carrickfergus, Antrim, Ireland, in 1710. At that time the home of James Haltridge was plagued by what modern experts in paranormal phenomena would call classic poltergeist activity: stones and household items thrown by an unseen hand, people feeling as though they were being hit or pinched for no apparent reason, cupboards slamming, and the like. In the eighteenth century such phenomena were usually attributed to witchcraft, which the Haltridge family believed was the cause of their misfortune.

The family's fear that a witch was attacking them via magic intensified after Haltridge's mother died and the violent poltergeist activity began to target one of the household servants, eighteen-year-old Mary Dunbar. Dunbar suggested that a group of witches had killed Haltridge's mother and was now sending demons to attack her. She named eight women as the culprits; seven were arrested and put on trial in March 1711. They were subsequently found guilty simply on Dunbar's word. However, their sentence was only a year in jail, although they also had to endure four sessions in a pillory, a wooden frame that locked around their head and hands, holding them in the public square for ridicule. **See also** Ireland, witch-hunts of.

magic

Magic as practiced by witches is the manipulation of unseen forces to achieve a desired result, such as the acquisition of personal wealth or the protection of a person, place, or thing. In their writings, most witches use the word *magick* instead of *magic* to refer to their witchcraft, to distinguish what they do from the pseudomagic used in stage tricks. The results of magic can be beneficial or harmful. Good, or white, magic yields beneficial results; bad, or black, magic, yields harmful results. Modern witches say they do not perform black magic, but they may perform countermagic, which is magic intended to neutralize or reverse another person's magic.

In practicing magic, witches use magic words, magic actions, magic rituals, and magic objects. Also called incantations or spells, magic words are a series of words or phrases that a witch chants, speaks, or thinks in a certain order while focusing mental energy on a desired result. A witch doing this is said to be casting a spell. Modern witches generally believe that the words in their spells are calling either on natural though mysterious forces within the universe or on deities such as the Goddess to bring about changes in their circumstances. In earlier centuries, however, they also considered their spells to be ways to summon good or bad spirits to do their bidding. During the Middle Ages and Renaissance, magicians, who were male specialists in magic, used spells specifically to call on demons or angels.

Magic actions are movements and gestures performed in accompaniment to the chanting, speaking, or thinking of a spell. For example, a witch might tie a knot or light a candle while casting the spell. Witches generally believe that without such actions some spells will not work or perhaps not work as effectively. In earlier times, many people also believed that if a spell and its accompanying gestures, movements, and activities were performed incorrectly, the person performing the magic might die.

When magic words and magic actions are used together, they embody a ceremony known as a ritual. The phrase "ritual magic" generally refers to magic that requires the spell caster to perform a complex series of magic actions, perhaps using detailed written instructions. This type of magic is also known as complex sorcery, ceremonial magic, or high magic. In contrast, low magic, also known as simple sorcery, practical magic, or folk magic, involves spells that require only simple magic actions or perhaps no magic actions at all. Modern witchcraft incorporates both kinds of magic, but in earlier times high magic was the sole domain of magicians and priests, while low magic was for witches. This distinction was related to gender, class, and literacy; most witches were uneducated women from the lower classes, and high magic was for well-educated, upper-class males who had access to occult manuscripts.

Both kinds of magic, however, employ magic objects such as amulets and talismans, which have been used by witches throughout history and are extremely popular in modern times. Witches "charge" small natural or man-made objects with magical power via certain rituals, then carry them to attract luck, good health, protection from evil, and other benefits. Witches also charge tools used in their rituals, such as candles and ceremonial knives, prior to their first use to imbue them with magic intended to keep away evil forces. Other items sometimes used in the practice of magic are herbs, dolls (called poppets), ropes, brooms, incense, and bowls of water.

Over the centuries, people have disagreed about the origin of the unseen forces that produce magic (if magic is indeed real, which has long been another point of contention). In ancient times, magic was viewed as being created by deities, nature spirits, and/or natural elements like moonlight, which the magician could learn to call upon to achieve desired results. By the thirteenth century, people had decided that the external forces that created magic were not natural but supernatural—specifically, either angels or demons. By the sixteenth century, the Catholic Church had decreed that all magic was the result of demonic forces.

During the seventeenth and eighteenth centuries, some people continued to believe that demons were the agents of magic, while others thought that spirits of the dead might be responsible. In any case, the prevailing view was that dabbling in magic could be dangerous. Cautionary tales of magicians who were injured or killed while calling on demons and spirits, perhaps because the magician did not recite a spell perfectly, were plentiful. In addition, it was believed that if a magician did not perform his spells within a protective magic circle, or if he allowed any part of his body to cross that boundary, a demon or spirit would grab him and carry him away to some otherworldly place.

During the late eighteenth century, however, people began to suggest that magic was created at least in part by energy com-

A witch performs an incantation to brew up a storm. While people disagree about the forces that produce magic, most believe that magic spells require mental energy and a summoning of energy in nature.

ing from within the magician, and by the nineteenth century this was the common view. In light of this new belief, though they still consulted ancient writings on magical systems such as the Kabbalah, occultists increasingly developed new ideas about how magic worked and should be performed.

In the early twentieth century, British occultist Aleister Crowley expanded on existing theories in proposing his own theory on how magic worked. He said that when a magician's personal will and imagination were heightened and focused through certain rituals, they could be used to access and direct nature's energy, thereby creating magic. Since Crowley was influential in the modern witchcraft movement, his beliefs increasingly led twentieth-century witches to emphasize the importance of the magician's will and personal spirituality as opposed to external forces.

Today, although modern witches acknowledge that nature's energy is still a part of magic and generally perform their magic at times when they believe this energy is at its peak, such as when the moon is full, they also believe that superior mental abilities, psychic talents, and other hereditary qualities make certain witches better at working magic than others. Moreover, because they believe that magic is largely dependent upon mental energy, modern witches often meditate, chant, go into a trance, or otherwise alter their mental state before attempting to work magic. They believe that these activities raise their power and perhaps connect them to deities.

Similarly, witches believe that the rituals, spells, and incantations involved with producing magic are there primarily to help them focus their mental energy so they can fully visualize a desired result. Some even think that the details of the rituals are unimportant; to them, spontaneity is acceptable as long as it helps increase mental energy. Their goal is to mentally turn a desire into concentrated energy—a "thought form"—and send it into the astral plane, which they believe is a receptacle for the energy of the universe. Once there, the thought form will theoretically manifest itself, in the form of the desire it represents, on the physical plane as well. This is one meaning of the common witch phrase, "As above, so below." **See also** Hermetica; magicians; sorcery; spells.

magicians

Magicians are male practitioners of magic, usually high magic, which involves the invocation of spirits and/or deities as part of complex, powerful magical rituals. Like witches, they cast spells in the practice of magic, but unlike most witches they do not typically honor goddesses. Instead most magicians believe that they derive their power from God, and some call on Christian angels or demons in their magical work.

Another common word for a magician is wizard, from the Middle English word *wisard*, which means "one who is habitually or excessively wise." Some people also use the term *sorcerer* interchangeably with *magician*, although when the word *sorcerer* was first used in the fourteenth century, it referred only to practitioners of divination and astrology.

The first magicians were Persian astrologer-priests who accompanied Persian king Xerxes I when he invaded Greece during the Persian Wars (500 B.C.–449 B.C.). The Greeks called them *magos*, from which the word *magician* is derived. From the time of the *magos* until the thirteenth century, magicians were highly respected for their skills and for their knowledge of the future and the workings of the universe. Many rulers therefore relied on magicians for advice. (Some historians believe that Merlin, who appears in Arthurian legends as adviser to King Arthur of England, was modeled on such an individual.) Nonetheless, in the thirteenth century the Inquisition of the Roman Catholic Church condemned magicians as devil worshipers and began putting them on trial for heresy.

However, church persecution of magicians never approached witch persecution in number or intensity. The fact that magicians were learned, respected men, whereas most witches were poor, uneducated women perhaps explains this prejudice. Indeed, some sixteenth-century magicians were so well respected, and usually politically powerful as well, that they could practice magic openly with little or no fear of arrest; these men included John Dee, Paracelsus, and Agrippa von Nettesheim. However, the church faithful spread stories about the dangers of practicing magic—such as tales about Faust, a magician who came to a bad end because of a pact with the devil—as a way to discourage others from following in these men's footsteps.

Still, the practice of magic continued, and by the seventeenth and eighteenth centuries, when witch-hunting had largely ended, magicians formed groups dedicated to the occult. These groups increased in popularity during the nineteenth century, and some remain in existence today. However, in the twentieth century the modern witchcraft movement attracted many participants who might otherwise have joined occult groups, and today there are more witches than magicians. **See also** Agrippa von Nettesheim, Heinrich Cornelius; Dee, John; Faust; magic; Paracelsus; sorcery; wizard.

maleficia

Maleficia refers to magic that is specifically intended to cause harm to people, animals, or property. The first trials against accused witches involved cases of maleficia, and of these the first complaints involved instances where one neighbor accused another of using witchcraft to destroy crops or animals. As time went on, witches were increasingly accused of committing murder by magic, particularly when an infant died of no apparent cause, and eventually other forms of calamity were suspected of being the result of witchcraft as well: problems with love or money, bad luck, bad weather, minor illnesses, and the like. For example, in seventeenth-century Germany, one man claimed that sixty-six-year-old Chatrina Blanckenstein was a witch because his cart had overturned in front of her house. She was also accused of murdering a baby via witchcraft because the child died four days after eating some of Blanckenstein's homemade jam.

Maleficia was also of great concern to the creators of laws related to witchcraft. Initially such laws distinguished between types of witchcraft that caused harm and those that produced no victims, such as various forms of divination. For example, the Carolina Code, a 1532 set of laws that governed entities under the control of the Holy Roman Empire, specifically stated that fortunetellers were not to be tortured, nor sentenced to jail if convicted. Instead they were only to be punished with whippings or fines, unless their actions had caused financial or personal harm, in which case jail might be appropriate. The same criterion was used to determine a convicted witch's sentence under the Carolina Code. A witch who had harmed others was to be burned to death, whereas one who had caused no harm would be spared to serve time in jail (the duration to be decided by the court) or to receive some other form of punishment. By the seventeenth century, however, these distinctions had been eliminated, largely under pressure from witch-hunters. Instead of requiring evidence of maleficia in order to condemn a witch, the new standard for conviction became proof of consorting with the devil. Such proof did not have to be hard evidence; many witches were executed based on another person's word that they had engaged in some kind of activity believed to involve or be sanctioned by the devil. In fact, some seventeenth-century witch trial judges considered feeding an evil spirit—which usually assumed the form of an ordinary household animal—a serious enough offense to warrant a death sentence. **See also** Carolina Code; persecution, witch; witch-hunter.

Malleus Maleficarum

The 1486 book *Malleus Maleficarum* (*Witches' Hammer*) by Heinrich Kramer and Jakob Sprenger is one of the most famous written works on the subject of witchcraft, and most likely the one that most influenced the witch persecutions in continental Europe. The book was essentially a guidebook on how to find and prosecute witches.

The book's contents were comprehensive. It described a variety of witches' activities, including infanticide, cannibalism, and all manner of sexual perversions, usually performed with demons. The authors advocated the use of brutal torture to extract confessions from suspected witches. The work also argued that witches were more likely to be women than men because the biblical tale of Eve in the Garden of Eden showed that women could not resist the devil's temptations. It further argued that most accused witches were guilty, even if the devil helped them disguise their guilt, and that the Bible commanded that all witches be put to death. The authors of *Malleus Maleficarum* also suggested that judges who did not convict witches might themselves be the devil's tools.

The ideas presented in the book not only justified but encouraged the mass execution of suspected witches. This was the intent of its authors. Kramer and Sprenger wrote *Malleus Maleficarum* while working as inquisitors in Germany, and they were displeased by the resistance they encountered to their witch-hunting efforts. After their book was published, support for witch-hunts increased throughout Europe. *Malleus Maleficarum* was extremely popular and went through over two dozen editions and multiple translations, although apparently no English version appeared until 1584. Nearly two hundred years later, the book was still popular and still inspiring witch executions. **See also** Germany, witch-hunts of; Inquisition; persecution, witch.

mandrake

Native to parts of southern Europe, the Mediterranean, and the Near East, the mandrake is a plant with an unusual-looking root that has been associated with magic since the Middle Ages. There are six varieties of mandrake comprising the Latin genus *Mandragora;* the shape of their roots vary, but in most cases it approximates the human form. Consequently some medieval Europeans believed that the right magic could turn the mandrake into a witch's or sorcerer's familiar, a servant who could do their bidding. During the seventeenth-century, several suspected witches on trial in Europe were accused of possessing mandrake familiars.

Mandrakes were also believed to have magical powers even when not turned into familiars. From the Middle Ages to the present, pieces of mandrake root have been carried as lucky amulets, and whole mandrake roots, particularly those most closely resembling tiny humans, have been prized as powerful attractants of wealth and good fortune in the areas of romance, sexuality, and fertility.

Acquiring mandrake roots actually requires no special skill, but in medieval times many stories sprang up about how difficult the job was. Historians believe that these stories were invented by mandrake sellers wanting to keep the high profits gained in their profession for themselves. It was said, for example, that the plant screamed when pulled from the ground, with a sound so loud and frightening that it could cause insanity or death. Death might also come if a person inhaled too much of the mandrake's powerful scent. Moreover, special rituals had to be followed to maintain the mandrake root's power while removing it from the ground. For example, some said it could only be removed as the sun set, after drawing three magic circles around the plants, and the root could only be loosened from the earth with an ivory staff. Furthermore, if someone touched the root during this process that person would fall dead. The most dangerous and consequently the most powerful root was said to be one that had grown at the base of an executioner's gallows.

Because of the supposed dangers, various means of pulling the mandrake root out of the ground without touching it were employed. One of the most common techniques mentioned in folklore was to tie the plant to a dog who would then tug it out and die. Once the root was up, the person who had acquired it for the purpose of creating a familiar was supposed to put the root in a glass jar filled with red dirt. Placed in sunlight and watered daily with human blood, the plant would come alive within a few days. Alternatively, someone who wanted the mandrake root as an amulet or talisman would not water it but let it dry out.

In Britain, where true mandrake does not grow, witches substituted the roots of a plant called a briony, which came to be known as the English mandrake. Their recipes for familiars required them to dig up the root under a full moon, carve it into the shape of a real mandrake (i.e., a tiny person), and then bury it again until the next full moon, whereupon it would be dried and placed in a box. If all went well, at the next witches' Sabbat the devil would turn the root into a familiar. In potions, English mandrake did not have the same medicinal powers as the real mandrake, but witches believed its magic would compensate for this shortcoming.

Real mandrake has long been used as a medicine. It was one of the first natural anaesthetics, administered in ancient times either as a drink made by boiling the root in wine or as an inhalant made by soaking a cloth in such a solution. Either would induce a deep sleep, although too large a dose could kill. In addition, ancient Greek physicians gave dental patients mandrake root to chew as an anaesthetic. Meanwhile the Arabs believed it to be an aphrodisiac and the Hebrews considered it to be hallucinogenic. **See also** familiar; herbs and other plants; poisons.

marks, witches' or devil's

During the witch-hunting times in Europe and North America, witch-hunters insisted that any unusual mark on a person's body was a sign that the person had made a pact with the devil and was therefore a witch. These marks, which were called witches' marks, devil's marks, or *sigillum diaboli* (Latin for "devil's seal"), included birthmarks, scars, and any scaly patches of skin that did not bleed when stuck with a pin. Some witch-hunters also included moles and pimples in their list of suspicious marks, although others ruled out such ordinary blemishes as indicators of a devil's pact. However, most witch-hunters agreed that a true devil's mark did not appear anyplace on the body easily seen by others. In other words, a strange pimple on the face was rarely taken to be a devil's mark, but the same pimple in an armpit was considered a sure sign of guilt. Other places the devil was thought to mark were within the genitals, under the breasts, within folds of skin, under eyelids, behind the ears, and behind the knees.

There were various stories about the methods that the devil used to make such marks, including licking, branding, beating, and clawing the witch. Some said that the marks were teats made by demons who suck witches' blood. In addition, most medieval people thought that the marks were part of a witch's initiation into a coven, which was presided over by the devil himself.

To find devil's marks, witch-hunters typically undressed suspected witches, shaved off all of their body hair, and subjected them to a thorough search, sometimes in public. In the early years of witch-hunting, only the most obviously unusual blemishes were deemed devil's marks, but over time witch-hunters broadened their criteria to include spots of skin that would not bleed when pricked with a pin and, later, callused spots that were merely insensitive to pin pricks. Again, these pin prickings often took place in public. Some historians have suggested that witch-hunters, financially motivated to prove witches guilty, used dull pins or even collapsing pins so that the accused witch would not feel anything when pricked. By the end of the witch-hunting period, witch-hunters were insisting that some devil's marks were invisible, making it even easier for them to label someone a witch. **See also** persecution, witch; pins; witch-hunter.

Martello, Leo (1931–2000)

Modern American witch Leo Martello was an influential author of books on witchcraft and a critic of Christianity. His many works include *Black Magic, Satanism and Voodoo* (1973) and *Witchcraft: The Old Religion* (1975). Martello wrote his first book, *Weird Ways of Witchcraft*, in 1969, whereupon he became involved in promoting witches' rights.

To this end Martello established two organizations, the Witches Liberation Movement and WICA (the Witches International Craft Association). In 1970 he began publishing a magazine, the *WICA Newsletter and Witchcraft Digest*, dedicated to sharing information about witches' issues and encouraging witches' activism. Shortly thereafter he established the Witches Anti-Defamation League, which was at the forefront for securing the same rights for American witches as are enjoyed by members of other, mainstream religious groups.

Martello also sought to educate the public about witches' rituals by sponsoring the first public magic circle, held in New York during the early 1970s. He continued such education projects throughout his life. In addition, he was an outspoken critic of Christian religions, particularly Catholicism, although he himself was raised a Catholic.

At age eighteen, Martello turned away from Catholicism and embraced the beliefs of one of his Italian ancestors, a Sicilian witch or strega. In 1951 Martello was initiated into a Sicilian coven. Four years later he became pastor of a nonsectarian worship group called the Temple of Spiritual Guidance, having received a doctor of divinity degree from the National Congress of Spiritual Consultants. Around this time he also began working as a hypnotist specializing in age regression. Martello left the temple and abandoned its beliefs in 1960. He then began searching for another form of worship to practice. In 1964 he went to Morocco to study its witchcraft; the following year he returned to the United States to study the Gardnerian, Alexandrian, and Traditionalist Witchcraft traditions, eventually becoming an initiate in each of them. These experiences explain why Martello's writings and political activism relate to a wide variety of beliefs.

See also Alexandrian Tradition; Gardnerian Tradition; Stregheria.

Mather, Cotton (1662 or 1663–1728)

New England Congregational minister Cotton Mather was one of the central figures in America's famous Salem witch trials. Like his father, Boston Puritan minister Increase Mather, Cotton Mather saw witchcraft as a serious threat to society. However, he was more aggressive than his father in opposing witches, calling for the extermination of all witches and personally intervening in witch trials to ensure convictions.

A Harvard graduate while still in his teens, Mather became involved in witch-hunting in his early twenties, when he was active in his father's ministry at Boston's North Church. He accompanied his father on investigations into cases of witchcraft and demonic possession, and over time he

Many scholars attribute the heightening of witchcraft hysteria in seventeenth-century New England to Cotton Mather's book Memorable Providences Relating to Witchcrafts and Possessions.

decided that his father was not strict enough in his dealings with suspected witches. During this period he also became fascinated with evil, reading and writing extensively on such subjects as murder and hell. He concluded that there was no such thing as a helpful, or white, witch; to him all witchcraft was connected to Satan. Moreover, Mather believed that all European witch executions were justified, as was the use of torture to obtain confessions. He expressed many of these beliefs in a 1689 book, *Memorable Providences Relating to Witchcrafts and Possessions*.

By the time Mather's book was published, New England had already experienced its first cases of witchcraft. However, many modern scholars believe that the work inspired witchcraft-related hysteria throughout the region. Mather also encouraged this hysteria personally. Considered a leading expert on witchcraft, he was often asked for advice by people conducting witchcraft investigations and trials. In such cases he always advocated harsh measures. Sometimes he even stepped forward with this advice without being asked. For example, when he heard that the life of accused witch Reverend George Burroughs was going to be spared, he approached the court trying the reverend's case and convinced its judges to execute the man instead.

When a rash of witchcraft cases developed in Salem, a town in the Massachusetts Bay Colony, Mather advised town leaders to proceed vigorously with investigations and trials. Shortly thereafter, the governor of the colony, Sir William Phips, appointed Mather to chronicle the events of the Salem witch trials. Mather took the opportunity to offer suggestions throughout the proceedings and was particularly vocal in expressing his opinion that the devil was responsible for the outbreak of witchcraft in the area. Mather did criticize one aspect of the trials, suggesting that spectral evidence—i.e., claims related to spirits supposedly seen by the defendants' accusers but not by anyone else in the courtroom—was unreliable. Yet he also pushed for convictions and executions of accused witches. For example, when one of the suspects demonstrated an ability to correctly recite the Lord's Prayer (normally considered proof of innocence), Mather argued that it meant nothing and the man was subsequently hanged.

After Salem's trials ended, Mather wrote about them in a book entitled *On Witchcraft: Being the Wonders of the Invisible World*, which was published in 1693. That same year, Mather became involved in yet another witchcraft case, this time in Boston. Again he encouraged aggressive tactics, but by this time the public was beginning to realize that the Salem witch trials had resulted in the deaths of many innocent people. In fact, even Mather's own father had begun to criticize the proceedings, and although he stopped short of saying that his son had behaved badly in advocating such harsh measures, people took his words as a condemnation of Cotton Mather. With so much criticism surrounding the Salem cases in general and Mather in particular, the leaders of Boston were not inclined to take Mather's advice.

As the months passed, Mather became the object not only of criticism but also of ridicule. The latter was fueled by the publication in 1700 of a book entitled *Another Brand Pluckt Out of the Burning, or More Wonders of the Invisible World* by Bostonian Robert Calef. Calef's title was a reference to Mather's book about Salem; *Another Brand Pluckt* made fun of the way that Mather had dealt with the Salem incident. Mather spent the rest of his life defending his actions as a witch-hunter, never publicly changing his views on how witches should be dealt with. Meanwhile, he lost the respect of both the public and the scholarly community. In his later years he watched other men receive honors that he felt would have gone to him but for the Salem trials. For example, he failed to get a coveted job as president of Harvard University, even though he was once considered an esteemed graduate of the school and his father had served as the university's president from 1685 to 1701. **See also** America, witch-hunts of; Bible; Mather, Increase; persecution, witch; Salem, witch trials of.

Mather, Increase (1639–1723)

New England Puritan minister Increase Mather wrote about witchcraft and gave sermons on that topic, suggesting that its spread was caused by Satan and that allowing it to continue would anger God. However, Mather also advocated caution during witch trials, saying it was better to allow a witch to go free than to convict and execute an innocent person.

Increase Mather attended Harvard University and was its president from 1685 to 1701. He was also pastor of Boston's North Church for much of his life. In 1684 he wrote *An Essay for the Recording of Illustrious Providences* to express his views on witchcraft. After the Salem witch trials, he wrote *Cases of Conscience Concerning Evil Spirits Personating Men; Witchcrafts, Infallible Proofs of Guilt in such as are Accused with the crime*, published in 1693, to call for greater care in future such cases. However, he stopped short of saying that the Salem witch trials were unjust or the executions unwarranted. Historians believe that Mather's reluctance stemmed from the fact that his son, Cotton Mather, had been an outspoken supporter of the trials. **See also** Mather, Cotton; Salem, witch trials of.

Merlin

Merlin is perhaps the most famous magician in literature, appearing in Arthurian legends as a powerful wizard and the personal adviser to King Arthur of England. Merlin was apparently Welsh, because his name appears to be derived from the Welsh name Myrddin. Some scholars think that the Arthurian Merlin was based on a real wizard who lived in Wales in the fifth century and specialized in divination. Others believe that the name Merlin was a common one for medieval wizards and that the Arthurian Merlin was a composite of many of these men. In either case, the person who seems to have first connected Merlin to Arthur was Geoffrey of Monmouth, who wrote several books about the wizard sometime in the twelfth century: *The Prophecies of Merlin* (supposedly a compilation of Merlin's prophesies), *The History of the Kings of Britain*, and *The Life of Merlin*. These books established Merlin's role in helping King Arthur acquire and hold on to his throne. **See also** wizard.

Midsummer

Also known as the summer solstice, Litha (apparently from the Anglo-Saxon word *lida*, for moon), or Midsummer's Eve, Midsummer marks the longest day of the year, which occurs sometime between June 20 and June 23. Midsummer is believed in many Witchcraft traditions to mark the time when the God is at his most powerful; from this point on, he grows weaker, just as the days grow shorter. Other traditions associate Midsummer with two kings, the Oak King (representing the lengthening of days) and the Holly King (representing the shortening of days), who are thought to fight each other until the Holly King wins the battle. Still other traditions associate Midsummer with fairies, believing that they are most powerful at this time of the Wheel of the Year.

Different Witchcraft traditions celebrate Midsummer in different ways. During Midsummer festivals, those who associate the time with the Holly King might perform ritual battles, while those who associate it with fairies might leave offerings for these magical creatures. Regardless of tradition, many witches consider healing magic to be particularly potent during Midsummer and believe that it is the best time to harvest magical herbs. In addition, most witches decorate areas intended for Midsummer festivals in the colors gold (for the God/sun), green (for the earth), and a variety of hues associated with fire, including crimson, orange, and yellow. They also light ritual bonfires and dance around them. Handfastings, which are Wiccan marriage ceremonies, are often held during these festivals as well. **See also** colors; fairies; handfasting; moon; Wheel of the Year.

Miracle of Leon

The Miracle of Leon was a 1566 exorcism in Leon, France, in which a woman was apparently cured of demonic possession. The focus of the Miracle of Leon was Nicole Obry, a young woman who began having convulsions, considered a sure sign of demonic possession, in 1565. She claimed that she had been possessed by the spirit of her dead grandfather, but a priest who attempted to communicate with the spirit declared that it was in fact a devil, Beelzebub. Obry was then subjected to a series of public exorcisms, first in her hometown of Vervins, France, and then in a cathedral in the city of Leon. Meanwhile her symptoms worsened; in addition to convulsions she cursed, shrieked, moaned, and spoke as Beelzebub, taunting those around her. By some accounts her tongue turned black and she developed the ability to levitate.

More important in terms of the history of witch persecutions, while speaking as Beelzebub Obry made statements that many thought implied that witches were involved in her demonic possession. Many of those who witnessed her contortions agreed that sorcery had to be involved. Some suspected that a Gypsy had bewitched Obry, others that her own mother was a sorceress who had directed the possession. Although no witch-hunts directly resulted from this case, long after Obry was finally freed of her symptoms, during an exorcism in February 1566, the belief that her now famous case of possession was tied to witchcraft persisted, and this undoubtedly influenced subsequent possession cases. **See also** devil; demonic possession; France, witch-hunts of; Gypsies.

moon

Perhaps because in ancient times moonlight was thought to be a source of magic, the moon is featured prominently in the practices of modern witches. They worship moon goddesses, hold rituals at key points in the moon's cycle, and associate each phase of the moon with a particular type of occult energy that strengthens certain kinds of spells.

The moon undergoes a total of four phases, also called quarters. In the first quarter, the time of the new moon, the moon appears as a crescent. In the second quarter, the moon grows from a crescent to a sphere; this is called the waxing period of the moon. In the third quarter, the time of the full moon, the moon appears completely round. Actually, it is only at its absolute fullest for one day, but witches believe that the power of the full moon, when the moon's energy is at its highest concentration, begins three days before it appears and lasts for three days after it begins to wane, providing seven days for full moon magic. In the fourth quarter, the moon shrinks back into a crescent; this is called the waning period of the moon. As the first quarter begins again, there are a few days when the moon is not visible because it rises and sets with the sun. Witches call this the time of the dark moon.

Witches associate the new moon, full moon, and dark moon with different phases in a woman's life: Maiden, Mother, and Crone. They also perform different types of magic beneath each of these moons, with the full moon being the most important in this regard. Every full moon is a time for an esbat, the witches' working meeting (as opposed to a Sabbat, which is a time for celebration), while the waxing moon is considered best for spells related to banishing negative energy. Other connections between lunar phases and Wiccan magic are as follows:

The Maiden. The Maiden is the new moon, a time for any magic related to new beginnings, new projects, personal growth, and creativity. Love and healing spells are also believed to be strengthened by the new moon, as is divination. The time when the new moon becomes the waxing moon is for spells and rituals related to change. Several goddesses represent the Maiden aspect of the Great Goddess, including Diana and Bridgit.

The Mother. The Mother is the full moon, a time for magic related to fertility and abundance, power, and protection. Many witches' rituals take place during the full moon, including cleansing and consecration rituals and rituals related to goddess worship, such as drawing down the moon. The goddess most commonly associated with this ritual is Selene, although other goddesses represent the Mother aspect of the Great Goddess as well.

Each of the thirteen full moons within a year is also associated with specific types of full moon magic. Although these associations vary according to Witchcraft tradition, in general January is for conception and protection spells; February for purification, cleansing, and healing rituals; March for spells related to growth (particularly of plants), exploration, and prosperity; April for spells related to creativity, love, and opportunity; May for nature-related spells; June for spells regarding personal decisions and strength; July for spells and rituals related to dreams and divination; August for health and family; September for endings and closure; October for peace and introspection; November for spirituality; and December for personal and spiritual transformation. Each year, one month has two moons; this second moon, called the blue moon, is believed to be the best time for divination. Every full moon is considered a good time to gather herbs that will be used in good magic.

The Crone. The Crone is the dark moon, a three-day period of no moon just prior to the appearance of the new moon. Unless a ritual requires the presence of the Crone aspect of the Great Goddess, often represented by Hecate, witches do not perform rituals or work magic at this time. **See also** coven; Diana; esbat; goddesses and gods; Hecate; herbs and other plants; rites and rituals; Sabbat; Selene.

Morgan le Fay

Morgan le Fay is one of the best-known sorceresses in Western culture. She appears in legends related to King Arthur of England as an evil woman—sometimes young, sometimes old, depending on the story—

intent on destroying him. However, on one occasion when Arthur was near death she magically healed him. According to some versions of the legend, she learned her sorcery skills from the wizard Merlin; according to others she learned them among nuns. Many modern scholars believe that the Arthurian Morgan le Fay has the same origins in myth as Celtic goddesses, fairies, and mermaids, the latter of which are called morganes in some ancient legends. Many witches, however, believe that Morgan le Fay was a sorceress who actually lived. **See also** Merlin; wizard.

An illustration of Mother Shipton. This famous English witch prophesied many events that apparently came true.

Mother Redcap

In England and Scotland, a redcap is a type of goblin, and since medieval times "Mother Redcap" has been used as a nickname for certain witches believed to consort with such goblins. Thus references to many witches named Mother Redcap appear in records of witch trials.

Mother Shipton (c. 1488–c. 1558 or c. 1448–c. 1518)

Mother Shipton is one of the best-known witches in English history, largely because of her skills as a fortune-teller. She first became famous by predicting the fates of individuals who came to her from all over the country. Today she is more famous for her prophesies related to world events, which many people believe accurately predicted events of the modern age. Although these prophesies, usually expressed in rhyme, are open to interpretation, many people believe that she accurately predicted such events as the invention of the automobile ("Carriages without horses shall go") and the Internet ("Around the world thoughts shall fly/In the twinkling of an eye"), the California gold rush ("Gold shall be found, and found/In a land that's not now known"), and the development of ships with metal hulls ("Iron in the water shall float/As easy as a wooden boat"). Other prophesies seem to have foretold the deaths of various English monarchs, major wars, the rise of feminism, and other important events. Some of Shipton's prophesies were clearly in error, however, including her prediction that the world would end in 1881. Still, the number of her apparent failures is so small that her supporters remain undeterred by them.

The details of Shipton's life are in dispute. Generally, however, people believe that Mother Shipton was born in a cave near the River Nidd in Knaresborough, Yorkshire, England; today the cave has been labeled a memorial to Mother Shipton and is a tourist attraction. Her mother was reputed to have been a witch, and according to some stories her father was the devil. Nonetheless, Shipton was raised in the local parish, according to one story, or by a local townswoman according to another. In either case, Shipton was apparently orphaned when her mother died while giving birth to her.

From the outset people said that Shipton had inherited her mother's ways with witchcraft. Even when she was a girl, rumors abounded about her use of magic to move things without touching them and to cast harmful spells on anyone who made fun of her appearance. (By all accounts, she was an ugly woman, and by some accounts she was physically deformed as well.) It was also said that a black dog—probably the devil in disguise, most said—often appeared at her side. When she married carpenter Toby Shipton in 1512, people said that she had certainly bewitched him, probably with a love potion, because she was so unattractive. By the time she was wed, Mother Shipton was already known for her prophesies. One of her predictions was that she would die when she reached seventy years of age, and this did indeed happen. Her death has been reported as 1558 or 1518, depending on whether her birthdate is stated as 1488 or 1448.

Many of Shipton's prophesies were collected and published in book form in 1641. Other collections appeared in 1667, 1668, and 1871. Modern scholars disagree on whether all of the verses in these books were really Shipton's or whether some were the creation of those who compiled them. **See also** devil; divination; England, witch-hunts of; potion.

Murray, Margaret Alice (1863–1963)

British anthropologist Margaret Alice Murray developed theories about the history of witchcraft that were highly influential in the modern witchcraft movement. However, most modern scholars have decided that her theories were wrong, although some witches still believe in them.

Murray studied archaeology at University College in London, then joined its faculty in 1899. She was initially a junior lecturer and later an assistant professor of Egyptology, a position she held until 1935. During her time at University College she went on archaeological digs in Egypt, the Mediterranean, the Middle East, and England; throughout her travels she studied various works related to witchcraft, witch trials, and ancient religions. These texts included *The Golden Bough; a Study in Magic and Religion* (1890) by Sir James Frazier and *Aradia: Gospel of the Witches* (1899) by Charles Godfrey Leland. Murray investigated various folk beliefs and witchcraft cases in England, then began investigating European cases as well.

In 1921 she wrote a book based on her research, *The Witch-Cult in Western Europe*, in which she theorized that a large, organized witch cult based on a pre-Christian fertility religion (most likely, she said, dating back as far as the Stone Age) existed during the centuries of witch-hunting. Murray reported that witches worshiped the goddess Diana, describing their activities in detail and providing such information as how many witches composed a coven, how covens were organized, and what kind of rites and ceremonies took place at coven meetings. Frazier and Leland had also suggested in their works that witchcraft could be traced to ancient times, but Murray's work was more detailed and seemingly better supported by facts. Consequently her theories were embraced by such modern witches as Gerald Gardner, who later asked Murray to write the introduction to his own influential book on witchcraft, *Witchcraft Today* (1954).

However, Murray faced serious criticism for her work because much of it was based on the records of witch confessions. Most of these confessions were obtained under either great duress or brutal torture, and witch-hunters extracting the confessions clearly had an agenda: to ensure that the people they wanted to execute as witches provided the same details about their activities as others who had been convicted as witches. Therefore Murray's critics argued that the circumstances by which the information was obtained invalidated it.

Murray anticipated these criticisms and addressed them in the introduction to her work. She said that no matter how they were obtained, the confessions were too similar to be dismissed. To her it was improbable that witch-hunters would have been interested in the details that many witches provided (such as the fact that covens had thirteen members), which appeared in many witch confessions from places geographically distant from one another. Moreover, Murray noted that witches from different locations and different time periods mentioned the same pre-Christian deities in their confessions, something that she believed was due to their religious beliefs rather than to witch-hunters' interrogation techniques. She was also struck by the fact that a few first names seemed to be extremely common to witches, something she believed was due to the fact that witches shared a common heritage and belief system.

In other words, Murray felt that there were too many similarities among the confessions to be dismissed as coincidence or the result of how the confessions were obtained. She persisted in believing that an organized witch cult had existed from the Stone Age to the present, and expanded on this theory in her next two books, *The God of the Witches* (1933) and *The Divine King* (1954). In the first, she discussed the Stone Age origins of the Horned God, and in the second she argued that all English kings from the eleventh to the early seventeenth centuries had practiced witchcraft in secret.

Murray also suggested that many of the deaths that occurred during these centuries among the upper classes, particularly those involved in politics, were the result of witchcraft. In 1945 Murray also theorized that a notorious murder in the Cotswold Hills area of England, a case that prompted many theories regarding the killer and motive but was never solved, was related to witchcraft.

Today most scholars completely reject Murray's theories regarding the practice of witchcraft. They simply do not believe that witch confessions are a reliable foundation for any such theory, regardless of their similarities, particularly since no other evidence has been found that corroborates Murray's conclusions.

Nonetheless, Murray's belief that witchcraft really was based on an ancient religion was adopted by those in the witchcraft movement of the 1960s. More importantly, modern witches used Murray's information about how ancient and medieval witches practiced witchcraft as a model for their own rites and rituals. Today their feelings about Murray's work vary. Some have decided that her theories were wrong, but they still value her contributions to their Witchcraft traditions, believing that the origin of such details as coven size are less important than the ancient religious beliefs Murray resurrected and promoted through her work. Other witches believe that many if not all of Murray's theories are correct or at least deserve closer examination. Some of these witches note that Murray's critics were primarily male, suggesting that the condemnation of her theories was yet another example of the same persecution of women by men that existed during witch-hunting years. **See also** Frazier, Sir James; Gardner, Gerald; Leland, Charles Godfrey.

Museum of Witchcraft

Located in Bocastle, Cornwall, England, since 1960, the Museum of Witchcraft houses over five thousand items related to witchcraft and the occult, including ritual tools, altar slabs, poppets, talismans, amulets, potions, herbs, books, manuscripts, and even the skeleton of a witch executed in 1582 in St. Osyth, England. Not all of the items in its holdings are on public display; nonetheless, the collection offers the largest number of such objects available for viewing. In addition, the museum uses mannequins to depict various scenes related to the practice of witchcraft and offers a great deal of information on the history of witchcraft.

The museum was founded in 1947 by occult expert Cecil Williamson using his personal collection of witchcraft-related items. These included many things given to him personally by prominent modern witches such as Gerald Gardner, Alex Sanders, and Aleister Crowley. Williamson faced great difficulty in trying to display these items, because in the 1940s most people still hated and/or feared witches. Consequently Williamson was forced to relocate his museum several times because community leaders objected to its presence in their towns.

The first home of the museum was Stratford-upon-Avon, England, which Williamson chose because, as the birthplace of playwright William Shakespeare, the town drew thousands of tourists each year. Two years later, Stratford-upon-Avon business leaders, who believed that a witchcraft museum was bad for the town's image, pressured Williamson to close it down. He reopened it at another tourist spot, the Isle of Man. By 1952 he had been forced to move again, this time to a location near England's Windsor Castle. As before, local businessmen pressured him to leave. After several more moves he finally settled in Bocastle, where he had room to display only a fraction of his extensive collection.

Williamson had other problems as well. In 1952 another witch, Gerald Gardner, had bought Williamson's property on the Isle of Man after the Museum of Witchcraft vacated it and established his own witchcraft museum on the site. He borrowed some of Williamson's amulets and talismans for his displays but died before he could return them. After Gardner's death in 1964 his heir, his high priestess Monique Wilson, claimed these items as her own and sold them to the owners of the Ripley's Believe It or Not! museums. Various stories exist regarding Williamson's attempts to get these items back from Wilson before the sale, involving a curse that he put on the woman and her ensuing miseries. There is no evidence that Wilson suffered from her claim of the amulets and talismans, but Williamson remained aggravated about the experience for many years.

Williamson sold much of his own collection in 1996, along with the museum buildings. His Museum of Witchcraft is now operated by its new owners, Graham King and Liz Crow. **See also** Crowley, Aleister; Gardner, Gerald; Sanders, Alex.

myrtle

The myrtle tree (*Myrtus communis*) has long been associated with fairies. According to folklore, fairies live in or near these trees. It is said that if someone wants to attract or appease fairies, all that person has to do is place a bowl of milk and honey, perhaps flavored with wine, beneath a myrtle tree. **See also** fairies; trees.

Mystery Tradition

The term *Mystery Tradition* is generally used in two ways. First, it is defined as the most advanced teachings of any secret occult or magical society or cult. Using this definition, some witches say that all Witchcraft traditions are part of the Western Mystery Tradition (as opposed to the Eastern Mystery Tradition, which encompasses various forms of Asian and Middle Eastern occultism). Second, the name Mystery Tradition refers to either the Men's Mystery Tradition or the Women's Mystery Tradition, two specific Neopagan traditions that feature teachings unique to the experience of being male or female, respectively.

In the Men's Mystery Tradition, initiations and rituals revolve around four essential elements of men's spirituality: Hunter/Warrior, Satyr, Divine King/Slain God, and Hero. Teachings related to the Hunter/Warrior involve tests of courage and physical strength; the Satyr explores sexual expression and restraint, the Divine King/Slain God self-sacrifice, and the Hero male nobility.

In the Women's Mystery Tradition there are three categories of spiritual experience: Triad Mysteries, Blood Mysteries, and Dark Mysteries. The Triad Mysteries are three aspects of daily life—forming the family, preserving the home, and performing acts of transformation (creating life, turning raw ingredients into food, yarn into knitted or woven cloth, etc.). Among some Women's Mystery groups the three aspects of the Triad are said to be Birth, Marriage, and Death. The Blood Mysteries involve rituals and magic related to menstruation and sex. The Dark Mysteries are teachings related to the moon, dreams, the Underworld, and the occult. **See also** aspect; Neopagans.

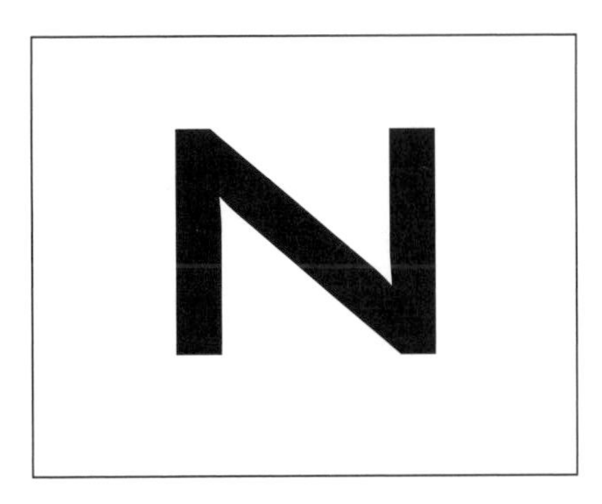

names, significance of

Names are extremely significant in the practice of magic. Since ancient times, magicians have recited the names of certain deities to draw on these deities' power or protection during the casting of magic circles and spells. This has been particularly common among practitioners of Kabbalah. Kabbalists believe that numbers, letters, and names hold great power, and that by calling out the secret names of angels and deities the magician can control them. Reciting secret names and other names of power is also a part of the ritual for necromancy, the magical raising of the dead.

Today many witches take secret names when they begin practicing magic. Such names are called eke-names or Witch-Names. These names are usually known only to other members of the witch's coven, or perhaps to other members of that coven's tradition. In selecting an eke-name, a witch uses numerology, the Runic alphabet, or another magical system to find the name believed to hold the most power and/or positive significance for the witch.

Numerology is also used to create a glyph, a magical symbol derived from a person's name. This symbol is marked on an object to create a personal charm against bad luck, illness, or psychic disturbance. In creating a glyph, each letter of a person's name is assigned a number from 1 to 9, and these numbers are added together until only one digit remains. For example, if the sum of the letters is 27, the digits 2 and 7 are added together to get 9. Each single digit corresponds to a particular glyph. **See also** Kabbalah; numerology; runes.

nature

A reverence for nature (typically capitalized among witches, to signify that it has a life force) is an important part of Wiccan beliefs. Most witches call upon nature spirits to aid them in their magical work, invoking them to enter magic circles prior to rituals, and generally believe that it is important to ask permission of nature before creating a magic circle outside or breaking off a tree branch to make a wand. In fact, some witches so revere nature that, in the case of the wand, they would take a branch from the ground rather than cut one from a tree.

Some traditions worship nature as Gaia, a Greek goddess also known as Mother Earth. Both Wiccans and Neopagans often invoke Gaia while performing magic or rituals related to the earth, herbs and other plants, and environmentalism. Because of their concern for nature, many witches are also politically active environmentalists. **See also** Gaia; Neopagans; trees.

necromancy

Necromancy is the magical raising of the dead in order to acquire some information from the spirits of the deceased, usually for the purposes of divination. In some cases, the corpse itself is actually said to be brought back to life; in others, only the dead person's spirit supposedly appears.

A kind of black magic, necromancy involves highly complex rituals, which since ancient times have been said to place the magician using them in grave danger. Usually a magician attempting necromancy does so within the protection of a magic circle; when cast properly, such a circle is said to ward off evil spirits. Because it is said to be so dangerous, most people believe that only a highly skilled magician would even attempt necromancy. In medieval times it was thought that only those who had made a pact with the devil were likely to survive the experience. Today, witches shun necromancy.

Over the centuries, a variety of published works and handcopied grimoires have included descriptions of necromancy and/or advice to magicians on the best ways to conduct their rituals. Some authors recommended certain times for necromancy, usually based on astrological influences. Others felt that the trappings of the rituals were most important. For example, it was recommended that necromancy be conducted in a graveyard, that the magician wear clothes taken from corpses—perhaps even from the body of the spirit being summoned—during the rituals or eat certain foods (particularly rotting ones) prior to performing necromancy. Some authors advised ringing a bell to awaken the spirits, others cited incantations, talismans, wands, or other ritual tools as critical to success. The number 13 was often said to be an important part of necromancy rituals, either because of the number's association with black magic or because there were supposedly thirteen people at the Last Supper, which preceded Christ's crucifixion and resurrection.

Many authors argued that necromancy would not work unless the spirit being summoned was from someone only recently deceased, under the theory that a person long dead would be neither willing nor able to return to the living. It was also commonly thought that the body should be subjected to certain practices after the necromancy rituals were complete. For example, some necromancers were advised to eat the corpse, others to burn it, still others to drive a stake through its heart. This was not true, however, with necromancy practiced to raise the actual body of the deceased rather than just the spirit. In such cases, the body was being raised to do the magician's bidding and had to remain intact. Such necromancy is a main part of the religion of vodun. **See also** devil; hand of glory; vodun.

Neopagans

Neopagans worship some form of pre-Christian pagan religion, or a blend of those religions, with modern adaptations; the term refers to a wide range of beliefs, rather than a single organized theology. Today experts in modern religions estimate that there are hundreds of thousands of Neopagans in the Western world. However, no reliable surveys have been conducted on this matter since 1981, when the Institute for the Study of American Religion used ownership of various classic texts for practicing Neopagans (who at the time simply called themselves pagans) as a way to determine that there were at least forty-thousand active Neopagans in the United States alone.

Scholars also do not have a complete picture of the worship practices of the pagans in pre-Christian Britain and Europe, whose beliefs form the basis for those of Neopagans. However, it is known that these ancient people were polytheistic, holding rituals to honor many gods and goddesses as well as nature spirits. It is also known that they recognized the importance of both the male and the female life forces.

It was during the environmental movement of the 1960s, when many people became interested in paganism because it emphasized a reverence for nature, that the Neopagan movement began. Neopaganism involves the worship of goddesses and nature spirits, and many of its members are active in feminism and environmentalism. Neopaganism also incorporates a collection of beliefs sometimes called New Age. In general, these include a belief in astrology, reincarnation, holistic medicine, the healing power of crystals, and personal spirituality.

Most modern witches also consider themselves Neopagans. In fact, many witches believe that their worship of male and female deities and nature spirits dates back to pre-Christian paganism, having been passed down from one generation of witches to the next. However, not all witches profess to be pagans. For example, Gavin and Yvonne Frost, who frequently lecture on Wicca-related topics, insist that although they practice witchcraft as Wiccans they are not pagans or Neopagans because they do not worship multiple gods and goddesses; for them, there is only one divinity, with male and female aspects within this one entity. In addition, other nonpagan witches practice witchcraft as members of religions other than Wicca.

There are also many ways to express Neopaganism. In addition to the form typically practiced by witches, other forms include Druidism, heathenism, shamanism, and Mystery Traditions. Druidism, or Druidry, is modeled after the paganism of the ancient Celts. Its followers use approximations of ancient Celtic rites, rituals, and storytelling practices. Some Druid groups also incorporate elements of early Christianity into their ceremonies, just as the ancient Celts eventually did. Heathenism is the contemporary term for the paganism of the ancient Scandinavians as practiced by Neopagans. It incorporates many Viking deities and beliefs as well as a belief in the power of runes. Shamanism is an ancient magical system, most likely from Central Asia, that includes the use of visions, altered states of consciousness, and a personal connection to nature deities. Mystery Traditions incorporate various rites drawn from ancient Greece, Rome, and Egypt. The Men's Mystery Tradition has rituals that center around issues related to masculinity, such as tests of a warrior's courage, and worships the Horned God. The Women's Mystery Tradition has rituals that center around issues related to femininity, such as menstruation and birth, and worships the Goddess.

Some Neopagans refer to themselves as pagans rather than Neopagans to connect themselves more directly to the religions of ancient times. Others refer to their beliefs as the European Traditional Religion, or the Old Religion. Those who avoid using any version of the word *pagan* typically object to its origin and history. The word came from the Latin word for "country dweller" and was first used to distinguish the folk beliefs of rural areas from the beliefs of the city dwellers, who were the first to embrace Christianity. Gradually the early Christians began to use the word in condescension, initially to suggest that pagans were inferior and later to suggest they were evil. **See also** Celts; Mystery Tradition; runes; shamanism.

New Reformed Orthodox Order of the Golden Dawn

Developed in the late 1970s out of a small group of occultists formed in the late 1960s, the New Reformed Orthodox Order of the Golden Dawn (NROOGD) is a Witchcraft tradition based in part on the occult teachings of a late-nineteenth- and early twentieth-century magical order known as the Hermetic Order of the Golden Dawn, which in turn based its teachings on ancient magical practices expressed in the Hermetica, the Kabbalah, and Abramelin writings. Members of the Golden Dawn stressed secrecy, and members of the NROOGD are secretive about their beliefs and practices as well.

Because of this secrecy, each NROOGD coven chooses its own deities and spirits to worship, and does not reveal the identity of these deities and spirits, even to members of other NROOGD covens. In fact, even the names of initiates are not disclosed to outsiders. Outsiders are also banned from viewing esbats, during which coven members work magic and/or celebrate their goddesses and gods.

However, at each of the eight Sabbats of the Wiccan Wheel of the Year, the group holds large public rituals open to anyone in the pagan community. These public rituals typically have three priestesses and one priest, while private NROOGD rituals involve only one priestess and priest. NROOGD rituals also feature numerous chants, and most ritual texts are in verse form.

As with many Witchcraft traditions, there are three levels or degrees of initiation within each NROOGD coven. The first initiation is the White Cord, which marks the member's entrance into either a particular coven or the tradition as a whole. The second is the Red Cord, which signifies that the initiate has fully learned the teachings of the tradition and is qualified to be an elder who can lead a coven and train and initiate others. The third initiation degree is the Black Cord. Also called Taking the Garter, this initiation is bestowed only by the gods; no one but the person receiving the degree can verify that it has been given, because this individual is alone when the gods bestow it. **See also** Golden Dawn, Hermetic Order of the; initiations; traditions, Witchcraft.

New Wiccan Church

Established in 1973 and currently located in Sacramento, California, the New Wiccan Church is an organization comprising people from several British Wiccan traditions, including Gardnerian and Alexandrian, who have been initiated into the third degree of Witchcraft. Called elders, these highly experienced witches join the New Wiccan Church for opportunities to meet others of like degree. The group sponsors local and regional meetings throughout the United States, maintains a library of witchcraft-related books and periodicals, and publishes a magazine called *Red Garters International*. It also helps people find covens within the member traditions to join. **See also** Alexandrian Tradition; Gardnerian Tradition; initiations.

Nordic Tradition

Also known as the Teutonic Tradition, the Nordic Tradition of Witchcraft is based on the beliefs and practices of pagans from Scandinavia and northern Germany. Its deities are the goddess Freya and the god Odin, and most of its rituals are connected to agriculture and the seasons. **See also** traditions, Witchcraft.

North Berwick witches

The 1590 to 1592 Scottish investigation into a group of people who became known as the North Berwick witches is among the most famous such cases in the history of witch persecution. There were anywhere from thirty-nine to seventy North Berwick witches, supposedly distributed among three separate covens. Their case initially attracted a great deal of attention because King James VI of Scotland (later King James I of both Scotland and England) questioned some of them himself, learned that they had been plotting to kill him via witchcraft, and strengthened his antiwitchcraft laws because of this experience.

The first of the North Berwick witches to come to public attention was Gilly Duncan in 1590. Duncan was a household servant who suddenly began exhibiting the skills of a healer. This unexpected onset of talent, along with her habit of going out often at night, caused her master, David Seaton, to suspect that she was involved in witchcraft. Since Seaton was the deputy baliff of his town (Tranent, near Edinburgh), he was able to confirm his suspicion by ordering that Duncan be tortured. Shortly after having her fingers crushed she admitted to being a witch; by this time, her tormentors had already discovered a blemish on the skin of her throat and declared it to be a devil's mark.

Duncan soon named dozens of others who practiced witchcraft with her, among them schoolmaster John Fian and midwife Agnes Sampson. It is unclear why Duncan named these particular people. Some modern scholars have suggested that Duncan really was in a coven with the people she named, while others think that when forced to provide names she chose respected people in hopes that they would escape persecution by virtue of their social standing. Unfortunately, once named these people were arrested and tortured in horrible ways. Sampson, for example, had her head repeatedly jerked by a rope, and the inside of her mouth was jabbed with sharp instruments. She was also kept awake for hours on end, and all of her body hair was shaved off so that examiners could look for devil's marks. (They later claimed to have found one on her genitals.)

Eventually Sampson confessed to over fifty witchcraft-related crimes, including the use of magic powders, keeping a familiar (a dog named Elva), and attending a Sabbat on All Hallow's Eve in North Berwick with two hundred other witches. Sampson reported that Gilly Duncan had been there too, as had the devil, and that all of them danced together. Both women said that Fian was the leader of their coven. He was tortured more brutally than anyone else involved in the case, and he too confessed to everything demanded of him.

Another key element of Sampson's confession was that her coven had attempted to kill King James using a variety of magical methods. They nearly succeeded, they said, by conjuring up major storms while the king was traveling at sea. Although such storms had indeed occurred, when Sampson first confessed to conjuring storms, King James, who heard her confession himself, thought she was lying. Then she told him something that he believed she could only know by magic: words that he had spoken to his wife on their wedding night. This knowledge of private information convinced the king that Sampson was a witch, and by extension that the people she had named as coven members were witches too. He insisted that the jurors in the case find all of the defendants guilty.

The jurors complied with the king's wishes, although many expressed doubt that the witches' confessions were valid because they were acquired under brutal torture. Once convicted of witchcraft, Sampson and Fian were strangled and their bodies were burned. Another defendant, Euphemia Maclean, was wealthy enough to afford numerous lawyers to fight her conviction, but ultimately she too was executed. Perhaps to punish her for the delay, she was burned alive rather than being strangled first. Another prominent defendant, noblewoman Barbara Napier, claimed that she was pregnant and was therefore spared. Defendant Margaret Thomson died under torture. The remainder of the roughly seventy defendants suffered a similar range of fates.

Of the other defendants, the most interesting is Francis, the earl of Bothwell, who was the king's cousin. He escaped from prison and fled the country. In *The Witch-Cult in Western Europe,* British anthropolgist Margaret Alice Murray argues that the earl not only played the role of the devil in rituals among the North Berwick witches but also instigated the covens' magic against King James. Murray suggests that Bothwell was already known for practicing witchcraft and thought to be bitter over not being king himself. Indeed, some sixteenth-century writings suggest that King James was afraid of his cousin. However, no scholars other than Murray believe that the earl used witchcraft to attack the king. In fact, most scholars do not believe there was a witch organization in North Berwick. They argue that the North Berwick witches were innocent victims of King James's paranoia. **See also** Fian, John; James I; Scotland, witch trials of.

numerology

Numerology is a method of divination based on the principle that numbers are mystical symbols that can tell people when to do things or that can influence people's characters. Under this system, each letter of the alphabet is sequentially assigned a number from 1 to 9, beginning with A assigned the number 1. (Thus the letters A through I are numbered 1 through 9, J through R the numbers 1 through 9, and so on.) The last letter, Z, is an 8. The numbers corresponding to the letters of any name are then added up and retotaled until a sum of one digit is achieved. For example, if the total of the letters is 32, the 3 and 2 would be added together to get 5. Depending on a person's beliefs, either the full name or just the first name is used.

Numerology associates an individual's "name sum" with certain qualities and results, as follows:

1 = Achievement-Oriented, Assertive, Stubborn.
2 = Artistic, Peaceful, Cooperative, Even-Tempered.
3 = Imaginative, Optimistic, Energetic, Witty, Creative.
4 = Practical, Patient, Calm, Cautious, Steady, Hard-Working.
5 = Adventurous, Restless, Risk-Taking, Versatile.
6 = Reliability, Balance, Domesticity, Loyalty, Affectionate Nature.
7 = Intuitive, Musical, Scholarly, Introspective.
8 = Materialistic, Forceful, Determined, Practical.
9 = Romantic, Charming, Compassionate.

Many witches use numerology to choose their Craft name, also called an ekename or Witch-Name. In selecting such a name using numerology, the witch experiments with different letter combinations to find the name believed to hold the most power and/or positive significance for the witch. Witches believe this name will affect their personality and consequently their magic. Some witches also use numerology to create a glyph, a magical symbol that represents a certain number, that is then marked on objects to create personal charms against bad luck, illness, or psychic disturbance. Others use numerology-related symbols drawn from the Kabbalah, a system of magic and mysticism created by ancient Hebrews.

In many magical systems, certain numbers are considered more powerful than others; 3, 7, and 13 are considered particularly special because of their significance to the natural world. Thirteen is the number of full moons in a year, 7 the number of days in a week as well as the number of planets known and considered sacred in the ancient world. Three is associated with certain trinities featured in pagan worship: new moon, full moon, and dark moon; birth, life, and death; Maiden, Mother, and Crone. In some magical systems, the number 9 is also thought to have magical powers because it is the result of multiplying the number three by itself. Accordingly, in some systems magicians write down nine magical numbers, arranged in the shape of a square with three numbers across and three down, while performing magic. **See also** divination; Kabbalah.

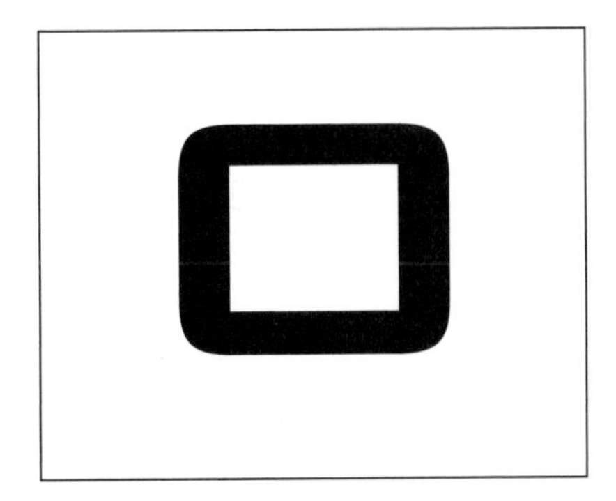

oak

Witches consider the oak (*Quercus petraea*) to be among the most sacred of trees, largely because it was the primary focus of tree worship among ancient pagans, particularly the Druids of Britain. Many ancient people viewed the oak tree as a symbol of fertility as well as of certain gods and goddesses, such as Zeus, Diana, and Bridgit, and held fertility rites beneath oak branches. There is some evidence that they also burned oak branches at certain festivals, and modern witches burn oak wood at their Midsummer and Yule festivals to honor this ancient practice.

Together with ash and thorn, the oak tree has also long been associated with fairies. Since ancient times it has been said that wherever ash, thorn, and oak trees grow together, fairies meet. Consequently some modern witches call these three trees the Fairy Triad. Ash, thorn, and oak also figure prominently in witches' spells to charge objects with magic. After saying such a spell, many witches state that it has been accomplished "by oak, ash, and thorn."

Some modern witches also carry an oak walking stick or staff, believing that it brings them positive energy. This practice dates back to ancient times, when priests in Britain and parts of Europe carried staffs made of oak to symbolize their role as an emissary of the gods. They believed that the oak tree was literally a god in physical form, and its wood therefore deserved reverence.

By medieval times, people no longer worshiped the oak, but they did still view it in positive ways. For example, people in Britain sometimes carried an acorn for luck. In particular, they believed that the oak's nut brought good health and dispelled evil spirits. **See also** ash; hawthorn; trees.

oils and ointments

Modern witches anoint themselves, their tools, and their altars with oils prior to conducting a ritual. In addition, they may anoint themselves during a ritual. Oils and ointments have been a part of magical and religious rites since ancient times. Ancient Greeks and Romans offered scented oils to the gods to honor them, while ancient Egyptian priests anointed themselves with oil prior to certain rituals. The Greeks considered olive oil to be particularly magical, and it is still the oil most commonly used by witches today. According to *A Witches' Bible* by Janet and Stewart Farrar, in the Gardnerian Tradition only pure olive oil is used to anoint ritual tools, whereas in the Alexandrian Tradition the olive oil is mixed with sweat from the high priestess and high priest. Witches often mix their oils with certain flowers, herbs, and other natural substances depending on the oils' intended use and the type of magic they want to work. Some substances are believed to confer good health, for example, while others bring romance. Herbal ingredients for oils intended for white, or good, magic are gathered during the full moon for maximum potency.

Ointments are also made with various flowers, herbs, and other natural substances, with various greases taking the place of oils. Like oils, ointments were first used ritually in ancient times. Modern witches do not use many ointments, if any, preferring oils. However, Gerald Gardner's Book of Shadows, as published in *A Witches' Bible*, includes a recipe for an anointing ointment employed during rituals that is made with animal grease, mint leaves, marjoram, thyme, and dried patchouli leaves. Numerous ointment recipes have survived from fourteenth- through seventeenth-century Europe. Their ingredients typically include noxious or toxic substances and/or blood and body parts, both animal and human. Some of these ointments were used to heal, but the majority of those mentioned in connection with witchcraft as opposed to medicine were said to effect murder by magic. Indeed, accusations involving these so-called killing ointments were featured prominently during witch-hunts. For example, in Milan, Italy, in 1630, several accused witches, including a city leader in charge of public health, were executed for applying a killing ointment to various walls in order to spread the plague.

During the same period throughout Europe, witches were also said to use ointments to enable themselves to fly, smearing it either on their bodies or their broomsticks or other flying tools. One ingredient commonly believed to be in flying ointments was bat blood. However, some recipes mention plants known to have hallucinogenic effects, leading modern scientists to suspect that the ointments did indeed enable witches to fly—in their imaginations. **See also** blood; flight; rites and rituals.

Old Religion

Old Religion is the term used by Wiccans to refer to an ancient religion on which many of their beliefs are based. Originally a fertility cult, this religion was expressed differently in different parts of pre-Christian Europe, the Mediterranean, and the British Isles. Generally, however, its followers worshiped both a goddess and a god as the personification of the female and male life force, with the Goddess being either superior or equal to the God, whom Wiccans call the Horned God for the staglike horns (considered a sign of virility) often depicted on his head. Ancient people viewed these deities as part of the natural world, believing that they controlled the seasons, the crops, and the cycles of life and death. The Goddess and the God were honored through festivals tied to various times of the year and aspects of nature.

Historians disagree on whether the Old Religion remained a viable religion after the advent of Christianity. In A.D. 324, Roman emperor Constantine declared Christianity the official religion throughout the Roman Empire, and imperial authorities began destroying ancient pagan temples or converting them to Christian churches. For a time some people continued practicing pagan rites despite Constantine's edict, particularly in Britain and northern Italy (the original strongholds of the Celts and Etruscans). By the eighth century, however, the Romans' tolerance of the Old Religion had ended, and the church took aggressive measures to stop pagan worship. In A.D. 743 the synod of Rome outlawed all offerings and sacrifices to pagan gods, and in 829 the synod of Paris issued a decree advocating that witches, sorcerers, and magicians—most of whom continued to worship multiple gods and goddesses—be put to death.

Given this level of persecution, historians disagree on what became of the Old Religion. Some have argued that witches kept the Old Religion alive throughout the centuries, bringing it to modern times essentially intact. British anthropologist Margaret Alice Murray theorized that this was done secretly through an organized witches' cult. Others think that witches kept elements of the Old Religion alive in a more haphazard fashion, primarily through folk magic and related practices.

A variation on this theory is that the Old Religion split into two factions, one worshiping the sun and the other the moon, and it was the sun cult that died out while the moon cult continued in secret. Murray's purported witch cult was dedicated to worshiping the moon goddess Diana, in large part because there is evidence that a Dianic cult actually existed among the witches of ancient Greece. The prevailing view among modern scholars, however, is that all organized pagan religions were effectively dead by the time of the witch-hunts, if not long before. In this view, modern Wiccans' religious practices are simply based on what prominent modern witches such as Gerald Gardner have said were part of pagan beliefs.

The first use of the term *Old Religion,* in the writings of the ancient Roman historian Seneca, applied to Etruscan rather than Celtic beliefs, and the Old Religion appears to have blended elements of both the Etruscan and Celtic cultures. It was also influenced by the Greeks and Romans as these peoples conquered the regions where the Old Religion had flourished.

The earliest manifestation of the Old Religion was in two religious cults that existed during the Neolithic period of the Stone Age, between 7000 and 3500 B.C., in Old Europe, which encompassed what is now Italy and Greece, as well as other areas along the Mediterranean and parts of Poland, Czechoslovakia, and Ukraine. One of these cults was the Cult of the Great Goddess; the other was the Cult of the Dead. The Great Goddess, responsible for fertility as well as death, was also connected with the moon, the frog, and the toad. The Cult of the Dead promoted the ideas that the human skull had power and that certain times of the year, such as the winter solstice, were spiritually significant.

Around 4500 B.C., human migration brought the Cult of the Dead to Spain and France. Around 3000 B.C., the Cult of the Dead reached Britain, and it appears that the Cult of the Great Goddess reached there as well. By 2500 B.C., goddess worship had largely died out in central Europe, a region conquered by a group of Indo-Europeans with patriarchal religious beliefs. In Italy, however, the Etruscans continued to worship a Great Mother goddess called Uni until they were conquered by the Romans in the first century B.C. The Etruscan people are therefore considered the heirs to the Cult of the Great Goddess that once dominated Old Europe.

Meanwhile, the Cult of the Dead lived on, although not in its original form, in the British Isles under the Celts. Emerging from central Old Europe in 700 B.C., the Celts invaded the British Isles sometime between 600 and 500 B.C., whereupon they conquered its people, built fortifications, and defended themselves aggressively from foreign invasion. Thus isolated from the influences of other cultures, the Cult of the Dead in Britain became uniquely Celtic. For example, whereas once the cult had emphasized the soul's journey to the afterlife, under the Celts its prevailing belief was that upon death a person's soul would be immediately reincarnated.

By the third century the worship practices of the cult had been taken out of the hands of most individuals and given over to the Druids, a separate priestly class. The Druids went into the woods to conduct secret ceremonies honoring nature spirits and deities, sometimes offering human sacrifices to them. Meanwhile, most Celts worshiped a variety of gods, goddesses, and spirits related to the natural world. Many of these deities and spirits figure prominently in modern Wicca, as do the moon, the frog, the toad, and the human skull featured in the Cult of the Great Goddess and the Cult of the Dead. **See also** Celts; paganism; Wicca.

olive

Many witches, particularly those in traditions that originated in or are based on pagan religions of Italy and Greece, consider the olive tree (*Olea europaea*) to be sacred and often use its oil to anoint ritual tools. The olive tree is also associated with moon goddesses and the goddess Athena. Its wood was used in ancient times to carve statues of these deities. **See also** trees.

Osborne, John (?–1751) and Ruth (?–1751)

In 1751, nearly forty years after the British government had stopped persecuting witches, John and Ruth Osborne were killed by an angry mob that suspected them of being witches. An impoverished elderly couple, the Osbornes had long been unpopular in their town of Tring in Hertfordshire, England, largely because they held political views different from those of their neighbors. Whenever some mishap occurred, townspeople typically blamed the Osbornes. One man, however, turned these minor grumblings into a witch-hunt. Cited in historical records only as Butterfield, he was a dairy farmer whose cows died of a mysterious ailment shortly after he refused to give Ruth Osborne free buttermilk. Without cows to provide income, he sold his farm and opened a tavern in a nearby town, whereupon he began having occasional convulsions. This too he blamed on Ruth Osborne's witchcraft.

When Butterfield complained about Ruth Osborne to his tavern customers, word quickly spread about the local witch. Somehow a rumor started that on a particular date—April 22, 1751—both Osbornes were going to be subjected to a traditional test to determine whether or not they were witches: swimming, whereby the suspected witch was bound and thrown into a body of water. Anyone who floated was considered a witch, while anyone who sank was considered innocent (but also most likely drowned before being pulled out of the water).

Local officials aware of this rumor hid the Osbornes, but on the appointed day a mob formed, tracked them down, stripped them naked, tied them up, and dragged them to a stream two miles away. Both were then thrown into the water. The leader of the mob was a chimneysweep named Thomas Colley, an extremely popular and boisterous man. He supervised the swimming test, and when Ruth Osborne did not sink he pushed her under the water with a stick until she nearly drowned. The crowd then dragged her out onto the bank and beat her to death, convinced from the test that she was a witch. They then dragged out her husband and beat him as well; he survived the experience only to die several days later.

Meanwhile Colley asked those who had witnessed the swimming test to pay him for the entertainment he had provided them. Colley believed himself a hero for ridding the area of two notorious witches, but government authorities did not view the incident in the same light. By this time, England had effectively ended witch persecution, and after investigating the Osbornes' deaths the authorities charged Colley and two other men with murder. Colley was the only one convicted; he was hanged for his crime on August 24, 1751. **See also** England, witch-hunts of; torture.

Ostara

Also called Eostar, the spring equinox, or the vernal equinox, Ostara marks the full return of spring, sometime between March 20 and March 23. Ostara is a Scandinavian goddess (called Eostar among Anglo-Saxons) associated with the spring and new life, including eggs and baby rabbits, chicks, ducks, and lambs. All of these are in keeping with the concept of Ostara as a fertility festival. In addition, it is traditional at Ostara to dye eggs, usually in red but sometimes in pastels. These colors, along with silver, are most commonly associated with Ostara. Many different kinds of spring flowers are also associated with this festival, including tulips and daffodils. Eventually, many aspects of Ostara were adopted by Christians and incorporated into the celebration of Easter. **See also** Wheel of the Year.

owls

In cultures around the world, owls have been associated with sorcery since ancient times. In some parts of Africa, they were believed to be the servants of wizards; in others, they were thought to be the sorcerers themselves, transformed either voluntarily in life or involuntarily as a spirit after death. The Aztecs of Mexico believed that an owl could actually be an evil spirit in disguise, and medieval, Renaissance, and Reformation Europeans thought that demons could take the form of an owl, particularly while accompanying witches in flight. Certain tribes of Native Americans also believed in the protective power of owls, although others thought that owls brought only evil. Similarly, in Scotland, England, and many other parts of Europe, it was (and for some, still is) considered extremely bad luck to see or hear an owl during the day. In fact, in most of these places the owl was traditionally called a harbinger of death.

The connection between the owl and death dates back at least as far as 2300 B.C., when the Sumerians depicted the goddess of death accompanied by a pair of owls. The ancient Egyptians used the owl to symbolize death as well. The ancient Greeks and Romans continued this association, but in addition they connected the owl to the goddess of wisdom and handicrafts, who was called Athena in ancient Greece and Minerva in ancient Rome. Representations of this deity often show her holding or accompanied by an owl. **See also** flight; goddesses and gods; wizard.

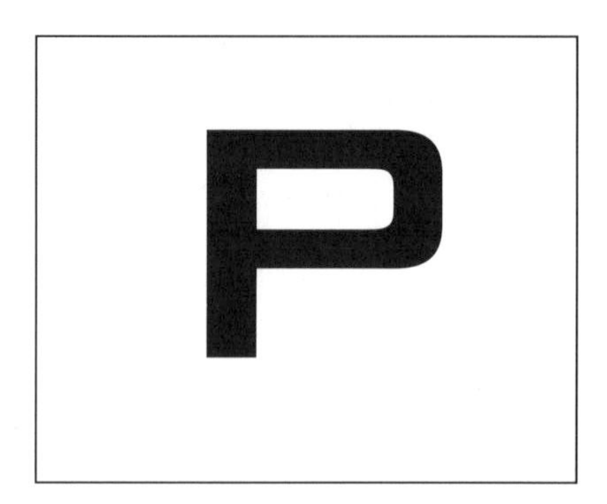

Pagan Federation

Founded in London, England, in 1971 as the Pagan Front, the Pagan Federation is a major organization of pagans that works internationally to educate the public about paganism and to promote religious freedom for all types of pagans. It also publishes a magazine called *Pagan Dawn*, formerly a newsletter called the *Wiccan*.

paganism

Paganism was the worship of multiple deities as part of a pre-Christian religion. The word *pagan* comes from the Latin word *paganus* for "country dweller" and was first used by early Christians seeking to distinguish their beliefs from those of rural people who were slow to embrace Christianity. Gradually the early Christians began to use "pagan" in condescension, initially to suggest that pagans were inferior and later to suggest they were evil.

Scholars do not have a complete picture of the worship practices of pagans in pre-Christian Britain and continental Europe, and there was no universal expression of paganism. However, it is known that pagans recognized the importance of both the male and the female life forces. Some groups celebrated the hunt, associated with the male life force, while others celebrated the growing seasons of the earth, associated with the female life force.

Paganism long held sway in Europe. Researchers have found evidence of pagan worship dating back to prehistoric times, and paganism remained popular in England until the seventh century, in Germany until the ninth century, and in Scandinavia until the twelfth century. As Christianity spread, Christians employed two tactics to eliminate the old beliefs: First, they portrayed paganism as evil, and second, they incorporated many elements of paganism into Christianity so that people could continue their traditional forms of worship. For example, Christians converted certain pagan deities and festival dates into Christian ones; the pagan goddess Bridgit, worshiped by Irish Celts, was said to have been baptized by the Christian Saint Patrick, whereupon she became the Christian Saint Bridgit.

After Christianity became the dominant religion in Britain and continental Europe, those who continued to practice paganism were persecuted for their beliefs. Often the persecution took the form of an accusation of witchcraft. Modern scholars have long debated whether the victims of witch trials were simply practitioners of folk magic or whether they were pagans as well (or, in some cases, instead). The extent to which paganism prompted witch-hunts is unclear, but it is clear that no one dared practice paganism openly during the time of witch hysteria for fear of being charged with and perhaps executed for heresy.

In modern times, of course, such fears are obsolete, and a new form of paganism called Neopaganism (meaning "new paganism") is practiced in many places. Particularly popular in the United States and Britain, it began during the environmental movement of the 1960s and 1970s largely because people associated paganism with a reverence for nature. This association stems from the fact that many deities worshiped by pagans were nature spirits. Neopagans (who sometimes continue to use the designation pagans) practice some form of earth religion, worshiping some aspect of nature and honoring the earth. Many are also witches, but the practice of witchcraft is not a necessary component of Neopaganism. **See also** Neopagans.

Pagan Way

Founded in approximately 1969, the Pagan Way was a Neopagan movement primarily intended to introduce people to witchcraft without the initiations, membership requirements, and other restrictive elements of Wiccan covens. The movement also sought to differentiate itself from Wicca by emphasizing nature worship rather than the practice of magic. This does not mean, however, that the Pagan Way was without magic rituals. The movement's founders, which included American witch Joseph B. Wilson, American Gardnerian high priest Ed Fitch, and British witch John Score, created group and solitary rituals specifically for the Pagan Way, publishing the material first in Wilson's magazine the *Waxing Moon*, and later as pamphlets and in books. These rituals had elements of Celtic and Gardnerian Traditions.

As the movement gained strength, it attracted a large number of solitary witchcraft practitioners who might occasionally mingle with others at an occasional Pagan Way event. Meanwhile, members attracted to the group experience met in clusters called groves. They encouraged the Pagan Way founders to add initiation rites to the movement and to increase its emphasis on magic, wanting to approximate the coven experience. Most of these members eventually decided to leave their groves to create their own groups and rituals or to use Pagan Way rituals in new ways. By 1980 most groves had ceased to exist, and the movement officially died out. However, its emphasis on the individual exploration of witchcraft, as opposed to the coven experience, still exists in traditions formed during the existence of the Pagan Way movement. **See also** Fitch, Ed; Gardnerian Tradition; Neopagans; Score, John.

Paracelsus

Born in 1493 as Philippus Aureolus Theophrastus Bombast von Hohenheim, Swiss physician and alchemist Paracelsus used what he called natural magic to heal people. In actuality, this "magic" was created not with spells but by making medicines of natural materials such as herbs and minerals. However, Paracelsus also routinely used talismans (objects charged with a spell designed to attract some kind of fortune to the person wearing or carrying it) in the belief that they increased the power of his remedies.

Because of Paracelsus's reference to magic, some people, both in his own time and since, believed that he was a magician. However, there is little evidence to support the view that he was anything but an innovative healer. Eager to experiment with various ideas for medical treatments, Paracelsus discovered mercury as a cure for syphilis, and he was the first person to recognize the medicinal value of zinc, still used today in treating the common cold. He was also the first person known to use chemical compounds as remedies, as well as the first person to understand that wounds needed only to be cleaned, drained, and kept clean to heal, rather than being cauterized and smeared with noxious ointments. In addition, Paracelsus was the first person to promote the idea that mental state affected a person's physical health.

Paracelsus was an innovative physician who discovered the power of many herbs and minerals in healing, leading many to label him a magician.

Paracelsus published some of his medical knowledge in a 1536 book, *Die Grosse Wundartzney*, which was extremely popular with physicians. Paracelsus, however, was personally unpopular. Since his youth he had been so obnoxious and pompous that few people could bear his company. In fact, he was so arrogant that after he received his doctorate in medicine (probably from the University of Ferrara in Italy) he chose the name Paracelsus for himself because it meant "superior to Celsus," one of the most esteemed physicians of ancient Rome. This arrogance, coupled with Paracelsus's notoriously violent temper, caused him a great deal of trouble. He was frequently embroiled in disputes and legal battles and was never welcome in one place very long. He traveled from one city to another throughout the late 1530s, and in 1541 he was apparently murdered while at the court of Prince Palantine, the Archbishop Duke Ernsty of Bavaria. **See also** magicians.

Paris Witch Trial

The 1390 witch trial of thirty-four-year-old Jehenne de Brigue, an event commonly known as the Paris Witch Trial, was the first witch trial in Europe prosecuted by civil rather than religious authorities. Conducted by the Parlement of Paris, it was also notable in that all of the authorities connected with the case scrupulously adhered to the laws and tried to be as just as possible, allowing de Brigue to have her own lawyers and examining witnesses carefully. Historians believe that the fairness displayed by judges in the case reflected their eagerness to prove that secular courts were capable of handling such matters in the future.

However, although it was fairer than previous bodies that had addressed witch cases, the Parlement of Paris still supported the idea of torturing a defendant until she confessed, and this essentially assured de Brigue's conviction. Upon her arrest the woman had immediately admitted to not saying her prayers as often as she should, and to using charms for luck and other benign purposes. In fact, she was originally arrested for using witchcraft to heal someone. But faced with the torturer's instruments she confessed to far more. (Historians disagree on whether de Brigue actually underwent any torture, or whether she confessed just prior to her torture session out of fear of what was to come.) In any case, de Brigue said that she was a witch and had consorted with the devil. She also said that she had used sorcery to make a man sick but then changed her mind and healed him. She named as her accomplice in this endeavor the man's wife, Macette de Ruilly, who was then arrested and tortured until she too confessed.

Both women later recanted their confessions, but it was too late. The court had searched their belongings and discovered locks of hair and other items used to make charms and possibly cast spells. The Parlement of Paris condemned the two women to be burned alive. Their sentence was carried out in August 1391. **See also** devil; France, witch-hunts of; torture; trials, witch.

Pendderwen, Gwydion (1946–1982)

Gwydion Pendderwen cofounded the Faery Tradition with Victor Anderson. Pendderwen did much to spread knowledge of the tradition throughout the Wiccan community, sponsoring Neopagan gatherings and recording songs about the Craft. In particular, Pendderwen gave the tradition much of its emphasis on elements of Welsh Celtic beliefs and practices, although the tradition includes other influences as well. Although Pendderwen was sometimes called the Faerie Shaman by those in his tradition, he called himself a *bhaird.* In ancient times, a *bhaird,* or bard, was a singer, poet, storyteller, and teacher who memorized long passages of text to pass on orally. Pendderwen passed on his own songs in a 1972 album entitled *Songs of the Old Religion.* He died in an automobile accident in 1982. **See also** Celts; Faery Tradition.

Pendle Forest, witch trial of

The 1612 trial of suspected witches in the Pendle Forest area of Lancaster, England, was one of the largest and most complex legal proceedings of its kind. There were twenty defendants from two families, and the sensational testimony attracted crowds of spectators. Perhaps more importantly, the case was the focus of a 1613 book by the court clerk, Thomas Potts, entitled *The Wonderful Discovery of Witches in the County of Lancaster*, which spread knowledge of the proceedings throughout England, thereby convincing many people that witchcraft was real.

The case began with two old, cantankerous women, Elizabeth Sowthern and Anne Whittle, from two different, large families. For a time they apparently worked together to make and sell magic potions, encouraging people to consider them witches in order to increase their sales. Then a member of one of their families accused a member of the other of stealing, and a major feud developed between the two families that lasted for several years. During this time, each side accused the other of all manner of witchcraft.

Hearing of these accusations, local authorities decided to step in, arresting Sowthern, Whittle, and nine of their relatives as witches. Thanks to the rival families' mutual animosity, the court had plenty of material on which to base charges. Sowthern was said to have magically sent a demon to kill a child and to have sent a familiar (in the form of a spotted dog) to kill a wealthy landowner. Various family members had also reported that Sowthern and Whittle made pacts with the devil and enticed others to do the same.

As the trial neared, officials learned that about twenty members of the two families who had not been arrested were conspiring to free the accused. Their plan involved murdering a guard and blowing up prison walls. Nine of the conspirators were caught and charged not only with attempting to free the prisoners but also with witchcraft, because authorities assumed them to be part of a coven led by Sowthern and Whittle. As part of these witchcraft charges, the new defendants were accused of using magic to kill sixteen people and several horses and cows.

At the trial, perhaps the most damning testimony was that of Sowthern's grandchild, Janet Device. Her mother, Elizabeth Device, sister Alison Device, and brother James Device were three of the original defendants in the trial. Janet was only nine years old, and as a witness for the prosecution she told elaborate stories about her relatives' activities as witches. For example, she reported that her mother used magic to kill three people. In the end, ten people were hanged as witches in August 1612. Another, Jennet Preston, was sent to another town to stand trial for a case of murder by witchcraft and hanged there in July 1612. Elizabeth Sowthern did not live to hear her sentence; she died in jail. One other defendant, Margaret Pearson, was convicted of magically killing a horse and sentenced to a year in prison. **See also** England, witch-hunts of.

pentacle and pentagram

A pentacle is a small, flat disk, usually made of wood, wax, clay, or some kind of metal, that displays a pentagram, the image of a five-pointed star, on one side. Sometimes the pentagram is drawn within a circle. Magical symbols might also be inscribed on the back of the pentacle as well.

In ancient times, magicians most often used pentacles as amulets to protect them from attack by evil spirits or as talismans that enabled them to conjure and command spirits. In modern times, pentacles are often used as amulets or talismans meant to protect the wearer or help the wearer achieve a specific desire, in which case the material chosen for the pentacle depends upon its intended magical use. Modern witches also wear pentacles as a symbol of the Wiccan religion, much the way Christians wear crosses to symbolize their faith.

Throughout history, the pentagram has been compared to a human figure, with one point as the head, two opposing points as arms, and two lower points as legs. Among modern American witches, pentagrams are always drawn with their "head" upright. Witches reason that this point represents pure spirit while the other points represent the four elements (earth, air, fire, and water). By placing the spirit upright, American witches intend to signify that it is more important than matter—i.e., than material gain. British witches, however, typically draw the pentagram with its "head" down, in keeping with long-standing tradition.

British witches are particularly dismayed that some Satanists have adopted the inverted pentagram as their own symbol. Witches do not practice devil worship (in fact, most do not even believe in the devil), so Satanists do not use the inverted pentagram because of its association with witchcraft. Instead they were inspired by early Christians who used the pentagram as a symbol of Christ, with its single point representing his head. To Satanists, the inverted pentagram is a mockery of Christ.

Witches routinely employ pentagrams in their rituals and magical work in ways thought to be positive. For example, they typically draw pentagrams in the air at each of the four directional points in a magic circle to consecrate the circle before beginning magical work. In addition, a pentagram is often displayed on the altar within the circle to protect those within and to strengthen invocations of the Goddess. The altar's pentagram is a place where ritual tools, amulets, and other items are typically laid during a ritual, and the image of the pentagram might be marked on ritual tools to confer strength, power, and protection to those items. In the practice of magic, witches typically employ the pentacle to represent the element earth, while the pentagram is a focus of concentration that helps witches turn thoughts and desires into reality. The circle typically drawn around the pentagram is believed to create a sacred space similar to that created within a magic circle, which means that it strengthens magic and protects the practitioner of magic.

The origin of the pentagram's association with magic is unclear. However, the symbol appears in writings related to an ancient Hebrew mystical system known as the Kabbalah, whose beliefs have influenced many modern witches as well as occult brotherhoods throughout history. A pentagram within a circle also appears on rings worn by members of a mystical brotherhood founded by the Greek philosopher Pythagoras (c. 570–c. 500 B.C.). **See also** elements, four; Kabbalah; tools, ritual.

Pentreath, Dolly (Dorothy) (1692–1777)

English witch and diviner Dolly (Dorothy) Pentreath is notable in that she was open about her use of magic yet was never persecuted for it. Perhaps even more surprising, when she died she was buried in her local churchyard. The circumstances of her life and death were both signs that witch persecutions had ended in eighteenth-century England. In fact, so accepted was Pentreath's witchcraft that her neighbors in Cornwall often sought her out when they wanted their fortunes told or needed a charm, spell, or some other manifestation of her magic. At the same time, townspeople were either afraid of Pentreath or disliked her, in part because of her reputation as a witch, but also because Pentreath had a foul temper, a foul mouth, and a foul odor about her. (The latter was most likely due to her occupation as a fishmonger.) **See also** England, witch-hunts of.

Perkins, William (1555–1602)

English Puritan preacher William Perkins is the author of *Discourse on the Damned Art of Witchcraft,* a popular guide to witch-hunting published in 1608. The book outlined the criteria by which someone could be suspected of being a witch; these criteria were so broad that they made it easy for someone to be falsely accused. For example, Perkins thought that anyone who closely associated with a witch was likely to be a witch too. This belief explains why most witch-hunters arrested the husband and children of suspected female witches. Perkins also said that if someone who was dying claimed that a particular person had bewitched him, this deathbed accusation warranted arrest and probably conviction. Similarly, if a person who was cursed later died, then the one who had done the cursing should be arrested for suspected witchcraft.

Perkins believed that all of the things he had heard about witches—that they consorted with the devil, for example, and could cast spells powerful enough to change the weather or kill someone—were true. Therefore, although he wanted witch trials to proceed as fairly as possible, he also wanted all convicted witches to be executed, and he saw nothing wrong with torturing accused witches to gain confessions. Moreover, he did not, like some of his peers, believe that certain kinds of witches were less harmful than others. While he did separate witches into different categories depending on the type of witchcraft they performed, he argued that all witches deserved equal punishment.

Perkins's views influenced public opinion for many years. In fact, his book was still being used as a guide for witch-hunters in the 1690s. However, Perkins did not live to see his work in print. He died six years before it was published. **See also** England, witch-hunts of; torture; witch-hunter.

persecution, witch

The organized persecution of witches did not begin until the late thirteenth century. Prior to that time, laws limiting or banning the use of magic applied primarily to witchcraft that was used to harm someone; it was not considered a crime merely to practice magic. In ancient Rome, for example, sorcery was forbidden because officials feared they might be assassinated by magic, but in practice this ban was applied only to evil, or black, magic, as opposed to good, or white, magic (i.e., folk magic used for healing).

This tolerance for white magic began to disappear under the influence of the Roman Catholic Church. From the outset, Christians felt that folk magic was a threat to their religion, because disbelievers suggested that Jesus Christ had healed through sorcery rather than through divine power. Moreover, wherever people looked to magic to solve their problems they were less likely to turn to Christianity.

As the Roman Catholic Church became more powerful, its leaders decided to stamp out not only all competing religions but also the practice of all forms of magic, particularly since witches typically worshiped pagan deities. Beginning in the eighth century, church leaders attempted to convince the public that anyone who practiced magic was a heretic, someone whose beliefs ran counter to church teachings. This was not an easy argument to make, since at that time people believed that heresy had to involve vocal opposition to the church's teachings, and most witches did not actively speak out against Christianity. However, a document called the Canon Episcopi, written sometime prior to the tenth century, answered that objection. Essentially, the canon stated that there was no such thing as witchcraft, because only God and Christ could have power over human beings. (Modern scholars believe that the church took this position in part to counter claims by disbelievers that Christ had been a witch rather than the Son of God.) Therefore anyone who claimed to be a witch or to have seen or experienced the effects of witchcraft had to be deluded. Moreover, the document also stated that anyone who believed in witchcraft was a pagan and therefore could be prosecuted as a heretic.

This position allowed the church to persecute witches, but it also made it difficult for church leaders to convince the public that witchcraft was dangerous, since the official church position was that witchcraft did not exist. When it became evident that the only way the public would support witch persecution was if people feared witches so much they no longer turned to them for healing spells, love potions, and similar folk magic, the church reversed its position to state, in a series of documents, that witchcraft was real.

Then in late-thirteenth-century France, some noblemen attempted to use witchcraft (specifically, poisons and image magic) to murder prominent politicians. This incident stirred up antiwitch sentiment, which had already been growing under the church's influence. Now the church had the public support it needed to target "heretical sorcerers" (as of 1335, defined as sorcery that included devil worship and attendance at Sabbats) for aggressive persecution. By this time, the church had already established a tribunal called the Inquisition to prosecute cases of heresy; now the Inquisition turned its attention to witches. As it had done with heretics, the Inquisition used brutal torture to extract confessions from people suspected of practicing witchcraft. With each forced confession the inquisitors amassed more evidence that witchcraft was a genuine, serious threat to society.

By the mid–fourteenth century, the public had been convinced that witches had real powers, and that these powers came from forces that were either angelic or demonic. By the fifteenth century, most people had concluded that all magical forces were demonic. Their opinion was shaped by the growing body of witch confessions (provided first by ecclesiastical courts and then, beginning in the late fourteenth century, by secular courts as well) which included accounts of witches meeting in large groups to worship the devil and plot against Christians.

Several books of the period also turned public opinion against witches. Of these, the 1486 book *Malleus Maleficarum* by two Dominican inquisitors, Heinrich Kramer and Jakob Sprenger, was considered the most influential. However, it was not the first book to offer descriptions of witches' activities, including devil worship and the casting of evil spells. Many historians believe that this distinction goes to the 1467 book *Fortalicium Fidei* (*Fortress of the Faith*) by Franciscan friar Alphonsus de Spina of Spain. It also identifies ten types of demons, one of the most significant of which is a demon that deludes women into believing they have magical powers such as the ability to fly. Works like these convinced the public that witches were depraved and dangerous devil-worshipers. Consequently, witch persecutions increased dramatically during the fifteenth and sixteenth centuries. In fact, the sixteenth century was a time of widespread torture and execution of accused witches.

The level of persecution varied considerably from one country to another. Germany was responsible for at least half of all witchcraft-related deaths during the years of witch-hunting (by some estimates, one hundred thousand of two hundred thousand total deaths), while France and Switzerland were responsible for much of the remainder. In Spain and Portugal, divination and healing were tolerated by church inquisitors, so there were far fewer executions. In Scandinavia, where torture was not used to extract confessions, there were only about two hundred executions. In Ireland there were only eight witch trials during the entire period of witch persecution, which scholars suspect was due to the country's isolation from the witch hysteria of continental Europe. This isolation was cultural as well as geographical; most people in Ireland did not have access to books that encouraged witch-hunting and the illiteracy rate was high. In England, where people had more access to witch-hunting material, there were at least a thousand witch deaths, most of them occurring after *Malleus Maleficarum* was translated into English in 1598.

In England, the legal system did not allow suspected witches to be tortured, although suspects might be kept awake, starved, or subjected to similar forms of coercion. However, in Germany and France torture was a common means of obtaining witch confessions and the names of accomplices. Also acceptable were courtroom procedures that put accused witches at a disadvantage. For example, in most places the defendant in a witch trial was not allowed to have a lawyer. Such tactics were one reason why German and French courts were more successful than others at convicting witches.

The methods employed to execute witches varied; witches were hanged in America and burned at the stake in continental Europe and the British Isles.

Another aspect of witch persecution that led to more convictions was the development of witch-hunting as a profession. Full-time witch-hunters went from village to village, presenting themselves as experts in witch investigations and prosecutions. Some of these witch-hunters worked for the church, but others were private businessmen who charged town leaders a fee for their services. These professionals saw to it that witches not only were found but convicted, since they often received a bonus on the conviction and/or execution of those they accused. One of the most prominent such men was Matthew Hopkins, who between 1645 and 1646 became wealthy by bringing about the executions of over two hundred accused witches.

Coinciding with the development of witch-hunting as a profession, several prominent men authored books opposing witch persecution. For example, in 1563 German physician Johann Weyer wrote *De Praestigiis Daemonum* (*The Imposter Demons*) to suggest that most people who displayed signs of demonic possession or professed to be witches were actually mentally ill and did not deserve to be on trial, and in 1584 English author Reginald Scot published *Discoverie of Witchcraft* to argue that it was unlikely any of the women condemned as witches had supernatural powers.

One of the things that disturbed such men was the fact that most of the victims of witch persecution were women. Church leaders presented a rationale for this: Women were more easily seduced by the devil, as evidenced by the biblical story of Eve's temptation by Satan in the Garden of Eden. However, to objective observers it seemed as though women without a man's protection—i.e., widows and spinsters—were pursued more aggressively by witch-hunters. Historians have noted that the basis for this disparity might actually be economic; the majority of witches were widows and spinsters who turned to folk magic as a way to earn their own living.

Another disparity in the level of persecution related to wealth. In many places, city or church leaders were allowed to confiscate the estates of executed witches, and towns usually charged accused witches or their relatives for all of the expenses related to their arrest, jail time, torture, trial, and execution. Therefore in some towns more rich people than poor ones were convicted; when witch-hunting became unprofitable—usually because all the rich people in the area had already been executed—witch persecution often came to an end.

Prominent citizens sometimes stepped up to complain about the unfairness of witch-hunts or even took action to stop them. For example, in England a prominent judge, Sir John Holt, was inclined to find most of the suspected witches who came before him innocent, which sometimes resulted in threats to remove him from the bench. Speaking out against witch-hunting could be dangerous; for example, in 1628 the vice-chancellor of Bamberg, a German city with a powerful witch-hunting organization, was accused, tortured, and executed along with his wife and daughter because he spoke out against the organization.

For the most part, however, witch-hunts proceeded not because few people objected to them but because they were popular. People often welcomed witch-hunts, providing they and their loved ones were not targeted, as a way to rid themselves of pesky neighbors or exact revenge on their enemies. Other motivations included the chance for monetary gain, a genuine fear that a witch would harm someone, and the desire to find a scapegoat for life's ills.

Children typically made witch accusations out of spite or as a bid for attention. Since most adults did not believe that children would make up stories about witches' activities, their testimony had great credibility. This was the case in Salem, Massachusetts, where children leveled charges that resulted in 150 witch accusations, 141 arrests, 31 convictions, and 20 deaths.

Approaches to witch execution varied. In America death was by hanging, but in continental Europe and parts of the British Isles the condemned were burned at the stake, usually alive but sometimes, as an act of mercy, after being strangled. Sometimes people were executed individually, while other times they were killed as part of mass witch executions.

In some villages, most of the population was wiped out because of mass executions. In one region of the Pyrenees Mountains, Basque sailors returned from a long voyage to discover that most of their loved ones had been killed. When witch persecution was limited to bringing about the deaths of a few village eccentrics or ill-tempered crones, the public accepted it. But once witch persecutions extended to upstanding citizens, such as the families of the Basque sailors, the public began to balk. Moreover, as witch-hunting eliminated more and more hardworking citizens, it began to have a negative impact on local economies and on church coffers.

Ultimately, witch trials became far less common. The last major cases took place in America in 1706, Ireland in 1711, England in 1717, Scotland in 1727, France in 1745, and Germany in 1775. But while witch executions ended, witch persecution did not. In 1736 the English passed a law mandating a year's imprisonment for anyone pretending to practice witchcraft (a way to punish witches without admitting that witchcraft was real). Meanwhile in Europe and America, individual witches were attacked either physically or verbally by townspeople.

The spiritualism movement of the nineteenth century helped lessen the number of these attacks, because it fostered an acceptance of, or at least an interest in, ghosts, fairies, and magic. Still, antiwitch sentiment remained strong until the mid–twentieth century, when England repealed its antiwitchcraft law. This enabled people to practice and write about witchcraft openly, thereby spreading interest in their activities. Consequently a modern witchcraft movement began, first in the British Isles and then in the United States.

This movement presented witchcraft as a religion, Wicca, and called for tolerance from people of other faiths. Gradually the American public came to accept this view, and in 1986 a U.S. appeals court ruled that Wicca is a legitimate religion, which means that its practitioners must be accorded the same rights and freedoms as practitioners of other religions in the United States. As a result of this recognition, the number of people practicing witchcraft has increased dramatically, and today some experts estimate that there are anywhere from two-hundred thousand to 1 million Wiccans in the United States alone. **See also** Bamberg, witch-hunts of; Basque region, witch-hunts of the; Canon Episcopi; Hopkins, Matthew; Inquisition; *Malleus Maleficarum;* Salem, witch trials of; Scot, Reginald; Weyer, Johann.

Pickingill, Old George (1816–1909)

Old George Pickingill was an English witch who established several covens in his native country, creating rituals that some people believe eventually became part of the Gardnerian Tradition of Witchcraft. Pickingill, who claimed to be a hereditary witch with ties to the Craft going back to the eleventh century, called for an end to Christianity and worked for decades to spread witchcraft throughout England. Ultimately he was responsible for the formation of nine covens in various regions throughout England, all of them led by those who, like himself, claimed to be hereditary witches. According to rumor, Pickingill was also the head of an all-female coven, representing the Horned God in various rituals. Pickingill believed that except for the role of the Horned God, all of the participants in these rituals should be women, although he did not exclude males from joining his covens.

Pickingill died in 1909 apparently having left behind little information about his witchcraft-related activities. However, in the mid-1970s a hereditary witch claiming an intimate knowledge of Pickingill and his covens reported that Pickingill had once initiated noted witch Aleister Crowley into one of his covens and that Crowley subsequently passed on details about this coven's rituals to Gerald Gardner, who in turn founded the Gardnerian Tradition. According to this source, E.W. Lidell (also known as Lugh), Gardner took some of Pickingill's rituals as his own. Modern witches disagree about whether Lidell was telling the truth, given that he could provide no proof of his claims. **See also** Crowley, Aleister; Gardner, Gerald; traditions, Witchcraft.

Pictish Wicca

Also called PectiWita or the Scottish Tradition, Pictish Wicca is a Witchcraft tradition based on the beliefs and practices of ancient Scottish pagans. For the most part, its practitioners are solitaries, and they employ few formal rituals. In fact, most Pictish Wiccans do not even cast a magic circle prior to performing magic. They do not believe that magic circles are necessary, and they cast spells without any preceding rituals. In fact, magic, not religion, is the main emphasis of the tradition. Healing and divination are also important, as are nature, animals, plants, and minerals.

Pictish Wicca has been growing in popularity, although its practitioners are still primarily located in Scotland and Canada. The spread of interest in the tradition is largely due to Raymond Buckland, who wrote about it in *Buckland's Complete Book of Witchcraft* (1986) and *Scottish Witchcraft: The History and Magick of the Picts* (1991). **See also** Buckland, Raymond; traditions, Witchcraft.

pins

Medieval witches used pins in the practice of magic, primarily as ingredients in potions. It was said that potions used in black magic required at least one crooked pin. Pins were also used for evil purposes in some types of image magic. For example, a witch might create a doll in the likeness of an intended victim, enchant the doll so that whatever happens to the doll happens to the person it represents, and then subject the doll to a variety of tortures, such as piercing the abdomen with pins in order to subject the victim to a series of sharp stomach pains or sticking it in the eye to cause the victim to go blind. Because of this association between witches and pins, whenever someone claiming to be possessed by demons vomited pins (a surprisingly common occurrence during the witch-hunting centuries), this was considered proof that the demons had been sent by witches. Today, however, witches no longer use pins for evil purposes. **See also** image magic; iron; poppet.

poisons

Most modern witches do not use poisons, because to do so would be a violation of the Wiccan Rede, or principle, that requires a witch to do no harm. However, for centuries witches did use poisons, and many witch trials have centered around cases of murder involving poison. For example, the trials of the Chambre Ardente, a court which sat in France from 1679 to 1682, concerned an international poisoning ring with numerous suspected or self-professed witches.

The most common types of poisons associated with witches of the sixteenth and seventeenth centuries were those made from certain plants in the nightshade family. Henbane, belladonna (also called deadly nightshade), and mandrake, all of which can be fatal if ingested in certain amounts, are members of the nightshade family.

Native to Europe, these three plants have been used as poisons since ancient times. However, witches also used them in lesser doses in brews and potions intended to aid clairvoyance, to act as an aphrodisiac, to cure lover's quarrels and infertility, and to bring good luck. According to witch-hunters, nightshade plants were also ingredients in witches' flying ointment, along with hemlock.

Hemlock is a poisonous herb often mistaken for parsley. Indeed, it is a member of the parsley family. Like plants of the nightshade family, it is native to Europe, so it was easily available to witches seeking to make poisons. Its efficacy in this regard was well known, since ancient Greeks used hemlock to create a poisonous brew given to criminals condemned to death. **See also** amulet; Chambre Ardente; herbs and other plants; Wiccan Rede.

poppet

A poppet is a small, handmade cloth doll, usually stuffed with herbs, that is used in image magic. In such magic, the poppet represents the person at whom the magic is being directed. (Sometimes a photograph of the person is pasted onto the poppet to make this connection clearer.) For example, a witch wanting to attract personal success might make a poppet stuffed with herbs and spices associated with success, which include bay, rosemary, and cinnamon. The witch would then use the poppet in casting a spell intended to bring good fortune, chanting over it and exposing it to smoke from certain incenses and candles. In casting a love spell, the witch might make two poppets, one representing each of the people intended to be drawn together. The most common type of poppet, however, is a healing poppet, stuffed with healing herbs such as ginseng, peppermint, and eucalyptus.

Modern witches use poppets in positive ways, but in earlier centuries witches sometimes used poppets to hurt people. For example, a witch might stick pins in a poppet's eyes to blind the person the poppet represented. Today the use of poppets for evil still exists among practitioners of vodun, a religion that combines elements of African paganism with Christianity. Such

Called voodoo dolls in the vodun religion, poppets are representative of a person for or against whom magic is performed.

poppets are called voodoo dolls. **See also** image magic; pins; vodun.

potion

A potion is an herbal concoction used in magical and healing rituals. Witches usually create it in the form of a tea, brewed in a cauldron while the witch says incantations over the liquid. In this way the witch directs magical intent into the potion, so that it is specific for one purpose. For example, there are love potions (also called philters), potions for youth and vitality, and potions to heal particular ailments. During the witch-hunting centuries, some witch confessions mentioned potions that enabled witches to become invisible or to fly. Witches have also long believed that potions should be prepared during the phase of the moon best suited for the potion's magical intent. For example, the new moon is thought to enhance love spells. **See also** cauldron; herbs and other plants; magic; moon.

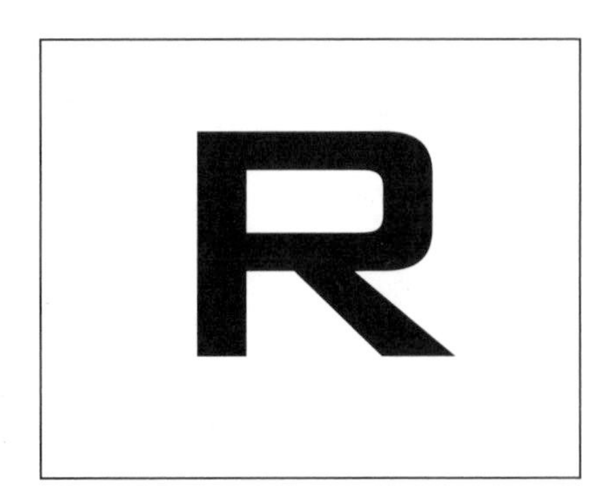

Ravenwolf, Silver (1956–)

American witch Silver Ravenwolf leads the Black Forest Tradition, which she established with her husband, Mick Ravenwolf. This tradition combines elements of the Gardnerian Tradition with a Pennsylvania healing tradition called Pow-Wow. Ravenwolf has also written numerous popular books on witchcraft-related subjects, including *To Ride a Silver Broomstick* (1993), *To Stir a Magic Cauldron* (1995), *Teen Witch* (1998), *To Light a Silver Flame* (1999), *Silver's Spells for Prosperity* (1999), and *Silver's Spells for Protection* (2000). She began her writing career in the 1980s with a small newsletter focusing on witchcraft, then went on to publish *Of Writers and Witches*, the newsletter of the Wiccan/Pagan Press Alliance. For fifteen years she was the director of this organization; today she concentrates her efforts on lecturing and teaching about Wicca and related subjects. **See also** Gardnerian Tradition.

Reclaiming Tradition

Established in San Francisco in 1980 and incorporated as a nonprofit religious group in 1990, the Reclaiming Tradition is a Witchcraft tradition that emphasizes personal empowerment. Its members believe that every individual embodies the divine and should be given the freedom to interpret spirituality in her or his own way. Covens of the Reclaiming Tradition therefore invoke goddesses and gods from many pantheons, working with both female and male elements of the deity. Rituals not only celebrate the seasons but also personal triumphs, and they raise the participants' energy levels to aid their practice of magic and healing. The four elements, air, fire, water, and earth, are an important part of Reclaiming rituals, and the tradition's approach to ritual magic shares many concepts with the Faery Witchcraft Tradition.

To be initiated into a Reclaiming coven, a person must petition a committee of teachers for permission to join. If and when these teachers decide that the petitioner is ready, they give the person a series of challenges to overcome before going through the initiation ceremony. These challenges are usually individually designed to encourage personal growth in the petitioner; they are difficult but not impossible for that individual to undertake. For example, someone who has exhibited a fear of heights might be challenged to go skydiving or hot-air ballooning. In the Reclaiming Tradition, conquering one's fears and inhibitions is an important part of becoming personally empowered.

The founders of the Reclaiming Tradition were American feminists Diane Baker and Starhawk, the latter of whom wrote many of the tradition's ritual texts. The two began by teaching classes in witchcraft, then added workshops in spiritual empowerment. Eventually they created a series of courses, hired additional teachers, and attracted an increasing number of students. These teachers and students formed the basis of their Reclaiming Collective, which later became the Reclaiming Tradition. Many original members were political activists involved in antinuclear and environmental issues, and their attitudes influenced the development of the tradition, as did the fact that Starhawk was originally trained in the Faery Tradition.

Today covens of the Reclaiming Tradition are involved in a variety of environmental, economic, social, political, racial, and gender issues and are particularly active in fighting discrimination against witches, women, and other minority or nonmainstream groups. The tradition's "mission statement" includes the unification of spirit and politics. The tradition also promotes the public dissemination of information on witchcraft. To this end, it publishes a newsletter, *Reclaiming Quarterly,* holds public rituals, and sponsors classes and workshops on the practices of magic and meditation. **See also** Faery Tradition; fairies; Starhawk; traditions, Witchcraft.

Reformation

The historical period known as the Reformation, which followed the Renaissance and encompassed the sixteenth century and the first half of the seventeenth century, was a time of transition in terms of witch-hunting. During the period, witch hysteria was waning in many parts of Europe, largely because Europeans increasingly realized that the typical approach to witch trials—that accused witches should always be presumed guilty and have fewer rights than other types of defendants—was wrong. This shift in opinion was understandable, given that by this time many people had lost a loved one to a witch trial or had experienced fear of being accused of witchcraft themselves. By the end of the period, doubts about the validity of witch-hunts were strengthened by new ways of thinking about science and religion. Science gradually replaced religion as the authority in people's lives, and this caused them to reject ideas born of faith rather than reason. This rejection continued during the Modern Age that followed. By 1688, witch-hunting had effectively ended in Europe and England, and shortly thereafter it ended in America as well. **See also** Renaissance.

reincarnation

Most modern witches believe in reincarnation, the idea that the soul lives on after death and is subsequently reborn in a new body. Most also believe that this process takes place so that the soul can learn and grow, and that when the soul has reached a certain level of growth it no longer needs to be reborn. Depending on the Witchcraft tradition, belief varies as to where the soul resides after achieving maximum growth. Also variable are beliefs related to how long and where the soul waits before being reborn and whether the soul must always be reborn into the same species. (Some people believe that the soul starts out in lesser forms of animals and works its way up to being human, while most people believe that a human soul has always been and always will be a human soul.) However, most witches agree that when a witch is reborn she generally remains within her own family. Therefore, a witch with an ancestor who was a witch often believes that her body contains that witch's soul, and some even claim to remember their past life as a witch. **See also** Summerland; rites and rituals; traditions, Witchcraft.

Rémy, Nicholas (c. 1530–1612)

French witch-hunter, lawyer, and judge Nicholas Rémy is the author of *Demonolatry*, a 1595 guide to witch-hunting. In the book, Rémy called for the execution of all witches and the punishment of their children, the latter of which was an unusual stance for the time but would subsequently be adopted by many witch judges. Rémy's book also offered detailed descriptions of witches' activities, including romps with the devil, spells, rituals, and the use of poisons, so that witch-hunters would be able to find them more easily. Rémy acquired these details via his own courtroom experiences, which lent authority to his information. Consequently, the work became extremely popular and was reprinted several times, not only in French but in German. In some parts of Europe *Demonolatry* came to be considered even more authoritative than *Malleus Maleficarum*, which many considered the leading handbook for witch-hunters and witch-trial judges.

During Rémy's career as a witch-hunter, he was responsible by some estimates for the execution of over nine hundred accused witches. The zeal with which he persecuted them was due in large part to his belief that in 1582 a witch used magic to kill his eldest son, as punishment for his own refusal to give the woman who had been begging the day before the money she had requested. Until his own death in 1612, Rémy continued to be merciless in his attempt to eliminate all witches. **See also** *Malleus Maleficarum;* trials, witch; witch-hunter.

Renaissance

The historical period following the Middle Ages, the Renaissance is characterized as a time when Europeans exhibited a renewed interest in all things related to the classical world of Greece and Rome. Generally, the period is considered by scholars to have spanned the fifteenth and sixteenth centuries.

The Renaissance was a time of many advances in the arts and sciences. However, it was also a time when the Catholic Church was both extremely powerful and relentless in persecuting witches and pagans. In many places this persecution continued into the subsequent historical period, the Reformation, even as the Catholic Church's political influence began to weaken. **See also** Reformation.

rites and rituals

Rites, which are ceremonies marking certain life events, vary widely among witches according to their Witchcraft tradition. Most modern witches, however, celebrate seven rites, also called rites of passage: Wiccaning, coming of age, dedication, initiation, handfasting, handparting, and passing over. Wiccaning is the rite whereby newborn babies are welcomed into the religious community and given a name. Alternatively, the infant (or sometimes an older child) might be given two names during the ceremony, one for public use and the other for use among witches. Coming of age marks the onset of puberty; during this ceremony, the young woman or young man is usually given a gift of some kind of jewelry significant to the tradition, representing either the female or male life force.

Dedication is the ceremony during which an adult dedicates herself or himself to studying Witchcraft. Usually the required period of study is a year and a day, whereupon the person undergoes the rite of initiation. This ceremony marks the person's formal acceptance into a tradition and usually into a particular coven as well (even if that person went through the coven's Wiccaning ceremony as a child, since witches believe that only an adult can make the decision to become a witch). After participating in this rite, the witch can choose to become part of a coven or practice the tradition as a solitary. In recent years, some would-be witches have used information found in books to perform a self-initiation rite, essentially avoiding having to adhere to the beliefs and practices of a particular coven or tradition.

The rites of handfasting and handparting are for witches who want to marry and divorce, respectively. In a handfasting, a man and a woman pledge to remain together

These modern Druids are performing a handfasting ceremony, in which a couple pledges to stay together as long as their love lasts.

only so long as their love lasts. In some Witchcraft traditions, it is customary to handfast for only a year and a day. When this time period is over, the couple undergoes a handparting ceremony that dissolves their marriage, though not necessarily their love for one another. In such cases, the couple can subsequently undergo a new handfasting if they wish. Both the handfasting and handparting rites are usually performed by a coven's high priestess and/or high priest. Members of the coven consider such ceremonies binding, and if the priestess or priest is registered with local government authorities as a member of the clergy, the ceremonies are legally binding as well.

The rite called passing over is performed upon someone's death. Since most modern witches believe in reincarnation, the ceremony is not one of mourning but of celebration. Participants honor the person who has "passed over" and encourage that person's spirit to continue on its journey to the next life.

Witchcraft rites are often performed within a magic circle and typically involve invocations, movements and gestures, chants, and the use of ritual tools such as candles, athames, and incense. This is also true of rituals, which are ceremonies performed for the purpose of worship or the practice of magic. However, rites usually involve a group of participants, whereas rituals are commonly performed by either groups or individuals. Moreover, whereas rites mark life events, rituals usually mark important times of the year, such as the appearance of the full moon and the arrival of the solstice and equinox. Modern witches also routinely employ rituals to raise magical energy just prior to spell casting. As with rites, rituals vary widely according to

Witchcraft tradition. Moreover, while some traditions require that certain rites and rituals be performed in certain ways, others encourage participants to make things up as they go along believing that such inventiveness is inspired by their deities. **See also** circle, magic; handfasting; traditions, Witchcraft.

Rituale Romanum

An official document of the Catholic Church written in 1614, the *Rituale Romanum* is a guidebook for priests that includes the church's first instructions on how to conduct an exorcism. However, recognizing the possibility that a victim of alleged demonic possession might actually be suffering from a mental illness, in the *Rituale Romanum* the church offered guidelines for assessing the victim's mental health and cautioned the exorcist not to be overeager in assuming that real demons were present. The *Rituale Romanum* also recommended that priests refuse to perform an exorcism involving a female victim without at least one other woman present, because of the possibility that the victim might make sexual overtures to the priest.

As for the precise exorcism ritual, the *Rituale Romanum* gave the exorcist wide latitude in deciding how to proceed, although it recommended a particular course of action. This included sprinkling holy water and making the sign of the Christian cross over the victim, reading aloud from certain biblical passages, praying, and repeatedly commanding the demon to leave the host body. In addition, the *Rituale Romanum* warned exorcists not to become too deeply involved in conversation with the demon, lest the priest himself be seduced to join the devil. The exorcist could, however, engage the demon in just enough conversation to determine how the victim became possessed in the first place. **See also** Bible; demonic possession; exorcism.

Robinson, Edmund (1624–?)

The case of Edmund Robinson illustrates how easily witchcraft-related hysteria was inspired in seventeenth-century England. Born in the Pendle Forest area of Lancashire, England, Robinson was nine years old when, he later said, he encountered two stray dogs that turned into humans. He claimed to have recognized one of them as a neighbor, Frances Dicconson, and insisted that she turned the other, a young boy like himself, into a horse that he then rode to a witches' Sabbat. When questioned further by judges, Robinson described the Sabbat and offered names of townspeople who had attended as practicing witches. On his word alone, over thirty people were arrested. Seventeen of them stood trial, although only one confessed to being a witch and consorting with the devil. This one confession, coupled with Robinson's testimony, was enough for the jury to convict all of the defendants.

However, fortunately for the convicted witches, the trial judge did not believe Robinson's story and set aside the jury's decision. He then sent Robinson and some of the defendants to experts in witchcraft for further examination. These experts concluded that Robinson had been lying. Shortly thereafter the boy admitted that he had indeed made up the entire Sabbat incident and falsely accused his neighbors. Various theories have been proposed for Robinson's motive for lying, ranging from a desire for attention to the fact that his father disliked Dicconson, but Robinson himself never offered a reason. Historical records do not indicate his fate. As for those he falsely accused, three died in prison while awaiting trial and the others were released. **See also** England, witch-hunts of; Sabbat; trials, witch.

Rosicrucians

The Rosicrucians was a secret occult brotherhood of the Middle Ages, the forerunner of a modern-day group called the Rosicrucian Order. Its members, also called Rosicrucians, devoted themselves to the study of magic, some say using teachings derived from texts from ancient Egypt, Greece, Arabia, and Morocco. These teachings blended the beliefs and practices of various ancient religions with a variety of medieval occult beliefs and practices.

The origins of the brotherhood are unclear. The earliest mention of the order appears in a 1614 manuscript entitled *Fama Fraternitatis* (*Account of the Brotherhood*). According to this document, the order was established by a German named Christian Rosenkreuz, who lived between 1378 and 1484 (making his age at his death 106); Rosenkreuz apparently traveled throughout the Mediterranean and Middle East, learning secret Eastern religious and magical practices. However, some people believe that the founder of Rosicrucianism was instead Paracelsus, a sixteenth century Swiss healer and alchemist. Still others think that Rosicrucianism actually began in ancient Egypt, despite the fact that no mention of it appears in documents from that time. People who support this theory argue that this lack of documentation is understandable given that the Rosicrucians was a secret brotherhood. **See also** alchemy; Paracelsus.

rowan

Rowan trees (*Sorbus aucuparia*) are among several trees that witches consider sacred. Many believe that the tree has protective powers, particularly against magic, and that this power is contained not only in its wood but in its berries. They might therefore sprinkle water in which rowan berries have been soaked around a home to protect it. Rowans have traditionally been planted near homes for the same purpose. In addition, carrying a twig from a rowan tree was once believed to protect people from being captured by fairies, perhaps because the tree is also said to be the home of good fairies.

In ancient times, the rowan was involved in pagan fertility rituals. For example, in spring rituals, animals were passed through hoops made of rowan to increase their fertility. In some legends, the rowan was associated with the female life force, with the ash being its male counterpart. For example, in Scandinavian mythology the first woman was created out of a rowan and the first man out of an ash. In Celtic mythology, the goddess Bridgit shoots arrows made of rowan, and rowan trees were said to be guarded by dragons. **See also** trees.

rue

Witches consider rue (*Ruta graveolens*) a sacred herb that possesses magic powers. In particular, rue can offer protection against evil magic, so witches sometimes carry pouches filled with rue as amulets. They might also use rue as part of protective spells. In Italian traditions, the herb is often ingested or used in charms to protect against enchantment and strengthen psychic abilities.

The idea that rue confers protection is ancient. The Greeks thought that rue placed in poison rendered the poison harmless, while the Romans thought that ingesting rue could protect eyesight. In medieval times, Catholics also believed that rue had protective powers and used a spray of rue to sprinkle holy water during church services. **See also** herbs and other plants.

runes

Runes are characters of the earliest written alphabet of Germanic peoples in Europe and Scandinavia. The word *rune* comes from the Old Norse word *run*, which means "secret"; this refers to the fact that when runes were first created, only pagan priests knew their meaning. They used Runic characters in making charms and magic spells, which is probably why runes have always been considered magic.

Throughout the centuries, the most common means of evoking the runes' magic has been to mark them on certain objects. Each Runic character is believed to be connected to a specific state of being, such as joy, prosperity, strength, or protection, and will theoretically confer that state of being to whomever or whatever bears that Runic character. For example, a necklace bearing the rune for protection is said to protect the health and well-being of the wearer. However, it is also said that the runes will not work without some effort on the user's part. In other words, a person cannot rely on the protection rune alone to ensure good health, but must also follow a healthy lifestyle.

The objects on which the runes have typically been marked have varied over the centuries. Vikings marked their weapons and homes with Runic characters to give them strength; modern witches, on the other hand, mark Runic characters on objects like ritual tools, ritual clothing, amulets, and talismans to "charge" these objects with certain types of power. They also combine characters in an artistic way, connecting or overlapping runes to create a new Runic image called a bindrune. A bindrune retains the properties of the individual characters from which it was created. Consequently a bindrune made from the Runic characters for prosperity and success would confer both qualities on the owner.

Both in ancient and modern times, people have also used runes in divination. For this purpose, Runic characters are typically marked on small stones, crystals, or sticks. Each of the states represented by these characters, such as joy, partnership, journey, strength, and protection, are believed to have complex meanings in terms of past, present, and future events. Guidebooks on runes offer detailed descriptions of these deeper meanings, and a person using the runes for divination often consults such a book during the process.

To begin the process of divination, a person selects a certain number of runestones, for example, at random—usually one, three, or five, depending on the method of divination being employed—and lays them out on a table. While selecting the stones, the person concentrates on a question related to whatever she or he wants to learn from the runes. For example, the person might silently ask the runes, "What will happen if I change jobs?" In determining the runes' answer, the person must consider not only the deeper meaning of each Runic character but also the order in which they were selected. In a divination process using three runes, for example, the first Runic character usually relates to the current status of the person's situation, the second to the past influences on that situation, and the third to prospects for resolving the situation in the future. Therefore a rune signifying prosperity will have a different meaning depending on whether it falls in the present, past, or future position.

Sometimes, however, the runes do not provide an answer to a question. One rune, called *wyrd*, is blank; its name means that the answer is unknowable because it is "up to the gods." In addition to the blank, there are twenty-four Runic characters, each with a different meaning. **See also** divination.

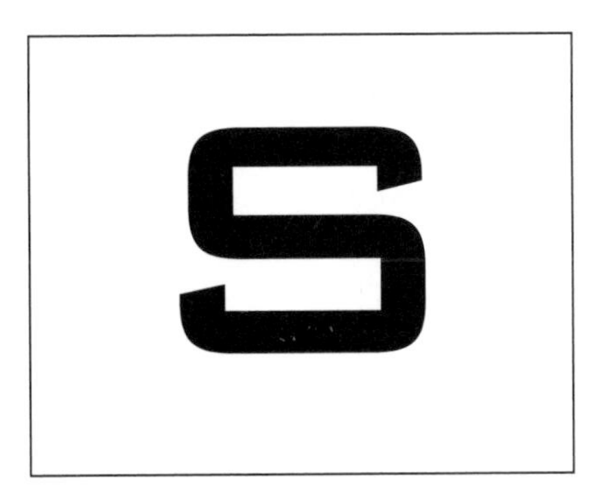

Sabbat

A Sabbat is a seasonal festival celebrated by Wiccans. There are eight Sabbats per year, four honoring the astronomical beginning of each season and four honoring ancient agricultural festivals. Those honoring the seasons are Yule, also called the winter solstice; Ostara, also called the spring equinox; Midsummer, also called the summer solstice; and Mabon, also called the fall or autumn equinox. Those honoring ancient agricultural festivals are Imbolc, which celebrates the birthing of the first lambs; Beltane, which celebrates new growth in the fields; Lughnasadh, which celebrates the time of harvest; and Samhain, which celebrates the time of slaughtering animals for food storage prior to winter. Some Witchcraft traditions, primarily those which have sprung from northern Europe, refer to these agricultural festivals as the Greater Sabbats and the remaining Sabbats as the Lesser Sabbats. Others, primarily those from southern Europe, reverse these designations.

Some witches believe that the word *Sabbat* is derived from the word *Sabbath*, a time when observant Jews believe no work is to be done. These witches therefore use the day to rest, reflect, and celebrate rather than to work magic. However, some Witchcraft traditions believe that Sabbats are the best time to work magic, because their significance adds power to a spell, as well as to honor deities.

In most traditions, Sabbats are also a time of rebirth, when witches can effect changes in their lives through either magical or nonmagical means. Various traditions mark these times of change in various ways. For example, some covens hold Sabbat ceremonies that involve walking under a veil to symbolize crossing from one reality to another. Others perform dances that move participants from one symbolic realm to another. Sabbat festivals might also feature chanting and the beating of drums, believed to alter states of consciousness.

Historians know that ancient pagans celebrated festivals at the same time of the year as do modern witches. However, they disagree on just how similar modern Sabbat celebrations are to their ancient counterparts. Much of the information about ancient pagan religious practices has been passed down orally, and many scholars believe that this information has been distorted along the way, particularly during the witch-hunting years.

During these years, the word *Sabbat* was often used to refer to any witches' gathering, not just those related to the eight festivals. This concept originated in the witch trials of mid-fourteenth-century Europe, when defendants began to confess under torture to meeting together in large groups. In most cases, it is unclear whether their meetings were tied to one of the eight festivals or were part of coven meetings held at other times of the year. Some of the witches confessed to participating in Sabbats once a week, while others said that they went only once a year.

Historians have disagreed on the extent to which Sabbat meetings were held and on their locations. Some say that there were no Sabbats held in Britain, while others believe that Sabbat festivals existed in both Britain and Europe. Some believe that Sabbats were seasonal, agricultural festivals related to pagan worship but not witchcraft. Such scholars do not believe that witches met in groups during this period at all, and said they did only to satisfy their interrogators.

Indeed, some of the witch trial defendants' other claims related to Sabbats were clearly either exaggerations or falsehoods. Many of them reported that they flew to their Sabbats on broomsticks, animals, or demons, or that they turned themselves into animals to fly to their meetings, which always took place at night on a distant mountaintop or deep in a forest, although sometimes caves were mentioned as well. Witches typically said that the devil presided over the revelries, which could include dozens or even hundreds of witches, and that demons were there as well. Their reported activities ranged from drinking, feasting, and sexual intimacies to blood-drinking rituals and human sacrifices. When such sacrifices were mentioned, they typically involved Christian infants that had not yet been baptized into their faith, and it was sometimes said that the revelers subsequently ate the infants.

Because of such lurid associations, some modern witches no longer use the Sabbat to refer to their festivals, seeking to disassociate themselves from an inaccurate history. There is no evidence that witches ever took part in the kind of demonic activities described in witch confessions. **See also** devil; Wheel of the Year.

sage

A plant belonging to the mint family, white sage (*Salvia apiana*) is featured in a purification ceremony performed by witches of many different traditions. The details of this ceremony, which is called the smudging ceremony or simply smudging, vary according to tradition. However, in most variations a small, short bundle of natural white sage sticks is lit and the fire then blown out, whereupon the sage continues to give off smoke. The bundle is then either placed in a bowl for the duration of the ceremony or waved around participants so that they are "smudged" with the smoke. In either case, the smoke is believed to eliminate negative energy from their bodies.

Salem, witch trials of

Lasting from 1692 to 1693 in Salem, Massachusetts, the Salem witch trials involved 150 accusations of witchcraft, 141 arrests, 31 convictions, and 20 executions, 19 by hanging and one by crushing. They were not the first witch trials in America (a distinction held by a 1647 witch trial in Connecticut), nor did they produce a large number of convictions compared with witch-hunts in Europe, which had been going on for roughly three centuries by the time the Salem trials occurred. Nonetheless, the Salem witch trials are perhaps the most famous witch trials in history, both because of the widespread publicity they received and because even before the trials ended it became obvious to most people that all of the defendants were innocent.

The witch hysteria that triggered the trials began in Salem Village (on the site of what is now Danvers, Massachusetts) in January 1692. On the most superficial level, it started when nine-year-old Betty (also known as Elizabeth) Parris, the daughter of the Reverend Samuel Parris, the town's Puritan minister, began exhibiting symptoms of having been affected by witchcraft.

During the day, Betty and Parris's

eleven-year-old niece Abigail Williams were cared for by Parris's slave, Tituba. Born in Barbados, Tituba told the girls stories of the magical practices on her native island, and they insisted she work magic with them and their friends: Ann Putnam Jr. (age twelve), Ann's servant Mercy Lewis (nineteen), Ann's cousin Mary Walcott (sixteen), Susannah Sheldon (eighteen), Elizabeth Booth (eighteen), Elizabeth Hubbard (seventeen), Mary Warren (twenty), and Sarah Churchill (nineteen). Together with Tituba, the girls performed divination and engaged in magic rituals, probably related to love spells. Shortly thereafter, Betty Parris began experiencing convulsions, and the other girls soon began having them as well. They also repeatedly crawled into holes or under tables and often spoke gibberish.

At first the girls were believed to be ill, but after physicians found no physical cause for their symptoms many people decided the girls were bewitched, even before stories of their magical play surfaced. Mary Walcott's aunt therefore ordered Tituba to bake a traditional English "witch-finding" cake, which, when fed to a dog, was said to make the animal the witch's familiar so that the dog would go directly to that person. Walcott's intent was to find the person who had bewitched the girls. However, her actions were condemned by Reverend Parris and others as opening the door to allow Satan to take hold of the town. New Englanders believed that any traffic with magic was an invitation to the devil.

Faced with such a threat, the townspeople naturally looked to God's agent—their minister, Reverend Samuel Parris. Immediately the man's status in Salem Village rose. Moreover, attendance at his worship services, which had been lagging in recent months, rose dramatically as people turned to the church for help with this clear crisis of faith.

Meanwhile the girls began naming their tormentors. The first people they accused were Tituba and two women who did not attend church, Sarah Good and Sarah Osborne. The women were immediately arrested. Good and Osborne protested their innocence, even after the girls fell into fits in their presence, but Tituba confessed that she was indeed a witch and had flown to Sabbats with Good and Osborne. Tituba further confessed that there was an active witch coven in Salem, led by a man in black who forced people to sign their names in the devil's book of pledged souls.

Given this information, town leaders pressed the girls to name more names and they obliged, with the help of Ann Putnam's mother, also named Ann Putnam. By this time the elder Ann had begun having fits along with her daughter, and the next women named as witches were people whom both Putnam women resented, Martha Cory and Rebecca Nurse. Cory and Nurse were respected churchgoing members of the community, but both had also experienced more good fortune than the elder Ann Putnam, who was reputed to be a jealous woman. Historians therefore believe Putnam made these accusations out of spite.

Nonetheless, once any of the accusations were made, the people of Salem were inclined to believe them, largely because of the efforts of Reverend Parris. In his sermons he began exhorting his parishioners to beware the cleverness of the devil, who concealed his agents well, implying that even the most respected citizen might be a tool of the devil. The minister also said it was not surprising that Salem Village had witches, given that the town had long been a place of contention.

There had long been two opposing factions in the town, and at the time of the Salem trials one of them supported Parris's ministry and the other preferred to worship in nearby Salem Town. Parris's primary supporters were also the main instigators of the witch trials; these included not only the senior Ann Putnam but also her hus-

The Salem witch trials are believed to have begun when a slave, Tituba, began telling children about witchcraft. Reportedly, the children began experiencing convulsions and talking gibberish, displaying signs of being bewitched.

band, Thomas Putnam Jr., who testified against several of the accused witches, and Thomas Putnam's brother Edward and brother-in-law Jonathan Walcott. Most of those accused of witchcraft were members of the anti-Parris faction. Historians do not believe this was a coincidence, suggesting that Salem's internal politics were a major reason the hysteria over witches took hold.

Parris, however, preached that Satan was to blame for all of the town's troubles, and said that the villagers would need to fight back if they were going to save the soul of their town. Many scholars believe that this encouragement was fundamental in keeping the witch hysteria going in Salem Village. Paul Boyer and Stephen Nissenbaum, in their book *Salem Possessed: The Social Origins of Witchcraft*, claim:

> Samuel Parris did not deliberately provoke the Salem witchcraft episode. Nor, certainly, was he responsible for the factional conflict which underlay it. Nevertheless, his was a crucial role. He had a keen mind and a way with words, and Sunday after Sunday, in the little Village meetinghouse, by the alchemy of typology and allegory, he took the nagging fears and conflicting impulses of his hearers and wove them into a pattern overwhelming in its scope, a universal drama in which Christ and Satan, Heaven and Hell, struggled for supremacy.

As Parris convinced the villagers that Satan was using their town for a dramatic battle between good and evil forces, they were more inclined to believe the bewitched girls' accusations even as they got wilder and wilder. The two Ann Putnams, Abigail Williams, Mary Walcott, and Elizabeth Hubbard all said that the specter of Rebecca Nurse had appeared to them to force them to sign the devil's book. When Rebecca Nurse's sister, Sarah Cloyce, and respected tavernkeepers John and Elizabeth Proctor suggested that "the afflicted," as those suffering from the fits were called, were lying, they too were accused of being witches. By this time, Tituba's husband, John Indian, had become one of the afflicted, and he joined Mary Walcott, Abigail Williams, the younger Ann Putnam, and Mercy Lewis in claiming that they had been tormented by the specters of Sarah Cloyce and the Proctors. While making these accusations, the younger Putnam and Abigail Williams said that they saw John Proctor's specter sitting in the rafters of the room. The afflicted also said that they had seen Elizabeth Proctor's specter force her maid, Mary Warren, to sign the devil's book.

This remark was clearly a clever calculation. Mary Warren was one of the afflicted until the Proctors had ordered her to stop having fits, which she then did. It was therefore vitally important for the afflicted to convince people that Warren had stopped not because she had been pretending but because she was under the control of the devil, who wanted the town to *think* she had been pretending. Moreover, if Warren had signed the book but was not one of the afflicted, she would be arrested as a witch herself. In a bind, shortly after the afflicted made this statement, Warren joined their ranks and confirmed everything they had said about the Proctors.

By this time, the investigation into Salem witchcraft had been moved to nearby Salem Town. The girls attended the formal interrogations of all those arrested, and whenever one of the accused witches was brought into the room the girls would immediately complain of being pinched, pricked, and otherwise tormented by the suspects' specters. If they touched the suspect, their symptoms would immediately cease. The court considered this to be ample evidence to hold the accused witches over for trial.

Eventually, the Massachusetts Bay Colony established a Court of Oyer and Terminer ("to hear and determine") in Salem Town under the supervision of Lieutenant Governor William Stoughton and several other learned justices. These men knew nothing of Salem Village's internal conflicts, so they proceeded on the basis of the afflicted girls' obvious physical symptoms. As each accused witch was brought into the courtroom, the girls created quite a spectacle, writhing, shrieking, convulsing, and claiming they saw specters. In at least one case, however, they did not do this—when the accused witch came into the courtroom from the back so they did not know she was there.

Such discrepancies in the girls' behavior made people suspicious, but since those who spoke out against the afflicted typically found themselves accused, few dared raise a protest. For example, when Justice Dudley Bradstreet, in the nearby town of Andover, refused to sign arrest warrants for people whom the girls had accused in his town, the girls accused him as well, but he fled before being arrested. The same threat loomed for members of the afflicted who began to feel guilty about their accusations and tried to go against the group. One such person was Sarah Churchill, who tried to take back one of her accusations but was threatened by her peers until she again stood firmly with them. Only when the entire group decided to let someone go free (usually because it was obvious that the person had powerful supporters and/or would never be convicted) would an accusation be recanted as a "mistake."

Most of those who were accused were found guilty. The first was Bridget Bishop, who was subsequently hanged on June 10, 1692. Shortly thereafter, one of the court judges, Nathaniel Saltonstall, resigned his

When bringing accused witches into the courtroom, the justices often relied upon the physical response of the town's young girls to determine guilt. If the girls began to convulse and shriek, the accused was found guilty.

position because he thought that at least some of the afflicted were lying. He was then accused of being a witch himself.

Saltonstall's doubt was inspired in large part by the fact that the afflicted girls kept saying they saw the spirits of the accused witches in various places. The girls also claimed that their "spectral sight" enabled them to see the activities of witches from far away. Because of this ability, they were able to accuse witches in distant towns without going there, which is what they were often asked to do once word of the Salem trials reached these places. Amid the resultant witch hysteria, distant townspeople who had suffered any kind of bad luck decided that they too had witches among them and petitioned the girls to identify the culprits from afar. At first the girls merely described people in general terms, and people fitting the description were then brought before the afflicted to see whether the girls would have fits in their presence. Later, however, the girls began identifying people from other villages by name (probably because someone had told them whom to name).

Some people believed in the girls' spectral sight, but others began to question its validity. Even the esteemed minister and witch-hunter Cotton Mather, called in to advise the court, expressed doubt over the reliability of spectral evidence. Still, he declared the proceedings essentially sound and justified, and the trials continued. In large part Mather's support was based on the fact that other townspeople did come forward to substantiate some of the girls' accusations. In all, approximately fifty people claimed to be the victims of witchcraft in the area.

Some of the accused witches actually confessed their crimes, both because they were mildly tortured while in jail and because it brought them mercy from the court. For example, almost everyone accused in the town of Andover, Massachusetts, was spared execution by confessing to being witches. In fact, so great was the incentive to confess that about fifty-five people accused during the period of Salem hysteria eventually did so. Most of their confessions contained details that were fairly standard for the period. For example, some claimed to fly on brooms, and most said they had seen the devil.

Others, like seventy-one-year-old Rebecca Nurse, protested their innocence to the end. In addition to Bridget Bishop, she and seventeen others were hanged: George Burroughs, Martha Carrier, Martha Cory, Mary Esty, Sarah Good, Elizabeth How, George Jacobs, Susanna Martin, Alice Parker, Mary Parker, John Proctor, Ann Pudeator, Wilmot Reed, Margaret Scott, Samuel Wardwell, Sarah Wilds, and John Willard. Twelve others were convicted but died in prison, escaped, or were later reprieved. Tituba was sent to prison rather than executed to reward her for her cooperation in destroying Salem's witch coven.

Of the deaths witnessed by assembled crowds, two were controversial even among those present. The first was the case of George Burroughs. Burroughs had once held the Reverend Parris's job, but had left his post and Salem Village when he became disgusted with the town's internal political conflicts. Some of the people who instigated the witch trials, however, still bore him ill will, so it is perhaps no surprise that he was tracked down and brought back to face trial as the leader of Salem's witch coven. While on the gallows waiting to be hanged, the former minister of Salem Village recited the Lord's Prayer flawlessly, which, according to popular belief, would not have been possible if Burroughs were really in league with the devil. Most of the people who witnessed his recitation therefore demanded that he be set free, but Cotton Mather, the witch-hunting expert, stepped forward to convince the assembly that the hanging should proceed, and Burroughs died on schedule.

The other death that raised an outcry was that of Giles Cory, an eighty-year-old man who refused to cooperate with court procedure. At the outset of the proceedings, each defendant was supposed to formally acknowledge that the court had jurisdiction over the case. Cory refused to do this, which delayed the start of his trial. To punish him for his obstinacy and force him to give his acknowledgement, the court ordered that he be laid down in a field and covered with a wooden board onto which heavy stones were gradually stacked. Called pressing, this punishment was illegal under a law established in England in 1641. Consequently, when Cory was crushed to death after two days of pressing, the public outcry in some quarters was great.

Meanwhile, Mather was facing criticism for his role in Burroughs's execution. Even his own father, Increase Mather, questioned whether the Salem witch trials were proceeding fairly (although, in deference to his son, he did not specifically mention the Burroughs hanging incident). In early 1693 Cotton Mather published a book entitled *The Wonders of the Invisible World* to defend his actions, but it did little good in repairing his now damaged reputation, particularly after Boston author Robert Calef published *More Wonders of the Invisible World* in 1700 to counter Mather's defense.

Others attacked the Salem witch trial proceedings as well. As more and more people were accused of witchcraft, a leading witch-hunter, the Reverend John Hale, said it was unlikely there could be so many witches and victims of witchcraft in such a small geographical area. Then some of the afflicted girls accused the wife of the governor of New England, Lady Phips, of being a witch, and people had finally had enough. Understandably, the governor, Sir William Phips, ordered that no new witch cases be brought before the Salem court, shut down the proceedings, and established a new court to consider the cases still awaiting trial. This new court refused to consider any spectral evidence, and all but three of the fifty-two remaining accused witches were found innocent. The governor immediately pardoned these three, as well as five people convicted by the previous court who were still awaiting execution.

This marked the end of the Salem witch trials, but their aftermath was prolonged. Remorseful over what had occurred, the colonial public no longer supported witch executions. In addition, in 1696 the jurors who had taken part in the Salem trials put forth a statement entitled "Confessions of Error" in which they publicly apologized for their actions and asked for the forgiveness of the victims' families. In January 1697, Salem Puritans held a public day of fasting and atonement to express their own remorse over the incident. In 1706, Ann Putnam Jr. publicly apologized to the town; however, she said she had been tricked by Satan into making her witch accusations, suggesting that she was not really responsible for what she had done.

Modern scholars have carefully examined the circumstances of the Salem witch trials in attempts to discover why those involved in the trials succumbed to witch hysteria. One theory is that the girls who instigated the trials began having fits as a way to gain attention and a sense of power. Alternatively, they might have made up their symptoms to exact revenge on certain people in their community. This clearly did occur as the witch trials wore on, and it is also possible that revenge was the initial spark that ignited the first accusations.

It is also clear that from the outset at least some of the adults dealing with the girls' situation exploited it for personal gain. Many scholars believe that the pro-Parris faction used the fits—and perhaps even invented the fits—to make witch accusations that would eventually crush their enemies. There was certainly precedent for this motive in European witch-hunts, and given the colonists' ties with England many undoubtedly had heard about some of these cases.

However, stories about European witch-hunts could also have triggered genuine witch hysteria in the colonies. Some scholars believe that the girls' symptoms, at least at the outset, were the manifestation of psychological trauma caused by Tituba's practicing witchcraft with them. In genuine cases of witch hysteria, people so convince themselves that they are bewitched that psychosomatic symptoms appear.

Still another theory is that the girls' fits were genuine physical symptoms of an unknown disease. For example, Laurie Winn Carlson, in her 1999 book *A Fever in Salem: A New Interpretation of the New England Witch Trials*, believes that the girls were suffering from a form of encephalitis, since animals in the community were experiencing the occasional fit as well. According to Carlson:

> Fits, hallucinations, temporary paralysis, and "distracted" rampages were suddenly occurring sporadically in the community. The livestock, too, seemed to suffer from the unexplainable illness. The randomness of the victims and the unusual symptoms that were seldom exactly the same led the residents to suspect an otherworldly menace. With the limited scientific and medical knowledge of the time, physicians who were consulted could only offer witchcraft as an explanation.

Scholars will undoubtedly continue to debate the possible medical, social, psychological, economic, and political factors most likely to blame for the Salem witch trials. But whatever the cause, Americans considered the outcome of the Salem trials so disturbing that even today they cite it as a cautionary tale against allowing emotions to override common sense. **See also** Mather, Cotton; Mather, Increase; trials, witch.

salt

From at least the Middle Ages to the present, salt has been used by sorcerers, magicians, and witches in the performance of magic. Medieval alchemists used white salt as an ingredient in the process whereby they attempted to use science and magic to turn base metals into gold, while modern witches often sprinkle salt or a solution of salt and water in an area where a magic circle will be drawn. Such witches believe that the salt will cleanse or purify the area. For the same reason, a bowl of salt is sometimes placed on an altar within the magic circle, both to keep the area pure and to represent the element earth in Wiccan rituals.

The idea that salt purifies is also the basis of the practices of using salt to rid something or someone of evil. For example, Roman Catholics mix salt with water to create holy water, which is thought to drive demons away during exorcisms. Similarly, the superstition of throwing spilled salt over one's shoulder originated with the idea that this practice would drive the devil away, although some said that it blinded him instead. Since ancient times, the Irish have traditionally given salt as a wedding present in the conviction that it keeps evil away from a household. Medieval magicians trying to raise the dead would avoid eating salt prior to performing their magic, believing that the presence of salt in their bodies would keep the deceased's spirit away. **See also** circle, magic; magic.

Samhain

Also known as Halloween, or All Hallow's Eve, Samhain is a fire festival celebrated on October 31, when large bonfires are traditionally lit and danced around. It is also the third harvest festival of the Wiccan Wheel of the Year, after Lughnasadh and Mabon, and is opposite Beltane on the Wheel; together Beltane and Samhain are the greatest of all witches' Sabbats. But whereas Beltane symbolizes fertility and new life, Samhain symbolizes death. In stories that tie the life cycles of the God and Goddess to the Wheel of the Year, Samhain is the time when the God is dead and completely lost to the Goddess, who has thrown herself into grief. The association of Samhain with death has led to many rituals regarding spirits of the dead. Some involve walking home with torches or lanterns to help guide the spirits there, welcoming spirits to feasts, or wearing masks to hide from or frighten away spirits. In some parts of Italy cakes, breads, and sweets are baked in the shape of skeletons, skulls, or corpses as a way to honor the dead. The colors most commonly associated with Samhain are black and orange, the former representing death and the latter fire. Samhain is also a time believed to strengthen a witch's skills at divination. **See also** Beltane; Lughnasadh; Mabon; Wheel of the Year.

Sanders, Alex (1926–1988)

British witch Alex Sanders founded the Alexandrian Tradition of Witchcraft in the early 1960s. He subsequently called himself "King of the Witches" and made media appearances promoting himself in particular and witchcraft in general. In the late 1960s and early 1970s he was the focus of numerous articles, a biography entitled *King of the Witches* by June Johns, and a film entitled *Legend of the Witches*. During this time he bragged about his sorcery skills and told elaborate stories about his initiation into the Craft as well as his experiences as a Wiccan who could effect miraculous cures.

One of Sanders's claims was that his grandmother was a hereditary witch who not only introduced him to the Craft but allowed him to copy her Book of Shadows. However, when Sanders later shared material from this book with others, it was discovered that much of it had been copied or derived from the writings of several other witches, primarily Gerald Gardner. Ironically, Gerald Gardner has been accused of copying much of his written material from other witches and occultists.

After witches discovered the true origin of Sanders's work, they doubted all of his stories, and many disassociated themselves from him. Nonetheless, his tradition took hold in Great Britain and spread to the United States, Canada, and Europe. In addition, many offshoots of the Alexandrian Tradition developed, most combining elements of the tradition with those of the Gardnerian Tradition. Consequently Sanders is credited with making important contributions to the Craft despite his disfavor with most witches. **See also** Alexandrian Tradition; Gardner, Gerald; traditions, Witchcraft.

Santeria

Santeria is a religion that combines the worship of African deities with elements of Catholicism. It developed among African slaves as they were exposed to Catholic beliefs during the Middle Passage transport to the Americas. Santeria then spread to other populations, particularly Hispanic cultures in areas where African slaves or former slaves resided. Today the religion is practiced in several major U.S. cities, as well as in Cuba, Jamaica, and parts of Central and South America.

People who practice Santeria are typically called Santeros, although in some places that word is reserved for Santeria priests and other worshipers are referred to as Santerians. Believers revere hundreds of gods and goddesses, some of which are identified with Catholic saints. These deities are thought to have very specific duties. For example, there is a god of smallpox, a god of doorways and roads, and a goddess of rainbows. Each river has its own goddess, as do other natural features. Santeria also has a complex hierarchy of priests, some of whom conduct ritual animal sacrifices to the gods. Images of certain animals are also used as talismans against evil magic.

Santero priests practice healing magic and are experts in the use of medicinal herbs. They also create amulets intended to bring good health. In addition, Santeros believe strongly in the power of image magic, whereby a representation of a person can be used to work magic against that person. For example, Santeros make dolls in the image of an intended victim, then enchant them so that when the doll is harmed the victim will be too. Similarly, Santeros think that objects that have come in direct contact with a person can be used to cast spells on that person. These objects include bodily matter such as nail clippings and pieces of hair, as well as jewelry, clothing, and other articles that have been worn by the intended victim. Because Santeria involves the use of magic, it is often mislabeled as a form of witchcraft.

Santeros who specialize in evil, or black, magic are called *mayomberos*, and there are many similarities between these people and witches as they were perceived in medieval times. For example, *mayomberos* brew poisons in cauldrons, steal parts of corpses from graveyards, sacrifice animals, and claim to consort with demonic forces. **See also** image magic; poppet; vodun.

Satanism

Satanism is the worship of Satan instead of God. Also known as the devil, Satan is the personification of evil according to Christian theology, which teaches that he was once an angel who opposed God's will and was therefore banished from heaven. Satanists, however, generally believe that Satan is God's equal and rival. In fact, some Satanists have suggested that according to the Bible, Satan is the rightful ruler of the world. To support their position they cite biblical passages that call Satan "prince of this world" (John 12:13) and "god of this world" (2 Corinthians 4:4).

Satanists also believe that Satan is not necessarily evil, just self-centered, which they believe is a positive attribute. To them he represents such qualities as pride and a desire for money, material possessions, and physical enjoyment. Satanists seek to emulate these qualities.

Satanists further argue that their beliefs constitute a viable religion, the antithesis of Christianity. To this end, they have established several satanic churches, of which the most famous is the Church of Satan, founded in 1966 by noted Satanist Anton La Vey. Many of the worship practices in such churches are intentionally patterned after Christian models, with Satan substituted for God. The Black Mass, for example, is based on the Catholic Mass, with Satanists reciting Catholic incantations backward during the ceremony.

Modern witches do not practice Satanism; in fact, most do not even believe in Satan, because of his ties to Christian theology. However, some occultists who influenced the modern witchcraft movement, such as Aleister Crowley, dabbled in Satanism, and this helped strengthen the connection between witchcraft and Satanism in the modern mind.

Originally, this connection was forged during the witch-hunting era, when Satanism was referred to as devil worship and viewed as a manifestation of Satan's still-ongoing attempts to thwart the will of God. At that time, witchcraft became synonymous with devil worship, in part as a way to justify witch executions. This association was also a way for the Roman Catholic Church to demonize and eradicate paganism, since most witches apparently worshiped pagan deities and not the Christian devil. **See also** devil.

Sawyer, Elisabeth (dates unknown)

The 1621 trial in England of accused witch Elisabeth Sawyer is particularly significant for inspiring a popular play, *The Witch of Edmonton,* that same year. This play, which used many details taken directly from trial records, presented the witch as an almost unwitting, misguided tool of the devil rather than as an inherently evil, intentional wrongdoer—an unusual view at a time when witches were generally seen as purposefully malicious. The playwrights who adapted Sawyer's story, poets William Rowley, Thomas Dekker, and John Ford, chose instead to make their agent of evil a black dog that was actually the devil in disguise.

Much of Sawyer's confession concerned this dog. She was originally accused of witchcraft when a neighbor fell ill after chasing Sawyer's pig off her property. The woman, Agnes Ratcliffe, soon died, whereupon other neighbors came forward to say that Sawyer had temporarily bewitched their children and/or livestock. At first Sawyer insisted that she had done nothing to hurt anyone. But after aggressive interrogation she admitted giving her soul and body to the devil, who had come to her as a dog. Sawyer added that the dog sucked her blood, and indeed upon physical examination she was found to have a strange mark where she said the dog's mouth had touched her skin. Moreover, her body was somewhat deformed (probably due to her advanced age and/or malnutrition), and this too was taken as a sure sign she was in league with the devil. Two days after she confessed she was condemned and immediately hanged. Her confessor, Reverend Henry Goodcole, then published an account of his dealings with Sawyer, and this text was later used to create the play about her life as a witch. **See also** devil; marks, witches' or devil's.

Saxon-Wicca Tradition

Also called Seax-Wicca, Saxon-Wicca is a Witchcraft tradition that encourages self-initiation and solitary practice. This tradition was founded in 1973 by Raymond Buckland, who had come to believe that the two prevailing traditions at the time, the coven-based Gardnerian and Alexandrian Traditions, were wrong in not allowing people to explore Wicca on their own. As its name implies, the tradition incorporates the beliefs and practices of Saxon pagans, although it includes elements of both the Gardnerian and Alexandrian Traditions it was meant to augment. **See also** Alexandrian Tradition; Gardnerian Tradition; traditions, Witchcraft.

Scandinavia, witch-hunts of

Like many other countries during the sixteenth and seventeenth centuries, Sweden, Norway (which was then united with Denmark), and Finland (then considered part of Scandinavia) held numerous witch trials, but far fewer than the number held in continental Europe. Scandinavians were slow to embrace the witch hysteria that was taking place elsewhere, and even when this hysteria finally took hold it was of shorter duration. Historians disagree on why this was so, but most believe that it was due at least in part to the fact that Scandinavian officials did not encourage people to accuse one another of witchcraft, nor did they torture suspected witches to obtain confessions.

In Sweden, for example, witch trials were forbidden until the reign of King Charles XI, when in 1669 rumors surfaced that witchcraft was being extensively practiced in the town of Mora. The king sent investigators to the community and within a short time, based on accusations made primarily by children, seventy people in Mora and neighboring towns had been accused as witches. Twenty-three of these people quickly confessed (without torture, which was forbidden in Sweden) to consorting with the devil, providing numerous details about their activities at Sabbats that had been attended by many of the children who had accused them. Fifteen of these children were eventually convicted and executed as witches, along with seventy adults. Afterward, however, King Charles learned that evidence against at least one of these adults had been fabricated by someone long jealous of the woman. Horrified that an innocent woman had been put to death, he banned any further witch trials.

The first witch trial in Norway took place in 1592. Between 1592 and 1622 there were only four more cases, and only a handful of cases after that. The last trial took place in 1684. There were no mass trials and no mass hysteria in the Norwegian cases, probably because although the Norwegians believed that witchcraft was real and that witches did commit evil deeds, most did not think that witches consorted with the devil. Instead they viewed a person who committed evil via witchcraft as equivalent to any other evildoer—in other words, a person whose motive for committing the crime was selfish rather than part of a larger battle between Satan and God. This brought witch cases down to the level of simple criminal matters, thereby minimizing hysteria.

The view was different in Finland, where the first witch trial took place in 1595. Like most Finnish witch trials prior to the 1680s, this trial involved a case of maleficia, which was punishable by death. In 1687 the death penalty was mandated as well for people convicted of making a pact with the devil, reflecting the changing emphasis of witch trials. More cases of diabolical witchcraft (i.e., witchcraft in which the devil was said to be involved) therefore went to trial. However, there were still no more than sixty witch executions in Finland during the witch-hunting years, probably because the country's ban on torture made it difficult to obtain confessions. **See also** devil; maleficia.

Score, John (?–1979)

British witch John Score, who also called himself "M," helped form two leading pagan organizations, one in the United States and the other in Great Britain: the Pagan

Way and the Pagan Front (later called the Pagan Federation) respectively. Beginning in 1968, he was also the editor of the *Wiccan*, one of the most widely read pagan periodicals. In his work he encouraged people to refer to witchcraft as the Old Religion, Wisecraft, or the Old Religion of Wisecraft. Outside of his pagan activities, he researched spirit communication, placing electronic equipment where he believed spirits were located in an attempt to record their voices. He was also an expert on natural healing. **See also** Pagan Federation; Pagan Way.

Scot, Michael (c. 1175–c. 1235)

Michael Scot was a Scottish astrologer, mathematician, and physician who wrote so knowledgeably about magic that his peers decided he had to be a powerful magician. Scot denied this repeatedly, and in fact spoke out against the use of sorcery. Nonetheless, his descriptions of magic rituals were unusually detailed. He also wrote about necromancy, astrology, astronomy, and other scientific and occult subjects. Educated at Oxford University in England and elsewhere in Europe, Scot served for several years as an astrologer for King Ferdinand II of Sicily. It was undoubtedly in Ferdinand's court that he gained much of his knowledge about sorcery, because the king surrounded himself with individuals well versed in the occult. In the last few years of his life, however, Scot lived in England and Scotland, concentrating on his writing. **See also** necromancy.

Scot, Reginald (1538–1599)

English author Reginald Scot protested witch persecution by self-publishing a book in 1584 entitled *Discoverie of Witchcraft*, in which he argued that it was unlikely any of the women condemned as witches had supernatural powers. Instead he considered them innocent victims or deluded, misguided ignorants. If they did knowingly commit what they said was witchcraft, Scot believed them to be frauds who had only pretended to know magic for financial gain, or perhaps evil people who killed with poisons but not by supernatural means. He accepted none of the typical elements of witch confessions—flying to Sabbats, dances with the devil, transformation into animals, and the like—as real. Boldly, Scot even criticized the pope for his support of witch persecutions and suggested that a biblical figure called the Witch of Endor, who raised Samuel from the dead in the Old Testament book of Samuel I, was a fake rather than a real sorceress.

No one knows exactly what prompted Scot to write *Discoverie of Witchcraft*, although many historians suspect it was his outrage over a particularly unjust mass witch trial in the English village of St. Osyth in 1582. In any case, once he decided to produce the work he studied existing literature, folk beliefs, and legal cases related to witchcraft, demonology, ghosts, magic, and similar subjects, paying attention to both sides of every argument. As a result, his book was extremely thorough and convincing—so convincing, in fact, that witch hater King James VI of Scotland (who later became James I of England) not only tried to destroy every copy but wrote his own book, *Daemonologie*, to refute Scot's work by arguing that witches had real and dangerous powers. **See also** Bible; coven; James I; Sabbat; St. Osyth, witch trial of.

Scotland, witch trials of

Prior to the sixteenth century, there were only a few witch trials in Scotland, because Scottish law made it difficult to gain convictions. Generally, evidence was required that the defendant had attempted to murder someone by magical charms, magical potions, or similar means. Moreover, many of the cases involved prominent citizens whose accusers were equally prominent personal or political enemies, making the trials less about witchcraft than about human emotions like revenge or greed.

In 1563, new Scottish laws broadened the criteria for prosecuting someone as a witch; the practice of any sort of magic, rather than just magic resulting in murder, was sufficient grounds for a trial. Consequently, the number of witch trials and subsequent executions increased dramatically. Witch hysteria was fueled even more by a sensational 1590 trial involving an alleged coven of witches in North Berwick, Scotland. Scotland's King James VI, who later became King James I of both Scotland and England, was personally involved in the case, which featured a plot to take his life via magical means. After the trial King James wrote a witch-hunting guide, *Daemonologie* (1597), that encouraged witch hysteria in general. In addition, he enacted a new statute in Scotland and England, the Witchcraft Act of 1604, that established harsher punishments for condemned witches and broadened the definition of prosecutable witchcraft. Previously, the emphasis in witchcraft trials was on maleficia, the causing of harm to people, animals, or property; judges based convictions on whether the accused witch had hurt anyone. Under James's new law, judges considered evidence related to devil worship, which made it possible to prosecute people even when there was no victim to lodge a complaint.

Interestingly, whereas in continental Europe the most aggressive witch-hunters were Roman Catholic, in Scotland it was the Presbyterian Church that led the efforts to stamp out witchcraft, along with numerous professional secular witch-hunters paid by towns and individuals to find and investigate witches and gain convictions. Their methodology was similar to that of Catholic and secular witch-hunters in continental Europe. In fact, witch investigations and trials in Scotland have often been compared to those in Germany, because both countries subjected accused and convicted witches to particularly brutal tortures and usually burned convicted witches alive. Both also required the heirs of executed witches to pay trial and execution costs.

Not until the early eighteenth century did witch hysteria in Scotland began to abate. The last witch trial in the country took place in 1727 and resulted in one defendant, Janet Horne, being burned alive for consorting with the devil. (A second defendant was found innocent.) Nine years later, King James's 1604 Witchcraft Act was replaced with the Witchcraft Act of 1736, and the witch hysteria was officially over. However, even in the twentieth century, Scottish trials still occasionally involved accusations of practicing witchcraft, although defendants had been brought to trial on other charges. **See also** James I; North Berwick witches; persecution, witch.

scrying

Scrying is a method of divination whereby the practitioner stares into a reflective object or container of liquid, both of which are called a speculum, until a vision appears. The most common speculums in modern times are black bowls of water; glass or crystal balls in colors such as dark blue, dark green, or deep lavender; mirrors whose backs have been painted black; and polished stones or gems. The visions provided by such objects usually appear within a speculum's reflective surface, but sometimes they appear only within the practitioner's own mind. In either case, they are typically employed to help the practitioner find the location of a lost object, make difficult decisions, or foretell the future. The vision might be a realistic representation of the desired information, or it might be a symbolic one. For example, a woman scrying to find a lost key might see the exact location of the key, or she might instead see something that symbolizes that location, such as a triangle if the key is beside a pine tree.

Many modern witches practice scrying, but they generally believe that certain practices must be followed for scrying to work. In particular, most witches believe that a speculum will do nothing unless it is first consecrated in a ritual performed under a full moon. They further believe that the speculum must never be exposed to bright light, particularly direct sunlight, or it will lose its power. Instead the speculum must be stored in a box or kept wrapped in a dark cloth, and it must be used in dim light. (Candlelight is believed best, with the light coming from behind the scryer.) Many witches think that the best place to practice scrying is within a magic circle. However, they warn newcomers that it takes time to develop the mental ability to see anything within a speculum, suggesting that unless a person is particularly gifted, only after repeated relaxed sessions of gazing into the reflective surface does a mist begin to form, followed by a vision within the mist. **See also** circle, magic; divination.

Believed to watch over all magicians and witches, Selene (pictured here on a vase) represents the full moon. She was worshiped by the Greeks as the sister of Apollo and by the Romans as the moon goddess Luna.

Selene

Selene is one aspect of a trinity of moon goddesses known collectively as the Triple Goddess. She represents the full moon, while the goddess Diana represents the new moon and Hecate the dark moon. Of the three, it is Selene who is usually called upon during a ceremony called drawing down the moon, in which the Goddess is asked to speak through the body of the Wiccan high priestess.

Selene originated in Greek mythology, where she is said to be the sister of the sun god Phoebus Apollo. (The ancient Romans worshiped her as the moon goddess Luna.) In one myth she falls in love with a handsome mortal, Endymion, and enchants him so that he remains forever asleep on a mountaintop, where she comes to gaze upon him every night. In part because of this story, as well as because of her connection to the moon, Selene has long been associated with enchantment, sorcery, and witchcraft. She is thought to watch over all those who practice magic. **See also** Diana; drawing down the moon; moon.

1734 Tradition

The 1734 Tradition is a major Witchcraft tradition that emphasizes meditation, vision quests, and other aspects of shamanism. Its members achieve altered mental states through chanting, dancing, focused psychic efforts, and, according to members, the active intervention of deities.

Some 1734 covens use standard texts in their rituals, but most believe in spontaneity. Unlike most other traditions, 1734 does not maintain a Book of Shadows. Instead, 1734 rituals are based on letters that British witch Robert Cochrane wrote while establishing the tradition. Cochrane wrote these letters during the mid-1960s, primarily to an American acquaintance, Joseph Wilson, to express his thoughts on witchcraft, and they are passed on by coven members much as the information in a Book of Shadows is passed on in other traditions. In addition, some individual 1734 witches have a personal Book of Shadows, in which they have made notations about Cochrane's letters as well as about other aspects of the Craft.

The 1734 Tradition is also unusual in that it requires potential members to solve cryptograms and riddles before they can be initiated into the tradition. In fact, the tradition's name is taken from a cryptogram that Cochrane designated number 1734, which when solved gives the name of the tradition's high goddess. Another cryptogram, 1737, gives the name of the tradition's high god. After solving these cryptograms, new initiates spend a year and a day studying and training in Craft practices before they attain the level of first degree within the tradition.

Cochrane developed the 1734 Tradition during the 1950s. Born in London, England, in 1931, he sometimes claimed to be a hereditary witch, and he first began participating in witchcraft rituals in 1953. Shortly thereafter he formed a coven that he named the Clan of Tubal Cain. Although originally rooted in the same British Celtic paganism as covens of the Gardnerian Tradition, over time Cochrane's coven became increasingly shamanistic in nature, largely because Cochrane wanted to distance his covens from the Gardnerian Tradition.

Interestingly, one of his coven members was Doreen Valiente, who once worked closely with Gerald Gardner to develop many of the Gardnerian Tradition's ritual texts. Valiente eventually left Cochrane's coven because of his disparaging remarks about Gardner, as did others. Shortly thereafter, in 1966, Cochrane died from an overdose of a poisonous plant, belladonna (also known as deadly nightshade). It is unclear whether or not this was an accident, because although friends said that Cochrane was suicidal he had also been experimenting with various types and dosages of herbal drugs. Today members of 1734 covens emphasize that their rituals do not involve the use of drugs, and that like other Wiccans they believe in the Wiccan Rede that commands witches to do no harm. **See also** Gardner, Gerald; Gardnerian Tradition; shamanism.

sexuality

Most witches criticize Christian religions for repressing human sexuality, believing that people should be comfortable with their sexuality and allowed to express it as they wish. The Wiccan religion is accepting of all types of sexual behavior and orientations providing people express their sexuality in ways that do no harm to others. In some traditions, Wiccans encourage a free-spirited approach to sexuality, which might include the performance of rituals in the nude (also known as skyclad). In a few Witchcraft traditions, rituals to honor the Goddess and Horned God, such as the Great Rite, might involve not only nudity but sexual acts, but coven members are not required to perform such acts against their will. **See also** Great Rite; skyclad.

shamanism

A part of hunter-gatherer societies for at least thirty thousand years, shamanism is a magical system whose primary purpose is healing. In tribal cultures, this healing magic is primarily employed against physical ailments, but in modern cultures the focus is on healing the spirit, psyche, or soul. In addition, modern witches employ elements of shamanism in their magic rituals because they believe that it strengthens their psychic power and therefore their magic.

Both traditional and modern shamanism require the practitioner, or shaman, to enter an altered state of consciousness to contact spirits in a place that many call the Otherworld. The spirits being contacted depend on the shaman's sense of identity. Shamans from agricultural societies, for example, typically contact agricultural spirits, whereas shamans from hunting tribes typically contact hunting spirits. Modern shamans usually contact animal spirits that act as their personal talismans and provide wisdom regarding the best methods of healing. Witches practicing shamanism typically contact goddesses strongly associated with witchcraft.

Whether traditional or modern, each shaman has at least one guardian spirit, which is often in the form of an animal. Shamans generally believe that their guardian spirit is the source of their healing power, also called medicine power. In fact, some shamans think that a guardian spirit takes over a shaman's body during healing rituals. A shaman might have only one guardian spirit in a lifetime, a series of them, or several at once, depending on their belief system.

Also variable are the cleansing rituals that many shamans perform prior to healing. However, most such rituals involve subjecting the shaman's body to heat and smoke in order to purify it by cleansing it of negative energy. Usually special herbs are burned during such ceremonies; they are thought to further prepare the shaman's mind for its contact with the spirits.

When shamans are ready to contact the spirits and perform healing, they use chanting or drumming to trigger their minds to enter an altered state. Some shamans employ drugs instead, but most witches who practice shamanism condemn the use of drugs on grounds that a self-induced trance is far superior to one created artificially. Once in the Otherworld, the activities and abilities of the shaman vary widely. Witches, however, typically travel to the Otherworld because they believe the journey raises their energy for magical work and healings.

Interestingly, just as witches employ magic circles for their rituals so too do shamans typically hold their healing rituals within a circle. This sacred space is usually delineated with rocks, and sometimes the directional points (north, south, east, and west) are marked as well. Native Americans call such circles medicine wheels.

Native American shamanism has been particularly appealing to American witches, as have South American and African shamanism. One Witchcraft tradition, Wiccan Shamanism, is a religion that combines Native American and African shamanism with elements of Wicca. Practitioners of Wiccan Shamanism take part in conventional Wiccan activities such as celebrations of festivals within the Wheel of the Year and the performance of rituals within magic circles, and they also use drumming and chanting to induce altered states of consciousness. In addition, they perform healing rituals and divination just as shamans do, although they use typically Wiccan tools such as crystals and Tarot cards, and they have personal guardian spirits, which they typically receive at the time of their initiations into the religion.

In traditional shamanism, shamans might also receive a guardian spirit after some sort of initiation ceremony. The most common form of this ceremony is the vision quest, which occurs after a person decides, or is selected by a tribe, to become a shaman and has been trained in shamanism. During the vision quest, the initiate goes off alone to fast, meditate, and sometimes undertake tests of endurance. If all goes well, the initiate will eventually fall into a trance, experience a vision, and encounter her or his guardian spirit. Sometimes, however, the shaman first meets this guardian spirit unexpectedly, in either the ordinary world or the dream world, when it arrives to tell the individual that he or she is meant to be a shaman. **See also** chants; circle, magic; Tarot cards; Wiccan Shamanism.

Sheba, Lady (?–late 1970s)

American witch Lady Sheba (originally Jessie Wicker) is best known for the 1971 publication of her entire Book of Shadows as *Book of Shadows*. No witch had ever before shared the full extent of her knowledge, and Sheba's decision to do so was controversial among Wiccans. Many witches felt that Lady Sheba was violating Wiccan codes of secrecy, since prior to this time only excerpts from witchcraft rituals and spells had been published. This controversy grew even more intense after Lady Sheba published *The Grimoire of Lady Sheba* in 1972 (reissued 1974), which provided still more information about secret witchcraft practices.

Shortly after *The Grimoire of Lady Sheba* was published, readers realized that some of its material was taken from the works of Doreen Valiente, a witch who helped establish the Gardnerian Tradition. It is unclear whether this plagiarism was intentional, since Lady Sheba was sharing information from the Gardnerian Tradition and Valiente had contributed so much to that tradition's written works. In any case, the incident tarnished Lady Sheba's reputation among some Wiccans. Others, however, laud her for helping spread the understanding of Wicca among the general public. They also acknowledge her work at the outset of America's modern Witchcraft movement, when she became one of the first people to gain a legal designation of religious group for a Wiccan organization—the Brotherhood of Wicca, located in Michigan. **See also** Book of Shadows; Gardnerian Tradition; grimoire; Valiente, Doreen.

Sherwood, Grace

Grace Sherwood of Princess Anne County, Virginia, was brought to court in 1706 on charges that she had used witchcraft against her neighbor, Luke Hill. Other neighbors had previously accused Sherwood and her husband, John, of bewitching their livestock; the Sherwoods had taken these people to court for libel but lost their cases. Grace Sherwood had also successfully sued Hill for assaulting her only a year before he took her to court. Therefore it is likely that Hill accused Sherwood of being a witch out of a desire for revenge over this earlier incident.

Sherwood's case is notable because it illustrates the extent to which witchcraft-related hysteria had subsided in America by the beginning of the eighteenth century. Just over a decade earlier, when the Salem witch trials were under way, the possibility that Hill's accusation was fabricated for revenge would probably have been ignored. Then, an accusation of witchcraft almost invariably led to a conviction regardless of circumstances. In Sherwood's case, however, the jury assumed her innocence from the outset of the trial, so much so, in fact, that the all-female jury balked at the judge's order that they examine Sherwood's body for devil's marks. So adamant were they that she did not deserve this treatment that the judge eventually had to impanel a new jury willing to perform the examination. After they did find marks on Sherwood's body, she was thrown into the water to see if she would float. When she did, this normally would have been considered proof that she was a witch. However, Sherwood continued to protest her innocence and jurors continued to believe her. Ultimately her case was dismissed. **See also** marks, witches' or devil's; Salem, witch trials of; water.

sigils

Sigils are marks symbolizing the secret names of angels, deities, or spirits, or alternatively an entire spell or concept. Used in ceremonial magic, when written and focused on, sigils supposedly call forth the beings they represent or bring about a desired goal. A magician practicing the Kabbalah, for example, might meditate on the sigil for the angel Gabriel to call forth that angel and command him. Similarly, someone focusing mental energy on a sigil of the Runic letter representing prosperity would theoretically attract wealth. **See also** Kabbalah.

silver

Silver has historically been used both by witches in their rituals and by many fourteenth- through seventeenth-century people attempting to defend themselves against witches. By the seventeenth century it was generally believed that a bullet made of pure silver, which most people considered to be inherently magical, was capable not only of killing a witch but of destroying that witch's evil, which was believed to remain after death. (The same logic led people to burn witches' bodies after executions.) Silver's magical qualities also made it valuable as a material for ritual tools, particularly chalices, and for amulets and talismans.

The association between silver and the tools of magic, an association that continues today, stems from the belief that silver is magically connected to the moon and its goddesses. This connection is said to imbue silver with the power to ward off attempts to enchant it. At the same time, it supposedly increases the power of any sign or symbol placed on it, or of an object or substance placed within it; hence its value as a chalice, amulet, or talisman. **See also** amulet; talisman.

Silver Circle

The Silver Circle began in 1979 as a coven formed by members of Gerald Gardner's first coven. Over the years the Silver Circle maintained the Gardnerian Tradition, without allowing other influences to creep in. Eventually the coven turned into a center for spreading information about the Gardnerian Tradition, particularly its religious aspects. Called the Silver Circle Center for the Old Religion, it is located in the Netherlands and run by witches Morgana and Merlin. The group publishes a bilingual magazine, *Wiccan Rede,* with articles printed in both Dutch and English in each issue. **See also** Gardner, Gerald; Gardnerian Tradition.

skull

For obvious reasons, the skull has been associated with death since ancient times. As such it was used in rituals related to the deities' powers over life and death. But because modern witches also believe in reincarnation, they see the skull not only as a symbol of death but also as a symbol of rebirth, renewal, and transformation. Some witches consider the skull a symbol of wisdom as well, because it once held the brain. **See also** Old Religion.

skyclad

The term *skyclad* is used among witches to refer to the nakedness of participants in a ritual or other expression of spirituality, as opposed to nakedness related to nonspiritual activities such as bathing. The word comes from the idea that naked worshipers in outdoor rituals are clad only in the sky. The practice of worshiping nude began in ancient times as part of fertility rituals, and ritual nudity is still practiced today among certain Witchcraft traditions, such as the Gardnerians and Alexandrians, both in solitary work and in coven work, as well as among Neopagans.

Many reasons are given for the practice of going skyclad. Most Wiccans who worship skyclad say that it brings them closer to nature and/or the Goddess and allows them more freedom of movement during various rituals. In addition, some Wiccans laud worshiping skyclad because it eliminates indications of wealth and social standing among coven members. **See also** Alexandrian Tradition; coven; Gardner, Gerald; Gardnerian Tradition.

solitaries

Solitaries are witches who practice witchcraft on their own rather than as part of a coven. Solitary practice of witchcraft is becoming increasingly common in modern times. In part, this trend is due to the easy availability of books on witchcraft, which allows people to learn rites and rituals without guidance from other witches. Until recently, it was difficult to obtain such material, so knowledge was passed on through covens. The Internet has also become a major source of information for solitaries. Witches who learn about the Craft online and/or participate in conversations and covenlike activities online are said to be practicing Cyber Wicca. **See also** Cyber Wicca.

Somerset, witch trial of

In 1664, sixteen women and nine men from the Somerset region of England, each believed to belong to one of two separate covens, were tried for witchcraft. Both covens were allegedly under the supervision of the devil himself, who appeared as a mysterious man named Robin. During their trial, the defendants gave detailed accounts of their Sabbats, initiation rituals (which they said included their being marked by the devil), familiars, and other aspects of their practice of witchcraft. One of the defendants, Elizabeth Style, also reported that she and other coven members would smear flying ointment on themselves and recite magic words whenever they wanted to fly.

The court handling the case of the Somerset witches apparently did not believe these confessions, because it dismissed the case before a verdict was reached. However, shortly thereafter, English cleric Joseph Glanvill argued that the Somerset case offered some of the strongest evidence that witchcraft was real and therefore should have been pursued.

Some modern scholars have suggested that the court's refusal to accept the confessions was not the result of disbelief but of a changing political climate, since during the mid–seventeenth century the general public in England and continental Europe no longer supported the prosecution of witches. Others have seen evidence of real witchcraft practices within the Somerset confessions. For example, they suggest that the "devil" who appeared to coven members was actually the coven's high priest, and that the flying the witches claimed to have done was part of a trance produced either through meditation or mind-altering herbs.

One of these scholars was British anthropologist Margaret Alice Murray, who relied extensively on the case of the Somerset witches in developing her theory that a witch cult actually existed throughout Europe during the time their trials took place. Murray was struck by the fact that various Somerset witches provided the same stories when questioned independently. Moreover, she noted that the details they provided were strikingly similar to those provided by defendants in witch trials elsewhere in Europe. **See also** devil; England, witch-hunts of; Glanvill, Joseph.

Sommers, Montague (1880–1948)

Twentieth-century English author Montague Sommers wrote numerous books on witchcraft in which he argued that all witches were not only evil but in league with a very real devil. These include *The History of Witchcraft and Demonology* (1926), *The Geography of Witchcraft* (1927), and *A Popular History of Witchcraft* (1937). He also translated several important fifteenth-, sixteenth-, and seventeenth-century texts on demonology, witchcraft, and witch-hunting into English. Of these, his most notable work was the translation of the 1486 book *Malleus Maleficarum* by Heinrich Kramer and Jakob Sprenger, which contributed a great deal to the study of the history of witchcraft. Sommers spent nearly his entire life writing about supernatural subjects, not only witches and demons but also werewolves and vampires.

Ordained as a Roman Catholic priest in 1909, Sommers believed that the witch-hunters of the fourteenth through seventeenth centuries had been justified in their actions because witchcraft was a very real threat. In fact, he thought that witch-hunting was inspired not by hysteria but by an increase in the number of witches and in malevolent acts caused by witchcraft. Sommers also did not accept British anthropologist Margaret Alice Murray's theory that the witches during that period of history were practitioners of an organized pagan religion. Instead he saw them as tools of the Christian devil. **See also** devil; *Malleus Maleficarum;* Murray, Margaret Alice.

so mote it be

Wiccans often use the ritual phrase "so mote it be" or "and as my will, so mote it be" at the conclusion of a magical spell to indicate that the spell has been "fixed," or put into effect. The use of "will" in the longer phrase refers to the fact that the spell caster's will, or mental energy and determination, are required to make the spell work. **See also** spells.

sorcery

Most people commonly use the term *sorcery* interchangeably to mean magic, which is the attempt to manipulate unseen forces to achieve a desired result, such as the acquisition of personal wealth or the protection of a person, place, or thing. People also commonly use the word for practitioners of sorcery, *sorcerers,* interchangeably with *magicians.*

In the sixteenth century, people divided sorcery into two different categories: simple sorcery and complex sorcery. Simple sorcery was magic whereby the sorcerer performed one physical act to produce another—untying a knot, for example, to magically produce a storm—and complex sorcery was magic whereby the sorcerer employed spirits, angels, or demons to produce the desired results. Today people commonly refer to simple sorcery and complex sorcery to mean low magic and high magic, respectively. Also called folk magic or practical magic, low magic involves spells that are cast with few or no accompanying magic actions. High magic, which is also known as ceremonial magic, requires the spell caster to perform a complex series of magic actions, perhaps using detailed written instructions.

Interestingly, the word *sorcery* was first used to distinguish one type of magic from another. It appeared in English in the fourteenth century to refer to divination and astrology. By the sixteenth century, however, the definition had broadened to include the practice of other forms of magic as well.

During the Middle Ages and Renaissance, complex sorcery was the sole domain of sorcerers, magicians, and wizards, who had the education necessary to read complicated texts explaining the rituals for calling spirits. These men were held in respect and/or feared for their ability to command great magical power and control the spirits; therefore they were rarely persecuted because of their magical practices despite their clear association with demons. Meanwhile, witches, who were largely illiterate, practiced only simple sorcery, yet were executed for their craft.

During the sixteenth and seventeenth centuries, however, sorcerers were increasingly viewed as evil and the public's respect for them decreased. In addition, stories spread about how dangerous it was to practice sorcery, which discouraged others from taking up the pursuit. For example, it was said that if during the conjuring of spirits a sorcerer placed even one small part of his body outside the magic circle he had cast to protect himself, the spirits would grab him and carry him away. Prior to the sixteenth century, the spirits said to be under the control of sorcerers were believed to be either angelic or a combination of good and evil, and therefore not particularly dangerous; later, due to the influence of the Catholic Church's teachings, sorcerers' activities came to be seen as evil.

Many non-Western cultures have connected sorcery with evil as well. For example, historian Jeffrey B. Russell, in his book *A History of Witchcraft: Sorcerers, Heretics, and Pagans*, reports that among the Zande people of southern Sudan in Africa, sorcery is defined as magic performed out of jealousy, greed, and other base human emotions in order to harm someone without just cause. The Zande people view sorcery as one of four types of magic, along with benevolent magic, used to perform divination, create amulets, or increase fertility; *bagbuduma*, or homicidal magic, used to seek revenge against someone who has murdered a relative; and witchcraft, which is an inherited power to heal. **See also** circle, magic; magic; magician; persecution, witch; witchcraft.

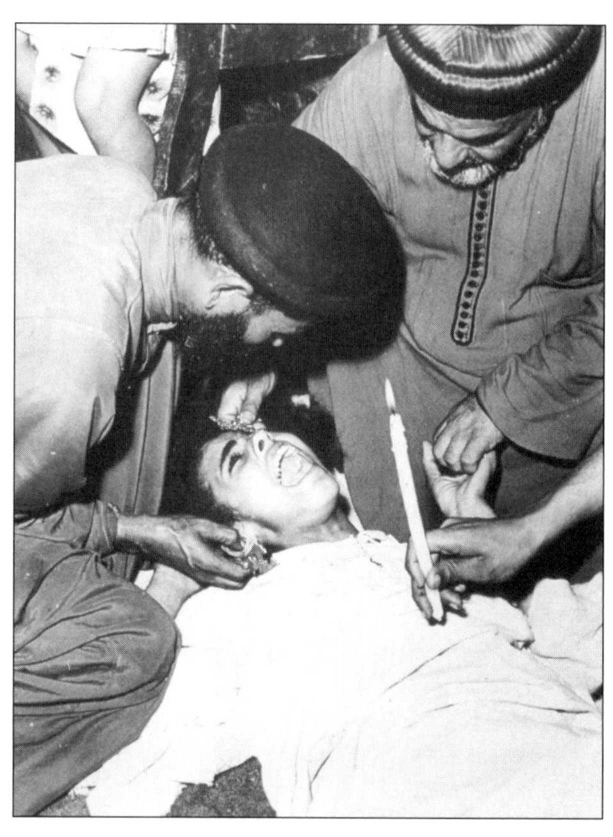

Those who believe in magic warn of the possible dangers in summoning evil spirits. This patient is allegedly screaming as an evil spirit escapes her mouth.

Spain, witch trials of

Spain's witch trials during the fifteenth, sixteenth, and seventeenth centuries were largely in the hands of the Catholic Church's inquisitors. However, the Spanish Inquisition was, in comparison with the Inquisition elsewhere in continental Europe, relatively fair, so that a great deal of proof was needed before a person was brought to trial and convicted as a witch. In addition, the accused in Spanish witch trials were usually charged with being involved in simple sorcery rather than complex sorcery, also known as diabolical witchcraft (i.e., witchcraft in which the devil was said to be involved). The exception was in the Basque region of the Pyrenees Mountains, where the Spanish believed the devil and his demons were active in spreading the practice of witchcraft. Consequently Basque people accused of being witches were persecuted much like those elsewhere in Europe, with torture and mass executions. **See also** Basque region, witch-hunts of the; devil; Inquisition.

spells

Also called incantations or magic words, spells are a series of words or phrases that a witch chants, speaks, or recites silently in a certain order while focusing mental energy on a desired result. This result can be for the person performing, or casting, the spell or for someone else. Sometimes this result is good, sometimes bad; however, most modern witches believe that casting spells to hurt someone else is wrong. This belief is expressed in one of their most important tenets, the Wiccan Rede.

Modern witches generally believe that the words in their spells are calling either on natural though mysterious forces in the universe or on deities such as the Goddess to bring about changes in their circumstances. In earlier centuries, however, they also considered their spells to be ways to summon good or bad spirits to do their bidding. During the Middle Ages and Renaissance, magicians, who were male specialists in magic, used spells specifically to call on demons or angels.

Some spells are fairly standard, passed from witch to witch. Other spells are written especially for a single occasion. In either case, many witches write the final version of their spell down (usually using pens, paper, and ink that have been magically "charged" through special rituals) and keep the paper in front of them while reciting the spell.

The words used for spells must be chosen very carefully, because they must be sufficiently specific, detailed, and clear to avoid bringing unintended results. For example, a spell that simply asks for a lot of money might bring about the death of a beloved relative who has included the spell caster in his or her will. Similarly, a spell asking simply for a husband might result in the person who cast the spell having a love affair with a married man. Again, without specific details—in this case, a description of the desired lover as being single—the spell can go wrong. To avoid these types of unpleasant outcomes, witches typically add some kind of phrase to a spell that asks that the intended result come about with joy and/or peace.

However, many witches advise that spells not be so specific that they limit the possibility of a better outcome than the person casting the spell can anticipate. For example, asking for a specific make, model, and year of automobile might bring that car to the person casting the spell but ultimately not be the best car for that person's needs. Some witches therefore advise creating a spell that asks not for a specific item but for the best item for a given situation. In the case of a car, for example, the spell might simply ask for a suitable car at an affordable price, in excellent mechanical and cosmetic condition, that will come with joy and peace.

Some witches would further suggest not asking for the best car but for the best mode of transportation to work, because such a spell might lead to the perfect carpool situation or to a new job within walking distance to work. Such witches generally believe that the deity knows the best way to bring satisfaction to the person casting the spell and should be given the widest latitude in accomplishing that goal.

Many modern witches cast spells designed to bring them certain items or life circumstances, not only cars but jobs, romantic partners, money, and fame, for example. Some witches, however, believe that spells should focus on less materialistic concerns, such as peace of mind and good health. Others believe that spells should primarily be used to benefit others, including the earth and its animals.

To cast a spell, the witch typically speaks, chants, or thinks it as part of a ritual, usually within a magic circle. A magic ritual involves a series of movements and gestures performed in accompaniment to the spell. For example, a witch might walk in a certain direction and/or manner while reciting a spell, or perhaps dance while doing so. Witches generally believe that without such actions some spells will not work or perhaps not work as effectively. In many cases, certain objects are also employed as part of the ritual. For example, a witch might tie a knot or light a candle while casting the spell. The purpose of these objects is to enhance or strengthen the spell. Sometimes witches "charge" these objects with magic power through a ritual prior to using them for spell casting.

Some witches believe that all rituals involving spells should be performed in a group, under the theory that the combined mental energy of several people makes the spell more powerful. Others prefer to work magic as solitaries. Such witches argue that being alone increases their ability to focus mental energy on their particular spell.

There is also debate over how uncrossing spells should be performed. Uncrossing is the act of breaking a harmful spell that has been cast on a witch by someone else. In an uncrossing ritual, the witch uses special oils, candles, or incense to banish negativity and evil spirits, thereby counteracting the malicious spell. Such rituals, which are usually performed at the time of the waning moon, might or might not include a new spell that redirects the evil back onto the person who originally caused the harm. Most Wiccans will not cast such a redirection spell, believing it violates the Wiccan Rede, but others believe that such spells are acceptable because they are not creating evil, only sending it back to the person who created it. **See also** magic; rites and rituals; Wiccan Rede.

spring equinox

Also called the vernal equinox, the spring equinox is one of two times of the year when the sun is precisely above the equator and the day and night are exactly the same length. (The other time is called the autumn equinox.) During the day in the spring on which this exact balance happens, witches celebrate Ostara, a festival that they also sometimes refer to as the spring equinox. **See also** Ostara.

Starhawk

Identifying herself as an ecofeminist, Starhawk is an American witch who has written extensively on Wiccan, pagan, and feminist subjects and is considered an expert on goddess worship. She was an influential member of the Faery Tradition and is now the leading theologian within the Reclaiming Tradition of Witchcraft, having written many of its ritual texts. In addition to these ritual texts, Starhawk is the author of such nonfiction books as *The Spiral Dance: A Rebirth of the Ancient Religion of the Great Goddess* (1979, 1989, and 1999); *Dreaming the Dark: Magic, Sex, and Politics* (1982); *Truth or Dare: Encounters with Power, Authority, and Mystery* (1987); and *Circle Round: Raising Children in the Goddess Tradition* (with Anne Hill and Diane Baker, 1998). She is also author of the novels *The Fifth Sacred Thing* (1993) and *Walking to Mercury* (1997). Starhawk co-owns a film company, Belili Productions, with director Donna Read, and together the two have collaborated on films related to women's spirituality. In addition, Starhawk teaches and lectures on goddess worship. She has a website at www.reclaiming.org/starhawk/. **See also** Faery Tradition; Reclaiming Tradition.

StarKindler Tradition

Established in 1987, the StarKindler Tradition is a Witchcraft tradition largely based on the Alexandrian Tradition. Its Book of Shadows developed out of the Alexandrian Book of Shadows, and its highly structured approach to initiation, coven establishment and governance, and other aspects of the Craft are also derived from the Alexandrian Tradition. The StarKindler Tradition also allies itself with the British Tradition, arguing that in fact all Wicca is essentially one with the British Tradition, and has close ties to the Pagan Way movement. The name of the tradition was taken from a coven whose members called themselves the StarKindlers. This coven was in no way related to the StarKindler Tradition, whose practitioners took the name simply because they liked it. **See also** Alexandrian Tradition; Pagan Way; traditions, Witchcraft.

stones

Many witches believe that stones, particularly gemstones, possess magical powers that come from the minerals' connection to energy vibrations of the earth, the sky, the stars, various planets, and perhaps even other realms of existence. They further believe that by wearing certain stones a person can direct this energy to heal the body or attract certain kinds of fortune. To these ends, they routinely employ stones to make talismans and amulets. Witches also use stones for various forms of divination. Perhaps the best-known stone connected to divination is the crystal ball, which is said to show images of the future. In addition, runes (symbols used for divination) are typically marked on stones.

Different types of stones are selected for different types of magic. For example, lodestone is connected to magic designed to help someone achieve or acquire something, probably because it has magnetic properties that can either attract or repel certain metal objects. The reasons for other associations between stones and their magical purpose are less clear.

Stones with vivid or striking colors tend to be valued more than others. For example, yellow citrine is considered a valuable aid to magic rituals, increasing the mental focus and therefore the magical powers of participants, while carnelian protects against negative energy. Carnelian is also used in magic intended to bring courage and/or sexual energy. Emeralds are for spells to bring monetary gain or love. Jade is for longevity and wisdom, while garnets are for strength and virility. Rubies are for personal power and wealth, topaz for peace and harmony. Sapphires are thought to bring the wearer visions during meditation and to enhance spiritual activity, while opals are believed to help the wearer with astral projection. Lapis lazuli is believed to protect against infidelity. Amulets of chalcedony or diamond are said to protect the wearer against a variety of ills, disasters, and evil spells. Witches who want to honor the Goddess often wear jewelry featuring moonstone, which some also believe increases the wearer's psychic abilities. Agate and amethyst are often used for amulets related to good health, as are many other stones. Amethyst is also associated with prophetic dreaming.

Although they are not gemstones, quartz crystals are considered by some witches to be the most powerful stones because they are associated with both fire and water. The connection with fire comes from the crystal's ability to act like a lens and start a fire when sunlight is directed through it and onto a combustible material like wood or dry grass. The connection with water comes from the fact that quartz crystals look like ice. Quartz crystals themselves are clear, but they take on certain colors when they develop among other minerals. Clear quartz crystals are used for crystal balls, into which people gaze to receive visions, while amethyst quartz is most commonly used to enhance the magic of a witch's wand or altar. Both types of quartz are believed to receive and transmit energy from other realms, and perhaps even magnify it. Other types of quartz are used for healing and protection.

Prior to using any type of gemstone a witch usually performs a ritual to dispel negative energy and charge it with positive energy. In general, only charged stones are made into amulets or meditated upon during spell casting. **See also** amulet; circle, magic; divination; magic; rites and rituals; scrying; spells; talisman.

St. Osyth, witch trial of

In 1582, St. Osyth, England, was the site of a notorious mass witchcraft trial involving approximately fourteen defendants, ten of whom were charged with committing murder by magic. The central figure of the trial, Ursula Kemp, provided a detailed confession—apparently without torture, although this point is in dispute by modern scholars—that featured her interaction with familiars. She claimed that she and fellow coven members kept a variety of imps disguised as animals to do their bidding. Kemp's included cats, a toad, and a lamb. She reported that one of her cats had killed a woman and that her lamb had injured a baby so severely that it later died. In addition, Kemp admitted to using witchcraft to worsen a woman's illness, the original charge that had brought her to trial.

Kemp had long made a living as a healer, and she had a reputation for using folk magic in her work. The person who had first accused her of maleficia—i.e., harmful witchcraft—was a former patient who had refused to pay her bill and thought that Kemp had made her sicker as punishment. Once the accusation was made, Kemp's eight-year-old son was coerced into offering detailed testimony about the witchcraft supposedly practiced in his home.

After confessing to being a witch, Kemp named four other women in her village as witches. She said that unlike herself, these witches met regularly as part of one of two covens in the St. Osyth area. These women were subsequently arrested, and like Kemp they too confessed and named still other women as witches. Meanwhile, the public decided that twenty-four deaths and several lesser misfortunes (including animal illnesses, ruined crops, and broken farm equipment) could be blamed on the witches' activities.

The roughly fourteen women ultimately identified as St. Osyth witches were put on trial together. In the end two of them—Kemp and Elizabeth Bennet, the latter of whom had been accused of killing a farmer and his family because the man had called her names—were convicted and hanged. Four other defendants were acquitted, two were released prior to the conclusion of the trial for lack of evidence, and the rest served various amounts of time in jail.

Because much of the testimony against Kemp had come from an eight-year-old, some people in England were uncomfortable with her execution. One of these people was Reginald Scot, who included his complaints about the St. Osyth trial in a 1584 book about the unjust persecution of witches, *Discoverie of Witchcraft*. Through this work, the Kemp case became the central focus in arguments regarding whether children's testimony should be accepted as solid evidence against witches in English and later in American courts.

Another controversy involving the Kemp case relates to whether or not her confession reflected the nature of witch practices of the period. It featured many elements common to other witchcraft confessions of the period, and some scholars believe that no such similarities could exist without some truth behind them. Such scholars suggest that Kemp and the other defendants in the trial were indeed guilty of practicing some form of witchcraft, although they might have exaggerated their abilities. Margaret Murray, one such scholar, took the theory one step further. In addition to saying that the St. Osyth witches really were practicing witchcraft, she argued that the case was evidence that witches during the period were well organized and therefore part of an ancient and widespread European witch cult. **See also** England, witch-hunts of; Murray, Margaret Alice.

Stregheria

The word *Stregheria* is commonly used to refer to all forms of Italian witchcraft as it is practiced today. Some scholars define the term in a more limited way, saying that Stregheria is an Italian American form of witchcraft developed by modern witches Raven Grimassi and Leo Martello, who used this witchcraft as the basis for several Italian Witchcraft traditions. Meanwhile, witches define Stregheria as the religious elements of Italian Witchcraft traditions, with *Stregonia*—Italian for "sorcery"—the magical practices of these traditions.

Grimassi, who established the first modern Italian Witchcraft covens, is still the leading expert on Italian witches. (Leo Martello died in 2000.) He reports that from ancient times to the present they have worshiped such goddesses as Hecate, Proserpina, and Diana. Italian witches also make protective amulets; heal using herbs, potions, and spells; and employ a great deal of knot magic. Many are hereditary witches, with information usually passed down from mother to daughter. This is how Grimassi believes that ancient Italian Witchcraft survived so well to modern times.

Grimassi also reports that there are several traditions of Italian Witchcraft, with variations in common practices depending on the region of Italy where the tradition originated. Grimassi believes that the tradition to reach modern times in the purest form is Sicilian Witchcraft, because the island of Sicily was more isolated from outsiders than the rest of Italy. However, Grimassi says that most Italian Witchcraft practiced in America is based on the Tanarra Tradition, which stems from the area around Naples, Italy. Two other forms of Stregheria, as described by Grimassi, are Fanarra from northern Italy and Janarra from central Italy.

Grimassi's critics have noted that none of these three tradition names have roots in Italian dialects, although *ianara* is the word people around Campania, Italy, use for *witch.* Critics have similarly noted that Grimassi's word for the leader of a coven in Italian Traditions, *grimas,* also does not appear in Italian dictionaries. However, these names do in more general ways suggest a connection to witches. The Italian word *grimo* means "wizened" or "wrinkled"—a popular image of a witch, and *Stregheria* comes from the Italian *streghe* (plural), which in turn comes from the Latin *striges*, meaning "screech owls." In ancient Rome, witches were sometimes called *striges* because they were thought to turn themselves into owls or other birds of prey, some of them horrific supernatural creatures, for night flight. Furthermore, after the Roman Empire fell, *strega* gradually came to mean "witch."

Grimassi and his followers believe that the witchcraft beliefs and folk magic practices of ancient Italy have been passed down to modern witches with few changes, providing evidence that a witch cult survived the centuries of witch persecution. At the very least, they believe that Stregheria became an organized religion in Italy sometime around 1353 and is therefore one of the oldest Witchcraft traditions in the world.

The first person to suggest that Stregheria had ancient roots was Charles Godfrey Leland. In his 1890 book *Aradia, or the Gospel of Witches*, he argued that a nineteenth-century Tuscan witch cult was the vestige of an ancient Etruscan religion. Grimassi has suggested that evidence of this religion can still be found in Italian folk practices. However, his critics argue that just because remnants of ancient folk practices still exist in modern times this does not mean that entire belief systems had survived. In other words, a person can continue to follow certain customs without adhering to or even recalling the religious beliefs that once inspired the custom. For example, Christians hide eggs at Easter, but this does not mean they are honoring ancient Roman gods in doing so, which is how this custom originated.

Using such examples in criticizing Grimassi, Martello, and others for suggesting that Italian folk practices are surviving elements of ancient Etruscan practices and beliefs, such scholars argue that centuries of influence from other cultures and religions, along with changes in Italy's social and political institutions and geographical boundaries, have caused so many distortions in folk beliefs and practices that it is impossible to rely on them to reconstruct an ancient mystical religion. Nonetheless, that is what Grimassi and other Italian Tradition witches have done. They admit that in establishing—or, they would say, in reestablishing—Italian Witchcraft they have been influenced by their own modern sensibilities as Wiccans, but they insist that Italian Witchcraft is still firmly connected to an ancient heritage.

Grimassi further suggests that certain amulets and charms common throughout the witch-hunting centuries were actually emblems of a secret witch cult. In the 1920s British anthropologist Margaret Alice Murray theorized that such a cult began in ancient times and continued to exist in secret throughout the witch-hunting years, but scholars immediately attacked her theory as unsupported by evidence, and today few historians take it seriously. Similarly, Grimassi's critics counter that the amulets and charms he suggests were witch emblems were actually evidence of simple folk magic, intended to protect the wearer from evil spells. In other words, they were not a witch device but an anti-witch device. **See also** Diana; Grimassi, Raven; Martello, Leo.

Summerland

Wiccans generally believe that the souls of the dead go to a place called Summerland, where they await reincarnation. The name comes from the concept that Summerland is a land of perpetual summer, where the sun always shines and the grass is always green. Some witches believe that it is also a place where mythological beasts such as dragons and unicorns went to live once they decided that the earth was no longer magical enough for them.

Various suggestions have been made regarding the location of Summerland. For example, some say it is in heaven, others that it is a magical realm beyond the north wind, and still others that it is an alternate reality on a different plane of existence. Scholars who do not accept the Wiccan belief in an afterlife suggest that the idea of Summerland came from ancient Celtic distortions of stories about Greece, which has a far milder climate than Britain.

In ancient times, another popular view of the afterlife, particularly among Italian witches, is that it was located in the light of the moon, which went from a crescent to a round ball as it was enlarged with souls. During the dark moon, when no light was visible, these souls were going through the process of reincarnation, returning to the earth en masse to live again. Therefore when the moon was once more visible it had returned to a crescent, empty of souls.

Not all Wiccans accept the presence of Summerland. Among some Witchcraft traditions, the afterlife is thought to be a dark realm deep within the earth, typically called the Underworld. In one story central to many of these traditions, the Great Goddess descends to this realm to ask Death to return her slain God to her or, in another version of the story, to learn various secrets from Death, with whom she then falls in love. In either case, the Goddess must pass through several gates to reach the innermost sanctum of the Underworld, and usually she is required to remove articles of clothing at each gate so that she arrives naked before Death. **See also** goddesses and gods; moon.

summer solstice

The summer solstice is one of two moments in the year when the sun is farthest from the equator; the other moment is the winter solstice. In the Northern Hemisphere, the summer solstice occurs on June 21 or 22, the winter solstice on December 21 or 22. (In the Southern Hemisphere, these dates are reversed.) On the day of the summer solstice, witches celebrate a festival which some call the summer solstice but most call Midsummer. **See also** Midsummer.

sword

Similar to the athame, the sword is a ritual tool of witchcraft typically decorated with magic symbols. But whereas most Craft traditions use the athame, the sword is falling out of favor. The sword's primary employment is like a wand in casting spells. It also sometimes rests on the altar during ceremonies. In medieval times, sorcerers might also use the sword much like a crystal ball, with the user looking into the blade to see the future.

Sylvan Tradition

Begun in northern California in the 1970s, the Sylvan Tradition of Witchcraft emphasizes nature worship, the practice of magic, and the existence of the fairy realm. There are generally no standard rituals; practitioners create their own as spontaneous expressions of the moment, arising out of a specific need or desire. The word *sylvan* means "part of the forest," and the natural world is honored above all. As part of the earth, the four elements are employed in many rituals, but Sylvan practitioners believe that because these elements exist everywhere they need not be assigned specific places or duties within a magic circle. Sylvan practitioners usually raise their magic circles outdoors. There they believe it is unnecessary to perform rituals that banish negative energy or protect against negative energy, because to them the earth is always a positive force within the magical space. **See also** elements, four; traditions, Witchcraft.

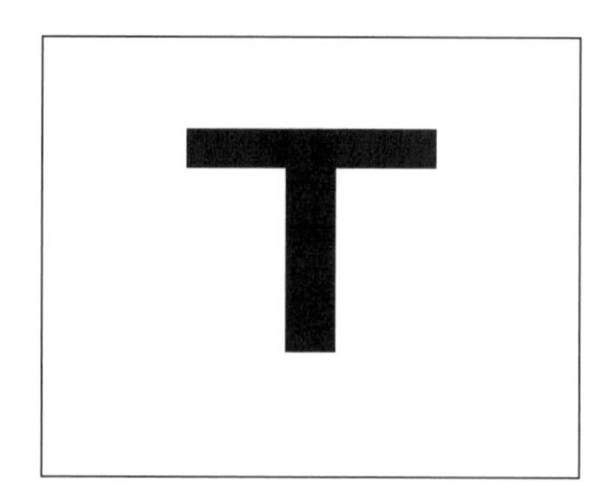

talisman

A talisman is an object—such as a disk worn as a necklace—that carries a spell designed to attract something to the person wearing or carrying it. For example, talismans are created to bring luck, prosperity, success in certain endeavors, or the strength to withstand particular trials or dangers. Many talismans are marked with symbols believed to be magical. Of these, perhaps the most popular is the pentagram, which is considered not only extremely powerful but highly protective of whoever wears it. To make a talisman, a witch performs a ritual designed to "charge" the object with magical power and link it to its purpose and user. Most witches believe that a charged talisman will require at least seven days to gain full strength and must occasionally be recharged if it is to serve a long-term purpose. **See also** amulet; magic.

Tarot cards

Typically used for divination, Tarot cards are a deck of seventy-eight cards portraying various images and symbols that are believed to be connected to ancient magic. There are two types of Tarot cards within one deck, the major arcana and the minor arcana, with twenty-two cards in the major arcana and fourteen cards of each of four suits in the minor arcana. (The word *arcana* comes from the Latin *arcanus*, meaning "hidden or secret knowledge.")

The suits of the minor arcana are the Wands, Cups, Swords, and Pentacles. Each suit represents one of the four elements used in magic, as well as a set of traits related to that element. Wands, which symbolize fire, represent power and energy; Cups, which symbolize water, represent emotions and good luck; Swords, which symbolize air, represent external pressures and bad luck; Pentacles, which symbolize earth, represent abundance and health.

Each of the twenty-two cards of the major arcana bears an image representing a person, object, or situation. They are the Fool, the Magician, the High Priestess, the Empress, the Emperor, the High Priest, the Lovers, the Chariot, Strength, the Hermit, the Wheel of Fortune, Justice, the Hanged Man, Death, Temperance, the Devil, the Tower, the Star, the Moon, the Sun, the Last Judgment, and the World. Some people perform divination, or Tarot readings, using only the cards of the major arcana. Most, however, use all of the cards in the deck.

Each image on each card has a meaning which the person performing the reading must interpret in relation to the life circumstances of the person for whom the reading is being performed. Each card has wide variations of meaning depending on the Tarot reader's personal beliefs. For example, the Death card might mean a physical death, a personal disaster, an ending of some circumstance, or a transition from one phase of life to the next. Some witches' interpretation of a particular card's meaning remains relatively constant from reading to reading, while others change the meaning in accordance with their intuition about what the card might be trying to say. Witches who vary their interpretations believe that they are being guided by psychic powers that have been enhanced by the cards.

Another factor that has bearing on a card's meaning is the order in which it has been pulled from the deck. Tarot cards are laid on a table face up in a prescribed pattern, and most Tarot readers believe that a card's position has particular significance. For example, one position in the layout might signify the past, another the present, and another the future—all for the same card. If the Death card, for instance, appears in a layout position representing the past, it would mean that the person for whom the reading is being performed has already gone through some sort of change or disaster, whereas if the Death card appears in a layout position representing the future it means that this event is yet to occur.

There are several ways to lay out the cards for divination, using various numbers of cards for different readings. There are also many different styles of deck, and the

Many witches use Tarot cards for divination. Pictured are Italian Tarot cards: On the left, the King, or Emperor, represents supreme civil authority; on the right, the Queen, or Empress, represents supreme civil and feminine authority.

artwork of the major arcana varies widely. However, their most popular style of deck is the Rider-Waite, created in 1910 by English occultist Arthur Edward Waite and artist/occultist Pamela Colman Smith.

The Rider-Waite deck draws its images primarily from the Kabbalah, a magical system believed to have been developed by the ancient Hebrews. Some people believe that Kabbalist symbolism has been associated with Tarot cards since their beginning. Under this theory, occultists from throughout the civilized world gathered in Morocco in approximately A.D. 1200 to develop a way to pass on their teachings, and the earliest Tarot cards were their solution; the occultists placed their most magical images and symbols on the cards, many of which came from the Kabbalah. This might explain why the major arcana numbers twenty-two cards. There are twenty-two letters in the Hebrew alphabet, each of which corresponds to a path on the Tree of Life used in practicing Kabbalah magic.

In recent years, however, many witches have chosen Tarot decks that use images drawn from other magical systems or forms of spiritualism. In such choices they are often guided by their Witchcraft tradition. For example, witches involved in traditions that employ shamanism might choose a deck depicting Native American drawings, while those in Witchcraft traditions that focus on fairies might choose a Tarot deck with fairy artwork. **See also** arcana; divination; elements, four; Kabbalah; magic.

Telesco, Trish (1960–)

Born in 1960, Trish Telesco is the author of several popular books on Witchcraft-related subjects, including *Kitchen Witch's Cookbook* (1994), *Goddess in My Pocket* (1998), *The Herbal Arts* (1998), and *Wicca 2000* (1999). A practitioner of Italian Witchcraft, she lectures on Wicca and writes regularly for several Wiccan magazines. **See also** Kitchen Witch Tradition; Stregheria.

threefold law

A major principle of Wicca, the threefold law states that any magic that a witch sends out to work good or evil will be returned to that witch threefold. In other words, if a witch casts an evil spell on someone, then that witch will personally experience three times greater evil in the near future. Conversely, if a witch casts a spell intended to benefit someone else, then that witch will personally experience three times the goodness in the near future. The first witch to write about the threefold law was Gerald Gardner, who made it one of the cornerstones of his Gardnerian Tradition of Witchcraft. Today witches of many traditions observe the law, which is why so many adhere to the Wiccan Rede admonishing them to "do no harm." However, some witches believe in a magical system that emphasizes the number 7 rather than 3, so to them the threefold law is the sevenfold law, whereby any magic sent out will come back sevenfold. Alternatively, witches who embrace Buddhist and Hindu concepts have adapted the threefold law to the law of karma, whereby any magic sent out will come back in equal measure. **See also** Gardner, Gerald; Gardnerian Tradition; Wiccan Rede.

tools, ritual

Ritual tools, also known as magic or magical tools or working tools, are tools that witches use during rituals. Some witches define them as objects held in a witch's hand during the performance of magic, such as knives, swords, and wands, while others believe that any object used to contain, direct, or focus energy during a ritual, such as a cauldron or candle, also qualifies as a ritual tool.

Some witches believe that magical tools are not essential to the practice of witchcraft. Most, however, believe they are necessary. In either case, ritual tools are thought to enhance the proceedings of a ritual and strengthen a witch's connection to the spiritual realm. In addition, each ritual tool is associated with one of the four elements—earth, air, fire, and water—based on its real or symbolic connection to these elements. However, witches disagree on the exact nature of this association. For example, some think that the athame (a short knife) is a tool of fire because its blade was forged in fire, while others think it is a tool of air because its blade slices the air during its use in a ritual. Similarly, some witches say that the wand represents fire because rubbing two sticks together creates fire; others say air because wands are typically made of tree branches that once swayed in the wind.

The number of tools employed during rituals depends on the Witchcraft tradition. In the Gardnerian Tradition, for example, there are eight working tools, whereas in the Saxon Tradition there are only three.

Prior to using a ritual tool, witches perform a ritual, typically called a rite of consecration, believed to eliminate negative energy within the tool, thereby making it an appropriate conduit for magic. For example, the athame might be ceremonially cleansed, whereupon certain words would be recited to call magical power into its blade. In many traditions, this cleansing involves sprinkling the tool with a solution of salt and water, then passing it through smoke created with incense.

A more elaborate ceremony is required for ritual tools that have never been used before. In such cases, the tool is typically exposed to representations of the four elements one after another, because these elements are believed to be integral to the practice of magic. For example, before employing a newly made athame blade for the first time, a witch might stick it into the earth, wave it in the air, pass it through fire, and dip it in or sprinkle it with water. In some traditions, incense is used to symbolize air and salt to symbolize earth.

Some witches purchase their ritual tools, often from merchants who specialize in such items. These witches believe that all of the ritual tools in a witch's collection must be personally selected, and that the Goddess guides a witch in making these choices. Most witches, however, believe that ritual tools should be handmade instead of professionally manufactured, and that a tool will have more power if it has been made by the person who will be using it, particularly if the tool is the athame or wand, both of which are considered highly personal items.

Covens might share the use of swords, cords, or other items, but most witches will not share their athame or wand. Although they have other purposes as well, both of these tools are used to direct energy from within the person wielding them into the area where magic is being performed, focusing power wherever the user points them. They are therefore intimately connected to a witch's personal power and are considered special by their owner, who often marks them with symbols of personal significance.

Because athames and wands are such personal items, some witches take great care in making their own, assisted by instructions in witches' guidebooks. For example, Raymond Buckland's *Complete Book of Witchcraft* offers instructions on how to forge, sharpen, harden, and temper steel for an athame blade, how to carve wood for its handle, and how to mark symbols on both handle and blade. Other guidebooks offer detailed instructions on how to make a wand out of metal, crystal, or wood. Some witches believe that wands should be a precise length, with the measurement depending on tradition, but others argue that any length that is comfortable to hold is acceptable.

In fact, some witches believe it is best to use instinct rather than rigid instructions in creating ritual tools. Even Raymond Buckland acknowledges this in his guidebook. He reports that arguments over how long a wand should be, for example, stem from concepts related to ceremonial magic rather than witchcraft; such magic was practiced by ancient occultists and magicians, who believed that if they did not follow certain prescribed instructions exactly while practicing magic, the spirits they were attempting to summon would kill them. Buckland argues that such notions have no place in modern witchcraft, which teaches that magic comes not from the ritual tool but from within the witch. **See also** athame; elements, four; wand.

torture

During the sixteenth and seventeenth centuries in continental Europe, various forms of torture were used to force people to confess to being witches and name accomplices. Even the simplest tortures could be extremely painful; these included flogging, forcing the victim to drink salt water and/or to eat salty food while denying them freshwater, making them stay awake and walk continually for hours or days without rest, stretching their limbs until their muscles tore and their bones broke, crushing their bones using vises or heavy objects, and brutally raping female victims. More severe tortures included the thumbscrew, a vise designed to crush a finger or toe, and the strappado, a process whereby the prisoner is tied up, weighted down, and repeatedly hoisted to hang from a ceiling so that her or his shoulders dislocate.

The most stubborn prisoners were subjected to squassation, an excessive form of the strappado. In squassation, the victim is fitted with weights as heavy as six hundred pounds and repeatedly dropped to the floor and jerked upwards, so that more than just the shoulder bones dislocate. When squassation was performed more than three times, the victim usually died.

Another horrible torture often employed in parts of Germany was an iron chair with spikes that pierced the person strapped into it. A fire was lit beneath the chair to intensify the victim's agony. Sometimes a victim's feet, shod or unshod, were stuck into a fire. Other methods of burning and scalding, particularly those involving caustic liquids, were also popular in Germany, as were various methods of flaying sections of skin. In fact, German witch-hunters employed the most sadistic tortures of the witch-hunting centuries; and their victims included pregnant women and children as young as two.

German witch-hunters also streamlined the process whereby an alleged witch was arrested, tortured, convicted, and executed. In the principality of Bamberg, for example, Prince-Bishop Gottfried Johann Georg II Fuchs von Dornheim established a witch-hunting organization in the 1620s comprising expert torturers, executioners, and attorneys whose goal was to gain witch convictions. He built a new prison solely to house accused witches, and he directed that all accused witches be tortured both before and after confessing their crimes. His mandated tortures were so horrific that few could resist confession; for example, von Dornheim's professional torturers dunked suspected witches in boiling water mixed with caustic lime, forced them to kneel on spikes, crushed their bones using various devices, and/or burned their armpits. Once suspected witches were found guilty, they might have their right hands cut off or their flesh pinched or pierced in various painful ways.

Although in some countries a person who went through three torture sessions and still refused to confess was deemed innocent, German witch-hunters tortured an accused witch until that person either confessed or died: A suspected witch resistant to torture was thought to be under the special protection of the devil or to have ingested something magical that allowed her to withstand the tortures. When a suspect did die during torture, some people said that the devil had killed the witch, either to prevent her from answering questions or to protect her from further harm.

As the witch-hunting years progressed, knowledge of European torturers' methods became widespread, and those arrested for witchcraft were terrified of what awaited

Witches were believed to be possessed by the devil. If a witch died from torture, many believed the devil had killed her out of mercy or to prevent her from answering questions.

them in the torture chamber. Sometimes an accused witch was so terrified that she had only to see the instruments of torture to confess. Anyone who recanted such a confession—or indeed, any confession—was immediately returned to the torture chamber for a fresh round of agony. For example, in 1637 one forty-year-old woman from Eichstätt, Germany, was subjected to the most brutal of tortures, including the repeated crushing of her legs, for two weeks before she confessed to consorting with the devil; her tortures then ended, whereupon she recanted her confession only to be tortured anew for what her judges called stubbornness. Finally, nearly insane with pain, she admitted all guilt and was executed.

Through such tactics, torture produced detailed witch confessions in great number, and with these numerous confessions came the public perception that witchcraft was rampant throughout the countryside. However, witch-hunters still sometimes faced criticism for their actions, and they wrote numerous books to defend themselves. For example, two Dominican inquisitors, Heinrich Kramer and Jakob Sprenger, who encountered resistance from local authorities displeased by their tactics, wrote in their 1486 witch-hunting guidebook *Malleus Maleficarum* that the only way to extract confessions from people in league with the devil was to torture them. Similarly, in his 1589 book *Tractatus de Confessionibus Maleficarum et Sagarum* (*Treatise on Confessions by Evildoers and Witches*), German bishop Peter Binsfeld argued that confessions acquired through brutal torture were valid, and that any recantations of such confessions should not be trusted.

Another work, the 1580 book *De la Démonomanie des sorciers* (*Demonomania of Witches*), advocated that witches be tortured as brutally as possible. Its author, French attorney Jean Bodin, suggested extremely painful methods and complained that the experience of burning witches alive did not last long enough. He also said that children should be tortured just as cruelly as adults to get them to speak out against their parents. He reported that as a trial judge he had often ordered that adults and children be burned with hot irons until they confessed to every charge put before them.

In addition to advocating torture, such books also provided guidelines on how to deal with witches during interrogations, and many of these suggestions were adopted throughout Europe. For example, a standard set of questions was routinely asked by interrogators—so standard that in some places the court identified them by number rather than restating them in official records. It was also common for suspects to be searched prior to torture, to make sure they were not concealing any charms or amulets that might help them withstand pain. For the same reason, some witches were shaved bald, because it was believed that tiny demons helpful to the witch could hide in hair.

With the number of witch-hunting guidebooks proliferating, countries that did not engage in witch-hunting and torture sometimes felt pressure to do so. This was the case in England, where some members of government and the public thought that more had to be done to fight English witchcraft. Nonetheless, witch torture was forbidden under English law, although it was still permissible for witch-hunters to starve, exhaust, or otherwise discomfit the suspect. One of the most successful English witch-hunters, Matthew Hopkins, would routinely tie up his suspects and throw them in deep water, until this too was forbidden under English law.

As the witch-hunting years progressed, learned men began to argue that witchcraft was not real and that confessions obtained under torture could not be used to justify executions. Their works influenced public opinion, so that both trial judges and the general populace began to doubt the veracity of any confession that came out of a torture session. Consequently torturers increasingly noted in official records that a suspect who had been brutally tortured had instead confessed without torture, so that the courts would think the confession was voluntary. These falsifications mean that historians will never know exactly how many suspected witches were tortured. **See also** Bamberg, witch trials of; Binsfeld, Peter; Bodin, Jean; Del Rio, Martin; Eichstätt, witch trials of; England, witch-hunts of; Germany, witch-hunts of; Hopkins, Matthew; Inquisition; *Malleus Maleficarum;* Scandinavia, witch-hunts of.

traditions, Witchcraft

Much like the sects of any religion, a Witchcraft or Wiccan tradition is a specific approach to the practice of Witchcraft that is passed on over time to other witches. Some traditions are based on the beliefs and practices of just one type of ancient pagan, such as the Irish Celts, while others draw on elements of Witchcraft from a variety of sources. Some involve the worship of just a few deities, while others worship many. A coven generally adheres to a single tradition; however, its approach to the practice of this tradition might change over the years.

The concept of a Witchcraft tradition arose in modern times, when some witches decided to create alternatives to the prevailing approach to Witchcraft, now called the Gardnerian Tradition; in earlier times, all witches were simply said to practice the Old Religion (or, alternatively, folk magic), with little or no effort made to distinguish variations among their beliefs and rituals.

Today there are numerous Witchcraft traditions; following are the most common:

Alexandrian Tradition. Originally established in the early 1960s by British witch Alex Sanders and his wife, Maxine, as an alternative to the Gardnerian Tradition, the Alexandrian Tradition is one of the most influential modern Craft traditions. The two traditions share many features, although the Alexandrian Tradition places a greater emphasis on ceremonial magic.

No two Alexandrian covens operate in exactly the same way, but generally Alexandrian Wiccans practice ceremonial magic based on the Kabbalah, Angelic Magic, and Enochian Magic. Most have a hierarchical structure, meeting at sacred times according to the Wheel of the Year as well as at the full and new phases of the moon. Some covens meet weekly as well. Many covens will allow interested guests to attend one of their circles, along with people who have not yet been initiated into the Craft but plan on doing so. Newcomers to the Craft are called noninitiates or neophytes, and once they have completed certain tasks and studied certain aspects of magic they are initiated into the first degree of the Alexandrian Tradition. Those who practice Alexandrian Wicca use basically the same tools as Gardnerians, although sometimes in different ways. The deities called upon by the two traditions typically differ as well.

British Traditional. British Traditional mixes elements of the Celtic Traditional and Gardnerian Traditions. In general, covens draw on the writings of Janet and Stewart Farrar for their rituals and follow a structured path to work their way up through the hierarchy of the group. Deities featured in rituals and festivals might come from throughout Britain or from a particular region of Britain, depending on the coven.

Blue Star Wicca. Blue Star Wicca is an American Witchcraft tradition that emphasizes the worship of gods and goddesses over the practice of magic, although witchcraft is still performed. Which gods and goddesses are worshiped depends on the coven; however, many choose Celtic, Greek, or Roman deities. Witches newly initiated into the tradition are called dedicants, who with time and training progress to becoming neophytes and then elders. The tradition is highly organized, with coven officers and a defined set of beliefs, and membership includes families with children as well as adults.

Celtic Traditional. The Celtic or Celtic Traditional Tradition is based on the religious beliefs of the ancient Celts and the practices of their Druid priests. Consequently its deities come from Celtic lore, and its rituals focus on nature worship, tree magic, and the four elements. Runes are also featured prominently in Celtic Traditional magic and divination.

Crystal Moon Wicca. Crystal Moon Wicca employs a variety of deities, including Celtic, Egyptian, Greek, and Roman goddesses and gods. Its members are allowed the freedom to choose their own practices, but generally Crystal Moon Wiccan rituals strongly emphasize nature, the moon, the four elements, and magic.

Dianic Wicca. Dianic Wicca is strongly identified with the American feminist movement, and many members of the religion are active in feminist politics. Accordingly, most of its practitioners are women and most Dianic Wiccan covens exclude men. The focus of Dianic covens is the Goddess, particularly the goddess Diana. They also generally celebrate the traditional Wiccan festivals of the Wheel of the Year, although covens vary widely regarding how they choose to celebrate and worship the Goddess.

Earthwise. Earthwise is based on the Alexandrian Tradition. However, unlike Alexandrians the members of an Earthwise coven believe that all members are equal and that each person must choose her or his own way to practice Wicca. At the same time, members must be formally initiated into the tradition, usually by a member of the opposite sex because the tradition believes in the balance of opposites. Once initiated, each member is considered a priestess or priest as well as a practicing witch. Moreover, unlike the Alexandrians, there are no other initiations that move a person up a hierarchy. Preinitiates, though, must spend a year and a day learning the rituals, herbs, spells, deities, and other aspects of their Craft before going through the initiation ritual. They must also handcopy the Earthwise Book of Shadows, which is largely Alexandrian in nature.

Eclectic Tradition. The Eclectic Tradition is a fairly recent Witchcraft tradition that mixes bits and pieces from many other Witchcraft traditions. It is primarily practiced by solitaries, who use information found in books and on websites to develop a unique version of Wicca. Practitioners of the Eclectic Tradition believe that there is no one right way to perform rituals or honor deities, and therefore each person must follow her or his own path.

Faery Tradition. The Faery Tradition employs Faery Power during rituals, believing that the participants in such rituals literally become enchanted and possessed by this power or spirit in a direct connection to the divinity. To encourage possession, the tradition's ceremonies rely heavily on invocation and feature many chants and poetical and liturgical material. In the working of magic, the Faery Tradition employs pentacles (both upright and inverted), visualization of a blue fire, secret names, significant colors, and various deities. Some of these deities can be found in other traditions, but most are unique to Faery. In addition, because each Faery Tradition initiate is encouraged to add something of her or his own interest into the coven, the tradition has developed many branches with influences as diverse as African and Haitian magic, Tibetan Buddhism, Native American shamanism, Kabbalistic magic, Santeria, and many other forms of magical and spiritual practice both ancient and modern.

Gardnerian Tradition. The Gardnerian Tradition is perhaps the oldest and certainly one of the largest modern Witchcraft traditions. Much of the Gardnerian Book of Shadows, particularly its liturgy, has been used in establishing other Witchcraft traditions; these include the Alexandrian Tradition, which shares many features with the Gardnerian Tradition. Gardnerian covens worship the Goddess and the Horned God, usually while nude (or skyclad) or in robes, perform a variety of rites to celebrate and honor various events, and practice magic using prescribed rituals established by British witch Gerald Gardner.

Georgian Tradition. The Georgian Tradition draws on material from several traditions, including Gardnerian, Alexandrian, British Traditional, and various other Celtic-based traditions. It can only be taught in a coven setting, with males instructing females and vice versa, and only someone who has been properly trained and initiated and has moved up the coven hierarchy to the priesthood can provide such training to others. In coven gatherings, Georgians worship both the Goddess and the God and practice magic as well. This magic is worked only for the benefit of coven members or for people who have requested the coven's help and can only be used for positive purposes. Each Georgian is encouraged to write her or his own rituals and spells and to develop an individual approach to witchcraft.

Green Wicca. Also known as Green Witchcraft, Green Wicca is a Witchcraft tradition that emphasizes herbalism, healing magic, and the worship of nature. Green Wiccans are attuned to the seasons, the phases of the moon, and other aspects of the earth's environment, and they are dedicated to worshiping earth gods and goddesses (primarily the goddess Gaia).

Hereditary Tradition. Practitioners of the Hereditary Tradition of Witchcraft are all hereditary witches who believe that their genetic connection to witchcraft has existed through many generations and who have been taught the Craft by a living relative. Their covens usually comprise only close relatives. Most believe that their knowledge and power as witches are inherited, although sometimes they adopt people into their coven if a family line is dying out.

Irish Faery-Faith Tradition. The Irish Faery-Faith Tradition is based on ancient Celtic religion, Irish folklore (both written and oral), and modern folk practices regarding fairies. Trees figure prominently in the tradition, and members associate each type of tree with a particular holiday, color, type of wisdom, etc. Each initiate into the Irish Faery-Faith Tradition selects one tree as a focus of study, then learns lore and magical skills and is tested on knowledge inherent in that tree. Members of the tradition believe that fairies guide them in their studies.

Kitchen Witch Tradition. The Kitchen Witch Tradition of Witchcraft involves rituals and magic related to domestic concerns, e.g., the home and healing. Herbs and plants figure prominently in this tradition, as does a respect for nature. In recent years, Kitchen Witches have applied their practice of magic to concerns of the workplace as well. It is primarily a tradition of solitary practitioners.

Ladywood Tradition. The Ladywood Tradition arose out of the Pagan Way movement and incorporates many aspects of other traditions into its practice of the Craft. However, it emphasizes healing magic and environmentalism more than many traditions. The Ladywood Tradition is also unusual in that it encourages its practitioners to open their rituals to the public, and it promotes various projects designed to educate the public about Wicca.

Nordic Tradition. Also known as the Teutonic Tradition, the Nordic Tradition of Witchcraft is based on the beliefs and practices of pagans from Scandinavia and northern Germany. Its deities are the goddess Freya and the god Odin, and most of its rituals are connected to agriculture and the seasons.

Pictish Tradition. Also called PectiWita or the Scottish Tradition, Pictish Wicca is a Witchcraft tradition based on the beliefs and practices of ancient Scottish pagans. For the most part, its practitioners are solitaries, and they employ few formal rituals. Magic, healing, and divination are the main emphasis of the tradition; there are few religious elements to the Craft.

Reclaiming Tradition. The Reclaiming Tradition emphasizes personal empowerment. Its members believe that every individual embodies the divine and should be given the freedom to interpret spirituality in her or his own way. Covens of the Reclaiming Tradition invoke goddesses and gods from many pantheons, working with both female and male elements of the Deity, and rituals not only celebrate the seasons and personal triumphs but raise the participants' energy levels to aid their practice of magic and healing. The four elements, air, fire, water, and earth, are also an important part of Reclaiming rituals. To be initiated into a Reclaiming coven, a person must petition a committee of teachers for permission to join. If and when these teachers decide that the petitioner is ready, they give the person a series of challenges to overcome before going through the initiation ceremony, because in the Reclaiming Tradition conquering one's fears and inhibitions is an important part of becoming personally empowered.

Saxon-Wicca Tradition. Also called Seax-Wicca, Saxon-Wicca encourages self-initiation and solitary practice. As its name implies, the tradition incorporates the beliefs and practices of Saxon pagans, although it includes elements of both the Gardnerian and Alexandrian Traditions.

StarKindler Tradition. The StarKindler Tradition is largely based on the Alexandrian Tradition. Its Book of Shadows developed out of the Alexandrian Book of Shadows, and its highly structured approach to initiation, coven establishment and governance, and other aspects of the Craft are also derived from the Alexandrian Tradition. The StarKindler Tradition also allies itself with British Traditional, arguing that in fact all

Wicca is essentially one with the British Traditional Tradition.

Stregheria. The word *Stregheria* refers to the many traditions of Italian Witchcraft, which vary widely in practice depending on the region of Italy that inspired each tradition. Most Italian Witchcraft practiced in America is based on the Tanarra Tradition, which stems from the area around Naples, Italy. Two other forms of Stregheria are Fanarra from northern Italy and Janarra from central Italy. American witch Raven Grimassi, often called the father of modern Italian Witchcraft, created two extremely popular Witchcraft traditions, the Arician Tradition and the Aridian Tradition, that combine Italian folk traditions with modern Wicca. Members of both traditions celebrate ancient Italian agricultural festivals. Those of the Arician Tradition also worship the god Tagni and goddess Uni, those of the Aridian Tradition the goddess Tana and god Tanus. Members of other Italian traditions worship such goddesses as Hecate, Proserpina, and Diana. Italian Tradition witches also make protective amulets; heal using herbs, potions, and spells; and employ a great deal of knot magic.

Sylvan Tradition. The Sylvan Tradition emphasizes nature worship, the practice of magic, and the existence of the fairy realm. There are generally no standard rituals; practitioners create their own as spontaneous expressions of the moment, arising out of a specific need or desire. The four elements are employed in many rituals, but Sylvan practitioners believe that because these elements exist everywhere they need not be assigned specific places or duties within a magic circle. Sylvan practitioners usually raise their magic circles outdoors. There they believe it is unnecessary to perform rituals that banish negative energy or protect against negative energy, because to them the earth is always a positive force within the magical space.

Welsh Traditional. Welsh Traditional, which actually began in the United States rather than in Wales, honors Welsh deities. The sword is the most prominent tool in Welsh Traditional rituals, and red the most significant color. Practitioners usually wear red robes during rituals.

Witta. Witta is based on Norse and Celtic Irish beliefs and practices, although its covens are primarily located in Texas and Ohio. Practitioners have secret names known only to themselves and their deities, most of whom are Irish. Covens have no hierarchies, and every member is encouraged to teach others the Craft. **See also individual traditions.**

trees

To many ancient pagans, trees were thought to be connected to certain gods—or in some cases, were gods themselves in physical form—and therefore magical. It was said that some tree roots reached all the way to the Underworld and some tree branches reached all the way to heaven, making trees the link between all elements of the spiritual realm. Others thought that trees had the power to bind evil spirits. Trees were also viewed as symbols of life and sacred knowledge. This plus their association with deities made them deserving of worship.

Certain individual trees were considered more sacred than others. In Ireland, for example, there were at least five great trees in ancient times—the Tree of Dathi, the Tree of Mugna, the Tree of Ross, the Tree of Tortu, and the Tree of Uisnech—each guarded by an Irish shaman-poet. Scholars believe that these men cut the trees down rather than let them fall under the control of early Christians. The ancient pagans considered certain species of trees more sacred than others. These trees are considered sacred by Neopagans as well, many of whom worship trees in outdoor rituals.

Many witches also incorporate elements of tree worship into their ceremonies and rituals, perhaps burning sacred wood at certain festivals or using the wood of sacred trees to make ritual tools. For example, birch wood is often burned at Beltane festivals, oak wood at Midsummer and Yule festivals. Birch twigs, willow cords, and ash branches are used to make ritual brooms. Ash branches are also used to make wands for magical rituals. Hazel wood is used for wands as well, and for divining rods and other tools of magic. Alder wood is sometimes used to carve ceremonial whistles and flutes, and the sap of the European alder (also known as the black alder) has been employed in a process to create red dye used to color ritual cords, ribbons, and bags. Walnut tree oil is sometimes used to anoint ritual tools, although in Italian traditions oil from the olive tree is preferred.

This nine-year-old is believed to have the ability to find water sources underground with a forked hazel twig.

In many Witchcraft traditions, trees are thought to be connected to certain deities. For example, in some traditions the willow tree is associated with the goddess Hecate. The elder is sometimes associated with goddesses of witchcraft or with the goddess Gaia, also known as Mother Earth. The oak, considered particularly sacred, is associated with a variety of goddesses, including Diana and Bridgit, and is featured in many witches' festivals and rituals.

Some witches also believe that certain tree trunks hold doorways into the fairy kingdom or are the home of certain fairies. These include the elder, the alder, the ash, the oak, and the hawthorn. Similarly, some witches believe that the elm is the dwelling of elves or holds a secret doorway to an elfin kingdom.

Some witches believe that trees not only harbor fairies, elves, and other spirits but are also repositories of ancient memories and knowledge. This belief originated among the ancient Celts, some of whom associated trees with an ancient alphabet called the Ogam. This alphabet was used by the bards of ancient Britain and Ireland to record and pass secret messages, some of which conveyed occult wisdom. The twenty or twenty-five letters of the Ogam were made by inscribing lines of various number, length, and angle on stone. In some regions where the Ogam was used, each letter was believe to represent an object, person, or place, but in most each letter stood for a particular tree. **See also individual trees**; broom; tools, ritual; wand.

Trèves, witch trials of

During the late sixteenth century, the city of Trèves (now Trier), Germany, then part of the Holy Roman Empire, was the site of an unusually large number of witch executions. In part this was due to witchcraft-related hysteria but it was also due to the fact that city leaders used witchcraft trials as a way to get rich. Most defendants were wealthy, and upon their execution their money and property were automatically confiscated by city officials. Consequently, according to one writer of the period, various members of the local government—particularly Trèves's executioner—quickly became the richest men in town.

In all approximately six thousand people were executed as witches in Trèves between 1587 and 1594. Witch hysteria actually began there in 1582, but the civil judge at the time, Dietrich Flade, refused to order execution for the condemned witches who came before him for sentencing; as punishment for his leniency, the prince-archbishop who controlled the region, along with its governor, dismissed Flade from the bench, and eventually ordered him executed as a witch. The grounds for Flade's execution was the supposition that only a witch would have sympathy for witches. Another man who expressed pity for condemned witches, Father Cornelius Loo, was banished from the country after he called the witch trials unjust. Meanwhile the trials continued until they ceased to be economically profitable. **See also** Flade, Dietrich.

trials, witch

From the thirteenth to the seventeenth centuries, thousands of alleged witches were placed on trial for their magical practices and beliefs. The motives of their accusers varied. Some truly believed that a particular witch had used witchcraft to harm them and wanted her punished under the law. Others were motivated by jealousy, spite, revenge, or hatred to make witchcraft accusations against people they wanted to hurt. Still others believed that all witches were in league with the devil and should be destroyed; they saw witch trials as God's work.

In the beginning, however, witches were not tried for practicing witchcraft. The first witch trials, which took place in southern France in the late thirteenth century, tried defendants on charges of treason rather than witchcraft. Although these defendants had attempted to murder prominent political figures using image magic and poisonous potions, they were treated as though they had tried to commit murder through nonmagical means.

In the fourteenth century, defendants in witch trials began to be charged with heretical sorcery—practicing magic in a way that violated the teachings of the Roman Catholic Church. In 1320 the Roman Catholic Church had decided to investigate and prosecute cases of heretical sorcery, which in 1335 it officially defined as sorcery that included devil worship and attendance at Sabbats. Folk magic, which involved using divination, healing, love potions, and other magic that did not involve complex rituals, was not seen as the domain of the devil and was therefore left alone.

At first the church's investigators, called inquisitors, looked strictly into cases of malicious witchcraft, or maleficia, where there was some physical proof that witchcraft might have been used to harm someone. Soon, however, what was at issue was whether or not the accused practiced any form of witchcraft, even the kind that left behind no traces and harmed no one. This was because the church had decided that all witchcraft was diabolical—i.e., involved the devil. Consequently, by the fifteenth century people practicing folk magic were as much at risk of being accused, prosecuted, and convicted of practicing witchcraft as those practicing other kinds of magic. In fact, oftentimes they were more at risk, because practitioners of folk magic were among the poorest, least well connected members of society and had few resources to defend themselves against witch accusations.

Having expanded its definition of prosecutable witchcraft, however, the church was unable to handle the flood of cases that resulted. Prior to this time, the church had used secular authorities to carry out its sentences, preferring to distance itself from actual executions. Now the church encouraged secular authorities to become involved in prosecution as well. The first secular witch trial took place in 1390 in Paris, and thousands followed throughout Europe, in Protestant as well as Catholic countries. However, secular authorities preferred to take on only those cases that involved maleficia, where there were clear victims of witchcraft, rather than cases involving beliefs, such as whether or not a particular person had made a pact with the devil.

In both secular and ecclesiastical courts, defendants in witch trials had fewer legal rights than other types of defendants. For example, throughout most of the witch-hunting years they were denied the right to an attorney, particularly in continental Europe, and in most places they were also denied the opportunity to call witnesses in their defense. Meanwhile prosecuting attorneys could call any number of witnesses to speak against the accused, including children, whose testimony was sometimes considered even more likely to be truthful than adults', and in many places these witnesses were allowed complete anonymity. This meant that it was often impossible for the court to determine whether a witness was testifying against the defendant for personal motives such as revenge or financial gain.

The reason that accused witches had fewer rights was because the courts generally believed that such defendants had an unfair advantage over prosecutors, judges, and juries, since witches could use magic and the help of the devil to influence the course of a trial. Only by making it more difficult for accused witches to be found innocent, officials reasoned, could fairness be achieved.

Convictions in most European trials depended on confessions extracted during torture. Without these, it was hard to prove cases of diabolic witchcraft, whereas once a confession had been obtained, a guilty verdict was inevitable. Consequently, some witch-hunters—particularly in Germany, where witch-hunting practices were the most brutal and unjust—continued to torture accused witches until they either confessed or died. During the sixteenth century, most European torturers followed a set of guidelines described in witch-hunting texts that provided them with questions to ask accused witches under torture. These questions eventually became so standardized that court clerks designated them merely by number in official records.

In some places, such as Scandinavia and England, the torture of witches was forbidden, on the supposition that any confessions obtained under torture were invalid. In England, however, throughout the witch-hunting years its politicians continued to debate whether its approach to witchcraft was too lenient. English and Welsh courts both considered witch trials a civil matter, and would not conduct a trial based on an unsubstantiated confession. There had to be some physical evidence of witchcraft for a trial to go forward, such as the discovery of witches' marks on a suspect's person or poisons, potions, poppets, or other tools of witchcraft in her home.

There was much public support for witch trials during the fifteenth and sixteenth centuries, but during the seventeenth century people increasingly began to argue that witch trials were unjust. For example, in 1631 German Jesuit priest Frederich Von Spee anonymously published *Cautio Criminalis* (*Precautions for Prosecutors*), to protest the way witches were accused and brought to trial. He particularly objected to the practice of torturing one suspected witch to get the names of others, believing that most of the people whose names were obtained in this fashion were innocent.

One reason for this change in public opinion was outrage over the many stories of witch-hunting injustices. Another reason was related to a movement called rationalism. Triggered by advances in science, this movement caused the majority of people to doubt the existence of magic and therefore the inherent guilt of accused witches.

Still another reason the public stopped supporting witch trials was the negative impact of witch-hunts on local economies. So many people were executed because of witch-hunting that in many places there were not enough workers to sustain a village. Moreover, the longer a witch-hunt went on, the fewer wealthy suspected witches there were to convict. This was a critical point in some places, because the courts were allowed to confiscate the property of anyone convicted of practicing witchcraft. It is no coincidence that many major witch-hunting efforts ended when witch-hunting was no longer profitable (and when towns had run out of victims).

The eighteenth century saw a general decline in witch-hunting both in Europe and America. The last major trials took place in America in 1706, Ireland in 1711, England in 1717, Scotland in 1727, France in 1745, and Germany in 1775. The following year, the English passed an antiwitchcraft law mandating a year's imprisonment for anyone pretending to practice witchcraft (a way to punish witches without admitting that witchcraft was real), but few people were prosecuted under this law. The most notable case, which took place in 1941, involved Helen Duncan, who was actually not a witch but a purported medium who earned her living contacting spirits on request. The last vestiges of antiwitchcraft legislation in England were repealed in 1951, and no other witch trials have taken place since that time. **See also** England, witch-hunts of; France, witch-hunts of; Germany, witch-hunts of; persecution, witch.

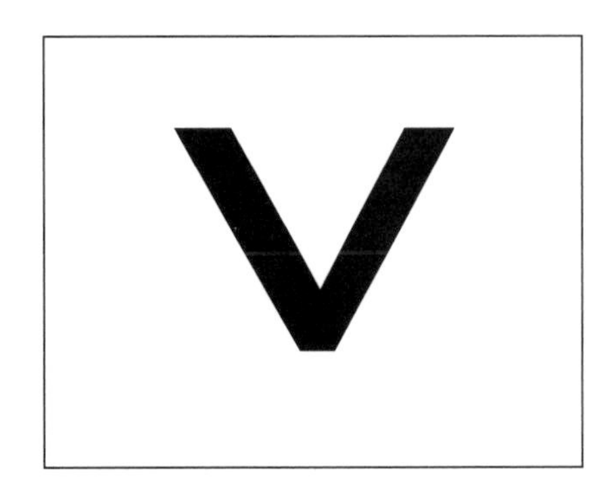

Valiente, Doreen (1922–1999)

Doreen Valiente was influential in shaping the Gardnerian Tradition, which is based on Gerald Gardner's Book of Shadows. Gardner claimed that his book had been given to him by hereditary witches, passed down from antiquity, but said its text was fragmentary. He therefore added to and rewrote parts of the material. When Valiente read Gardner's work, she realized that he had copied parts of it, intentionally or unintentionally, from the published works of another witch, Aleister Crowley. She offered to rewrite these passages, and with Gardner's permission went on to rewrite other sections and add new material. She then worked with authors Janet and Stewart Farrar to publish Gardner's book within the Farrar's 1984 book *The Witches' Way*. Valiente herself subsequently wrote several books about witchcraft, including *Witchcraft for Tomorrow* (1978) and *An ABC of Witchcraft Past and Present* (1973; republished as *An ABC of Witchcraft* in 1986). **See also** Crowley, Aleister; Farrar, Janet and Stewart; Gardner, Gerald; Gardnerian Tradition.

Venus

The Roman goddess of love, sexuality, and beauty, Venus (or her Greek counterpart, Aphrodite) is often invoked by witches casting spells related to love and romance. She is also associated with magic related to fertility, divination, and prosperity. **See also** goddesses and gods.

vodun

Also known as voodoo, voudoun, or vodoun, vodun is a religion that combines elements of African paganism with Christianity. Vodun practitioners worship hundreds of uniquely vodun gods and goddesses derived from those of West African religions. Among the most prominent deities, or *loa*,

This vodun priestess, Camille Perez, practices a religion that integrates elements of African paganism with Christianity.

are Ayida Wedo, Damballah, and Erzulie. Ayida Wedo and Damballah are a goddess and god, respectively, of Haitian voduns. Ayida Wedo is a rainbow-colored serpent goddess (although she is sometimes depicted as a dragon or snake instead) often seen on vodun temples, and Damballah, also a serpent, is her consort. Erzulie is the vodun goddess of love and fertility. Depicted as a beautiful woman, she is the consort of two gods, Agwe and Ogoun.

Vodun priests, who are usually called witch doctors, not only worship vodun deities but also use magic for healing and divination. Their name comes from the concept that most of the illnesses they cure are believed to have originated from witches' evil spells. Consequently they routinely employ magic and the summoning of gods and spirits to protect *against* witchcraft or to work good or evil.

Vodun priests also perform secret rituals and blood oaths, and their ceremonies feature chanting, animal sacrifice, and participants' possession by gods or ancestral spirits. They employ image magic to create "voodoo dolls," dolls in the likeness of their intended victims that, when injured, cause the victim to be injured. In addition, they are reputed to be able to create zombies, walking corpses that serve as slaves. Researchers have discovered that these people identified as zombies are not actually "the living dead" but instead have been subjected to a toxin.

Transported to the West Indies and America in the seventeenth and eighteenth centuries by African slaves, today vodun is primarily practiced in Haiti and New Orleans, Louisiana. However, there are pockets of vodun practitioners in a few other major U.S. cities, including New York City. **See also** image magic; witch doctor.

Von Schultheis, Henrich (dates unknown)

Seventeenth-century judge Henrich Von Schultheis is the author of *Detailed Instructions How to Proceed in the Inquisition Against the Horrible Vice of Witchcraft*, a 1634 book that advocated the most brutal of tortures for accused witches. Von Schultheis did not believe the accused deserved any protection under the law, because in all likelihood they were guilty and therefore in league with the devil, and the devil would stop at nothing to thwart the legal system. Von Schultheis further suggested that God would be pleased to see accused witches subjected to brutal treatment. Moreover, he said that anyone who spoke in favor of an accused witch might be an agent of the devil and therefore deserving of prosecution. As for condemned witches, Von Schultheis argued that all should be executed, preferably in the most gruesome manner possible. Von Schultheis himself saw to it that this was done, not only as a judge but also as secretary to several German bishops who themselves persecuted witches.

Von Spee, Frederich (1591–1635)

Jesuit priest Frederich Von Spee of Germany is the author of *Cautio Criminalis* (*Precautions for Prosecutors*), a 1631 work that protested the way witches were accused and brought to trial. He particularly objected to the practice of torturing one suspected witch to get the names of others, believing that most of the people accused in this fashion were innocent. In fact, having acted as confessor to condemned witches in Würzburg, Germany, the site of a series of witch trials during the 1620s, Von Spee believed that nearly all of the people deemed witches as part of a witch-hunt were innocent.

Von Spee had long noted that once a woman was accused of being a witch, it was almost inevitable that she would be condemned and executed. Any sign of goodness in her was taken as counterfeit, a trick to make people think she was innocent; even a refusal to confess under torture was considered proof that she was in league with the devil, who it was said had given her the strength to bear pain. Von Spee also revealed that in most cases, official documents stating that the accused had confessed voluntarily were fraudulent, because some form of torture was always used during witch-hunts of the period. He criticized all witch-hunters but especially those who were leaders of a church, arguing that men of God should not be involved in such injustice and brutality. Moreover, he accused these religious leaders of being motivated by profit rather than a desire to fight Satan, because most witch-hunters earned money for their work and/or received the property of executed witches.

In attacking witch-hunters, Von Spee knew that he himself would come under attack, and perhaps even be branded a witch. To protect himself, he published *Cautio Criminalis* anonymously; nonetheless, many of his Jesuit peers suspected him of writing it, and his relationships with them suffered. Shortly after the book's publication his superiors sent him to work as a confessor to plague victims in the German city of Trèves (now Trier). There he contracted plague and died in 1635. Meanwhile, despite church attempts to keep Von Spee's book from being reprinted, it was translated into sixteen languages and widely read throughout Europe. Some scholars believe that it contributed to the gradual decline of witch-hunts during the late seventeenth century.

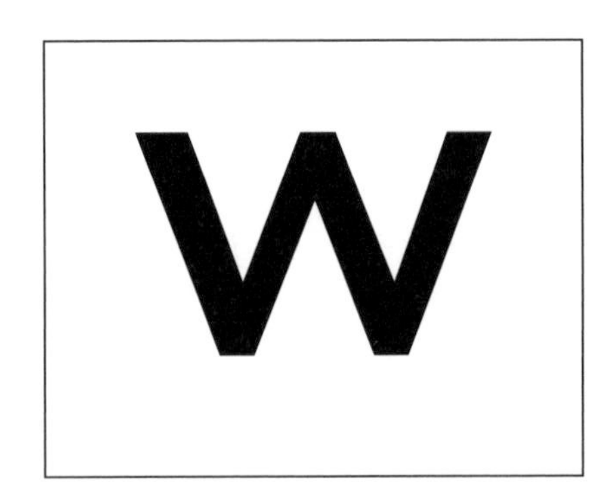

walnut

The walnut tree (*Juglans regia*) is prominently featured in Italian Witchcraft traditions. Its wood is considered sacred and its oil is used to anoint ritual tools. The tree is also associated with fertility, divination, and fairies. **See also** Stregheria; trees.

Walton, Charles (1871–1945)

Charles Walton is thought to be a modern-day victim of a witchcraft-related murder. In 1945 he was found dead in the Cotswold Hills of England on Candlemas, a day sacred to Wiccans. His body exhibited signs of a ritualistic killing performed specifically to end a witch's life, confirming the area's reputation as a place where witches gathered. No one was ever charged with the murder, so the exact connection between the crime and witchcraft remains a mystery. **See also** Cotswold Hills.

wand

The wand is a tool used to direct the user's energy during a ritual or spell casting. Although wands can be any length, modern witches typically prefer wands that are twenty-one inches long because they believe this was the length of wands used by witches in ancient times. However, some ancient writings prescribe a nineteen-and-a-half inch wand for drawing magic circles, while others suggest that wands be made in a length determined by measuring the distance from the owner's elbow to the end of the longest finger. Also variable is the material from which a wand is made. Some witches prefer them to be iron or some other metal, others choose crystal, but the majority select wands of wood, most typically ash, hazel, or willow. Indeed, the oldest wands were all made of wood from certain trees sacred to pagans, leading most scholars to believe that their use originated with tree worship.

Among sorcerers, wands made of cypress wood have long been associated with black magic and spells involving the dead. In fifteenth-century writings, wands were said to be the devil's gift to his new worshipers. More commonly, though, wands have been associated with white magic. In addition to drawing magic circles and directing energy, they are employed to trace magic symbols on the ground during rituals, to call the gods, to bless objects, and to stir cauldrons brewing magic potions, particularly those related to healing. The connection between wands and the healing arts goes back to ancient times; some scholars suggest that this connection is the reason why physicians of the sixteenth through eighteenth centuries traditionally carried walking sticks regardless of whether they were needed.

Like other tools used in Craft rituals, wands are believed to have a connection to one of the four elements: earth, air, fire, and water. However, witches disagree on whether wands represent fire (because rubbing two sticks together creates fire) or air (because wands are typically made of tree branches that once swayed in the wind). In any case, witches believe that new wands have no power until certain rituals are performed to awaken their magic. Such rituals vary, but generally they involve saying words or names thought to be magical over the wand. Many witches also cleanse the wand prior to each use. **See also** circle, magic; elements, four; magic; tools, ritual.

Warboys Witches, trial of the

The trial of the Warboys Witches, which took place in Huntingdonshire, England, in 1593, was one of the most sensational legal cases of its time. As such, it influenced subsequent witch trials, and many scholars believe that it was a major factor in the passage of the 1604 Witchcraft Act encouraging witch-hunts. The Warboys Witches, as the defendants came to be known to the English public during their trial, were seventy-six-year-old Alice Samuel, her husband, John, and her daughter, Agnes.

The incident preceding the trial began in 1589. At that time, Alice Samuel had the misfortune of visiting the estate of neighbor Robert Throckmorton of Warboys just as one of his daughters, ten-year-old Jane, began having what historians now believe was an epileptic seizure. Jane immediately blamed Samuel, and within a short time the other girls in the family, ranging in age from nine to fifteen, began having fits and blaming Samuel for them as well. Their more enlightened parents, however, doubted that witchcraft was the cause of their daughters' distress. Wealthy and well connected, they summoned the best doctors to examine the girls. Unfortunately, the physicians could find no medical cause for the girls' symptoms, and the fits were becoming more frequent and violent. Moreover, other women in the household (servants and the girls' aunt), most likely affected by mass hysteria, began having fits as well. At first these fits occurred at random, but after a while they occurred only when Samuel was visiting. (She was repeatedly asked to come to the Throckmorton estate as various people tried to figure out what was causing the girls' problem.)

Eventually the Throckmortons decided to see what would happen if Samuel stayed with them, thinking that the girls could not keep up the fits day in and day out. Their theory was correct—the fits did sometimes cease—but now the girls started seeing demons. Then a visitor, Lady Cromwell, tried an experiment; she burned some of Samuel's hair in the common belief that doing so could weaken a witch's power. Not only did the experiment fail, but Lady Cromwell later claimed that Samuel had appeared to her in a dream the night after the experiment and attacked her. When Lady Cromwell died after a long, unexplained illness a year later, people remembered this dream and blamed Samuel for bewitching the woman.

By 1592, the Throckmorton girls were still having fits, seeing demons, and generally being tormented by what they said was Samuel's witchcraft. Tired of her ordeal, Samuel finally lost her temper and ordered the girls to stop their nonsense, and to everyone's surprise their symptoms stopped. This was taken as proof that Samuel was a witch, since she seemed able to control the girls' bodies. Shortly thereafter, Samuel herself began to wonder whether she did indeed have some kind of magical control over the girls, and she expressed her worries to a local clergyman. When he shared her concerns with others, a formal investigation into the Throckmorton girls' apparent bewitchment was opened.

A confused, pressured Samuel soon confessed to practicing witchcraft, perhaps hoping that she would be dealt with mercifully. Instead she was placed on trial, not only for the girls' bewitchments but also for the murder by magic of the recently deceased Lady Cromwell. In addition, in keeping with the common belief that when the woman of a household practiced witchcraft other family members, particularly her daughters, were likely to be practicing witchcraft as well, Samuel's husband and daughter were put on trial too, even though both insisted they were innocent. All three were convicted and hanged in April 1593, whereupon the Throckmorton household became free of all symptoms of bewitchment. This cessation led people of the period to conclude that Samuel really had been a witch. Modern scholars, however, suggest that Samuel's death merely triggered the end of the witch hysteria that had accompanied her appearance—or perhaps the girls simply decided not to pursue their attention-getting antics with another victim. **See also** demonic possession; England, witch-hunts of.

warlock

A derogatory term first applied to male witches by Roman Catholic witch-hunters, the word *warlock* comes from the Old English *warloghe*, meaning "an oath breaker" or "a traitor." Witches themselves do not use the word. In fact, many Wiccans find it highly offensive. Nonetheless, nonwitches have added the word to the modern vernacular through portrayals of witches and witchcraft in the popular media.

warts

A wart is a hard growth on the surface of the skin that may appear anywhere on the body. The size and shape of warts vary considerably, and warts on the face can sprout hairs. Modern physicians know that warts are caused by viruses and will disappear if the body develops an immunity to the virus. When this does not happen spontaneously, doctors can remove the wart through chemicals, freezing, lasers, or surgery.

From the fourteenth through eighteenth centuries, people believed that warts were marks of the devil. Since witches were believed to consort with the devil, anyone who exhibited a wart was thought to be a witch. Consequently it was dangerous for someone to display a wart, and people tried all kinds of strange cures to rid themselves of one. For example, in Britain one remedy was to rub the wart with a piece of raw meat, then bury the meat; supposedly as the meat decayed the wart would shrink and eventually disappear. In America a similar remedy called for wiping the wart with a rag that was then buried at a crossroads, preferably at midnight. Throughout the Western world, people believed that anyone who touched a toad would get warts, probably because toads were associated with witchcraft and because a toad's skin appeared to be covered with warts. **See also** frogs and toads; marks, witches' or devil's.

Watchers

Some witches believe the Watchers were members of an ancient race of magical beings, perhaps related to fairies. Others say they are the spirits of the four elements. Still others believe that the Watchers are deities or spirits associated with certain stars. This concept is derived from ancient pagan religions in which the Watchers were deities who stood watch over the entrance to heaven or over certain stars. Later religions associated the Watchers with angels. In Judaism, for example, the Watchers are angels who sit in judgment of human actions, while to early and medieval Christians they were either angels who conferred wisdom to human beings or, more commonly, fallen angels who caused problems for humanity. **See also** elements, four; fairies.

water

Water is one of the four elements typically employed in the practice of magic.

Modern witches typically associate each of these elements with ritual tools; in the case of water these tools are the chalice and cauldron. The element of water is thought to embody the Goddess and the forces of birth and fertility. During magical rituals it balances fire and stabilizes air. It is connected with the colors green and blue in various shades; the direction west; the astrological signs Cancer, Scorpio, and Pisces; and the metal silver. The gemstones associated with water include the aquamarine, moonstone, and pearl; the plants associated with water include the aloe, cucumber, gardenia, lily, and willow. The incense and fragrances used in water magic include aloe wood for love and luck; cherry oil and incense for love and divination, respectively; gardenia incense, rose oil, and jasmine oil for love; and lilac oil for protection.

Water also has great significance in terms of the history of witch persecutions. Because of the connection between water and certain rites and rituals of the Roman Catholic Church, particularly baptism, witch-hunters of the Middle Ages through the eighteenth century were convinced that water repelled witches. This belief inspired a common witch test in which the suspected witch was tied up and thrown into deep water. Anyone who floated was considered guilty, because water would supposedly reject a witch. Similarly, medieval people believed that witches, demons, and ghosts could not cross streams or rivers, and that if a body was buried beneath water its spirit could not come back from the dead to haunt people.

The most powerful deterrent to witches and demons was holy water, a mixture of salt and water that had been blessed by a priest. It was used to drive away demons during an exorcism, and some witch-hunters routinely carried a vial of it to protect themselves from evil spells. What medieval witch-hunters believed notwithstanding, in fact, many witches use a mixture of salt and water as part of their rituals, believing that by sprinkling the solution they are cleansing and purifying ritual areas and tools. **See also** cauldron; chalice; elements, four; salt.

Webster, John (1610–1682)

English physician and author John Webster wrote a 1677 book entitled *The Displaying of Supposed Witchcraft* in which he suggested that although people might claim to be witches, it was unlikely that they had any magical powers at all. He attributed witches' and witch-hunters' claims of real witchcraft to imagination, hysteria, or fraud, describing specific witch trials in making his points. Many modern scholars believe that Webster's arguments did much to convince his peers that witch-hunts should end, because shortly after his book's publication the aggressiveness with which witches were pursued and prosecuted in England diminished. **See also** England, witch-hunts of; persecution, witch.

Weinstein, Marion (birthdate unknown)

Modern American witch Marion Weinstein has written numerous books on witchcraft, including *Positive Magic* (1978; revised edition 1981), *Earth Magic: A Dianic Book of Shadows* (1979; newest edition 1998), *Magic for Peace* (1991), and *The Ancient/Modern Witch* (1991; revised edition 1993). She also hosted a New York City radio program on occult topics, *Marion's Cauldron*, from 1969 to 1983, and has performed stand-up comedy routines based on her experiences as a Wiccan. Prior to developing her witchcraft-related career, Weinstein worked as a commercial artist, then performed in improvisational theater before becoming a radio host and stand-up comic. In the late 1970s she established her own company, Earth Magic Productions, to produce books, videos, and audiotapes related to witchcraft; it is currently headquartered in Oregon.

Weir, Thomas (c. 1600–1670)

Scottish soldier and respected public figure Thomas Weir became the central focus of a witch trial after he began displaying erratic behavior at the age of seventy. Until this time he had led an exemplary life, both in the military (where he attained the rank of major) and as a leading figure in the Presbyterian Church of Edinburgh, Scotland. Consequently when Weir began saying odd things and acting out of character, his peers accepted these behaviors merely as the eccentricities of old age.

Then Weir suddenly confessed to practicing black magic and engaging in a variety of lewd sexual activities, including the molesting of young girls. The citizens of Edinburgh were stunned, and at first refused to believe Weir, suspecting mental illness. Several physicians examined him and declared him sane, whereupon town leaders felt they had no choice but to arrest him as a suspected witch. They also arrested Weir's sister Jane, with whom he had claimed to be sexually intimate throughout their childhood and much of their adulthood.

For reasons that are now unclear, Jane Weir quickly confessed that both she and her brother were witches who had signed pacts with the devil, but insisted that all blame for her involvement should be placed squarely on her brother. When the two went to trial, however, only Jane was charged as a witch. Thomas Weir was accused only of various forms of sexual misconduct, because prominent members of his church did not want any mention of black magic made in connection with a leading Presbyterian like Weir. Both Jane and Thomas were convicted; in April 1670 Thomas Weir was strangled and burned and Jane Weir was hanged. **See also** devil; persecution, witch; trials, witch.

well-worn path

Among witches, the phrase *well-worn path* refers to following the practices and beliefs developed by other Wiccans. Most believe that only after following this path to its end—in other words, becoming familiar with the accumulated wisdom of previous generations—can a new trail be blazed. Some Wiccans, however, argue that the practice of witchcraft need not be based on everything that has come before. They take a different, more experimental approach to the Craft, blazing a new trail before fully reaching the end of the old.

Welsh Traditional

Welsh Traditional is a Witchcraft tradition that actually began in the United States, not in Wales or other parts of Great Britain. It developed out of the efforts of Ed Buzynski and Herman Slater, who owned a store in Brooklyn Heights, New York, called the Warlock Shop. Although the store was originally simply a place to buy witchcraft-related books and materials, it quickly developed into a networking opportunity for witches throughout the country. Buzynski and Slater organized meetings for people interested in witchcraft as part of the Pagan Way movement, published a journal called *Earth Religion News*, and were instrumental in establishing several covens in the New York area. Buzynski wrote the Book of Shadows for these covens, forming the basis of Welsh Traditional beliefs and practices. Some of these covens are still in existence in New York and have inspired the creation of other Welsh Traditional covens elsewhere in the United States, particularly in Georgia, California, and Washington State. All of the deities involved in Welsh Traditional rituals are Welsh; the sword is the most prominent ritual tool and red the most significant color. Practitioners usually wear red robes during rituals. **See also** Pagan Way; traditions, Witchcraft.

Weschcke, Carl (1930–)

Magician and former Wiccan high priest Carl Weschcke is president of Llewellyn

Worldwide, Ltd., a leading international publisher of books on witchcraft, the occult, paganism, and New Age topics. He was also at the forefront of the Neopaganism movement of the 1970s.

Weschcke was first exposed to the occult as a child; his grandfather was an occultist and his parents professed to be telepathic. However, he did not acquire a serious interest in the occult until adulthood. At the same time, he was deeply committed to the idea of becoming a publisher and began searching for a suitable company to buy. He purchased the Llewellyn Publishing Co. (the firm's official name includes the abbreviation) in 1960, six years after the death of its founder.

Weschcke immediately relocated the business from Los Angeles to St. Paul, Minnesota, and added titles on a variety of occult subjects. Soon he published a magazine, *Gnostica*, as well, and in 1970 he opened the Gnostica Bookstore in Minneapolis, where he sold his books and also sponsored occult-related activities. In 1971 he began hosting an annual festival there, originally known as the American Aquarian Festival of Astrology and the Occult Sciences but later called the Gnosticon. The following year he established the short-lived Council of American Witches, which was dedicated to delineating the defining principles of modern Wicca. These principles continue to define Wicca, and they have been included in U.S. military handbooks for chaplains that describe various religions.

Weschcke was once extremely active in the American Celtic Tradition of Witchcraft, into which he was initiated in 1972. That same year he met and married Wiccan priestess Sandra Heggum, becoming high priest of her coven. The two held meetings in their home until they had a son, Gabriel, and decided to end their association with the coven, at least until he was older. In the mid-1970s Weschcke sold his bookstore to concentrate more on his publishing enterprise. For a short time he also served as Grandmaster of the Aurum Solis, a magical order based in St. Paul, Minnesota, but founded in Great Britain in 1897. In 1991 Weschcke quit the order, and since then he has not been active in any other Craft-related group, although he continues to be active in the running of his publishing company. **See also** Council of American Witches; traditions, Witchcraft.

Weyer, Johann (1515–1588)

German physician Johann Weyer is the author of *De Praestigiis Daemonum,* a 1563 book that argued that most people who displayed signs of demonic possession or professed to be witches were actually mentally disturbed and should not be tried for witchcraft. This was a revolutionary position for the time in Germany, when witch-hunts were widespread.

Weyer did, however, believe in the devil and his power to influence human behavior. In fact, Weyer so strongly believed in demons that in 1568 he published the *Pseudo-Monarchy of Demons*, a guide to Satan's realm which described a hierarchy of 1,111 divisions of 6,666 devils and demons each. Weyer also classified the human beings who he believed really did work for the devil. Those who came before the courts as true witches, he said, did not actually use magic in their work, despite their claims of great power. Instead, Weyer said, they employed poisons and other ordinary means to commit murder and mayhem. The remainder of those who worked for the devil were male sorcerers with genuine magical powers. Weyer considered these people to be truly dangerous, but he argued that they rarely came before the courts, being too clever and too powerful to be caught. Consequently, Weyer suggested, the criminal justice system was only dealing with the most trivial of sorcery cases, along with many cases of mentally ill, elderly people who did not deserve prosecution. Weyer, who was

Protestant, blamed the Catholic Church for causing the witch hysteria under which such people were put on trial.

Weyer's position was not only unusual but very unpopular. People wanted to believe that all witches used magic, that the cases before their courts were serious matters, and that their witch hysteria was valid. Consequently, when Weyer's views became widely known, many people called for his execution for expressing sympathy for witches. Some also called for his books to be burned. Fortunately for Weyer, as a physician he had influential friends, including his patient William, the duke of Cleves, in the Netherlands. Duke William not only protected Weyer but also was apparently swayed by his arguments. As a result, Dutch officials adopted an attitude of leniency toward elderly women who were either accused or confessed witches. Eventually, however, the duke's protection was not enough to keep Weyer safe. Angered by Weyer's anti-Catholic statements, the Catholic duke of Alba forced him to leave the country. **See also** trials, witch.

Wheel of the Year

The Wheel of the Year refers to the seasons or cycles of nature, which occur at key points in the sun's journey across the sky. Wiccans celebrate these points via Sabbat festivals, and they use a visual representation of the Wheel of the Year, a symbol first used by ancient Greeks prior to 600 B.C., as a calendar to mark these points.

Said to turn as the year progresses, the wheel has eight spokes, each one equidistant from the next just as each Sabbat is equidistant in time from the next. Each spoke represents a different season or celebration. The spokes are created by drawing one cross to divide the circle of the wheel into quarters and then another cross to cut each of those quarters in half. The four spokes that divide the wheel into quarters are called the quarters, while those that divide the quarters are called cross-quarters. Quarters and cross-quarters alternate around the wheel.

The quarters represent four moments that mark the astronomical beginning of each of the four seasons: winter, spring,

Many witches celebrate the four seasons with festivals called Sabbats. Pictured are Druids celebrating the autumnal equinox, called Mabon, in London.

summer, and fall. The Sabbats that honor these moments are Yule, also called the winter solstice; Ostara, also called the spring equinox; Midsummer, also called the summer solstice; and Mabon, also called the fall, autumn, or autumnal equinox. The cross-quarters represent four times of year when witches believe that ancient pagans held agricultural festivals. The Sabbats that honor these times are Imbolc, which celebrates the birthing of the first lambs; Beltane, which celebrates new growth in the fields; Lughnasadh, which celebrates the time of harvest; and Samhain, which celebrates the time of slaughtering animals for food storage prior to winter. Some Witchcraft traditions refer to the cross-quarters as the Greater Sabbats and the quarters the Lesser Sabbats; others reverse these designations.

Many witches view the wheel not only as a calendar but as a symbol representing the role of the Goddess and God at certain times in the year's cycle. Each tradition has its own set of myths regarding this role. One of the most common beliefs, however, is that the wheel represents a myth in which the Goddess gives birth to the God, who grows up, unites with her, creates a new child, and dies, whereupon she awaits his birth so the cycle can begin anew. At the same time, witches find it greatly significant that the wheel has no beginning and no end, so that all life is part of an endless circle. **See also** autumnal equinox; Beltane; Imbolc; Lughnasadh; Mabon; Ostara; Sabbat; Samhain; spring equinox; summer solstice; winter solstice.

Wicca

Wicca is a religion based on pre-Christian nature religions now classified as pagan. Most but not all modern witches practice Wicca. Of those witches who do not practice Wicca, most adhere to another type of paganism, while a few are members of more mainstream faiths. However, witches who participate in mainstream religions usually reject their notion that the deity is male, believing instead that the divine force has both masculine and feminine elements.

In fact, the main difference between mainstream religions and Wicca relates to the gender of divinity. Whereas the traditional emphasis in most religions is on a male God, Wiccans focus on worshiping and honoring the Goddess. However, they also recognize a male aspect of divinity. Some Wiccans believe that this male aspect is separate from the Goddess and functions as her consort. Called the Horned God, he is viewed as inferior to the Goddess by most Wiccans, equal to her by others. Alternatively, some Wiccans suggest that the Goddess holds both the masculine and the feminine energy of creation within her. In other words, she has no need of a male consort.

Wiccans worship the Goddess in many different ways, depending on the Witchcraft tradition with which they identify. In many traditions, the Goddess is worshiped as having more than one state of being, or aspect—such as Maiden, Mother, and Crone—and many personifications. In recognition of the many forms in which the Goddess appears, they might worship goddesses from many pantheons (e.g., Greek goddesses, Roman goddesses, Celtic goddesses, etc.) rather than confine their worship to just one pantheon or goddess. However, certain goddesses have been more popular with Wiccans than others. In the 1960s, most American Wiccans worshiped the goddess Diana and other deities from Greece and Rome. In the 1970s the American Wiccan focus turned to Celtic deities. Today there is much interest in Eastern deities as well as in Celtic, Greek, and Roman ones.

Most Wiccans also worship nature spirits, or at least honor nature in their rituals. In part because of this reverence for nature, environmentalism is a fundamental part of Wiccan belief. Many hold their worship rituals outdoors, perhaps in the nude—which they call skyclad—to feel closer to nature. Many witches call on certain aspects of nature, such as the elements of earth, air, fire, and water, as part of their rituals. Many Wiccans consider these and other aspects of nature to be part of the divine forces of the universe.

Wiccans also believe that the divinity exists within themselves. They honor this divinity in many ways. For example, most treat their bodies with the same respect and reverence as they treat the earth, eating healthy foods and otherwise taking good care of themselves. Most also adhere to the Wiccan philosophy to do no harm, because they believe that acting intentionally to injure another person damages their own spirit, will, or psyche. Moreover, most Wiccans think that any evil deed will come back to punish the perpetrator of that deed threefold.

For these reasons, Wiccans do not generally perform evil, or black, magic. (A few Wiccans, however, do not believe there is such a thing as good or evil magic; in their minds, magic is simply magic, with all forms a natural part of the forces of the universe. Nonetheless, they do not practice what others would call black magic, because to do so would cause harm.) Wiccans do practice many other types of magic. Herbalism, simple spell casting, divination, and other magical practices known as folk or low magic are common, but are usually combined with elements of high magic (i.e., magic involving rituals and the invocation of spirits and/or deities). Rituals are also performed to honor deities and celebrate certain times of year. The Wiccan calendar of these times is called the Wheel of the Year.

Until recently, most Wiccans belonged to a coven, a group of usually three to thirteen witches, and/or to a Wiccan church or organization. Today, however, an increasing number of Wiccans choose to practice their religion alone. Called solitaries, these people rely on the numerous books available on witchcraft-related subjects, many written by Wiccan priestesses or priests, to guide them in their practice of Witchcraft. The Internet has also provided valuable resources for solitaries, as Wiccan organizations like the Covenant of the Goddess (www.cog.org) increasingly offer websites devoted to helping people learn about Wicca.

Because of such resources, in recent years the Wiccan community has grown extremely diverse. However, this community has always been more diverse than other religious communities, as the Council of American Witches discovered in 1973–1974 when it met to identify common Wiccan beliefs. Although the council did succeed in finding commonalities among Wiccans, it also found many points on which Wiccans disagreed.

Some of the most protracted disagreements involve semantics. Wiccans have long argued over what to call themselves and on what the name of their religion means. Some think that *Wicca* comes from the Old English root *wic*, which means "to turn, twist, or shape." Others believe that it comes from the Old English verb *wiccian*, which means "to cast a spell." Still others argue that the word *Wicca* was derived from the Celtic word *witan*, meaning "to know," and therefore means "a wise person." Scholars have largely discounted this latter view, although they too disagree on other origins. In any case, in Old English, a *wicca* (pronounced *WITCH-a*) was a male witch and a *wicce* (pronounced *WITCH*-eh) a female witch.

Wiccans similarly disagree on whether the words *Wicca* and *Witchcraft* are synonymous. Witches first began capitalizing Witch and Witchcraft in the 1960s to indicate that these words referred not only to the practice of magic but to a body of religious beliefs. In the 1970s, many witches began using Wiccan and Wicca as replacements for Witch and Witchcraft to disassociate themselves from the negative images historically associated with witches and witchcraft. Once Wicca was recognized by the U.S. government as a valid religion in 1986, witches again began using the names Witch and Witchcraft, this time to distinguish members of the religion (which includes the practice of magic) from people who practice magic but do not hold Wiccan beliefs. Today some people maintain this distinction, although they might not capitalize the word *witch,* while others use the words Wicca and Witchcraft interchangeably. **See also** goddesses and gods; coven; magic; traditions, Witchcraft.

Wiccan Rede

The Wiccan Rede is a major principle of Wicca that guides most witches not only in their practice of magic but also in their daily lives. It states, "An' it harm none, do what thou wilt." Witches disagree on what this means. Some say that the Rede allows people to do whatever they like as long as their actions do not hurt anybody else. Others think that the Rede obliges people to do what the deity intends for them to do, because following this path will surely harm no one. A variation of the latter is expressed in Raven Grimassi's book *The Wiccan Mysteries*:

> To do as one wills to do actually means to find one's purpose (one's True Will) and to fulfill it. This is intended to be for the benefit of the person but not to the detriment of another person. In a higher sense this Wiccan tenet is related to Eastern Mysticism. It is the work of the neophyte [a beginner on the Wiccan path] to master his or her physical senses and to pass into nonattachment. Once the student has risen above the desires and needs of the flesh, then he or she can view the world with detachment and so discover their true Will or Purpose.
>
> At this stage there is no greed, envy, or jealousy, and therefore the person can act through knowledge of his or her own pure will, which then naturally causes no harm to another because it is not centered on any relationship, personal prestige or any personal gain within a society. It is the true will of the divine nature within the person, acting in accord with its purpose in this lifetime.

The issue of whether or not a Wiccan may intentionally cause harm is controversial within the religion. Some believe that doing harm is perfectly acceptable in self-defense. Others think that it is always wrong to do harm, no matter what the reason. Still others think that the "do no harm" edict applies only to the realm of spell casting. In other words, they believe that the act of harming someone, either intentionally or unintentionally, only violates the Rede if magic is used in the commission of that harm. Their reasoning is based not just on morals but on their belief in a law of magic known as the threefold law, which states that any harm done by magic will come back to harm the magician in a way three times worse.

Wiccans have also disagreed over the origin of the Wiccan Rede. Gerald Gardner, who incorporated it into his own Witchcraft tradition, claimed that he uncovered it while studying pagan legends. However, he apparently took it from the writings of modern witch Aleister Crowley, who advised: "Do what thou wilt shall be the whole of the Law." For his part, Crowley claimed that this law, which he called the Law of Thelema, was given to him as part of a manuscript dictated to him by a spirit named Aiwass in April 1904. Not every Wiccan believes that Crowley actually communicated with a spirit, however. Some think he came up with the Law of Thelema on his own, while others think he discovered it in ancient manuscripts he did not want to reveal. **See also** Crowley, Aleister; Gardner, Gerald; Grimassi, Raven.

Wiccan Shamanism

Created by Selena Fox, a Wiccan high priestess and a leader in the modern Neopagan movement, Wiccan Shamanism is a religion that combines elements of Wicca with those of Native American and African tribal spiritualism. Practitioners of the religion, called Wiccan Shamans, take part in conventional Wiccan activities such as celebrations of festivals within the Wheel of the Year and the performance of rituals within magic circles; therefore while Wiccan Shamans generally practice their religion only among other Wiccan Shamans, they can also be members of covens within Wiccan traditions that allow diversity in their rituals. This tolerance for diversity is necessary because, unlike other Wiccans, Wiccan Shamans incorporate elements of shamanism into their practices, using drumming and chanting to induce altered states of consciousness. In addition, Wiccan Shamans perform healing rituals and divination just as shamans do, although they use typically Wiccan tools such as crystals and Tarot cards. Also like shamans, many Wiccan Shamans have personal guardian spirits, which they often receive at the time of their initiations into the religion. Initiations into Wiccan Shamanism usually require the initiate to go through an experience much like a vision quest, spending a night alone in order to gain self-awareness. **See also** Fox, Selena; shamanism; Wicca.

willow

Since at least the times of ancient Greece, the willow tree (*Salix alba*) has been believed to have magical properties; therefore its wood is a popular material for the construction of a variety of witches' tools, such as wands. From medieval times witches' broomsticks have also been made using willow; a willow cord fastens birch twigs to a stick taken from an ash tree. In certain Witchcraft traditions in which whips are employed in rituals, these tools are manufactured using strips of willow. Several goddesses have historically been associated with willow trees. In particular, the tree is believed to be sacred to the goddess Hecate and therefore is sometimes considered a symbol of the Underworld. **See also** broom; Hecate; trees.

winter solstice

The winter solstice is one of two moments in the year when the sun is farthest from the equator; the other moment is the summer solstice. In the Northern Hemisphere, the winter solstice occurs on December 21 or 22, the summer solstice on June 21 or 22. (In the Southern Hemisphere, these dates are reversed.) On the day of the winter solstice, witches celebrate a festival which some call the winter solstice but most call Yule. **See also** Yule.

WITCH

Begun on Halloween of 1968, WITCH (Women's International Terrorist Conspiracy from Hell) was a short-lived American feminist organization that viewed witch-hunting in terms of male oppression, given that far more women than men were executed as witches. Members of the group used witches as a symbol of feminism, dressing in the stereotypical costume of witches—flowing black robes and tall pointed hats—to stage feminist demonstrations and sometimes calling out what they thought were witches' curses. However, the group displayed a complete lack of understanding of modern witches and witchcraft, so most witches felt the group was exploiting their beliefs for political purposes. During the short time the group existed there was a growing interest in witchcraft among young people, some of whom were attracted to WITCH under the mistaken impression that it was connected to Wiccan worship. **See also** hats.

witchcraft

Witchcraft with a lowercase "w," also called spellcraft by some modern witches, is the practice of magic as it is performed by witches. In general, witchcraft involves divination, the use of herbs and potions for healing, and folk magic (also called practical magic or low magic) with simple spells and without elaborate rituals. In modern times, those practicing witchcraft have combined ancient folk magic practices from Europe and Britain with the magical practices of Western occult societies. Modern witches also believe that witchcraft requires certain psychic powers attuned to the forces of the universe.

Witchcraft with a capital "W" is the practice of magic combined with the worship of ancient deities, primarily goddesses rather than gods. This distinction between witchcraft and Witchcraft was designed by modern witches, who use Witchcraft to indicate that their magical practices are an expression of their religious beliefs. The religion of most witches is some form of Wicca, but a witch need not be a Wiccan to practice Witchcraft. Many witches think that their religious beliefs are closely tied with the beliefs of pre-Christian religions, while many scholars argue that Witchcraft as it is practiced today is a wholly modern invention.

In practicing Witchcraft, witches not only participate in magic rituals, in which they recite magic words, perform magic actions, and use magic objects, but also participate in various ceremonies intended to honor deities. These ceremonies vary according to Witchcraft tradition. In addition, prior to or during the practice of magic, many witches call on certain spirits or deities, primarily the Goddess, to be present. Once a ceremony is complete, participants often offer cakes and wine to the spirits or deities that were invoked and thank them for their presence.

During the Renaissance, people considered any worship of deities other than the Christian God to be connected to the devil. Therefore they assumed that witches consorted with Satan during their rituals and/or signed pacts with him to be his slave. Anthropologists refer to the type of witchcraft associated with such beliefs as diabolic witchcraft. During the witch-hunting years in Europe, people were routinely accused of practicing diabolic witchcraft—and sometimes confessed to doing so, usually under torture—but it is unclear whether devil worship was ever really a part of their witchcraft, or whether they instead worshiped pagan deities much as modern witches do.

Anthropologists also disagree on whether other Renaissance beliefs related to witchcraft were real or imagined. By comparing and contrasting those beliefs with long-standing witchcraft-related beliefs in parts of the world, they have found some striking similarities, which some modern witches have interpreted to mean that witchcraft has historically been universal, constant, and real. One of the most interesting of these comparisons is one between Western witchcraft and African sorcery. Jeffrey B. Russell, in his book *A History of Witchcraft: Sorcerers, Heretics, and Pagans*, explains:

> The similarity between many African witch beliefs and those of historical Europe are pronounced. Both African and European 'witchcraft' include the following characteristics: the witch is generally female and often elderly. The witches meet in assemblies at night, leaving their bodies or changing their shapes in order to fly to the meeting-place. The witch sucks the blood of victims or devours their organs, causing them to waste away. Witches eat children or otherwise cause their deaths, sometimes bringing their flesh to the assembly. They ride out on brooms or other objects, fly naked through the air, use ointments to change their shapes, perform circular dances, possess familiar spirits. . . . Of course, no one group of sorcerers is supposed to do all these things, but all these beliefs may

> be found in Europe as well as in Africa. In all, at least fifty different motifs of European witchcraft can be found in other societies.

Scholars debate whether these similarities were due to some contamination of one society by another. However, witches dispute any evidence of this, and argue that such similarities cannot be a coincidence. **See also** devil; persecution, witch; sorcery; torture; Wicca; witches.

witch doctor

A witch doctor is a practitioner of magic in the tribal cultures of Africa, South and Central America, and the West Indies. Priests in two religions to come out of these regions, vodun and Santeria, are also called witch doctors, as are some practitioners of folk magic living in the Appalachian Mountains of the eastern United States.

Perhaps the most famous witch doctor in the United States was Doctor John, a former African slave who practiced vodun out of New Orleans, Louisiana, during the nineteenth century. Like most witch doctors, he primarily used his magic for healing, fortune-telling, love potions, eliminating curses, and exorcising spirits, but he was particularly noted for being able to rid homes of poltergeists. Other witch doctors have been famous for their poisons, sometimes used as part of evil spells and curses. Appalachian witch doctors specialize in countermagic, whereby they cure victims of evil spells. Similarly, African witch doctors spend most of their time curing illnesses believed to have been brought on by witches. **See also** Santeria; vodun.

witches

The modern definition of witches is either women or men who worship both nature and a female divinity (and usually, though not necessarily, a male divinity as well) and who practice magic as part of their religion. Sometimes the definition of a witch includes a mention of psychic powers, because witches believe that human thought can produce magic and that the physical world is only a small part of reality.

An alternate modern term for witch is Wiccan. Wicca is the religion of Witchcraft, recognized as such by the American government in 1986. At one time, all American witches considered themselves Wiccans, but in recent years an increasing number of people consider themselves witches but not members of the Wiccan faith. They practice magic either as part of a non-Wiccan form of paganism or without incorporating many, if any, religious elements into their magic rituals. **See also** magic; persecution, witch; Wicca; witchcraft.

witch-hunter

Also called a witch-finder, a witch-hunter was a person who worked either independently for profit or as an official of a court to ferret out witches in communities throughout fourteenth- through seventeenth-century Europe, and to a lesser extent in fourteenth- through seventeenth-century Britain and seventeenth-century America. Their usual method was to single out odd, ostracized, quarrelsome, or otherwise nonconformist individuals within a town and encourage the townspeople to view these people as witches who deserved to be arrested and interrogated about their activities. Alternatively, a witch-hunter might start with one witch accusation, made either before or after he came on the scene, and by brutally torturing the arrested witch extract a confession that led to mass arrests of supposed accomplices, who in turn were tortured to name other witches. This method worked because in most places suspected witches could be arrested on the flimsiest of evidence or even with no evidence at all.

Moreover, since witch-hunters were paid for each witch arrest, it was obviously in their best interest to force a convicted witch to name as many cohorts as possible. For example, seventeenth-century English witch-hunter Matthew Hopkins charged towns 40 shillings for each witch investigated, usually with a bonus for each witch convicted. Depending on how many witches he could uncover and convict, his profit per job was anywhere from 4 to 26 pounds, or 160 to 1,040 times what the average worker made in a day. In just one town—Suffolk, England—he investigated approximately 200 people as suspected witches, arresting about 125 and gaining convictions and death sentences for 68.

In most cases, witch-hunters like Hopkins were called into a town by local authorities who were already caught up in witch hysteria. Sometimes, however, they turned up uninvited and created the hysteria to increase their profits. Once they realized what the witch-hunters were doing, some town leaders bribed a witch-hunter to leave their community alone. For example, in Rheinbach, Germany, in 1631, town leaders offered witch-hunter Franz Buirmann money to abandon his witchhunt there and move on. (Although he accepted the bribe, Buirmann returned in 1636 and this time he went ahead with his witch-hunt. By some estimates, the Rheinbach witch trials of 1631 and 1636 led to the execution of 150 people out of only 300 families living in the region.)

In addition to Hopkins and Buirmann, other notable witch-hunters include

Witch-hunting became very popular when the witch-hunters were paid generously for each arrest; little evidence was needed to convict a witch, and few attempted to defend the accused.

American theologian Cotton Mather and France's Pierre de Lancre. De Lancre operated primarily in the French Basque region of the Pyrenees Mountains, while Mather figured in America's notorious Salem witch trials. Other famous witch-hunters were the authors of popular guidebooks on witch-hunting. These include Nicholas Rémy, who published *Demonolatry* in 1595, and Heinrich Kramer and Jakob Sprenger, who published *Malleus Maleficarum* in 1486 (with twenty more editions published by 1669). **See also** Buirmann, Franz; de Lancre, Pierre; Hopkins, Matthew; *Malleus Maleficarum*; Mather, Cotton; Rémy, Nicholas.

witching hour

A time when witches' spells are believed to be most powerful, the witching hour occurs during the hour of midnight on a night with a full moon. The concept of the witching hour is undoubtedly derived from ancient pagan rites and rituals devoted to honoring the goddesses of the moon, including Diana, Selene, and Hecate (known collectively as the Triple Goddess), who later came to be associated with witchcraft. **See also** Diana; Hecate; Selene.

Witta

Established in the United States during the 1960s, the Witchcraft tradition of Witta is based on Norse and Celtic Irish beliefs and practices. Its covens are primarily located in Texas and Ohio. Practitioners have secret names in addition to their regular ones; these secret names, which are used during the practice of magic, are known only to themselves and their deities, most of whom are Irish. Covens have no hierarchies, and every member is encouraged to teach others the Craft. **See also** traditions, Witchcraft.

wizard

A wizard is a male practitioner of magic of a type requiring a high level of skill and knowledge. In ancient times, wizards were among the best-educated men in a community; hence the word *wizard*, which was first used in fifteenth-century Britain and continental Europe to refer to village sorcerers, comes from the Middle English word *wisard*, which means "one who is habitually or excessively wise." Wizards have historically practiced various forms of magic, ranging from high magic (i.e., magic involving complicated rituals and the invocation of spirits) to folk magic (i.e., magic involving simple spells, potions, image magic, divination, and healing) to a mixture of both.

Perhaps the best-known wizard was Merlin, a figure from Arthurian legend. Both powerful and wise, Merlin was the personal adviser to England's King Arthur. Some scholars think that he was based on a real wizard who lived in Wales in the fifth century and specialized in divination. Others believe that the name Merlin was a common one for medieval wizards and that the Arthurian Merlin was an amalgam of many such men.

Another famous wizard is Gwydion, a mythological Celtic figure whose adventures have been told and retold among the people of northern Wales. Said to be the son of a Welsh goddess named Don, he employed his magic either helpfully or mischievously, depending on the deservedness of the person asking for his assistance. Modern witches in Celtic-based traditions sometimes call on Gwydion to join their initiation rites.

Today few people call themselves wizards (Wiccans generally shun the term); most male practitioners of magic are witches, magicians, sorcerers, or occultists. In the sixteenth and seventeenth centuries, though, the term was quite common because it was applied to all sorts of men (and a few women) who practiced magic. Such people did not have the education of ancient wizards, and they were typically paid small fees for their services, which included divination, exorcism, and the making of potions and amulets. However, they were well-respected in their villages and often called on to settle disputes.

Wizards were generally spared persecution during witch-hunts. Historians have suggested that because village wizards were extremely popular they had many defenders, some of them influential with witch-hunters and the courts. Feminists, however, argue that wizards were spared because of their gender, since most of those persecuted were women and almost all wizards were male. **See also** magic; magicians; Merlin; persecution, witch.

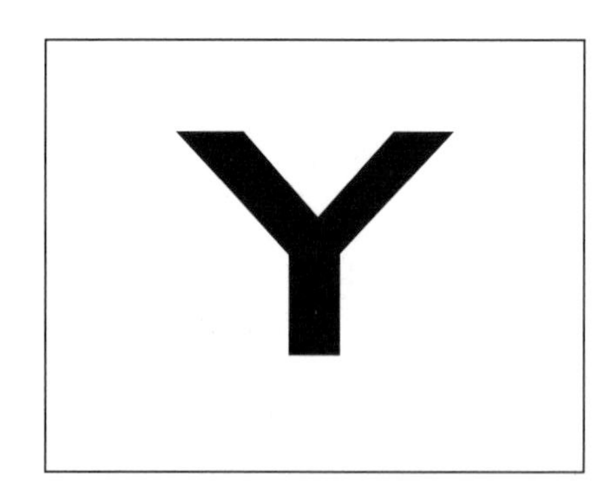

Yule

Also called the winter solstice or Yuletide, Yule is celebrated on the shortest day of the year (and the longest night), which falls sometime between December 20 and December 23 in the dead of winter. This is the time when, according to some stories, the God (who represents the sun) is born of the Goddess (the moon), and along with him the promise of the coming spring. To celebrate the birth, signs of nature's continuing fertility—i.e., plants that still grow in winter—are brought inside: mistletoe, holly, ivy, and bay leaves. Among witches and Neopagans who view the God as the Horned God, the reindeer symbolizes the deity at this time of year. Colors associated with Yule celebrations are silver (for the moon/Goddess), gold (for the sun/God), green (for the earth), and red (for fire).

Indeed, fire is integral to Yule festivals. A Yule log, usually of oak or birch, is burned as a symbol that the sun will continue to grow and thrive. After burning, many witches spread the Yule log's ashes in their gardens, believing that it will increase the fertility of the soil. They also traditionally save a piece of that year's Yule log to light the new log the following year; this piece is believed to bring good luck for the next twelve months. Another tradition is to write wishes down on bay leaves and throw them into the fire, in the belief that the magic of the day will help them come true. In addition, many witches burn bayberry candles at Yule time to bring prosperity for the coming year.

Christians also burn bayberry candles at this time of year. In fact, many Yule traditions have been adopted in the celebration of the Christian Christmas. **See also** Wheel of the Year.

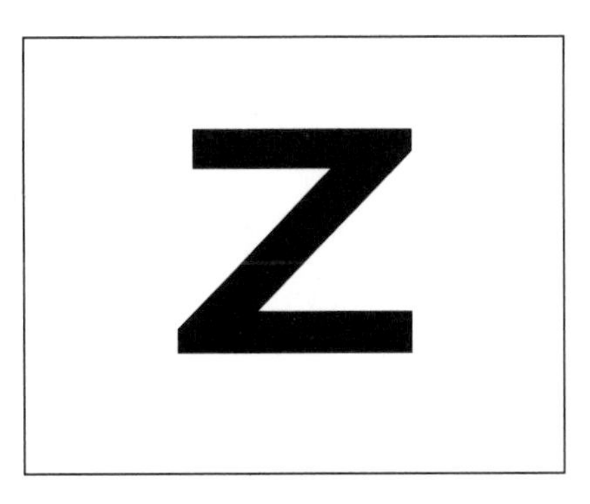

Zell-Ravenheart, Morning Glory (1948–)

Born Diana Moore, Morning Glory Zell-Ravenheart is one of the foremost experts and lecturers on Neopaganism and Goddess worship in the United States. She herself has worshiped the Goddess as a ritual priestess in the Church of All Worlds (CAW) since 1974. She is also a frequent contributor to a magazine entitled *Green Egg: A Journal of the Awakening Earth*, which she once helped edit and produce, and she has provided information to the authors of many books on the subjects of Wiccan and pagan magical practices. Zell-Ravenheart is married to Oberon Zell-Ravenheart, the founder of CAW, but has other mates as well, in keeping with her belief in polyamory, or multiple love (a term she invented as an alternative to *polygamy*, which means multiple spouses). She conducts workshops on polyamory and relationship issues as the Priestess of Aphrodite (the Greek goddess of love).

However, Zell-Ravenheart is perhaps best known among nonwitches for her unicorns. In the 1980s she and her husband (who was then using the name Otter G'Zell) used a secret technique to create four unicorns out of four Angora goats. Scientists speculate that the couple surgically removed the hornbuds of the infant goats and reattached them at the center of their foreheads, placing the two buds so close together that as the animal grew the horns fused as one. The couple then sold these animals to the Ringling Brothers and Barnum and Bailey Circus, which in 1985 put them on display individually billed as "the Living Unicorn." Animal rights activists were outraged, arguing that an animal should not be disfigured and subjected to unnecessary surgery and pain merely for economic gain. In the wake of the negative publicity, Ringling Brothers stopped displaying the animals, but Zell-Ravenheart and her husband continued to produce unicorns for their own enjoyment for many years. **See also** Neopaganism; Zell-Ravenheart, Oberon.

Zell-Ravenheart, Oberon (1942–)

Formerly known as Otter G'Zell, Oberon Zell-Ravenheart is the founder of the Church of All Worlds (CAW), a pagan church, and a leader of the Neopagan community. In fact, Zell-Ravenheart was one of the first to refer to the nature religions that developed in the United States during the 1960s as pagan, and he was the first to coin the term Neopagan to distinguish these new versions of paganism from ancient ones. His forum was a pagan magazine named *Green Egg: A Journal of the Awakening Earth*, which he established in 1968. This magazine helped turn Neopaganism into a widespread American religious movement, as did CAW and Zell-

Ravenheart's other pagan projects. These include the establishment of the Council of Earth Religions, an organization that offers support to many forms of paganism.

Zell-Ravenheart, who has been initiated into several different Witchcraft traditions, calls himself a wizard. He has also practiced psychology. He established CAW in 1967, and in 1970 it became the first pagan church recognized as a valid religious group by the U.S. Internal Revenue Service (IRS), which exempts such groups from federal income taxes. Also in 1970, Zell-Ravenheart began writing about environmentalism, proposing that the earth's ecosystem is a living entity that consciously keeps its atmosphere and other components in balance. This idea became the foundation of the Gaia theory (Gaia is the goddess also known as Mother Earth) developed by environmentalists of the 1970s and 1980s and still popular today. Zell-Ravenheart continues to write about environmentalism, as well as about paganism. In addition, he and his wife, Morning Glory Zell-Ravenheart, hold public earth-healing rituals and ceremonies honoring the seasons. They also sponsor pagan retreats. The two became famous among nonwitches during the 1980s by surgically creating unicorns from Angora goats; Oberon Zell-Ravenheart, who is an accomplished sculptor and painter, features unicorns in much of his artwork. **See also** Neopaganism; Zell-Ravenheart, Morning Glory.

zombies

Zombies are dead people believed to have been reanimated via vodun magic. Although nonbelievers think of these walking corpses as the stuff of horror movies, in Haiti, where vodun is widely practiced, many people claim to have seen zombies or even to be one themselves. Believers in vodun are certain that zombies are created via black magic, but researchers have found a scientific explanation for the phenomenon. The supposedly dead person, they say, is not truly dead, but is simply a victim of a poison that temporarily paralyzes the body until a vodun priest can remove it from its tomb.

Regardless of the method used, upon being reanimated the zombie—who at first exhibits the glazed eyes, shuffling gait, and disorientation of the typical movie zombie—is by custom bound to be the priest's slave. To guard against this type of enslavement for their loved ones, relatives of the deceased sometimes stab the body in the heart, slice its throat, or even decapitate it prior to entombment. Alternatively, various charms are used to protect the body, which is only believed to be vulnerable for seven days. After that, its spirit has traveled beyond the reach of the vodun priest. **See also** vodun.

FOR FURTHER RESEARCH

Katharine Briggs, *An Encyclopedia of Fairies*. New York: Pantheon, 1976.

Robin Briggs, *Witches and Neighbors: The Social and Cultural Context of European Witchcraft*. New York: Viking Press, 1996.

Scott Cunningham, *The Truth About Witchcraft Today*. St. Paul: Llewellyn, 1999.

Gerina Dunwich, *The Wicca Garden*. Secaucus, NJ: Citadel Press, 1996.

Sybil Leek, *Diary of a Witch*. New York: New American Library, 1969.

Charles G. Leland, *Aradia: Gospel of the Witches*. Custer, WA: Phoenix, 1990.

Edain McCoy, *Inside a Witch's Coven*. St. Paul: Llewellyn, 1997.

Patricia Monaghan, *The Goddess Path: Myths, Invocations, and Rituals*. St. Paul: Llewellyn, 1999.

Teresa Moorey, *Witchcraft: A Beginner's Guide*. London: Hodder & Stoughton, 1999.

Ann Moura, *Green Witchcraft: Folk Magic, Fairy Lore, and Herb Craft*. St. Paul: Llewellyn, 1996.

———, *Green Witchcraft II: Balancing Light & Shadow*. St. Paul: Llewellyn, 1999.

———, *Green Witchcraft III: The Manual*. St. Paul: Llewellyn, 2000.

Silver Ravenwolf, *To Light a Sacred Flame: Practical Witchcraft for the Millennium*. St. Paul: Llewellyn, 1999.

Carol Rose, *Spirits, Fairies, Leprechauns, and Goblins: An Encyclopedia*. New York: W.W. Norton, 1996.

Patricia Telesco, *Spinning Spells, Weaving Wonders: Modern Magic for Everyday Life*. Freedom, CA: Crossing Press, 1996.

Denise Zimmermann and Katherine A. Gleason, *The Complete Idiot's Guide to Wicca and Witchcraft*. Indianapolis: Macmillan USA/Alpha Books, 2000.

WORKS CONSULTED

Books

Anton and Mina Adams, *The Learned Arts of Witches and Wizards: History and Traditions of White Magic*. New York: Barnes and Noble, 2000.

Margot Adler, *Drawing Down the Moon: Witches, Druids, Goddess-Worshippers, and Other Pagans in America Today*. Rev. ed. New York: Penguin, 1986.

Bengt Ankarloo and Gustave Henningsen, eds., *Early Modern Witchcraft*. Oxford: Clarendon, 1993.

———, *Witchcraft and Magic in Europe, Ancient Greece, and Rome*. Philadelphia: University of Pennsylvania Press, 1999.

Julio Caro Baroja, *The World of Witches*. Chicago: University of Chicago Press, 1975.

Anne Llewellyn Barstow, *Witchcraze: A New History of the European Witch Hunts*. San Francisco: Pandora/HarperCollins, 1994.

Paul Boyer and Stephen Nissenbaum, *Salem Possessed: The Social Origins of Witchcraft*. New York: MJF, 1974.

Elaine G. Breslaw, *Witches of the Atlantic World: A Historical Reader and Primary Sourcebook*. New York: New York University Press, 2000.

K.M. Briggs, *The Fairies in Tradition and Literature*. London: Routledge & Kegan Paul, 1978.

Raymond Buckland, *Ancient and Modern Witchcraft*. Secaucus, NJ: Castle, 1970.

———, *Buckland's Complete Book of Witchcraft*. St. Paul: Llewellyn, 1999.

———, *Witchcraft from the Inside: Origins of the Fastest Growing Religious Movement in America*. 3rd ed. St. Paul: Llewellyn, 1997.

Laurie Cabot, *The Witch in Every Woman: Reawakening the Magical Nature of the Feminine to Heal, Protect, Create, and Empower*. New York: Delta, 1997.

Pauline Campanelli, *Rites of Passage: The Pagan Wheel of Life*. St. Paul: Llewellyn, 1994.

Joseph Campbell, *A History of Magic*. New York: Taplinger, 1977.

Laurie Winn Carlson, *A Fever in Salem: A New Interpretation of the New England Witch Trials*. Chicago: Ivan R. Dee, 1999.

Edward Carpenter, *The Origins of Pagan and Christian Beliefs*. London: Senate, 1996.

Chas S. Clifton, *Shamanism and Witchcraft*. St. Paul: Llewellyn, 1994.

Chas S. Clifton, ed., *Witchcraft Today: Book One: The Modern Craft Movement*. St. Paul: Llewellyn, 1993.

Vivianne Crowley, *Principles of Paganism*. London: Thorsons/HarperCollins, 1996.

———, *Principles of Wicca*. London: Thorsons/HarperCollins, 1997.

———, *Wicca: The Old Religion in the New Age*. New York: Sterling, 1989.

Arnold and Patricia Crowther, *The Secrets of Ancient Witchcraft, with the Witches Tarot*. Secaucus, NJ: University Books, 1974.

Patricia Crowther, *Lid Off the Cauldron: A Wicca Handbook*. York Beach, ME: Samuel Weiser, 1989.

Scott Cunningham, *Cunningham's Encyclopedia of Crystal, Gem, and Metal Magic*. St. Paul: Llewellyn, 1987.

———, *Magical Herbalism*. St. Paul: Llewellyn, 1982.

———, *Wicca: A Guide for the Solitary Practitioner*. St. Paul: Llewellyn, 1988.

Phyllis Curott, *Book of Shadows: A Modern Woman's Journey into the Wisdom *of Witchcraft and the Magic of the Goddess*. New York: Broadway Books, 1998.

H.R. Ellis Davidson, *Myths and Symbols of Pagan Europe*. Syracuse, NY: Syracuse University Press, 1988.

Owen Davies, *Witchcraft, Magic, and Culture 1736–1951*. Manchester, England: Manchester University Press, 1999.

Mike Dixon-Kennedy, *Celtic Myth and Legend*. London: Blandford, 1997.

Gerina Dunwich, *Wicca A to Z: A Complete Guide to the Magickal World*. Secaucus, NJ: Citadel Press/Carol, 1999.

———, *The Wicca Sourcebook: A Complete Guide for the Modern Witch*. Secaucus, NJ: Citadel Press/Carol, 1998.

W.Y. Evans-Wentz, *The Fairy Faith in Celtic Countries*. New York: Citadel, 1994.

Janet and Stewart Farrar, *A Witches' Bible: The Complete Witches' Handbook*. Custer, WA: Phoenix, 1984.

———, *The Witches' Way: Principles, Rituals, and Beliefs of Modern Witchcraft*. London: Robert Hale, 1984.

Gavin Frost, *The Magic Power of White Witchcraft: Revised for the Millennium*. Paramus, NJ: Prentice-Hall, 1999.

Gerald Gardner, *The Meaning of Witchcraft*. New York: Samuel Weiser, 1959.

———, *Witchcraft Today*. Secaucus, NJ: Citadel, 1973.

Gilbert Geis, *A Trial of Witches: A Seventeenth-Century Witchcraft Prosecution*. London: Routledge, 1997.

Migene Gonzalez-Wippler, *The Complete Book of Spells, Ceremonies, and Magic*. St. Paul: Llewellyn, 1999.

———, *Santeria: African Magic in Latin America*. New York: Original Products, 1981.

Raven Grimassi, *Encyclopedia of Wicca and Witchcraft*. St. Paul: Llewellyn, 2000.

———, *Hereditary Witchcraft: Secrets of the Old Religion*. St. Paul: Llewellyn, 1999.

———, *Ways of the Strega*. St. Paul: Llewellyn, 1995.

———, *The Wiccan Mysteries: Ancient Origins and Teachings*. St. Paul: Llewellyn, 1999.

Rosemary Ellen Guiley, *The Encyclopedia of Witches and Witchcraft*. 2nd ed. New York: Facts On File, 1999.

Graham Harvey, *Contemporary Paganism: Listening People, Speaking Earth*. New York: New York University Press, 1997.

Gustav Henningsen, *The Witches' Advocate: Basque Witchcraft and the Spanish Inquisition*. Reno: University of Nevada Press, 1980.

Christina Hole, *Witchcraft in England*. London: B.T. Batsford, 1947.

Ellen E. Hopman and Lawrence Bond, *People of the Earth: The New Pagans Speak Out*. Rochester, VT: Destiny, 1996.

Charles Alva Hoyt, *Witchcraft*. Carbondale: Southern Illinois University Press, 1989.

Ronald Hutton, *The Pagan Religions of the Ancient British Isles*. Cambridge, MA: Blackwell, 1995.

Michael Jordan, *Witches: An Encyclopedia of Paganism and Magic*. London: Kyle Cathie, 1996.

Amber K., *True Magick: A Beginner's Guide*. St. Paul: Llewellyn, 1999.

Richard Kieckhefer, *Magic in the Middle Ages*. Cambridge: Cambridge University Press, 1997.

Anthony Kemp, *Witchcraft and Paganism Today*. London: Michael O'Mara, 1993.

Francis X. King, *Witchcraft and Demonology*. New York: Exeter, 1987.

William E. Monter, *European Witchcraft*. New York: John Wiley & Sons, 1969.

Teresa Moorey, *Witchcraft: A Complete Guide*. London: Hodder & Stoughton, 2000.

Michele Morgan, *Simple Wicca*. Berkeley, CA: Conari, 2000.

Margaret Alice Murray, *The Witch-Cult in Western Europe*. 1921. Reprint, New York: Barnes and Noble, 1996.

David Pickering, *Dictionary of Witchcraft*. London: Cassell, 1998.

Ken Radford, comp., *Fire Burn: Tales of Witchery*. New York: Wings, 1989.

Israel Regardie, *Ceremonial Magic: A Guide to the Mechanisms of Ritual*. Wellingborough, Northamptonshire, England: Aquarian Press, 1980.

———, *The Golden Dawn*. 5th ed., St. Paul: Llewellyn, 1986.

Russell Hope Robbins, *The Encyclopedia of Witchcraft and Demonology*. New York: Crown, 1959.

Jeffrey Burton Russell, *A History of Witchcraft: Sorcerers, Heretics, and Pagans*. 1980. Reprint, London: Thames and Hudson, 1999.

———, *Witchcraft in the Middle Ages*. Ithaca, NY: Cornell University Press, 1972.

Lady Sabrina, *Secrets of Modern Witchcraft Revealed: Unlocking the Mysteries of the Magickal Arts*. Secaucus, NJ: Citadel Press/Carol, 1998.

———, *The Witch's Master Grimoire: An Encyclopedia of Charms, Spells, Formulas, and Magickal Rites*. Franklin Lakes, NJ: New Page Books/Career Press, 2001.

Lewis Spence, *An Encyclopedia of Occultism*. Reprint, New York: Carol, 1996.

Merlin Stone, *When God Was a Woman*. San Diego: Harcourt Brace Jovanovich, 1976.

Doreen Valiente, *An ABC of Witchcraft Past and Present*. Custer, WA: Phoenix, 1973.

Victor Walkley, *Celtic Daily Life*. New York: Quality Paperback Book Club/Dove Tail Books, 1997.

Marion Weinstein, *Earth Magic: A Dianic Book of Shadows*. Custer, WA: Phoenix, 1998.

Selma R. Williams and Pamela J. Williams, *Riding the Nightmare: Women and Witchcraft*. New York: Atheneum, 1978.

The Witches' Almanac. Middletown, RI: Witches' Almanac, 2000.

Zolar, *Encyclopedia of Signs, Omens, and Superstitions*. Secaucus, NJ: Citadel Press/Carol, 1997.

Internet Sources

Covenant of the Goddess website. www.cog.org.

Sabina Magliocco, "Spells, Saints, and *Streghe*: Witchcraft, Folk Magic, and Healing in Italy," Virtual Pomegranate website, www.interchange.ubc.ca/fmuntean/POM12a1.html.

INDEX

PICTURE CREDITS

Archive Photos, 253
© Bettmann/CORBIS, 99
© Raymond Buckland/Fortean Picture Library, 47
© Kevin Carlyon/Fortean Picture Library, 57
Dover Publications, 51, 67, 119, 133, 164, 197, 243
Express Newspapers/Archive Photos, 230
Fortean Picture Library, 13, 28, 70, 82, 127, 138, 174, 201
Hulton Getty/Archive Photos, 16, 79, 87, 110, 243, 249, 262
Image Club Graphics, 105
Library of Congress, 19, 45, 144, 170, 192, 214
North Wind Picture Archives, 37, 63, 154, 212, 269
© Clive Odinson/Fortean Picture Library, 205
© Philip Panton/Fortean Picture Library, 93
Pierpont Morgan Library/Art Resource, NY, 239
© Gerald Ponting/Fortean Picture Library, 35
Scala/Art Resource, 223

ABOUT THE AUTHOR

Patricia D. Netzley is the author of over thirty nonfiction books on a wide range of topics. Her works include *The Encyclopedia of Special Effects* (Oryx Press Hardback, 1999; Facts On File Paperback, 2001), *The Encyclopedia of Women's Travel and Exploration* (Oryx Press, 2001), *Environmental Literature: An Encyclopedia of Works, Authors, and Themes* (ABC-CLIO, 1999), and *Social Protest Literature: An Encyclopedia of Works, Characters, Authors, and Themes* (ABC-CLIO, 1999). She is currently working on *The Greenhaven Encyclopedia Of Ancient Egypt* as well as several other fiction and nonfiction projects. Netzley lives with her family in Southern California, where she and her husband are the proud parents of three children—Matthew, Sarah, and Jacob.